Gilbert Stuart

Also by CHARLES MERRILL MOUNT

John Singer Sargent, a Biography

[*Frontispiece*]

GILBERT STUART

Recently identified as a self-portrait

Reproduced by courtesy of the Trustees of the Tate Gallery, London

Gilbert Stuart

A Biography

by

Charles Merrill Mount

NEW YORK

W·W·NORTON & COMPANY·INC·

To my daughter

Contents

Illustrations

Preface

ONE OF THE most incisive portrait painters of all time, founder of the American artistic tradition, Gilbert Stuart made the leaders of the American Revolution more vivid to posterity than any comparable group in history. George Washington and his generals, Adams, Jefferson, Madison, and Monroe, their wives, Cabinet members, and friends have a unique historical vitality, overshadowing the Royal Governors who preceded them and the pale figures who later filled their places, precisely because they were preserved as complex living human beings in Gilbert Stuart's portraits. This enigmatic genius returned to his native shore in 1793, bringing the most accomplished technical powers and artistic intellect America had ever seen. With him too came tales of a fabulous career on distant shores that ever since have seemed as suspect as his own too numerous portraits of Washington.

Lack of substantial knowledge concerning Stuart has not been a credit to American scholarship. The precedent for future appraisals was set by William Dunlap, who gathered anecdotes reflecting Stuart's high spirits and ambiguous character, without noting the compensatory balance of his genius and lordly austerity. Fifty years after her father's death, Jane Stuart attempted to set the record straight. Three articles embodied her pious effort before she yielded to George Mason, who produced a rambling, uncritical volume with the redeeming virtue of preserving valuable materials.

The established interpretation of Stuart already showed an indolent and thoughtless eccentric, with a gift for painting heads, and this was complacently accepted by generations of Americans. The "lost years" of Stuart's life remained lost, and conspicuously unsought—while hundreds of unedifying accounts, alternating between parody and mockery of a great artist, mushroomed in references, texts, and "authoritative" works on American art. And ignorance of Stuart has remained profound. For seventy years it has been a commonplace of criticism that his best-known larger work, the full-length portrait of Washington, was based on an earlier French picture. Critics have repeated the fact as though it were the discovery of a knave in the American ancestral heritage. The shame lies not with Stuart, but with those generations who failed to trace whether he had employed this source elsewhere in his work, what other sources he employed, or whether these sources also were reflected in the parallel works of his contemporaries. Thus, 135 years after his death we first discover that Stuart was a brilliant exponent of a fantastically accomplished eighteenth-century school that fed on earlier works. By training and belief and by his profoundly intellectual approach to art, Stuart was a *Georgian* painter. Like the masters of the Renaissance and certain later eras, he systematically employed the best works of other artists as sources for the perfection in his own. In an artistic Valhalla reserved for the most learned masters he expected to encounter the sculptors of antiquity, in company with Raphael, Titian, Rubens, Van Dyck, Rigaud, Lely, Vigée-Lebrun, Gainsborough, Romney, Reynolds, West, and Copley—from *all* of whose works he had borrowed.

The greatest need has thus existed for an entire revision of the prevailing superficial ideas concerning Stuart. Predicated on intensive research and a sound historical approach to the whole of his life and career, the "lost years" in England and Ireland had to be found and fitted into place, and sources of every sort searched for and sifted, to evaluate, verify, discard, and correlate in the desire to present an authentic and historically sound biography. Important new materials have been found, including many letters, receipts, accounts, diaries, leases, the full text of a memoir by his Irish assistant James Dowling, and private papers located in England, Ireland, and the United States.

My long residence in England and Ireland has facilitated this work immeasurably by providing opportunity for indispensable field research; unknown and long-neglected and misattributed works have been rediscovered; and finally, an intimate knowledge of painting techniques (for this work has been accomplished in the intervals of a portrait-painter's life) has made it possible for me to reconstruct Stuart at work. Erroneous attributions have been removed from the appended catalogue; even so, it will be seen that methodical ransacking searches through English collections and Irish country houses have materially enlarged the known quantities of Stuart's portraits. These searches were sponsored in part by the Archives of American Art, who have registered the discoveries. I am exceedingly grateful for the encouragement of the Archives and especially that of its director, Mr. Edgar P. Richardson.

From these studies eight essential points have developed: (1) Stuart was a highly trained artist in the specialized *Georgian* mode; (2) during his first abortive career in London he was the obvious heir to the British school; (3) by his alliance with the Shelburne Whigs he ran Reynolds hard, and deprived Gainsborough of male sitters; (4) he became the quasi-official painter of the Irish Parliament, laureate to the Ascendancy, and holds a place in Irish history as significant as that in the United States; (5) despite his deliberate falsifications, he painted George Washington from life only twice; (6) he was the most naturally gifted painter and portraitist of his time, but never developed to the full extent that his early career showed possible; (7) he had a romantic attachment; (8) he was the victim of his own unstable character.

It is my hope that this work will show Stuart's true status altered from that of an historic monument to that of the great master of portraiture he was: a brilliant exponent of a movement we have too long overlooked; a *Georgian* painter, trained to intellectual habits and studio procedures, dependent on references like a modern historian. Subtle and highly developed, his art cannot be appreciated without understanding.

Charles M. Mount

May 19, 1963
Ashford, Co. Wicklow

Gilbert Stuart

PROLOGUE

The Georgian Portrait

AMONG THE most conspicuous monuments of English history are the gracious portraits of the Georgian age. These convey to us still an extraordinary impression of the culture and elegance and established power of that world. The ladies, with magnificent self-assurance, dominate carefully tended landscapes; the gentlemen stand gracefully in their frames, their attitudes of nonchalance belying a worldly competence at politics and business and the resourcefulness which secured a far-flung empire. Officers in battledress, the sprinkling of dark and slant-eyed faces, recall the realities of an imperial era. Apart from their beauty, these remarkable pictures have the second distinction of expressing perfectly the life that inspired them. Landscape, so essential a part, symbolized the strong roots in the earth of an essentially agrarian kingdom. At least half of a gentleman's life was spent on his estate, from which his wealth was drawn and where, discarding powdered wig and silk hose, he supervised the planting of crops and handling of cattle. His gun and hunting coat were part of the normal costume, his horse a mark of service performed freeing the land of foxes or officering a regiment.

These gracious, airy portraits, designed to take their place in the stately comfortable homes architecturally appropriate to this life, are intimately associated with the long reign of George III and were the product of deliberately evolved artistic principles. Though the prototype can be traced to Titian and sources more remote, it was first brought to England by a Fleming, Anthony Van Dyck, in the seventeenth century. Nurtured at classical sources by Rubens, his master,

Van Dyck placed on portraiture the gentle, firm stamp of his distinctive personality. The clarity of his heads, the elegance of his hands, the Italian skies and landscapes that peeked from behind his columns and draperies, but most of all the quiet majesty of his mood, left an indelible impression on English aristocratic taste. From Titian Van Dyck had learned economy of modeling: a head gained in beauty when its forms remained pure, simple, and flat, its lines crisply traced around areas of clean bright flesh. To eliminate half-tones and any but one strong shadow beneath the nose assisted the impression of clarity, and successive generations made this a formula to which painters strictly adhered.

Further refinement came with Sir Peter Lely, a Dutchman, who added his own solidness, accomplished technique, and gloss. The German Sir Godfrey Kneller reduced these to a formula rapidly assembled for vast repetition. Despite vicissitudes at the hands of less well-endowed practitioners, a special character for portraiture became fixed. This art was distinguished by largeness of vision, bold design, flat, simple lighting, and the utmost restraint in three-dimensional form.

The long tradition at last came into the hands of native-born English artists in the second half of the eighteenth century. Filled with the sense of cultural inferiority that is England's special invention, they dared not deviate from their continental models. The practice Rubens had developed of rummaging through the works of older masters, taking whole sections from some works, and from others a fragment, an idea, or an arrangement, became a firm artistic principle. And engravings developed a half-mystic significance that neither Rubens nor Van Dyck would have understood. A higher development was brought about by three men of genius who, in violation of all probabilities, were of the same generation and worked at the same time in London—Reynolds, Gainsborough, and Romney. For literalness of appearances these men substituted a new aesthetic at once more abstract and more sophisticated. They did so with a profusion that is startling, leaving one aghast that they could be so prolific while practicing a craft so delicate, demanding, and highly wrought. Curious also is that these men lived in the belief that they worked at a lesser branch of art. Painters of the time were urged by the examples of the Italian masters to devote themselves to scenes from history and mythology. However, the practical English patrons preferred to see recognizable persons in their pictures. To this economic circumstance the world is indebted for the most perfect flowering of English pictorial genius, the Georgian Portrait.

In an intellectual sense, as well as through his professional dominance, Sir Joshua Reynolds became the established leader of English art, and by his example he elevated the status of his fellows. On his return from Rome, in 1753, Reynolds quickly gave a new impetus to English portraiture and formed it in the mode most readily remembered. That the landscape setting became a principal attribute was due to him alone. The heroic military portrait against battle-smoke and the gentleman seated in his library were equally his inventions. Because of Reynolds' desire to emulate Raphael, English mothers caressed the nudity of their young babes in a manner without precedent in English art.

Rivals competed with Reynolds, but as creator of the modes his contemporaries adopted, he remained their primary master. In addition to obvious organizational genius, as a portraitist Reynolds had a remarkable if unsubtle sense of character. His ladies are charming, his dowagers forceful, his Bishops properly sententious. Parallel with a painting tradition he also founded one of taste and criticism, and the supremacy of his position made possible the formation of a Royal Academy with sponsorship from the throne. Though George III warmly detested him, Reynolds was chosen first President and given a knighthood; his addresses delivered to the Academy remain the fullest expression of eighteenth-century orthodox dogma.

The rival art of Thomas Gainsborough was at once less grandiose and more personal. His was an expression of the characteristic English gift for handling pigment with grace and brilliance. Lacking the constructional genius of Reynolds, Gainsborough yet followed the conventions he fixed, feeling perhaps more fully the French elegance of which Reynolds betrayed an oblique awareness.

George Romney's superior color and craftsmanship made him a strong contender in a three-sided contest. His was an artistic conscience which forbade the employment of assistants, and he developed a convention all his own by painting hands, figures, and draperies from living models who posed in the studio; the best known of these was Emma, later Lady Hamilton. Romney's works thus often have a proficiency which those of Reynolds lack, foreshadowing the new nineteenth-century integrity of working solely from the living model, which colors still our ideas of propriety in portraiture.

To whichever of these distinguished artists the patron went, procedures were uniform. "It requires in general three sittings," Reynolds wrote to an applicant; "about an hour and a half each time. But if the sitter chooses, the face could be begun and finished in one day; it is divided into separate times for the convenience and ease of the person who sits. When the face is finished the rest is done without troubling the sitter." Prices were well-known in the society from which applicants were drawn, and at the first sitting payment of half the fee was demanded. Customarily, portraits were done in four sizes, which simplified the procedure for patron and frame-maker alike. Most common was the bust, on a canvas twenty-five by thirty inches. Slightly larger, and higher in proportion to its width, was the kit-kat. The three-quarter portrait showed the subject to the knee, whether standing or seated, and was less in demand than the full-length, to which both artists and patrons were specially dedicated. In large measure it was by their success with full-length portraits that artists were judged.

Each sitter was asked whether he preferred to be shown standing or seated, indoors or in landscape, and a portfolio of engravings, after the artist's own works and those of older masters, was proffered to aid his selection. In three sittings, often arranged to fall at different hours several days apart, a finished head was produced on an otherwise bare canvas. Confident that a likeness had been secured, and that in a few weeks' or months' time his completed picture would be delivered, the sitter departed. An artist might receive as many as six sitters in a day, each of whose portraits was in some different stage of development. Every morning the artist's dry pigments were measured out and ground with oil by an assistant, pupil, or apprentice until they were of good consistency to be placed in orderly arrangement on his palette. Romney liked his whites made thick and pasty, to churn well under pressure from bristle brushes. Gainsborough and Reynolds, who in the normal usage of that time employed brushes of sable hair, were less exacting about the consistency of their colors; though Reynolds kept his media, oils, and varnishes locked away in a cupboard, so that even favored assistants were unable to learn with what he worked.

After the last sitter had departed, figures and backgrounds were advanced. According to rigid aesthetic principles, the artist made a conscientious effort to borrow heavily from older sources, employing the perfections of earlier works to guarantee the quality of his own. A classic statue might provide the "attitude" for a figure, or it might derive from Van Dyck. Well-disposed hands were sought in the works of Raphael, Lely, and the French court painters; graceful legs were found in Van Dyck's cavalier portraits; a column and a drape were taken from Rigaud; trees suitable for the landscape were searched for in engravings after Claude and Rubens. Such was the force of their belief in this mode of constructing a portrait and so remarkable their intellectual application that a fine picture usually evolved. The method was essential to the work. The point was nicely put by a contemporary of Reynolds: "When a single posture is imitated from a historic picture, and applied to a portrait in a different dress, this is not plagiarism, but quotation; and a quotation from a great author, with a novel application of the sense, has always been allowed to be an instance of parts and taste, and may have more merit than the original." A later critic wrote more simply that Reynolds "borrowed to improve," which has equal truth, for in fact he did improve both the source and his own work.

Through supreme understanding, ability, and craftsmanship, these borrowed accessories when used in a conventional but contemporary manner added a sense of classic grandeur. Likenesses ceased to be essays in reportage and became works of imaginative power, expressive of that gentle, earthy, aristocratic age. This is most clearly recognized when finished pictures are compared with the uncompleted sketches left behind. And finally, the fact that accessories were taken from engravings had the virtue of keeping these secondary elements flat and weightless, thus contributing their decorative beauty to the ensemble without distraction. Wrought so deliberately to the temper of its time, the Georgian portrait was the perfect expression of its world of graces, occasional crudities, and classic orientation. It brings us, better than its contemporary literature, furniture, or architecture, an immediate insight to the period. And if it was an expression of a world, a society, a mentality, and a way of life, it was more. It was the first complete avowal of intellect as an artistic element, and of the supremacy of style. For the first time we come on the principle that style is everything: the classic allusion of these portraits, the bold brushing, carefully arranged dress, juggling of pictorial elements, and arbitrary use of color show them to be works designed along principles of the artist's self-interest. The subject is held secondary to the artist, who has ceased to be subordinate, and for the first time has become the dominant personality of the two.

By 1782 King George III had been on his throne twenty years, America was lost, and the art and literature associated with his long reign were in full flower. The three men whose art best expressed this epoch neared their final rewards. Trained in the studio of Reynolds, John Hoppner appeared to be the natural successor, until in that year he was thrust aside by the spectacular success of a newer, more vigorous young American. For a short time this American was heir apparent to British art and its Georgian portrait: his name was Gilbert Stuart.

PART ONE

The Kingdom and the Glory

I

Over the Sea to Skye

HIS FIRST brilliant success was delicious to Stuart, for his
road to it had been painful and had left scars that never
healed. The seeds of his strangely unbalanced career and
personality lay in obscure beginnings, which must be examined with
particular care, for at no time was his genius the attribute of an entirely normal person. He was born near Newport, Rhode Island,
December 3, 1755. When the cold of winter abated, the four months'
old infant was duly carried to the Old Narragansett Church of St.
Paul's, where, on April 11, 1756, he was baptized by the Rev. Dr.
McSparren, whose aged apple-cheeks and toothless mouth are recorded by the brush of John Smibert. Though Dr. McSparren thereafter passed from the scene, his deed, performed on Palm Sunday,
was remembered; and like many persons whose birth was recollected
by an association, Stuart celebrated his birthday at Easter.

Although Stuart was born into the artisan class, the cultivation he
later displayed was suggestive of higher origins, and in fact such seem
to have existed. Successive authors have scoffed at the family traditions, but there is nothing intrinsically unbelievable in the tale that
his father, also named Gilbert Stuart, or more properly *Stewart*, was
born in Perth, Scotland, the son of a Presbyterian clergyman who
had him educated for the ministry. Details recorded by the family
are distinctly corroborative when viewed against the period of Scotch
history that followed the defeat of English arms at Fontenoy.

This proudest of Louis XV's personal victories took place in 1745,
when under his royal eye a hard-pressed French army, led by Marshal

de Saxe, Europe's best general, administered to the English a crushing defeat. Scotland rejoiced to see its oppressors humbled, and when shortly afterward a Stuart Pretender to the English throne, the glamorous, heroic, half-legendary Charles Edward, arrived in Scotland to assert his claims, the Highlands rallied to his banner. They did not do so from any loyalty to a Catholic Prince whose forebears their own Scottish army had destroyed, but out of the discontent of an increasing poverty. In this context the assertion by a later member of the family that the elder Gilbert Stewart "was in opposition to the father on the subject of politics, [and] joined the standard of the Pretender" strikes the correct note. An educated young man, lacking a church appointment from the Newcastle administration in London, he would have felt strongly his own discontents and those of his fellow Scots. Given the rabid enthusiasms of the family, he might well have joined the Pretender. It would have been strange had he not, once the vigor and spirit of that movement had carried it to a conquest of all Scotland, and an invasion of the English midlands. The elder Stewart's father, a Presbyterian clergyman, more easily saw the distinctions between a Highland uprising and the creation of a Catholic king opposed to his Presbyterian church; for the return of the Stuarts meant Catholicism and subservience to France.

The inevitable followed. England stood firm. At Culloden the Pretender was defeated; he retreated and fled. The Highlands were remorselessly reconquered and as the years passed became a barren waste. The elder Stewart, father of the painter, is believed to have been present at Culloden, and it may be supposed that the brutal reprisals and proscriptions were the cause of his taking ship to America. In the new country his first-born son was baptized James, and the second, named Gilbert after himself, to which later was added Charles; the royal names of the Stuart dynasty.

The place where the elder Stewart landed in America and the date are facts lost in the mists of time. Undoubtedly Stewart himself was responsible for this absence of detail. Passage money to America averaged six to eight pounds sterling, a sum not easily found by defeated and impoverished Scots. An agreement usually was made with a ship's Captain whereby the non-paying passenger was indentured on his arrival in America. His buyer accepted obligation for the transportation and, after four to seven years, the immigrant was freed from service and equipped with a new suit of clothes. In essence such indenture was parallel to an apprenticeship at home; and as Stewart's first years in America remain unaccounted for, and he then appeared in Rhode Island with the new trade of mill-wright after an elapse of years sufficient for a term of indenture, his story was probably typical of other luckless and poor.

He appears to have borne his trials with an exemplary courage, as befitted a man trained for the ministry, and when his service ended, about 1751, to have re-asserted his social status by moving to the Scottish colony at Newport, Rhode Island. There he met a learned physician named Thomas Moffat, who in a community of English Quakers and Scotch Presbyterians was distinguished by having studied at the famous Boerhaven medical school at Leyden. Uncongenial to his sober Quaker neighbors because of his dress and manners, Moffat was unable to make his way as a doctor. He sought another gentle existence, and began cultivating tobacco for the manufacture of snuff.

The custom of taking snuff was widespread, and no gentleman was properly outfitted without a sea-shell, or a silver or gold snuff-box peeking from the pocket of his waistcoat. Fashion made the cost of snuff high; once established, the taking of this stimulant was an unbreakable habit. In the American colonies snuff was imported by sea from Glasgow.

At Dr. Moffat's suggestion, Stewart, described by a contemporary as somewhat imprudent but attractive and ingenious, agreed to undertake the cultivation of tobacco and to build a snuff-mill at the head of Petaquanset Pond in North Kingston County. Before entering into a written partnership with Dr. Moffat, Stewart, on May 31, 1751, married Elizabeth Anthony, the pretty daughter of a family with substantial land holdings. Though not a brilliant match for her, for Stewart, marriage into a family which shared his own respectable origins and which had been associated with Dean Berkeley when that notable cleric dreamed of a utopian colony on their land, confirmed his status as a well-bred artisan. Recorded in the Land Titles as a Mill Right, the registered partnership he entered into November 5, 1751 shows Stewart to be an equal partner with Dr. Moffat. A third partner, Edward Cole, is described with eighteenth-century frankness as "gentleman." The record clearly states that the intention of this partnership was "to erect an engine for the manufacture of snuff"; and in the two-story building with gambrel roof, a large, high framed structure, the mill-wright's famous son was born four years later.

A century and a half had passed since white men first landed in the American wilderness, and their work had been accomplished well. The boyhood of Gilbert Stuart was little different from what it might have been were he born to a family of similar circumstances in England, Scotland, or Ireland. Living far from town, the Stewarts were dependent on their garden for vegetables, their yard for poultry, and a butcher's shop for meat, unless they followed the custom of killing their cows in winter and salting the meat. Indians existed, but a hundred miles distant, in the uncleared forests of the "west." The greatest danger was from French incursions in the north and west, and these were effectively dealt with by British regulars and the stronger colony of Virginia.

Only the slightest impression could have been made on the young Gilbert Stuart by this mill in which he was born, despite a heavy scent that rose when tobacco was ground on the lower floor. Prosperity seemed not far distant; some of it appears to have reached Dr. Moffat—the mill-wright less. Lack of glass containers, in which snuff ordinarily was sold, brought failure. Stewart remitted his interest in 1761, and with his wife, elder son James, daughter Anne, and five-year-old Gilbert, moved to Newport. In doing so, as a final assertion of loyalty, he defiantly altered the spelling of his name from Stewart to *Stuart*. The inclination to stiffen his pride in adversity was something he passed on to his more famous son; hopeless impracticality was another characteristic; absentmindedness a third. Stuart's wife recounted with obvious pleasure how she once started off to church with him, riding behind on the same horse. Lost in reverie, he allowed her to slip to the ground from the jogging beast. Only after some minutes did he sense her absence and ride back to find her resting complacently on the road, enjoying the anticipation of his surprise. "God's-my-life," he cried: "Are you hurt?"

What occupation the elder Stuart followed at Newport is uncertain. At one period he invented a machine for loading vessels, by which some other party was enriched; his genius was of that quality, and this too was transmitted to his son. His wife was given land, presumably from the holdings of her family, and this, it is assumed, they farmed. Their poverty was relative, but not without some graces, for Mrs. Stuart's family remained one of means, and she herself owned a slave woman who had a child. A township called Newport was laid out in Nova Scotia at the time the partnership was dissolved, Stuart's name appearing among the grantees. Probably he considered moving north, but fourteen years later was still at Newport, Rhode Island, described again as a "snuff-maker," which implies that he continued working at his trade.

Stuart the artist later described the family abode as "a hovel on Bannister's wharf." When five years old he became a charity scholar at the Parochial School of Trinity Church. Here he learned the beautifully articulated script that distinguished him, and he was taught the rudiments of Latin. His mother, ignorant of that language, studied it herself to assist him, not without comic results. And from the earliest time he demonstrated an observant eye and a desire to draw. When a very rare execution occurred at Newport the town turned out to watch the solemn procession of criminal and hooded hangman, wondering who had been induced to perform the awful deed.

"Oh, I know who it was," is the earliest recorded quotation from this precocious child.

"What put that into your head?" he was asked.

"I knew him by his *sues* [shoes]," came the confident reply.

THE EARLY death of his elder brother James left Charles Gilbert an only son, the joy of both father and mother and the leader in every mischief among his friends. An early description finds him "a very capable, self-willed boy, who, perhaps on that account, was indulged in everything, being an only son; handsome and forward, and habituated at home to have his own way in everything, with little or no control from the easy, good-natured father." For a time he boarded at school, where his unfettered imagination made him a problem. Betrayed in one exploit by a local shoemaker, he vowed vengeance; armed with an old gun, blood from a butcher's shop, and a syringe, he led a mighty plot. The blood was mixed with warm water and put in the syringe, the gun given a liberal charge of powder. On a summer evening Stuart and a friend crept to the open window of the shoemaker's establishment, near which the cobbler was at work. One boy fired the gun, while the second squirted warm blood on the cobbler's bald head.

Startled by the explosion and finding blood trickling down his neck, the shoemaker rolled over among his lasts and lap-stones, calling out that he was murdered. With assistance he was got to bed, where his wife proceeded to explore in vain for the wound. When in a short time the shoemaker felt as comfortable as ever, the trick was suspected. Immediately he ran to school, where Stuart and his friend were discovered in bed wearing shoes; the customary application of birch followed, without achieving any moral purpose.

He was a leader among his friends, easily communicative, and had a decided charm in his twinkling, handsome face. One can only surmise what influence on his character was exerted by the deformity of one leg that in after life was noticeably leaner than the other. The boy was at one period attended by Dr. William Hunter, a Newport physician who retained an interest in him, but whether a hereditary defect or acquired through childhood illness, his infirmity failed to hamper youthful spirit. Later it received notice, and that he never mentioned it himself, except during his last illness, implies sensitivity. From this infirmity it is possible that his craving for sympathy developed, and to it also is attributable the special degree of parental affection he received. To his parents an obvious intelligence and the artistic inclinations of the sensitive were blissful compensation.

Young Stuart learned to play tunes on the flute and harpsichord, and continued to draw. Like any provincial center, Newport possessed a share of pictures carried from its inhabitants' older, more distant homes. Occasional visits from itinerant artists, who treated the American colonies as an extension of their rambles through the English provinces, provided an additional stimulant. The same pictures were found at Newport as at Bristol, Edinburgh, Cork, or Kilkenny, and it is recorded that a group of these paintings were in possession of the family on whose wharf the Stuarts lived; Mr. John Bannister's house stood a mile from town. There the boy undoubtedly beheld a three-quarter-length portrait of Charles I, and another of Henrietta Maria, while a reputed Van Dyck self-portrait introduced him to that master. More current fashions were manifest in portraits by Robert Feke, and between past and present were examples by Sir Godfrey Kneller, whose portrait of the Czar Peter was at the home of Isaac Hart. At thirteen one of Stuart's friends noted his greater interest in drawing; he copied, probably in pencil, a few of the pictures he saw, and a little later was emboldened to essay pencil portraits. Soon a side of the family barn was covered with sketches in charcoal and chalk.

Thus passed a childhood that does not appear to have been unhappy. Whatever his artistic essays, young Stuart was mainly oc-

"I wish so too . . . but I am determined not to . . . affect raptures for music I do not feel."

STUART's portraits were becoming increasingly accepted at New-port. His ability to catch a likeness was noted by his mother's younger brother, Joseph Anthony, a prosperous Philadelphia merchant, who on a visit admired a picture executed from memory of the young man's grandmother. Stuart also painted his own father, and John Bannister. An aching primitive intensity appears in these laboriously wrought pictures, each part of which is rendered minutely, with detriment to the whole. Only in the eyes, which shine with frank self-assurance, can one detect the gift that was to mature. His next sitters were drawn from the Jewish merchants of Newport; a por-trait of Jacob Rodriguez Rivera is known, others have disappeared or remain unrecognized, and only the name Lopez, and Stuart's as-sertion that he painted a rabbi, have survived.

His activities would indicate a minor prosperity, until, inevitably, too much was asked of him. Mention of a full-length portrait froze him with fear; one suspects he already had experienced failure with these difficult works, probably at Edinburgh. "A committee of the Redwood Library, of Newport," Benjamin Waterhouse remembered, "waited upon him to engage him to paint a full-length of its founder, Abraham Redwood, then living next door to the painter, for which the young artist would have had a generous reward. But [despite] all that his parents and the rest of his friends could say, he declined it in sullen silence, and by so doing turned the popular tide in some degrees against him . . . This occurrence cooled the zeal of many of his friends." By its very abnormality the reaction demands inspection; *he declined it in sullen silence* well notes his trauma at the thought of the full-length portrait, normally considered the particular glory of an artist's skill. When first we find him faced by such an effort he al-ready was deeply scarred.

He did in fact paint a half-length portrait of Redwood, but the damage to his Newport patronage had been done. Soon after, the young artist set up in Boston, to profit, perhaps, from the recent de-parture of Copley. Again almost no facts are preserved, except for the recollection of a lad to whom he gave instruction. "Stuart was the first person who learnt me to draw at about twelve years of age in Boston. He lived then," wrote Mather Brown, "near Mr. Whiting's, a print-seller near Mill Bridge."

If, as seems evident, Stuart was aware of Copley's colonial renown, for the portrait of Francis and Saunders Malbone, painted at this time, is strongly influenced by Copley, then Stuart also knew that in June 1774 this brightest son of native American genius sailed from Boston to England. Copley's departure had been dictated by a growing desire to perfect his art; he acted on the advice of Reynolds and Benjamin West, with whom he had long been in correspondence. That a consignment of tea addressed to his father-in-law, Richard Clarke, was thrown into the Boston harbor at that most famous of tea-parties probably did no more than unsettle him. Even before Copley departed, on May 17, 1774, the first of many calls issued from Providence for an intercolony Congress. By September the delegates who met at Philadelphia topped their recommendations by advising the people to arm. The winter that followed was an angry truce; then in April, 1775, at Lexington, began the war fated to last eight long years.

As Massachusetts broke into armed conflict Stuart found himself caught in the besieged city of Boston. He struggled to find a way out, and on June 7, ten days before British regulars charged colonial troops on Bunker Hill, he made his dash back to Newport. No trade awaited a returned portrait-painter. Whether rich or poor, merchants saw ruin in a war that prevented ships from entering their ports. Loyalties conflicted; some saw virtue in adherence to the monarch, others saw profit in denying him. But at Newport the Scottish colony stood true to a Hanoverian dynasty it had reviled thirty years before.

While Stuart was absent in Boston his friend Benjamin Waterhouse had departed for England, armed with the hope that he could study medicine, and carrying a recommendation to his rich cousin, the famous Quaker physician, Dr. John Fothergill. Stuart sorely missed his friend, "for, beside me," admitted Waterhouse, "he had no associate with whom he could expatiate and dispute upon painting and music." A more serious loss ensued when shortly Stuart's own father slipped out of Rhode Island to take up the lands he had been granted in Nova Scotia a dozen years before. These he began to clear and to stock with cattle, in preparation for his family. But the feckless, charming, and ingenious man who was his father had passed from Gilbert Stuart's life, for Nova Scotia, a new wilderness, offered no hope of employment to an artist. His work had shown considerable improvement since he studied the example of Copley, and now that he was unemployed in Rhode Island, possibly the example of Copley's action suggested itself. Nearly possessed of the Bostonian's skills, as he imagined himself, in England he could accomplish whatever Copley could. Early in the summer of 1775 he took a fateful decision: he would go to England.

His mother, to whom he was much devoted, hated the plan. Her fears, however, were quieted by the elder Waterhouse, who, in a true Quaker vein, likened their sons to David and Jonathan. But passage to England in the face of rebellion and the teeth of blockade required means sadly lacking at Newport. An arrangement was made with Mrs. Stuart's younger brother, Joseph Anthony, for Gilbert to go to Philadelphia. Elated by the prospect, he passed most of the night before his departure playing his flute beneath the window of a young lady.

"His uncle . . ." Waterhouse remembered, "was proud of his ingenious nephew, and employed him to paint a portrait of himself, and of his wife and children," and an entry in Anthony's account books shows his nephew's presence in Philadelphia during July, 1775. By then, at Cambridge, the military destiny of the American colonies had been placed formally in the hands of George Washington. The artist whose name is inextricably associated with Washington's meantime fled south into Virginia. At Norfolk, where he retained earlier acquaintances, he awaited an England-bound ship in which he took passsage.

II

In the Wilderness

WEEKS stretched into months as the slow sailing vessel wallowed toward England. Accounts do not agree how late in 1775 land hove in view, but it was probably autumn when for the second time in his short life Stuart disembarked on a foreign shore and made his way to London to join Benjamin Waterhouse. Equipped for his courageous undertaking with but one known letter of introduction, without acquaintance in England, he was entirely dependent on his friend. Disappointment awaited him. Uninformed of Stuart's intention, Waterhouse had gone north, to the medical school at Edinburgh. "Your father was at our house just before I left home," the youth wrote balefully after his vanished friend. ". . . He said Gilbert and Ben are so knit together like David and Jonathan, that if you heard from one, you would also hear from the other."

The gentle warping process had begun. Separated from his family and the one friend on whom he depended, at twenty Stuart was faced again with the dismal prospect of making his way in a foreign land. He seems to have been disheartened from the start. Cheap lodgings were found, probably with a tailor called John Palmer, in York Buildings on Buckingham Street near the Strand, and there he began the lonely battle with fortune for which he was so ill-equipped. The quaintness of his colonial attire, a generation behind London's fashion, presented the first obstacle to be overcome, and he acquired a new stylish green overcoat. Though better dressed, he remained still an artist scarcely competent by London standards, and one who lacked the necessary contacts to enter the world of fashion where alone portraits were a part of life. Now and again he did receive an order, which he executed at a price so low it scarcely provided for food. Better artists than this ill-trained youth found it expedient to emigrate to India or Dublin. The English provinces were the best he could hope for, a knowledge that itself eluded him. Ignorant of the craft as well as the scope of his profession and the conditions necessary to it, he remained frozen to London, and under the harassments of the ill-fortune that found him, his belief in himself crumbled rapidly.

"I don't know the day of the month or even what month, and I have no one to ask at present, but the day of the week is Tuesday, I believe," he appended to another letter sent Waterhouse. A too-frank cry for sympathy, his emotional indulgences are instructive of his state; exposed to an unrelievedly grim prospect, faced by the same debacle that overwhelmed him in Edinburgh three years before, and, equally powerless to stave it off, he sank into dejected self-pity. Years later he recalled how "destitute of the means whereby to support himself, or pay his landlord for board and lodging, already due, [he was] walking the streets without any definite object in view."

Even a return to Newport was impossible. In February 1776 Stuart's mother petitioned the Rhode Island General Assembly for permission to leave the colony. She expressed herself "willing to give the amplest security that nothing but the wearing apparel and household furniture of the family and the necessary provisions for the voyage shall be carried . . ." And her own plight in Rhode Island was well suggested; "exclusive of the impracticality of her supporting herself and her family in the said colony, which strongly impels her to follow her said husband, she is very desirous of joining him, which she is bound in duty to do if possible." The petition was granted, and probably in early March, 1776, Stuart's mother, sister Anne, and whatever smaller children were referred to, sailed to Nova Scotia.

Ignorant of these events, Stuart managed to exist through his first shattering winter in London. Waterhouse returned from Edinburgh in the summer of 1776 to find him still lodged with the tailor, his easel occupied by an unfinished portrait. The sitter was probably Sir Alexander Grant, a former patron of Cosmo Alexander, to whom Stuart had brought his only letter of introduction. Sir Alexander had paid the needy young man in advance. His fee realized, Stuart lost interest; the picture "remained long in his lodgings, and I am not sure that it was ever finished," recalled Waterhouse.

Waterhouse's return eased his sad plight and had the parallel advantage of holding him in check. For short periods Stuart wriggled free from melancholy, and when he did an obsessive gaiety took hold of him. Together the two rambled London, for a guide using Maitland's *The History of London from Its Foundation to the Present Time*, and:

> agreed to devote one day a week to viewing pictures, wherever we could get admittance . . . We made it a point also to walk together through all the narrow lanes of London, and having a pocket map, we marked such streets and lanes as we passed through with a red lead pencil, and our map was full two-thirds streaked over with red when we received some solemn cautions and advice to desist from our too curious rambles. We were told by some who knew better than we did that we ran a risk of bodily injury, or the loss of our hats and watches, if not our lives, when we gave up the project. We had however, pursued it once a week for more than two years, and never experienced other than verbal abuse, chiefly from women, and saw a great deal of that dirty, monstrous, overgrown city, containing, to appearance, no other people than the natives of Britain and Ireland, and a few Jews, not laughing and humming a song like the populace of Paris, but, wearing a stern, anxious, discontented phys[iognomy].

Much like any tourist, Stuart made foolish jokes of the statues at the British Museum. One in particular reminded him of a Newport personality famous for his arithmetic powers. "I see you have a head of *Calculating Jemmy* here," he quipped to the guard.

"Calculating Jemmy!" came the scandalized response. "That is the head of Sir Isaac Newton."

A propensity to bait those about him, not always within the limits of good taste, was further evident when he boarded a coach. His fellow passengers were strangers, gentlemen it seemed, and one, finding his talk amusing, ventured to ask his occupation. With grave face and serious tone Stuart replied that he sometimes dressed a gentleman's or lady's hair.

"You are a hairdresser, then?"

"What!" said he. "Do you take me for a barber?"

"I beg your pardon, sir, but I inferred it from what you said. If I mistook you, may I take the liberty to ask what you are, then?"

"Why, I sometimes brush a gentleman's coat, or hat, and sometimes adjust a cravat."

"Oh, you are a valet, then, to some nobleman?"

"A valet! Indeed, sir, I am not. I am not a servant,—to be sure, I make coats and waistcoats for gentlemen."

"Oh, you are a tailor?"

"Tailor! Do I look like a tailor? I assure you, I never handled a goose other than a roasted one."

By this time all in the coach roared.

"What the devil are you then?" asked another.

"I'll tell you," said Stuart. "Be assured all I have said is literally true. I dress hair, brush hats and coats, adjust a cravat, and make coats, waistcoats, and breeches, and likewise boots and shoes, *at your service*."

"Oh, a boot and shoemaker after all!"

"Guess again, gentlemen. I never handle boots or shoes but for my own feet and legs, yet all I have told you is true."

"We may as well give up guessing."

Stuart forced himself to cease laughing, and renewed his flow of spirit with a large pinch of snuff. He then addressed his fellow-travelers very gravely.

"Now, gentlemen, I will not play the fool with you any longer, but will tell you, upon my honor as a gentleman, my *bona fide* profession. I get my bread by making faces."

With this he screwed his features into such contortions that his fellow-travelers were overcome by laughter. Each took credit to himself for having suspected all along that he belonged to the theater. To their utter astonishment Stuart next informed them he was never on the stage, and very rarely saw the inside of a playhouse. The trip drew to a close; before stepping from the carriage he explained.

"Gentlemen, you will find that all I have said of my various employments is comprised in these words; *I am a portrait painter*. If you will call at John Palmer's, York Building, London, I shall be ready and willing to brush you a coat or hat, dress your hair à la mode, supply you, if need be, with a wig of any fashion or dimension, accommodate you with boots or shoes, give you ruffles or cravats, and make faces for you."

The passengers all repaired to an Inn, for a parting glass. A chance question, concerning in what part of England he was born, launched

Stuart on new patter. He told them he was not born in England, Wales, Ireland, or Scotland.

"Where then?" he was asked.

"I was born in Narrangansett."

"Where's that?"

"Six miles from Pottowoone, and ten miles from Poppasquash, and about four miles from Conanicut—not far from the spot where the famous battle with the warlike Pequots was fought."

"In what part of the East Indies is that, sir?"

"East Indies, my dear sir! It is in the state of Rhode Island, between Massachusetts and the Connecticut River."

THE EXCESSES of Stuart's gaiety were as unhealthy as his despair, and born of the same mechanism. "With Stuart it was either high tide or low tide. In London he would sometimes lie abed for weeks, waiting for the tide to lead him on to fortune," recalled Waterhouse. His sufferings were no less acute for their nervous origins; he could see no future, and at the same moment he was capable of entire improvidence. He neglected what work he received, had constant difficulties over money, and twice was seized by bailiffs who confined him in "sponging houses," from which Waterhouse was forced to release him by the payment of his debts. "Of my allowance of pocket money he had two thirds, and more than once the other third." Waterhouse also did service as artist's model, and represented "to him what Rembrandt's mother was to that wonderful Dutchman, an object at hand on which to exercize a ready pencil. I once prevailed on him to try his pencil on a canvas of three-quarters size, representing me with both hands clasping my right knee thrown over my left one, and looking steadfastly on a human skull placed on a polished mahogany table." Waterhouse's description is the only knowledge we have of this work, and all the pictures of this period. However many Stuart began or completed, their nature and appearance are as lost to us as the pictures themselves. The period, one of grave significance in the moral and psychological development of the artist and man, is graced by no preserved works.

Waterhouse's singular resource in England remained his rich Quaker relative, Dr. John Fothergill; a small, withered, ascetic man, whose enormous medical practice netted him upwards of £7,000 a year. Unmarried, distinguished in his profession, respected for his creed, a friend of Benjamin Franklin, with whom he negotiated to prevent war in America, Dr. Fothergill not only admitted his young kinsman to his bounty, but Stuart as well. By courtesy of Dr. Fothergill, that summer of 1776 Waterhouse was granted privileges in the London hospitals. He took quarters with a linen-draper married to Fothergill's niece, but the new abode in Gracechurch Street "was about three miles from Stuart's lodgings, an inconvenience and grievance to us both as we could not see each other every day. Therefore measures were taken to procure him [Stuart] lodgings between the houses of my two cousins, Mrs. Freeman and Mrs. Chorley, nieces of my kinsman and patron Dr. Fothergill. This was the best I could do for my friend."

But it was not all. Soon Stuart was directed by Dr. Fothergill to paint a portrait of Waterhouse, though no one who visited the doctor's Harpur Street house caught sight of the picture. Eventually the gesture was recognized for "a delicate mode of giving the young American artist ten guineas." Dr. William Curtis, an associate of Dr. Fothergill's, became another sacrificial lamb; and soon Stuart was asked to paint two Quaker sisters, who, in the manner of the time, were to impersonate *The Comic and Tragic Muses.* Events moved more swiftly through the autumn: a full-length portrait of Dr. John C. Lettsom came next, and though Quakers were not attached to the arts, which accounted for Dr. Fothergill's unwillingness to hang pictures, Waterhouse skillfully employed his contacts to keep Stuart "even with his landlord and washerwoman, which was doing better than he had done."

Stuart's modest abilities unfortunately were exceeded by the demands of Dr. Lettsom's full-length. At Newport he had already "declined in a sullen silence"; now he dared not treat friends with rebuff, nor could he finish. Struggling with problems of drawing, altering perspective, and composition, he brought failure on himself. Nor did the picture of the two sisters progress; to make a unified composition of them was beyond the capacities of an unnerved young man; the putative muses melt into forgotten history. Dr. Lettsom's picture became a cause célèbre that opened his wounds. Forever after a full-length filled him with icy terror; at the time his disgrace was complete, and in his dramatic display of dejection, he failed to begin a portrait of Dr. Fordyce for which Waterhouse had collected half-guineas from the subject's students:

> I was unwise enough to let my needy friend have the greater part of it before he commenced the painting, which I never could induce him even to begin. This was a source of inexpressible unhappiness and mortification, which at length brought on me a fever . . . After my recovery I had to refund the money, when I had not a farthing of my own, but what came from the thoughtful bounty of my most excellent kinsman, Dr. Fothergill, who would never afterwards see Gilbert Charles Stuart.

THE LITTLE bubble of Stuart's patronage had burst in shame and humiliation. Everyone now saw the awful incompetence he only then admitted to himself; but the realization of his limits only shook him further, leaving him too dazed and rigid to function with practicality. To seek advice the ever-solicitous Benjamin Waterhouse approached another distinguished Quaker, Benjamin West, who appears to have asked that Stuart visit him personally. Absorbed in the pleasures of his pain, Stuart's own hopes were placed in his uncle; the receipt of funds from Philadelphia, or a return thither, probably were the limits of his ambitions, and though Waterhouse pressed him to see West, he shrank from the cruel necessity.

As his circumstances deteriorated, finally Stuart took hold of himself, and went to West's fashionable house in Newman Street. The moment was singularly well chosen, for West was at dinner with American visitors, including Joseph Wharton, a Philadelphia merchant associated with Joseph Anthony. The servant who opened the door went to inform West he had a caller.

"I am engaged," he answered, but after a pause enquired, "Who is he?"

"He says, sir, that he is from America."

West left the table, and on returning spoke to Wharton. "There is a young man in the next room, who says he is known in *our* city. Go you and see what you can make of him."

The merchant found a handsome, pale, sad-looking youth, with sullen uneasiness about his eyes, who was dressed in a fashionable green overcoat; he explained in forthright fashion he was sent to

see what he could make of the caller. "You are known in Philadelphia?" he commenced.

"Yes, sir."

"Your name is Stuart?"

"Yes."

"You have no letters for Mr. West?"

"No, sir."

"Whom do you know in Philadelphia?"

"Joseph Anthony is my uncle."

"That's enough—come in," Wharton later recalled, "and I carried him in, and he received a hearty welcome."

In West's presence Stuart spoke, possibly disingenuously, of a long
desire to see him, and of his wish to improve himself in the arts. West
listened with kindness and attention, then asked that something Stuart
had painted be brought, so that he could form some judgment; he
may also have given Stuart the three or four guineas mentioned by
Waterhouse. On this satisfactory note the interview ended. Stuart
presumably returned with an example of his skill, and West, leader of
a deeply cultivated movement, advised him to copy the masters and
bring the results to him. West's quiet benevolence impressed Stuart,
and his paternal tone gave comfort. Aware of West's position, and
humbled by his own failures, he seems to have found a new determination.

Nothing material had been gained, however, and existence remained
grim. He found himself still aimlessly walking London's streets, "destitute of the means whereby to support himself, or pay his landlord
. . ." In one street, possibly Foster's Lane, he heard the notes of an
organ, and paused to listen; music was one of his own accomplishments, the organ an instrument he played. The sound led him to a
church. It appears to have been St. Vedast's, to which two years before
a new instrument had been given by William Duncombe, who undertook to play himself, or find an able performer in his place. Inside the church, trials for the vacant organist's post were taking place;
Stuart was asked if he wished to compete, and on agreeing proved
superior to the other candidates. As a reference to his good character
he gave a name, perhaps Sir Alexander Grant's, and was given the
position. His salary, possibly less than the thirty pounds a year he
later recalled, was the start toward a livelihood; but he later recollected as well that his valuable services were discontinued after three

months.

Benjamin West, who had detected unfavorable characteristics in Stuart too, continued to treat him with avuncular care—and to hold him at a distance. That Stuart won an appointment as organist he refused to believe until the note was shown him, nor did he know what to think when suddenly Stuart spoke of making music his career. However, the organist's position and musical ambitions then vanished, suddenly as they had appeared. His fortunes deteriorated still further, and by Easter of 1777 Stuart was in still worse straits. Reduced to one meal a day, and sometimes not that, having exhausted the patience of Waterhouse and his Quaker connections, his only avenue of appeal was to West. That Quaker gentleman continued to receive him kindly, to assist with advice, but remained distant. For others he had done more.

The Easter season, which launched Stuart on what he counted his twenty-first year, was disheartening. Hungry and miserable, unable to face West, and probably incapable of calling on him to explain his plight, the day after Palm Sunday he began a letter. At first he intended to pose and preen like a gentleman. In his most elegantly drawn script, generously flourished with round copper-plate decorations, he wrote *Mr. West, Sir;* then the violence of his emotions carried him away in an eruption of impassioned pleading.

> Monday Evening No. 30
> Gracechurch Street

Mr. West

Sir,

The benevolence of your disposition encourageth me, while my necesity urgeth me to write you on so disagreeable a subject. I hope I have not offended by taking this liberty; my poverty and ignorance are my only excuse. Let me beg that I may not forfeit your good will which is to me so desirable.

Pity me good sir. I've just arrived at the age of 21, an age when most young men have done something worthy of notice and find myself ignorant, without business or friends, without the necessities of life so far that for some time I have been reduced to one miserable meal a day and frequently not even that, destitute of the means of acquiring knowledge, my hopes from home blasted and incapable of returning thither, pitching headlong into misery I have only this hope. I pray that it may not be too great; to live and learn without being a burden. Should Mr. West in his abundant kindness think of aught for me I shall esteem it an obligation which shall bind me forever with gratitude. With the greatest humility

> Sir, Yours at Comd
> G. C. Stuart

To receive such a letter may have been no less frightening than to write it. Well-expressed, with a ranting display of colorful phrasing that betokened a cultivated mind, it betrayed too clearly Stuart's taste for misery. Sensitive, high-strung, neurotic, Stuart's letter was expressive of his own pleasure in pain for the joy of it. His motivation, as so often before, may have been a partly disingenuous desire to evoke pity, but West must have wondered what strange sort of person this was. He did not immediately offer to make a pupil of Stuart; he did, however, provide for him by giving employment in his studio as a copyist. To be nearer West, Stuart again found quarters off the Strand, at 27 Villiers Street, where Charing Cross Station now stands. Under West's sponsorship Stuart's *Portrait of a Gentleman* was admitted to the annual exhibition of the Royal Academy in May. The contumely of its reception ended finally his pretensions to being a portrait painter of professional qualification; he settled down to learn, and, growing calmer and somewhat more assured under West's paternal eye, and impressing the master more favorably now, Stuart accepted an invitation to become a pupil.

III

West, Copley, and Rigaud

THE NEWMAN Street residence of Benjamin West was appropriate for a personal friend and principal history painter to King George III. The central passage was hung with his studies, and led to a large gallery, where in a perfect diffused light, West's enormous epic paintings of religion and ancient lore were displayed. Casts of Venus and Apollo guarded the entrances to his various painting-rooms, and behind all, small but elegant, in the Italian taste of the time, was his garden, surrounded on three sides by an arcade studded with classic sculptures.

Barely forty, West was affluent if not rich, enjoying the most favored patronage an artist could have. Nevertheless, he retained a bearing of simplicity and quiet dignity. His manner was easy, his words few; his Quaker sobriety seemed little elevated by constant intercourse with royalty. Indeed, he was reputed to travel from his gallery in Newman Street to Windsor, and back again, with the staid demeanor of one of the brethren going to chapel. Of his importance at court he was willing enough to speak, though in a mild and meek way, affecting somewhat the vague diplomatic language of official men dealing with high matters. Since 1769 West had received orders from His Majesty in person; together they planned the subjects and set the prices. In addition to one thousand pounds a year paid on account, West received whatever more, and it was never much, might be due him for completed canvases. Fees for portraits, copies, and engravings after his historical works, provided the bulk of his income.

West's Pennsylvania twang revealed that his origins were comparable to those of his new pupil, and in the wilderness of his native colony
the Quaker conscience had been troubled by the revelation of his gift.
From books he early conceived the curious notion that artists were
exalted beings, and when, before he had reached man's stature, he
proclaimed "a painter is the companion of kings and emperors," the
brethren thought him surely mad. Their faith in his ability was not
lacking, however, and after a period as a primitive, when he cadged
instruction from whatever itinerant could be made to speak of his
craft, cribbed their pictures, and took orders from anyone who offered to pay, he found the means to study in Italy. His candor
astounded Rome; the Apollo Belvedere he likened to "a young Mohawk warrior . . . I have seen them often standing in the very attitude of this Apollo, and pursuing with an intense eye the arrow
which they have just discharged from the bow." The error, one of
natural frankness, was not repeated, for in Rome he encountered the
rising tide of a neoclassic revival, the theories and practices of which
he made his own. After three years of intense study and application,
crowned by success, esteem, honors, and a wide acquaintance among
visiting English gentry, he went to London, where he was a breath
of something fresh and new.

West's simple dignified ways, his "barbaric" origins, and the severe
classicism of his brush, suited the philosophic sophistry of that day.
Quickly he was introduced to Reynolds, Dr. Johnson, and Edmund
Burke, then had offers of employment from Burke's patron, Lord
Rockingham. He painted portraits while contemplating higher endeavors, and for Dr. Drummond, Archbishop of York, painted an
Agrippina With the Ashes of Germanicus which this good prelate
brought to the attention of the King. To this introduction, and the
consequent Royal favor, West owed his reputation and his employment.

If in his person West seemed remote and impassive, his art suffered
from the same defect. His was a rebirth of the spirit of Poussin, with
awe and grandeur as deliberate goals. His art aimed to instruct; to
make the lesson stronger he believed in the efficacy of enormous scale,
and though aware that inflation brought artistic dangers, he modestly
believed himself immune from them. Like the Georgian portraitists,
whose theory of art was closely related, West's compositions were
derived from elements separated from older works; his figures fre-

quently hark back to ancient sculpture; his skies speak of Poussin, his foliage of Claude, his women belong to Raphael, his men to Carracci and Michelangelo. The whole, when diligently planned and painted on enormous scale by West's corps of assistants, became a unique art, expressive of his own temperament and scholarship. Perhaps it bore less stamp of genius than he himself believed, but it succeeded in its major function of instructing, for West spread through England and the world classic lore and classic arts, an awareness of both, and a classic taste.

By entering West's house Stuart moved from the position of a provincial outsider to the inner currents of art. As a teacher West was not at his ease. To add wings to those whose imaginations were fit for flight was beyond his poor verbal power. He was again remote, sensible, instructive, with no unstudied felicities of phrase or aptness of illustration, and little vigor of thought. "No Negro boy ever had more difficulty expressing himself," Stuart noted, realizing that "this came from a want of literature." Nonetheless, West's teaching was reputed to be the best in England, based on carefully calculated rules from which the pupil was quoted "chapter and verse" for any problem that arose. Immune from artistic jealousy, West hid nothing from his pupils—unlike Reynolds, who seemed to care not at all whether his pupils advanced and who locked his paints-cupboard so that they could not see his materials. West exerted his influence to obtain permission for Stuart to see the Royal collections. Stuart's own enthusiastic anticipation is apparent in a note he sent Waterhouse:

Friend Benjamin,
By no means disappoint me, but be at my lodgings precisely at three o'clock, to go to the Queen's Palace.

Yours,
G. Stuart

Saturday afternoon

and long afterward, Waterhouse recalled, "we found nothing to equal the collection at Queen's Palace, or Buckingham House."

Stuart accommodated himself to the routine of West's house, carefully paced to the master's production. West rose early, studied before breakfast, at ten descended to the studio where he began to work on one of his enormous canvases. He painted with little interruption until four, then washed, dressed, and saw visitors. His house was a gathering-place for Americans who came to England, and he did not permit the American rebellion to alter his mode of hospitality; he invited guests to dinner, and having dined, resumed his studies. The regularity of this existence, and Stuart's sheltered position within it, eased much of his previous emotional stress. Routine and defined goals brought him greater stability. At West's suggestion he carried out simple exercises in drawing and painting, such as the representation of some object, or a piece of cloth carelessly thrown over a chair. And at anatomical lectures given by Dr. Cruikshank, to which West had recommended him, he made the acquaintance of William Coates, a medical student who recently had passed the examination for Surgeon's Mate in the Royal Navy. When shortly Waterhouse went to Leyden to continue his own medical studies, Coates replaced him as boon companion to Stuart.

In company with West's young son, Raphael, he attended classes at the Royal Academy in old Somerset House. Student habits are unchanging, and it was typical that in the hallway of the academy Stuart became involved in a discussion of the great masters. Each pupil disclosed some favorite painter along whose path he had determined to march: "the titanic Michelangelo," "the gentle divine Raphael," "the glow and sunshine of Titian's coloring," and "Rembrandt's chiaroscuro," were the themes mentioned. Stuart, in turn, expressed a determinedly iconoclastic view: "For my own part I will not follow any master. I wish to find out what nature is for myself, and see her with my own eyes. This appears to me to be the true road to excellence. Nature may be seen through different mediums. Rembrandt saw with a different eye from Raphael, yet they are both excellent, but for dissimilar qualities."

Gainsborough chanced to come by while Stuart was speaking. "That's right, my lad. Adhere to that and you'll be an artist," he said, with a reassuring pat on the shoulder.

THOUGH Stuart retained his own lodgings, he probably slept under West's roof during the summer months, when the West household, including Mrs. West, sons Raphael and Rubens, and pupils and apprentices moved to Windsor. From his spacious establishment on Park Street Benjamin West had easy access to a painting-room in the castle, granted him by an enthusiastic King. Conveniently close to his friendly sovereign, West received a more royal encouragement than any English artist since Van Dyck.

Of his place at court everyone, even the Queen's attendants, was fully conscious. "The Queen was most brilliantly attired; and when she was arrayed Mr. West was allowed to enter the dressing-room, in order to give his opinion of the disposition of her jewels . . ." recorded Fanny Burney. Politics, especially with regard to the rebellious American colonies, were spoken of in West's presence, and his opinions regarding personalities across the Atlantic were sought. For this purpose West kept in touch with any American of consequence who came to London, and maintained a minor intelligence system that serviced both the King and American interests.

To Stuart the summers away from London must have been an especial pleasure, as was his closeness to court circles. He must often have seen the King and Royal family, though it is doubtful whether so junior a pupil was present when George III visited West's painting-room. During Stuart's second year at Windsor, West brought to a conclusion his first series of Royal portraits. To assist the elaboration of these large canvases, West produced from his portfolios a sumptuous steel engraving by Pierre Imbert Drevet, one of the most celebrated French craftsmen. Drevet's steel had been cut from a portrait of the renowned Catholic theologian, Bishop Bossuet, painted generations before by Hyacinthe Rigaud, official portraitist at the later court of Louis XIV. This was Stuart's first introduction to Rigaud's elaborate art, so deliberately calculated to please a French monarch to whom splendor was a passion. Rigaud gave new bite to techniques inherited from Rubens and Lely, much heightening their styles with dazzling adaptations of Bernini's baroque spirit; and wedded to Rigaud's ostentation and pure magnificence was an acid candor that fixed forever the worldly cunning of the grand monarch's immediate circle. His strength lay in devastating portraits of men—women were left to the softer pomp of Largilliere.

West's attitude toward Rigaud's lofty achievement is unrecorded; officially he expressed himself as uninterested by the French school. Now, however, Stuart saw his master carefully study and develop certain elements from the engraving for Queen Charlotte's portrait. Rigaud's four columns were reduced to one, which, with a flattened perspective, West placed behind the Queen. He also drew upon the

engraving for a fantastic snapping baroque curtain, whose major
lines and forms were retained, though color and texture were transformed and plausible new folds invented. The Bishop's cloak, so
inappropriate to the portrait of an English sovereign, West found too
attractive to ignore. Again with perfect plausibility he transformed it
into a velvet table-covering that filled a corresponding section of
his canvas.

Unsatisfied, West turned next to an engraving after Van Dyck's
double portrait *The Duke of Bedford and the Earl of Bristol.* Hung
across the Duke's crooked arm he discovered a velvet cloak inter-
sected at the floor by a steel breastplate. He transferred the cloak to
his own canvas, where it dashed out, unexplained, from beside the
Queen's elbow; and curiously, West considered the steel armor-piece
so inextricably woven into the drapery rhythms that he fashioned
its shapes into a continuation of the crescendo of tumbling cloth.
Finally, to complete an ensemble of calculated splendor, West carefully elaborated a carpet beneath the Queen's feet.

Minor portions of this picture were entrusted to Stuart, and the
lesson he learned far outweighed his actual participation. One does
not know whether West thereupon presented his pupil with the
cherished engravings from Rigaud and Van Dyck, or whether Stuart,
on his return to London, sought out copies of his own. From that
time forth, however, the Drevet engraving after Rigaud was the
young man's most significant possession.

SURROUNDED by the most high-flown art England ever had known,
Stuart never lost his essential interest in the portrait. That it was the
most profitable branch of the arts a glance toward Sir Joshua Reynolds, whose ostentatious carriage and team daily passed through
London streets, was sufficient to demonstrate. But to a colonial like
Stuart, or John Singleton Copley, whom he now encountered working among West's assistants, portraits were the fundamental of art.
From their youth it had been the one acceptable form of artistic
commerce.

To perfect himself as a portrait painter required that Stuart apply
his intellect more than his hand. Even today, to the less sophisticated,
the most significant content of the portraitist's art is thought to be
character. For this the earliest examples show Stuart to have possessed

an abundant natural gift, which, held to its proper place in the balance of skills, would one day be decisive. The stress too often laid on character, however, is a primitive intellectual concept. This is best demonstrated by the fact that, reduced to simplest form, it places caricature in a higher category than the greatest works of Van Dyck. The remarkable Fleming, however, had a refinement of skills derived from generations of artistic experience. He knew instinctively, and transmitted to his English heirs, that *style*—the ability to do a thing well, with precision, ease, grace, and dexterity, to synthesize and suggest, add subtlety and subtract all that was vulgar and commonplace; to build forms that had beauty, to stress graceful lines and shapes, color harmoniously, and create a picture that was a thing of beauty because it was an expression of a cultivated artistic mind working in harmony with a skillful hand—that this use of *style* was the highest content of the portraitist's art.

To arrive at this high goal it was necessary for Stuart to learn that the head was not a collection of features, as Cosmo Alexander had painted it, but a single fused form; its tissue of flesh rose and fell by skillful variation of tints: contours were the subtle definition of planes. West's own portraits, originally conceived in a harsh linear manner that recalled Raphael, were only just coming to this point of greater fluency. Quickly, aided by a new ease with pigment, Stuart was in advance of his master. The earliest work preserved in this newly sophisticated manner, a portrait of himself painted in 1778, shows both remarkable growth and the filial piety with which he now viewed Benjamin West.

True to the Georgian mode of designing a picture from another of proven worth, Stuart used a self-portrait by West for his model. Though West's mode had been Raphaelesque, and his picture reflected the sweetness of a self-portrait by that Renaissance master, West blended this primary source with the more powerful Rubens self-portrait at Windsor. The result, painted in his own bright clear coloring, became Stuart's point of departure. His own face he turned to match West's coy posture; West's Rubens-inspired hat he sketched on his own head; but the clarity, directness, and intensity of his approach indicated the born portrait-painter. Contours that West had lost in shadow Stuart kept clear. Petty forms and nasal lines that West copied, Stuart wiped away in the sweep of his brush. His searching gaze into the mirror before him is recorded with startling immediacy, and with perfect objectivity he notes that his mouth had dropped open. A brilliant work, summarizing his lessons, Stuart finished the portrait by gracefully balancing a fat highlight on the nose-tip, an expression of his own emerging artistic personality.

West, who at first had viewed his pupil as a dubious quantity, now took pride in him. And the growing respect of others had tonic effect on Stuart. A gay, boyish, high-spirited nature again asserted itself. A wordy fellow, frequently Stuart appeared to be out to impress by his conversation, and equally often, one wondered where he acquired his showy erudition. At other moments it was obvious that he had set out to charm, and sometimes he succeeded; Mrs. West, who daily sat sewing in the Newman Street parlor, and who became the recipient of some of the affection he felt for his own distant mother, was his special target.

The slightest offense, or hint of offense, brought forth an immediate rejoinder from Stuart. One morning Dr. Johnson called on West to converse on American affairs; after some little time West remarked he had a young American in his studio, from whom information might be obtained. He introduced Stuart, and the conversation continued, until Dr. Johnson, noting Stuart's remarkably clear, educated British accents, remarked on them to West. Next he somewhat abruptly asked Stuart where he had learned to speak as he did. "Sir, I can better tell you where I did not learn it. It was not from your dictionary!" was the instant response.

Though on occasion he lectured his pupil severely, West remained tolerant and patient. Perhaps he realized the best balm Stuart could have was his present security under a paternal eye. Alone in the world, frightened, defensive, and essentially lonely, Stuart found it necessary to establish human contact with those about him. Whether in the studio, traveling by coach, or visiting a museum, he would make an effort to strike up conversation, and his easiest route had always been through humor. A smile and a bright word quickly brought warm response. The habit led to abuses, and too often degenerated into bantering that disturbed those about him.

When in good humor, and less inclined to plague his associates, Stuart retained an essential charm that since earliest childhood had made him likable. While West painted *The Battle of the Boyne* he followed the normal procedure of pressing his entire studio into service as models. Stuart's thin leg excused him from the worst of these chores, but for hours he was made to lie on the floor, dressed in armor, as the Duke of Schomberg.

"Are you dead, Stuart?" West called at last.

"Only half, sir," was his merry reply, and quite true it proved, for the heavy armor had deprived him of sensation in his limbs.

FOR JOHN SINGLETON COPLEY, pre-revolutionary America's greatest artist, life in London had not proved easy. Humorless, small, quiet, studious, with intense little eyes that often seemed a day's march into his head, at the time Stuart joined West's studio in 1779 Copley still frequently passed the odd week there, happy to have payment for his labors. Possessed of greater skill than the ordinary assistant, aware of his superior abilities, and possessing too a touch with the brush that everywhere left his individualized mark, Copley felt no pleasure in his day-work for others. West's generous nature was seen to advantage when, on Copley's return from two years' study in Italy, he secured for him the privileges of an Associate Membership in the Royal Academy, to which he was elected November 4, 1776. Though some portrait orders came to him, Copley still had to struggle to support his family, and when West was unable to employ him he visited other studios. Nathaniel Dance, friendly and conscious of merit, sometimes hired Copley to paint hands and draperies, and during 1779 Copley worked for Reynolds too.

Despite differences of personality, in the confines of West's studio Copley and Stuart had the same lessons to learn. Each acquired from West the classic lore that was the alchemist's stone of their world. Sorting through West's large collection of Italian engravings they were shown how Raphael, when designing his gracious *Sistine Madonna*, derived its stance and bared feet from the Apollo Belvedere. A cast of this ancient work, which stood at the angle of West's gallery, was the surety of his wisdom and the touchstone of his taste. In quiet, grave Pennsylvania accents, West instructed them in the uses to which ancient sculptures and Renaissance engravings were put; the hand of a Raphael, graceful drapery from some saintly handmaiden, and the stance of a Grecian masterwork, were united into pictures of Georgian beauty. The stylish perfection obtained was universally admitted to be unmatchable by mere improvisation from nature, for the human figure had been used by artists of sublime genius; one humbly revered their works, and hoped by study and labor to equal them. Reynolds, the epitome to which every portrait painter aspired, was an inexhaustible store of classic invention, even if, unlike West, he debased his genius by ignoring sublime themes. Albano, Correggio, and Guercino could all be seen hovering behind Reynolds' felicitous arrangements, nor could one desist from admiring his ability to use a hand from Raphael or Van Dyck or Lely, and draperies from them all.

On the common ground of West's studio even such disparate personalities as Stuart and Copley could collaborate. Copley executed a head for a *Peter Denying Christ:* working at his own snail's pace he developed the image of a strongly shadowed, aged apostle. Neither deliberately pathetic nor completely restrained, it was distinguished by brilliantly rendered loosened flesh that was the ultimate of Copley's special powers. Earlier he had employed this same head for his own *Samuel and Eli*, which Stuart, with newly acquired understanding, noted was patterned on Titian's *Pesaro Altarpiece*, with a stunning hand added from Guercino's *Jacob Blessing the Sons of Joseph*. To the neophyte Stuart it was obvious that Copley was very posh; when he was able he added an engraving of the Titian work to his own small collection. Consistent with West's design, Stuart advanced the canvas, adding two figures in his own thinner facture. Broader, more stylized, less diligent than Copley's *Peter*, they show a rapid development of the younger man's skill. One feels no need to deny that the head of Christ that Stuart fashioned from a likeness of West was a compliment deliberately intended, nor that it was an unconscious gesture to paint himself as a callow apostle.

Long a master in his own right, Copley continued his advantageous employment in West's studio. There he saw something that had filled him with wonderment at Boston—how groups of figures were planned and executed. Nor did Copley fail to note that while West had classic knowledge superior to his own, he himself possessed far greater manual skill. Soon Copley was planning vast historical compositions in his own studio, and West generously saw that his new rival was elected, February 9, 1779, to full membership in the Royal Academy.

If Stuart also had ambitions the road was clearly marked out for him, and his fluent brush was the marvel of West's studio. Once designs were cast by West himself, work on them was parceled out among assistants. Stuart found himself entrusted with entire compositions of remarkable complication: five panels West designed for the lecture-room ceiling of a rebuilt Somerset House, to which the Royal Academy moved in 1780, demonstrate his further progress. Filled with an assortment of nude and half-draped figures, cherubs and animals, all resting contentedly on cloud-banks, the panels bear the inimitable mark of Stuart's brush. John Trumbull, son of the Governor of Connecticut, who arrived late in 1780 with a letter of introduction from Benjamin Franklin, noted Stuart's special eminence. West told the new arrival he had another American in the studio, then conducted him to Stuart, who had a room of his own. That he was without funds was obvious from the tattered black coat he wore, one side "torn off the hip" and held up by a pin.

To piece out his finances Stuart now painted an occasional portrait, three of which were exhibited at the Royal Academy of 1779. They attracted no attention, and the year following he did not bother to send more. But to Trumbull, as to others in the studio, Stuart remained a constant source of amazement. Upon mention of Benjamin Franklin Trumbull was startled to hear Stuart say: "Linnaeus is right. Plato and Diogenes call man a biped without feathers—that's a shallow definition. Franklin's is better: 'a tool-making animal.' But Linnaeus is best: '*homo*, animal mendax, rapax, pugnax.'" On observing a drawing of Trumbull's Stuart was at first puzzled, then burst out, "Why, Trumbull, this looks as if it was drawn by a man with but one eye."

Much hurt, Trumbull replied, "I take it very unkindly, sir, that you should make the remark."

Stuart asked what he meant.

"I presume, sir," Trumbull responded, "that you know I have lost the sight of one eye, and any allusion to it in this manner is illiberal."

"Now," Stuart recalled in after years, "I never suspected it, and only the oddness of the drawing suggested the thing."

OTHER stray shafts Stuart recounted himself:

"I used very often to provoke my good old master, though heaven knows, without intending it. You remember the color closet at the bottom of the painting room. One day, Trumbull and I came into this room, and little suspecting that he was within hearing, I began to

lecture on his pictures, and particularly upon one then on his easel.
I was a giddy foolish fellow then. He had begun a portrait of a child,
and he had a way of making curly hair by a flourish of the brush,
thus, like a figure of three.

" 'Here Trumbull,' said I, 'do you want to know how to paint
hair? There it is, my boy! Our master figures out a head of hair like
a sum in arithmetic. Let us see—we may tell how many guineas he
is to have for this head by simple addition,—three and three make
six, and three is nine, and three are twelve—.'

"How much the sum would have amounted to I can't tell, for just
then in stalked the master, with palette knife and palette, and put to
flight my calculations.

" 'Very well, Mr. Stuart,' said he—he always *mistered* me when
he was angry, as a man's wife calls him *my dear* when she wishes him
at the devil.—'Very well, Mr. Stuart, very well indeed!'

"You may believe that I looked foolish enough, and he gave me a
pretty sharp lecture without my making any reply. When the head
was finished there were no *figures of three in the hair* . . . Mr. West
treated me very cavalierly on . . . [another] occasion, but I had
my revenge.

" 'Stuart,' said West, 'it is a pity to make His Majesty sit again
for his picture; there is the portrait of him that you painted. Let me
have it . . . I will retouch it and it will do well enough.'

"Well *enough!* very pretty, thought I; you might be civil when you
ask a favor. So I *thought*, but I *said*, 'Very well, sir.'

"So the picture was carried down to his room, and at it he went.
I saw he was puzzled. He worked at it all that day. The next morning,
'Stuart,' said he, 'have you got your palette set?'

" 'Yes, sir.'

"Well, you can soon set another; let me have the one you prepared
for yourself; I can't satisfy myself with that head.'

"I gave him my palette and he worked the greater part of that day.
In the afternoon I went into his room, and he was hard at it. I saw that
he had got up to the knees in mud.

" 'Stuart,' says he. 'I don't know how it is, but you have a way of
managing your tints unlike anybody else—here—take the palette and
finish the head.'

" 'I can't, sir.'

" 'You can't?'

" 'I can't indeed, sir, as it is, but let it stand 'till tomorrow morning and get dry, and I will go over it with all my heart.'

"The picture was to go away the day after the morrow, so he made me promise to do it early next morning. . . . He never came down into the painting room, at the bottom of the gallery, until about ten o'clock. I went into his room bright and early, and by half-past nine I had finished the head. That done, *Rafe* and I began to fence; I with my mahl-stick and he with his father's. I had just driven Rafe up to the wall, with his back to one of his father's best pictures, when the old gentleman, as neat as a lad of wax, with his hair powdered, his white silk stockings, and yellow morocco slippers, popped into the room, looking as if he had stepped out of a band-box. We had made so much noise that we did not hear him come down the gallery or open the door.

" 'There, you dog!' says I to Rafe; 'there I have you, and nothing but your background *relieves* you!'

"The old gentleman could not help smiling at my technical joke, but soon, looking very stern, 'Mr. Stuart,' said he, 'is this the way you use me?'

" 'Why, what's the matter, sir? I have neither hurt the boy nor the background.'

" 'Sir, when you knew that I had promised that the picture of His Majesty should be finished today, ready to be sent away tomorrow, thus to be neglecting me and your promise! How can you answer it to me or to yourself?'

" 'Sir, said I, 'do not condemn me without examining the easel. I have finished the picture; please to look at it.'

"He did so, complimenting me highly, and I had ample revenge for his 'It will do well enough.' "

IV

Chief Assistant to West

B Y TACT, good sense, and his personal friendship with the King, West remained unmolested, though his homeland was in revolt and allied with England's hereditary enemy. He deliberately made himself useful, and surely his contact with the King was a constant pledge of loyalty from one who, it was known, never ceased to reserve sympathies for his native land. Stuart was shielded by West's position, and the peculiar circumstance that his family was presumed "loyalist" through its departure from Rhode Island. His own presence in London thus was easily explained.

Early in 1778 West accepted as his pupil Ralph Earl, a loyalist refugee from America. By his own admission, he had informed on the Americans to the British; slight though his services were, he had been hunted by his countrymen and sought refuge with the Quarter-Master General of Burgoyne's army, who found him a "persecuted man." After reaching England disguised as this officer's servant, he industriously petitioned the Lords Commissioners of the Treasury for compensation of losses sustained in support of the English cause.

Ralph Earl's presence in West's studio might have been less awkward had not a committee of American Loyalists existed in London, guided by Joseph Galloway, former member of the First Continental Congress, and ex-President of the Pennsylvania Assembly. Galloway had advised the British during their attack on Philadelphia, and under their subsequent occupation was port superintendent. After October 1778 he was in England, constantly expressing outrage at the kindnesses George III showed to West. When John Trumbull arrived in London in 1780, Galloway's full quota of spleen was vented; son of the "rebel" Governor of Connecticut, and himself an aide-de-camp to General Washington, Trumbull's arrival while hostilities were still continuing was an act of audacity. Galloway immediately notified the Secretary of State, who returned the amused reply; "You are late, gentlemen; Mr. Trumbull arrived yesterday at three o'clock, and I knew it at four." But the government showed no inclination to interfere with an art student, until four months later, when, after the death of Major André at American hands, Trumbull was summarily arrested. His papers were seized, and as these included a letter from Benjamin Franklin's grandson and secretary, William Temple Franklin, he was charged with treason.

What use would Galloway now make of this arrest for treason of an American who had been received under West's roof? Might West be implicated and similarly charged; and what of Stuart? In haste West made his way to Buckingham Palace, where he requested an audience with the King. The monarch received him kindly, and West explained what had induced him to take the liberty of an intrusion: his anxiety lest Trumbull's arrest might involve his own character.

"West, I have known you long," assured King George, "and have conversed with you frequently. I can recollect no occasion on which you ever attempted to mislead or misinform me, and for that reason you have acquired my entire confidence. I . . . assure you that my confidence in you is not at all diminished by the unpleasant occurrence. I am sorry for the young man, but he is in the hands of the law, and must abide the result. I cannot interpose. Do you know whether his parents are living?"

"I think I have heard him say that he has very lately received news of the death of his mother; I believe his father is living," replied West.

"I pity him from my soul," mused the King. Then, "But West, go to Mr. Trumbull immediately, and pledge him my promise, that, in the worst possible event of the law, his life shall be safe."

By this understanding West, and Stuart under his protection, lived out the remaining three years of the war. The lesson to Stuart was a great one, and ever after he exercised an extreme caution when confronted by politics.

STUART probably was delegated to carry the King's message to Trumbull, incarcerated in Bridewell Jail, behind Buckingham Palace. The

Older likenesses, or miniatures, can partly allay the unusual problem of a posthumous portrait, though Stuart's manner of proceeding implies that the aids supplied him were few. The deceased doctor's most trenchantly recalled characteristics were a long overhanging nose and wide-stretched mouth. Sittings from Waterhouse provided a mask of the face; his contours, forehead, eyes, jaw, and chin, are all present. Over these he brushed the long spear of West's nose, strongly accented to persuade of a likeness. To the curious amalgam he formed, Stuart then added a widely distorted version of West's mouth. The enormous, richly curled, and white-powdered peruke Dr. Fothergill had worn in defiance of Quaker simplicity came to Stuart's assistance, for he was able to paint this lavish headpiece from the article. The employment of his normal skill and dexterity greatly enhanced an illusion of life.

But no great ingenuity was expended on the arrangement of a composition. The dead man was granted one book, and a single carefully studied hand; perfunctory clothing finished the task, except for the final addition of a flourished indulgence of pigment, intended to simulate the texture of an awkwardly placed chair-back. Every picture he painted for himself at this period showed an area in which pigment was thus daubed, a mannerism taken from Copley, demonstrating another direction in which the young Stuart's eyes wandered.

CURIOUSLY compounded of West and Waterhouse, and sworn to represent the deceased Dr. Fothergill, the portrait found a place at the Royal Academy exhibition of 1781. The subject's eminence surely was responsible, for few pictures Stuart had painted were quite so grotesque. With it the Academy hung his portrait of Benjamin West, an easy, dexterous performance, granting more charm than West perhaps possessed. Both pictures received attention, and Stuart experienced a minor success. At the exhibition West discovered him standing before his portrait. Familiarity with Stuart's heady behavior prompted a severe tone: "You have done well, Stuart, very well; now all you have to do is go home and do better." Not by dashing off rapid portraits was Olympus scaled!

Stuart's was a new talent however, as the newspapers made clear: "An excellent portrait of Mr. West, indeed I do not know a better one in the room," announced the critic of the *St. James's Chronicle*.

This was praise indeed at an exhibition where Gainsborough and Reynolds were in full flower, the latter showing his triple portrait of *The Ladies Waldegrave*. Stuart's two subjects, one transplanted to the hereafter while the other devoted his talent to it, gave rise to a certain obvious humor: "The last is Dr. Fothergill, and this, as well as the other portrait, shows to our observation something like *a good painter hereafter*," was the not too successful bon mot of *The Public Advertiser*. An independent pamphlet devoted to comments on the exhibition was especially kind. "Mankind are much obliged to this artist, who has paid the debt of gratitude to the memory of Dr. Fothergill. He who has rescued so many from the grave is now restored to life by an admirable pencil. Death, which generally terminates all friendly recollection, has not prevented Mr. Stuart from doing what Dr. Fothergill would not permit when he was alive."

Trumbull was released from imprisonment as the exhibition closed, for a short time to take his place again in West's studio. Stuart worked five mornings on his likeness, which, saying he could do nothing with his "damned sallow face," he left for Trumbull to complete himself. This dual performance and probably other of Stuart's works figured that September 1781 in a display held at West's gallery.

Though still an assistant, Stuart continued to attract attention. While working alone in his room one day a gentleman entered, and after inspecting various works, seated himself. Stuart felt embarrassed, but continued to work, and West, who shortly entered, introduced the seated guest as Nathaniel Dance, the Academician who sometimes employed Copley. "Young man, you have done everything that need be done; your work is very correct," the veteran told him, and as always in the face of praise, Stuart was delighted.

Another of those who took interest in him was Alderman John Boydell, the publisher of prints. As was the case with Gainsborough, Romney, and Reynolds, a large part of West's income came through engraving rights attached to his pictures. When sold separately, to some publisher like Boydell, these were the source of considerable profits. Under agreement with the painter, Boydell contracted with the best engravers of the day to engrave plates from which prints were made; these he published in large numbers throughout the world. A new portrait of the King, a successful General or Admiral, the picture of a stirring battle by land or sea, could make the fortune of the painter. But Boydell's special position in London rested on his enterprise, for he was not content just to seek out pictures that might stir the public. Boydell's frequent practice was to commission works he believed would prove profitable as prints. In his gallery he displayed the canvases ordered from leading artists, to stimulate sales of his prints made after them. West's biblical subjects were popular, as were beautiful and titled ladies by Reynolds. A sea battle would be ordered of Dominic Serres almost as soon as its report reached London; and in that year of 1781, following an unsuccessful French attempt to storm St.-Heliers on the Island of Jersey, Boydell commissioned Copley to paint the encounter. *The Death of Major Pierson,* perhaps the greatest of all battle pictures, is equally a monument to Boydell's enterprise and Copley's skill.

Quick to seize on new talent, Boydell had Stuart paint himself, his nephew and associated engraver Josiah Boydell, and Dominic Serres. These portraits were intended to acquaint visitors to his gallery with those responsible for the production of their engravings. Alderman Boydell's enormous prestige thus became attached to Stuart.

To UNDERSTAND the sudden vogue that swept in upon Stuart the winter and spring of 1781–1782, one must take a broader look at portraiture as it then existed in England. The theories of art held by West and Reynolds dominated their profession completely, but to find adequate expression required acres of canvas. The full-length portrait had assumed its monstrous importance because it was the fullest expression of the Georgian mode; in the smaller realm of the bust portrait much of the classic allusion was not applicable, and in this minor realm no real master existed. The genius of Reynolds was not adapted to catching a likeness. For this, in fact, he was often thought to have less ability than meaner rivals; Gainsborough, Romney, Copley, and Nathaniel Dance were more satisfactory, and less costly. All of them were in a sense Reynolds' followers, sharing with him certain characteristics that were Stuart's as well. Notable among these was a sensitivity to character in older persons; a desire to paint women in a flat, shadowless light to soften features and allow the artist to luxuriate in clear complexions; and a tendency to view children in idealized detachment.

Stuart broke into this scene with characteristics of his own that essentially altered the eighteenth-century formula of head-painting. His particular genius permitted him to show the features of a person fused together, as they appeared in normal vision. All that was merged and indistinct to casual sight remained so in his portraits. The man whose colorless mouth was a blur beneath his nose found himself painted so; if in the fusion of normal vision his eyelids did not entirely separate from his brow, Stuart had the unexpected skill to keep them as they were. He preserved the truth of appearances as no one else in London attempted to do, and from this unusual skill grew both a likeness stronger than that to which the English public was accustomed and a more profound cast of expression.

The origin of Stuart's innovation was essentially technical, a strength grown from the weakness of his training. Whereas the normal portrait painter built heads from the drawn line, finding it necessary to distinguish the edges of all features, Stuart, who worked from an oval of pigment spread on his canvas, shaped it entirely by variations of color: he thought not in terms of line at all. His procedure was an entire reversal: from the flat tone laid on his canvas he worked *toward* definition, stopping short of the arbitrary hardness of line on which most painters depended for likeness. A new beauty and a new delicacy existed in works where forms and edges melted away only to be found again. In later years he explained that his method was to create an effect of *projection*, instead of depending on the accuracy of the outline; by projection he meant the rise and fall of planes merging smoothly one into another; what in fact distinguishes the greatest masters of portrait painting.

An essential corollary was that Stuart's portraits had a sense of expression that resided not in carefully traced mouth or eyes but in the play of light on the muscles of the head's larger masses. While accurately recording an undulating tissue of flesh, he committed to canvas the habitual disposition of the face, a coordination of parts that gave truthful analysis. Nothing escaped him; in truth, at this early part of his career he may have been unable to avoid frank statement. And startling realism was further enhanced by an unusually fresh, crisp color. Into a carefully pitched general tone, spread on the canvas, he gently worked gradations of color and hue to mold the head into its proper spheroidal shape. His pigments were applied in touches that mingled only on canvas, where they formed a clear, fresh substance exquisitely simulating the texture of flesh itself. Not the indirect methods of Reynolds, whereby drawing and color were separated into different stages, nor the fat unctuous pigment of Romney, nor the transparent layers of Gainsborough have the same impact as Stuart's perfect flesh. "It's no use to steal Stuart's colors," West told his other pupils, possibly recollecting a sad experience of his own. "If you want to paint as he does you must steal his eyes."

Equally attractive was the new fluid bravura of his execution. Costumes, wigs, the highlights of faces, were touched in by a marvelous swordsmanship, and in the simplest of his endeavors, by drawing on the standard off-balance placements known to every London painter, he created fine little pictures. Only his first efforts at composition betrayed awkwardness; once the trickery of Dr. Fothergill's head had been accomplished Stuart failed to seek a graceful design for his picture, and his profile of Alderman Boydell is equally gauche. The dash and exuberance of his informal study of Dominic Serres quickly redeemed him, and the portraits of that winter were a striking revelation of new talent. In the cynical world of the studios Stuart had detractors too, who said that he "made a tolerable likeness of a face, but as to the figure, he could not get below the fifth button"; a jibe no less damaging for being true.

STUART had achieved a modest fame, but if he wished to make his way in London he would have to be wary. Half an artist was not sufficient, though his training from West was exactly such as would put at his disposal the entire resources of the artistic world. If he had learned the classic lesson well, he could now be the equal of anyone —but Stuart was not anyone. His strange youth had left him with an inexplicably convoluted nature. He was subject to feelings of harassment that put him to bed when no physical malady could be found. At times it required all his strength to rouse himself from reverie and the indolence that overcame him. Somewhere deep inside his psyche were open wounds, ready to bleed afresh. One of these was the portrait of Dr. Lettsom he had been unable to finish. It was a recurrent nightmare to him; and at Newport, he had offended a delegation from the Redwood Library rather than attempt the full-length requested. This aberration imbedded in his nature twice bore down on him in disgrace. The second time it had defeated him utterly, and driven him like a famished mendicant to the door of Benjamin West.

Now a formidable technician at the height of new form, that *sine qua non* of English life, art, and fashion returned to haunt him. He was asked to do a full-length portrait. The request came from Mr. William Grant, of Congalton, of whom little else is known. Stuart admitted to feeling great diffidence and doubtless experienced panic. An appointment was made and Mr. Grant arrived, but on entering Stuart's room at West's house, he regretted the appointment because of the excessive cold, observing the day was better suited to ice-skating than sitting for one's portrait.

The excuse was sufficient. Stuart turned conversation to skating by telling Grant he was an expert from his American childhood. Years before Benjamin West, then unknown in London, had made a minor reputation by demonstrating fancy skating on the Serpentine. That history was well known, and now together Stuart and Grant went off to try their skills in the same place. A crowd of curious onlookers was attracted by the handsome young artist, who cut figures in the ice. Grant followed his example, and though a well-made, graceful man, he proved less proficient than his twenty-seven-year-old companion. When a crack developed in the ice it was only by fast thinking, and instructing Grant to hold on to his coat-tails, that Stuart brought his patron off the river, to avoid catastrophe.

One suspects that on returning to West's house in Newman Street Stuart's eye fell again on the cast of Apollo in the angle of the gallery. What statue had been used in so many guises? Intended for a Greek godhunter, he had been made a Madonna and mistaken by West for a Mohawk warrior! Reynolds patterned male and female figures on it indiscriminately, and his curious Grecian sandals were not unlike the fastenings of skates: could the Apollo Belvedere be made a skater too? Grant composedly took his place in a studio chair, his eyes receded in deep shadows cast from his brows by the room's top-light. Three or four sessions were sufficient to produce an incisive image of his well-cut face and cleft chin, the dark eyes averted. And when the artist mentioned the unusual posture of skating, Grant made no objection. With that he withdrew.

Alone with his canvas, Stuart's first necessity was to invert the Apollo in a mirror, to fit it under the head painted from his sitter. The reversed outline was transfered to canvas; great care was required, but Stuart was now well acquainted with this studio process. Apollo's upraised rear foot was given a skate; the forward foot, on which all weight rested, took the imposition with equal grace. But the motion of the figure now was at odds with the outstretched bow-arm of a hunting Greek; he improvised a cross-armed pose, such as skaters frequently adopt, strengthening the balance of the picture. To give an air of nonchalance Stuart's own rough wide-brimmed hat with buckled band was sketched onto the head, its lines imparting the correct touch of grace to wide and squarish shoulders.

Now the young man began to use pigments. At first all went well; shoulders and arms were blocked in with ease, but this deserted him when he turned to the legs. Contour lines were kept hard and clear, and once he succeeded in covering these extremities with pigment he feared to return to them. Fat touches gave point to the skates and shoes, but he dared not trifle with the flat, overly correct execution of the legs. Even so, when he stood back the picture was a marvel. It had indeed taken on the appearance of a man skating!

"What a charming picture!" cried Barretti, the Italian author and lexicographer, friend of Reynolds, who wandered into Stuart's room. He had come to call on West, and finding him absent was sauntering about the studio. "Who but the great West could have painted such a one!"

Stuart said nothing. Between his chores for West he continued to work on his big portrait. The obsessive problem of the figure successfully overcome, he was able to elaborate it at ease, painting a scribbled winter landscape, and spectators who watched two rapidly twirling skaters; reference to Mr. Grant and himself on the Serpentine. Again Barretti called, and coming into Stuart's room, blurted, "What, young man, does Mr. West permit you to touch his pictures?" This time Stuart replied that the picture was his own. "Why," said Barretti, "it is almost as good as Mr. West can paint."

V

Independence

THE ROYAL ACADEMY exhibition of 1782 brought Stuart his first taste of acclaim. It did not come unbidden, for the group of portraits he sent in support of the skating picture's dashing bravado marked the effort's careful calculation. Dominic Serres, whose sea-pictures had such popularity, was a subject certain to attract attention; as was Caleb Whitefoord, whose literary reputation was broadened by his position as Secretary of the British Commission negotiating peace with the Americans. While casting the gauge to official quarters, Stuart also sent a fourth work, a portrait of a gentleman with Swedish associations, who may have been Sir William Chambers, the architect and highly influential Royal Academician.

None of these carefully selected escorts overshadowed the importance attached to the skating picture, which, from the first, was greeted as an astonishing achievement. The attention it attracted at Somerset House was general and electrifying, and the subject found himself sharing in it when he came to view the exhibition. Horace Walpole, whose presumably impeccable taste guided aesthetes, wrote "very good" in his Academy catalogue, and surely he spread this opinion through the proper quarters of London. The Duke of Rutland ran direct from Somerset House to Leicester Fields on opening day, to urge Sir Joshua Reynolds: "I wish you would go to the exhibition with me. There is a portrait there you ought to see—everyone is enchanted with it." Asked by Reynolds who painted it, the Duke replied, "A young man named Stuart." Even in private letters comment is found: "One would have thought that almost every attitude of a single figure had long been exhausted in this land of portrait painting," penned Sir John Callum. "One is now exhibited which I recollect not before—it is that of Skating. There is a noble portrait, large as life, thus exhibited, which produces the most powerful effect."

Newspapers reflected the general clamor: "If we are informed aright this is the gentleman's first essay in this branch of the art; at all events it does honor to his pencil, from the novelty of the design and the neatness of the execution"—*neatness* was a hidden dart, aimed at Reynolds' rough and hasty execution. Another paper as furtively rebutted the prick: "Mr. Stuart seldom fails of a likeness, but wants freedom of pencil and elegance of brush." To know something of the young man was suddenly a mark of distinction. *The St. James's Chronicle* easily won this contest with its unblushing comments of May 2, 1782:

> Mr. Stuart is in partnership with Mr. West, where it is not uncommon for wits to divert themselves with applications for things they do not immediately want because they are told by Mr. West that Mr. Stuart is the only portrait painter in the world; and by Mr. Stuart that no man has any pretentions in history painting but Mr. West. After such authority what can we say of Mr. Stuart's painting?

Despite the presence of fourteen works by Reynolds, including his fiery full-length of Banastre Tarleton, recently returned from marauding cavalry actions in Virginia, and the general impression that ". . . Gainsborough treads hard on the heels of Sir Joshua," the one admitted result of the Academy exhibition of 1782 was Stuart's establishment. John Hoppner, long Reynolds' assistant, and considered heir apparent to the splendid artistic estate of his master, was swept aside. Speculation was rampant concerning Stuart's next move. Rumors were heard that he intended to take a great house, as Reynolds did early in his own career; but those closer to Stuart were aware of terrible indecision.

Nathaniel Dance, who had the distinction of early recognizing Stuart's promise, now spoke with him about his prospects. The advice he gave was definite and forceful, for it seemed madness to throw away his sudden success. "You are strong enough to stand alone," he urged. "Take rooms; those who would be unwilling to sit to Mr. West's pupil will be glad to sit to Mr. Stuart." John Hoppner's part-

American wife, conscious of her husband's eclipse, kept careful watch. June third she wrote, "Tuesday the exhibition closes . . . Stuart has taken a house, I am told, of £150 a year rent, in Berner's Street, and is going to set up as a great man." Her information, which would have settled Stuart near Sir William Chambers, was inaccurate. In the end, frightened, unwilling to turn aside the advice and good wishes received, yet fearful of detaching himself from the shelter he had found with West, Stuart compromised by taking rooms near his master in Newman Street.

STUART's emergence from West's studio saw a return of his former instability, though its character was altered by the effects of prosperity. To distinguish himself from the better-known Edinburgh historian *Gilbert Stuart* he variously called himself *Charles, Gabriel,* and *George* Stuart; part of his charm was that he never became hardpressed for variations on fact. His celebrity altered him in every exterior aspect; he began by pulling together the long dark hair that had curled about his neck, and powdering it white in the fashion for gentlemen. His torn coats were replaced; one of gray-lavender became conspicuous, as did another of royal blue in the newest sleek cutaway vogue; a shining barrage of brass buttons sparkling down the front, and tinkling across slit cuffs. Added to these splendors were yellow and white waistcoats, the latter with enormous triangular lapels turned out over his coat. In a land of fine plumage Stuart rapidly made himself the fanciest bird of all, resplendent in stiff linen cravats whose bows framed his chin and dangled fringes to play across his chest. Most gorgeous of all his new finery, and most proudly worn, was an extravagant chemise trimmed by a thick ruffle of Brussels bobbin lace at breast and wrists.

Like ruffles to a man who wants a shirt, this magnificent new Stuart now returned at night to rooms in Newman Street barren of all save the most meager furnishings. A dog assuaged his renewed loneliness, but how good a companion "Dash" proved is unrecorded, except that like his master he sometimes barked at sitters. Furniture remained a problem; only a few doors from West's spacious gallery, Stuart received sitters with only one chair of elegance in which to place them. Nathaniel Dance came to his rescue. His own career was drawing to a close; he had married a rich widow, and was in the process of retiring to the country and a life of politics. Aware of Stuart's precarious beginnings, he invited the younger man to help himself to anything serviceable from his house. Stuart had the ill-fortune to call on Dance in his absence, and, uneasy in the role of applicant, all he dared take were a palette and some brushes. When told of this moderation, a day or two before the sale of his furnishings Dance sent Stuart a mass of materials. Many were not immediately useful, but all were far more costly than Stuart could have afforded. The palette, Dance later told him, was the one formerly used by Hudson, his own and Reynolds' teacher.

Alterations in Stuart's fortunes and his external image were celebrated in the second surviving self-portrait, which shows what a splendid young chap he was at this first exuberant moment in his London career. Handsome, a sarcastic twist to his well-formed mouth, a twinkle in his eye, he viewed the world with considerable satisfaction, and had every reason to do so. His anxieties over patronage were quickly resolving; and the impression that he was heir-apparent was accentuated when in November Sir Joshua Reynolds suffered a paralytic stroke. Reynolds' friends were more alarmed than himself; Dr. Johnson wrote from the country, where he was staying, "I heard yesterday of your late disorder, and should think ill of myself if I heard it without alarm. I heard likewise of your recovery, which I wish to be complete and permanent. Your country has been in danger of losing one of its brightest ornaments . . ." Though in fact Reynolds did recover, his health ever after remained uncertain.

Those acquainted with the great Sir Joshua were casting about for his successor, and in that year of Stuart's first triumph it was to him they looked. Aware of the phenomenon, the crafty Reynolds put up his prices still further, though it already was said in the politest of drawing-rooms that they were "shameful." A bold assertion of supremacy by an ill man being run hard by three serious rivals, his gesture served also to lessen the flow of applicants to Leicester Fields. In Newman Street, the future decidedly seemed Stuart's, and Alderman Boydell was surely of this opinion when he asked Stuart to continue his portraits of artists. William Woollet, the engraver, particularly upset Dash, who barked furiously, and had to be put out of the room; later the animal seemed anxious to chew apart the finished picture when it stood glistening on the easel.

The report that West and Stuart were in partnership, though

written as the chaff of journalism, had an essence of truth. When time hung heavy Stuart still took his place in West's working rooms. West seemed perpetually astonished by the flourishing abilities of his pupil. Persons who applied to him for portraits more often were sent to Stuart, among them the Cartwrights, for whom West previously had done an elaborate group of five children. Stuart now painted the Cartwrights' blond son William Ralph holding a fishing pole and wearing the hat that previously had figured in the *Skater*. Through continued friendship with William Coates, occasional naval officers began to appear in Stuart's rooms. Among them was Sir Harry Parker; and Lord Grantham, who had greeted West and made introductions for him in Rome twenty years before, also came for one of Stuart's rapid, telling likenesses, accomplished with much audacity of brushing. Captain Richard Coffin was the subject of an equally dashing performance. Even so, among these first works are some, like Parker and Master Cartwright, that betray the artist's laborious care; an impression perhaps accentuated by comparison with the more brilliant works to follow.

STUART had achieved his first acclaim with a boldly conceived full-length portrait. It was natural that further such orders would be forthcoming: two appear to have been offered him immediately. Henrietta Elizabeth Frederica Vane, a pretty little child and niece to the Earl of Darlington, was only ten years old. This order proved Dance had been correct in surmising that Stuart was strong enough to draw sitters direct from exhibitions at the Royal Academy—a world beyond that of his own few contacts and the clients sent by Benjamin West. Even better proof was his second large order, the subject for which was Richard Brinsley Sheridan.

Stuart made no effort to exercise again the elusive popular appeal of the *Skater* for his portrait of little Miss Vane. In that rigidly confined century the canons of taste for a child's portrait were different. Simplicity, sweetness, comical conceit if possible, but withal a candid treatment, was demanded. These he gave, with direct painting and his own characteristic effulgence. Stuart was aware that whatever he did in this first year of his public notice would be contrasted with the best of Reynolds, Gainsborough, and Romney, and he again became uneasy.

He now owned a print of the Drevet engraving after Rigaud's *Bishop Bossuet*, the same that West has used for his picture of Queen Charlotte. Tradition, however, required that a child's portrait be painted in landscape—Rigaud was no help to him—unless the elements of architecture could be transformed into elements of landscape.

The column standing at left of Rigaud's picture quite naturally reached Stuart's canvas as a tree. His rapid touch easily made curtains rustling behind the Bishop into foliage; and the corded tassels on their long leads became a vine that twirled about the tree. The base of Rigaud's column-turned-tree was hidden by an assortment of ragged-edged volumes, which, to suit his childhood context, Stuart altered to a basket of flowers. Then, recalling how in West's picture the Queen's contour had been lent an extra grace by extraneous draperies, Stuart felt the need of something to bind his summery little white-clad figure into its landscape. West's solution had come from Van Dyck: Stuart remained true to Rigaud. His engraving turned side-wise, he selected a portion of the heavy episcopal cloak to brush beside little Miss Vane. The effect was of singular felicity, and working with West's sources, Stuart began to feel the same security he had derived from the presence of his master.

This second effort at the full-length, like his first, was a startling success, perfectly in the tradition of Georgian portraiture; and while accomplishing it Stuart discovered in the Bossuet portrait the key to his own anxieties. With the accrual of a minor fame, patronage, financial independence, and the feeling he was a gentleman and a beau, he must also have felt that at last he had conquered his fears before large canvases. What pleased him less was his manner of handling pigment. Despite the grace of his brushing, it remained the flat manner acquired in West's studio. Critics had noted that he lacked freedom of brushing; his surfaces, he thought, must be uninteresting against the roughened torrents of Reynolds' pigmentation, or the lusciousness of Romney's. A first hint of Stuart's research into techniques had appeared in the portrait of William Ralph Cartwright, for which the whites were ground with more than usual stiffness, as was Romney's custom. On canvas these produced an attractive pasty quality, and he learned too that if applied with turpentine, rather than oil, this special mixture dried to a more buttery consistency. He adapted Romney's characteristic placement of heads to one side of the canvas, and frequently imitated that painter's sometimes-scribbled, sometimes-hatched rendering of wigs.

But the real test of how much he was now master of himself came when he finished his portrait of Sheridan. Seven feet of blank white canvas, near its top a head carefully painted, still was frightening. The use of *Apollo Belvedere* gave his *Skater* great distinction: a new effort could not have less of that elusive quality. The portfolio of engravings he was assembling included a print after Van Dyck's portrait of the *Prince d'Arenberg*, whose forward-pitching stance, the entire weight uneasily balanced on the balls of his feet, made it peculiarly attractive. Here again was something with the audacity that had made his *Skater* notable. In the best eighteenth-century mode he determined to employ each of the three sources now familiar to him.

A torso and akimbo arm was provided by Van Dyck's *Duke of Bedford;* hips and legs were sketched onto this from the *Prince d'Arenberg,* and he found these precisely right to draw out the torso's long lines. A graceful twist of the back that materialized from the joining of elements gave unexpected elegance, and the figure stood wonderfully well. Stuart began to apply pigment, garbing Sheridan in his own finery: his fashionable new blue coat with brass buttons, the stiff linen cravat worn belligerently high about the chin; the latest mode in scanty light-colored smallclothes clung to the figure, white stockings and deep-cut pumps completing its raiment. Legs, rather too elegantly precise, closely followed Van Dyck's, varied only slightly by study from Stuart's own too-thin ankles. The whole of the figure in fact bore a strong resemblance to Stuart's own slim athletic form, from which, before the mirror, the clothing was painted. Next he referred again to Rigaud. The Frenchman contributed little this time except major horizontal and vertical divisions, a heavy tassel, and flowing draperies. Statuary probably came from Lely.

Like the portrait of little Miss Vane, this rendering of Sheridan was a cleverly knowledgeable reorganization of elements from classic sources, an excellent piece of pictorial conjuring in the best eighteenth-century manner. Curiously, it betrays a sensitivity to line, and a firm, bold, attenuated usage of it unique in English art. That he also created a faithful image of his model can be seen from Fanny Burney's impression of Sheridan himself; ". . . a very fine figure, and a good though I don't think a handsome face. He is tall, and very upright, and his appearance and dress are at once manly and fashionable . . ."

THE PRESENCE of Richard Brinsley Sheridan, the most conspicuous and successful theatrical writer of that age, in his rooms at Newman Street gained considerable prestige for Stuart. Sheridan's two wit-pitted plays had given new life to a theater that for generations had existed on mediocre sentimental comedies and adaptations of Shakespeare. *The Rivals* proved so successful when performed in 1775 that Sheridan purchased the retiring David Garrick's share of the Drury Lane Theatre. Two years later he acquired the second half. Meanwhile his personal brilliance had lifted Sheridan from obscure Dublin origins into the world of fashion, and through it to politics. Never averse to an adventure, he escorted the beautiful and compromised sixteen-year-old singer Elizabeth Linley to a convent in France, marrying her en route; on his return he fought two duels. In 1780, having established himself and his wife in Orchard Street, Portman Square, where he dispensed hospitality on equal footing with the nobility, while creditors waited in other rooms, he entered Parliament.

To Stuart, Sheridan's progress through London demonstrated how far a man could rise were he able to assume the habits and attitudes of the ruling classes; a stylish appearance, polished words, and a glib tongue to cast off epigrammatic shafts were as requisite as the gift of living without means. If in addition to these a man had genius, he could rise far, and Sheridan provided the model for the next phase of Stuart's climb. The playwright's unfortunate habit of speaking in half-truths and his artistic re-arrangements of fact was a contagion to which Stuart had no resistance; tedious veracities lacked the artistry he was able to give them. Sheridan's manner of giving gentle offense to social superiors to demonstrate his own lounging ease amongst them was also readily acquired.

Contact with Sheridan brought Stuart into two worlds previously inaccessible to him. The doors of Drury Lane Theatre, with its mysterious nether regions of back passages, libraries and offices, and the frowsy glory of its dressing-rooms, were thrown open. In its dashing, unreal atmosphere he found himself elbowing nobles, painters like Reynolds, whose stall was reserved, musicians, and the glamorous creatures, male and female, from behind the proscenium arch. Sheridan's entertainments at home were another world into which Stuart happily entered; and in both places he gained a newer, more intimate view of British politics than ever was derived from the sober mind of Benjamin West.

The future belonged to the Whigs, to whom, as an ally of Charles James Fox, Sheridan had attached himself. That same year, 1782, the great political blow fell; Lord North's Ministry, like the American war it upheld, collapsed. He was replaced by Lord Rockingham, about whom gathered the many separate threads of Whig thought. Fox joined him as a Secretary of State; the Earl of Shelburne accepted a parallel post on condition that the King recognize the United States. Thus, near to the summit of his own career, there entered Stuart's the vain, hypocritical, callous, self-centered Lord Shelburne, who, in his strange wisdom, both established the United States and gave it her artist-laureate.

Conflicting views dissevered the Whig camp internally. Lord Rockingham, the Prime Minister, led the most powerful group, among whom figured Edmund Burke. But at Bowood, his country home, Lord Shelburne gathered leading philosophic dissenters, among them Dr. Joseph Priestley, a nonconformist parson who was a political pamphleteer and the discoverer of oxygen. Attached to him by political patronage, private pensions, or positions in his household, Shelburne brought such men together with Jeremy Bentham, creating a link between the philosophic reform movement and parliamentary circles. While Edmund Burke purged the Royal household of funds that had allowed the King to control Parliament, Shelburne and Fox, each steadily intriguing against any move made by the other, opened preliminaries for peace with America: such information as was desired to reach the King passed through Benjamin West. But with the death that July of Lord Rockingham Whig factional disputes burst into the open. Motivated by his personal hatred of Fox, who systematically debauched the Prince of Wales, King George sent for Lord Shelburne, avowed admirer of Washington and friend of America, to form the new Ministry. Fox resigned from the government, and the lines were drawn that would divide British politics for the balance of the century.

"Lord Shelburne may negotiate with Franklin as long as he pleases, but he will not succeed 'till France is satisfied; for I am persuaded both Washington and the Congress are in the pay of France . . ." wrote Lord George Germain, whose ministerial failures contributed largely to the military disaster. The truth was diametrically opposed, for the French and Spanish, whose fleets sealed the fate of Cornwallis at Yorktown, now considered American claims excessive. Undaunted, John Adams, Benjamin Franklin, John Jay, and Henry Laurens negotiated directly with Lord Shelburne, and had their way.

The American peace that followed was a severe blow to the King; the war had been his personal policy, carried on by a Ministry supported by the majorities in Parliament his funds provided. Parliamentary distaste for his personal rule had taken the American question as its point of opposition, and, resistance to the Royal prerogative so long centering about America, it now followed that Americans in England, like West, Copley, and Stuart, were assumed to be in alliance with the Whig party. This became clear even during the brief Rockingham administration when the Lord Chamberlain, the Duke of Manchester, applied to Stuart for his portrait. Patronage from such a personage was of considerable consequence; another new sitter, again illustrative of the trend, was William Wyndham Grenville. Twenty-four years old, and since February 1782 the Member of Parliament for his elder brother's "Borough of Buckingham," he was a close friend and relative to Lord Chatham's still unknown son, William Pitt. Whig forces were welcoming the young artist introduced to them by Sheridan: yet, like West, Stuart was forced to smile on all and evade open acquiescence, or the appearance of an alliance. Copley also straddled the fence, painting an American patriot like Elkanah Watson before the newly unfurled banner of stars and stripes at the same time he had sittings from the deposed Lord North.

For over a year the government remained exceptionally insecure. Fox and his followers, among whom Sheridan was a close lieutenant, stood in opposition to Lord Shelburne. North and his followers were in opposition too; the King still had considerable influence, and built more through seats in the Commons controlled by his nobles. Sheridan filled subordinate ministerial positions and refused £20,000 proffered by the American Congress in recognition of his services to the peace. In this quagmire of treachery it was necessary for Stuart to tread gently. He was too young and ill-established to have any importance, but he could damage himself irreparably were he to take a wrong step.

VI

Pressing Forward

HIS IMPRESSIVE victories over two enormous canvases gave
Stuart new confidence. His hand moved more surely and
forcefully, and enameled surfaces gave way to fresher textures marked by vigorous touches of creamy impasto that tripped
effortlessly from his brush. London was unaccustomed to portraits so
fresh, bright, vivacious, or with the sense of a thing *seen:* robust realism, personal revelation, Van Dyckian distinction, and Georgian elegance had coalesced in works of remarkable taste and appeal. But the
increasing assurance found in his work had its counterpart in the
attitude he brought to his life, and in that realm he was less a master,
for efforts to emulate the frothy example of Sheridan gave him a
slightly supercilious air. His hair was now worn longer, carefully
powdered, and formed into bulging rolls strung over his ears. His
nose, a long straight wedge, too bulky for a thin youthful face and
crammed with snuff, he carried high in the air: his snuffbox was a
part of him almost as prominent. The snuff habit, acquired early in
life, now was allowed free rein, as he joined a world that exuberantly
cultivated its vices.

Though his entrée to smarter society attached to the theater was
sufficient excuse for certain extravagances in Stuart's appearance and
dress, there was further purpose. When each sitter departed, the
canvas left on his easel showed no more than a deftly painted head.
To this Stuart drew shoulders and formed a composition; then the
mirror came into play. Stuart's wardrobe, reflecting the new trend
to cutaway coats, was put to account, and added largely to the stylish-

ness of his pictures. In those rare instances when he painted women, procedures were altered, for he had no model on whom he could make call. He had acquired engravings after the works of Vigée-Lebrun, Marie Antoinette's official painter, and to these he turned as needed. Other additions were being made to his engravings portfolio also, for the Duke of Manchester, garbed in his appropriate Peer's gown, had held his wand of office in a hand conspicuously derived from Lely, above which fluttered Stuart's own ruffles of Brussels lace.

Stuart left nothing undone that might advance his career, but he often lacked the tact and sense of fitness that came to others through long apprenticeship in their own class. Raised far away, forcing entry by the strength of his personality as much as his obvious genius, attempting to hold his own with those to whom this life was effortless, he could not avoid appearing ridiculous; and this was exaggerated by the way success had gone to his head. Benjamin West looked on, quietly. "It will eat itself out," is his only recorded comment, for West doubtless was also aware how closely Stuart sought for advantages. Early in 1783, when the Incorporated Society of Artists, a group previously run to ground by the formation of the Royal Academy, again became active, Stuart's proclivity to seize an opportunity became conspicuous.

In 1768 Benjamin West, together with the architect Sir William Chambers, Francis Cotes, and Moser the enameler, had planned the formation of the Royal Academy. A prudent man, West then called on Reynolds and in a two-hour conference persuaded him to join them. West and Chambers then sought Royal sponsorship, which, when gained, deprived the Incorporated Society of the patronage it formerly held. West did not harbor professional jealousies, but Reynolds had fought hard for his pre-eminence, and was intent upon keeping it. Inside the Academy, of which he became the first President, he exercised a despotism that was complete. Cotes graciously removed himself from any strife by an early death. Against Gainsborough and Romney, his two remaining rival portrait painters, Sir Joshua kept up harrying tactics that deprived Romney entirely of the opportunity to exhibit in London. West, an amiable man and no rival in portraiture, still occasionally dined with Reynolds, swallowed the faint praises meted out by the President, and maintained outward appearances of friendship. But it was a Reynolds axiom that two painters in the same branch of art could not live in friendship.

Stuart's path would be made more stony than his master's, especially as it was necessary for him to advance within an Academy over which Reynolds presided. The dormant Incorporated Society of Artists, once a flourishing concern, had never disbanded; funds from its formerly profitable exhibitions still were intact. Now it proposed to lease back its own splendidly built galleries in the Strand for an exhibition competitive with the Academy.

The success of such a venture could only be assured by the participation of notable painters, and dissident elements within the Academy were willing to take part. Stuart realized that, if he chose to gamble with his future, he could be the most outstanding among them. No venture could be more bold, for Reynolds was a formidable antagonist: yet for Stuart the opportunity was enormous. Should the Incorporated Society establish itself in public favor, he, Stuart, easily could become its chief attraction and dominant force. In May 1783, by his own reckoning just twenty-eight years of age, Stuart made his bold bid. He turned his back on the Royal Academy, where only a year before he had won his first success, and sent nine works to the Strand galleries of the Incorporated Society of Artists.

Most prominent among Stuart's canvases was the portrait of the Duke of Manchester, which proclaimed the noble and political nature of his patronage. A portrait of a clergyman made obeisance to that considerable market for likenesses. Two accomplished portraits of artists, seen at their work, added that note of informality and whimsy that Reynolds had used to profit; they also brought the firm assurance that Alderman Boydell considered their painter a man of artistic worth. Gay in her summer frock and twinkling landscape, little Miss Vane added a note of sensitivity and sweetness; her portrait also demonstrated his gifts as a children's painter, and was an example of the all-important full-length. To represent the thespian world was a picture of Mrs. Wilson, the first member of Sheridan's acting company at Drury Lane to have attracted Stuart's attention, and possibly his gallantry. Hannah More, whose plays were performed at Bath, represented the intellectual ranks of social reform, and gave token of how Stuart treated less beautiful members of her sex. Two portraits of gentlemen, indispensable and unidentifiable, completed the assemblage.

STUART had cast his net wide to solicit patronage and to demonstrate the full scope of his talents. In that day when portraits were exhibited discreetly without names, the Duke of Manchester was widely recognized, gaining for Stuart the particular accolade he sought; "No. 260 is a portrait of the Duke of Manchester—esteemed an excellent likeness and certainly an excellent picture," said the *St. James's Chronicle*. But otherwise contemporary journals took little notice. Sir Joshua Reynolds and friends of the Royal Academy found such an exhibition, assembled in defiance of the Academy, in bad taste. Few persons outside the profession understood that opposition to Reynolds arose from grounds more profound than mere jealousy. The unique result of this great effort was Stuart's further emergence as a force in London; what he coveted most, an increased patronage from elevated circles, followed quickly. Among the fresh applicants were Lord Sydney, another of the personalities involved in Whig ministerial intrigues, and after whom the Australian city was named. Admiral William Hotham was the first of four distinguished brothers to arrive in Newman Street, and a few naval figures followed, among them Sir John Dick. Orders from Alderman Boydell confirmed that Stuart would be well occupied through the winter, and certainly he had achieved much of what he wagered for by turning his back on the Academy.

Matters had run better for him, however, than for the Incorporated Society itself. Though it elected Stuart to membership in December, that gesture took on the nature of a parting favor, for the Society's coffers had emptied, and faced by disapproval, it gave up hopes of further exhibitions. What had appeared another giddy success thus, in retrospect, was seen to have been a debacle for its young hero, who had led the way to destruction. It was a false step of large and adverse consequence in his march forward, for naturally his action had offended influential members of the Academy, and now he was obliged to return to that fold—if he could. The imponderable Sir Joshua, grown more combative since his illness, was always to be considered. No cause existed for immediate alarm, but a wise man would give heed.

The new portraits ordered by Boydell included one of the engraver John Hall, who earlier had cut the plate of West's famous *William Penn's Treaty with the Indians*, a portion of which is glimpsed behind him. West himself also had been added to Boydell's list, a company become increasingly distinguished, representing all those who in their various capacities participated in the Alderman's enterprises. Since Stuart last painted him, two years before, West had put aside his wig, allowing the softened outline of his own carefully powdered hair to bring to his temples a more mature dignity. Such alteration alone cannot account for the enormous advance of this second portrait over the first, for Stuart's art and his sensitivity to individuals showed increasing maturity. His rapid brush no longer required stiff-ground whites to leave a personal mark, nor did he now paint his sitters' eyes averted. To West's keen glance he gave a sense of the unsmiling wisdom he respected in his master. Brushed more easily than *John Hall*, the composition was not essentially different; partly revealed behind West's inclined figure is a *Moses* that long before, under very different circumstances, Stuart himself had painfully executed from West's design. Probably it was the first composition West entrusted to him; a happy recollection, especially when larger variations on the same theme still were developing in West's rooms.

Not the only hint at filial respect and affection is found in this reference to an earlier relationship. Though Stuart portrayed his master fingering an edition of Boydell's Bible, thus tactfully genuflecting both to his present employer and West's Quaker piety, his master's hands also hold the pen with which he idled away the unaccustomed leisure of his sittings. Peering at Stuart against the light, West drew the ludicrous figure before him—seated cross-legged, dressed as though for a ball, his hair disheveled, his expression grim, a pot of oil balanced precariously on the edge of his seat. That Stuart was deeply troubled West saw and recorded in a hollow grimacing face: twenty years' intimacy with Reynolds made the reasons obvious, and they had taught West much about the character of the President, to whom he felt a conciliatory gesture was due. Stuart, however much he regretted the necessity, must go to Reynolds. Those who, like Romney, were too proud were beaten at the start. "Some choice colors" that West proposed to give Sir Joshua could be made the excuse for Stuart's visit.

Reynolds could not have been unaware what brought Stuart to his house in Leicester Fields, nor was he averse to giving this ambitious young man a lesson. He had just begun one of his proudest efforts, a portrait of Sheridan's newest star at Drury Lane, Mrs. Siddons, whom he was painting as *The Tragic Muse*. No ordinary picture of an actress, for Reynolds drew upon his full armory of pictorial magic. Mrs. Siddons was shown seated on an elevated throne framed in eerie lights whose flashes revealed shadowy forms symbolizing Crime and Remorse. A frank effort at the sublime, this was the branch of his art in which Reynolds felt confident no one could approach him, and when he escorted Stuart to his painting room it was in expectation the young man would be properly overwhelmed. Reynolds was not disappointed. What pupil of West could do aught but admire a work daring to employ a *Sybil* by Michelangelo as its source, intensifying its wild majesty, and simultaneously transforming it into an epitome of drama? So far beyond his own essays, the sight of this unfinished canvas gave Stuart enormous new respect for Reynolds' achievement. The President had hoped for nothing more; as a parting thrust he extended an invitation to see the picture when finished.

To cultivate Reynolds now was essential: happily Stuart accepted the offer which permitted him to call again. Probably he chose his moment badly, however, for when he next appeared at Leicester Fields he found Sir Joshua in testy humor, still working at this canvas, though his stockings sagged and his wig was disheveled. The instant Stuart shifted his glance from Reynolds to the easel he involuntarily caught his breath with disappointment. Sir Joshua noticed immediately. Sensitive, he tried to prod assurance by asking Stuart if he had not improved it.

"It could not have been improved—why did you not take another canvas?" blurted Stuart.

"That's true," Sir Joshua replied. He was familiar with his own inclination to over-paint canvases; of another major work he later said, "There are ten pictures under it, some better, some worse."

But Stuart immediately realized what a liberty he had taken in speaking to Reynolds as he would to an equal. He was exceedingly abashed, and Sir Joshua appeared to bear the criticism amiably. The effort to appease, however, had failed.

LIKE ANY sudden new fashion, Stuart was widely imitated in London. Though he had exhibited only twice, other artists filled their pictures with adaptations of his mannerisms. Mather Browne, to whom he first gave tutelage in Boston, had followed on to London in 1781, where he joined West's studio. Browne was a direct and avowed emulator of Stuart's every nuance. More surprising was that John Hoppner, rudely displaced in the race to succeed Reynolds, also was veering over to his rival's manner. Abandoning the heavy finish of Reynolds, Hoppner developed a light touch similar to Stuart's, especially notable in crisp, clean handling of whites. And when, more rarely now, Stuart appeared at West's studio, he was treated as a person of distinction. One day as John Trumbull struggled with a hand posed by a newer pupil, William Dunlap, Stuart was asked how he liked the work in progress:

> Pretty well, pretty well, but more like our master's flesh than nature's. When Benny teaches the boys he says, "Yellow and white there," and he makes a streak; "red and white there," another streak; "blue-black and white there," another streak; "brown and red there for a warm shadow," another streak; "red and yellow there," another streak.
>
> But nature does not color in streaks. Look at my hand;—see how the colors are mottled and mingled, yet all is clear as silver.

His own brush increasingly motivated by frenetic energy, Stuart could not help marveling at the wonderful, slow industry of Copley, whom he now painted for Alderman Boydell. In Copley's large house at George Street, Hanover Square, one saw a progression of grave, dignified portraits at full-length, among them the American Peace Commissioners John Adams and Henry Laurens, and an equally superb portrait in progress of the Earl of Mansfield, Lord Chief-Justice of England. This last order had come to Copley through his *Death of Lord Chatham,* for which Mansfield, like a majority of the House of Lords, had given sittings. The Lord Chief-Justice, impatient and tired of long, boring sessions, failed to pose for his hands. Neither Reynolds, West, nor Stuart would have been troubled; Copley, deeply committed to his own concept of authenticity, complained that Mansfield's hands were especially fine. Examination of the portrait reveals Mansfield wearing Stuart's ruffled cuffs of Brussels lace; and that Copley once irritated the impatient Stuart by keeping him too long while painting a bit of his lace is known.

Though they did not represent a separate faction, the three principal American painters in London were much thrown together. Copley was shy, diligent, and easily vexed; Stuart flamboyant; together they taxed West's powers of tact and persuasion, yet he watched over both with typical care, and Stuart found that association with his master was still advantageous. To patrons it gave a needed assurance. Sir John Dick wrote, concerning his own portrait, December 14, 1783; "The painter's name is Charles Stuart, an American—was some time at Edinburgh, where he did several pictures,—since that time has studied under Mr. West, and is, I think, one of the best portrait painters here." Nor was he the only Scot to evince interest, for an increasing number of Stuart's portraits were carried north, where by 1784 Henry Raeburn attempted a small picture of the Rev. Robert Walker, seen skating on Duddingston Loch; a work which, even though miscarrying into the realm of humor, was the first northern effort to emulate the artist electrifying London. Raeburn's further efforts were more successful, and from Stuart he developed his own rapid brevity.

A celebrity beyond the confines of London, Stuart now received an order for a group, to represent a family of two adults and two children, with a horse. Copley had demonstrated striking fertility of invention in this field, and it is surprising that, with the sense of fitness normally distinguishing him, West had not directed this order to the Bostonian. That Stuart received it may only imply his rapid brush was more free than that of Copley. The family that now appeared for sittings in Newman Street centered about William Bingham, a Philadelphian, who during the recent war, while engaged in diplomatic work in the Caribbean, increased an already large fortune by judicious investment in privateers. A man of undeterminable principles, Bingham's multiple activities were laying the foundation for a later generation more frankly labeled Robber Barons. His saving grace, beyond political acumen, was an enchanting wife, whose loveliness paved his way through society and quickly captivated Stuart. Rather than jeopardize a large canvas, he began individual studies of Bingham, his engaging wife, and their two infant daughters, then transferred these to the larger canvas, on which rough outlines of a composition were sketched.

Sir Joshua Reynolds was adept at cruel devices by which fellow artists and possible rivals were eliminated from the ranks of the Royal Academy over which he presided. That year, while being painfully, even pedantically honorable, he contrived to have a Gainsborough portrait of the King's three eldest daughters so unflatteringly hung that the artist withdrew it in a rage. That Reynolds dared offend even Royal quarters was an omen that Stuart could hope for no mercy, and, bowing to the inevitable, in 1784 he appears to have submitted nothing to the exhibition.

With Gainsborough a recruit, late in April the Incorporated Society held another meeting. Stuart, Romney, Wright of Derby, and Downman were the nucleus, but time in which they could act was lacking: the Academy exhibition already was hung, and soon opened. Reynolds craftily exhibited *Mrs. Siddons as the Tragic Muse*, backed up by the *Prince of Wales*, and, most significantly, *Charles James Fox*, who, it was widely believed until a few days before the exhibition opened, would topple the Shelburne Whigs to become Prime Minister. The election results revealed in April, 1784, surprisingly made young William Pitt the Premier, but few thought he could last long against the forces Fox then disposed. Sir Joshua, by exhibiting Fox's portrait, had the advantage of showing the man of the hour, and surely his position at the top of the heap was as unassailable as ever. The Incorporated Society could assemble no rival exhibition in time to compete, and whatever hopes it may have entertained soon vanished.

Whether by accident or design, or through the paradoxes of nature, the sitter next suggested by Alderman Boydell to Stuart was Reynolds himself. One dislikes to consider it pure chance that now brought together these two men for the long, quiet hours necessary to reach an accommodation. Boydell himself was too intimately involved in Stuart's fortunes to wish him to languish outside the natural arena of the Royal Academy; and West, who provided many of Boydell's finest subjects for engraving, kept benevolent guard over his pupil. Destitute of sitters in the heat of July, Reynolds agreed, setting aside three early morning appointments. Conversation was not aided by Reynolds' deafness, nor did Stuart set about to portray the President with any special tact. Turned to hide his scarred upper lip, painfully searching the younger man's face for words he could not hear, Reynolds was all tension; nor did Stuart hide that his parsimonious adversary wore a wig grown too small for fleshy temples. A profound statement, and the portrait by which Reynolds is best seen, Stuart's wonderful likeness failed to please the subject, who proclaimed it bore no resemblance!

Though Reynolds was equally adamant towards Gainsborough and Romney, the failure of the Incorporated Society was less critical to them than to Stuart. Older, better known, each with an established clientele among the great families and contacts in the world of fashion, those men kept private galleries in their houses, where recent works were hung and seen by the public. For Stuart, domiciled in rooms a few doors from West in Newman Street, this was not possible. He understood that if he had the will to succeed he was obliged to follow the example by keeping his own private gallery. This overpowering necessity forced the young man to extend himself, by seeking a house of his own. He discovered and negotiated for an imposing structure at number 3, New Burlington Street, near Piccadilly. It was beautifully proportioned and fashionably located; his heart swelled with pride when he contemplated its three stories of graceful comfort. At the top were small dormered servants' quarters, and on the second floor, behind an ironwork grill that hooded the entrance, the large pedimented window of a room about to become his studio: a drawing-room already famous by its inclusion in Isaac Ware's *Complete Body of Architecture*. Though requisite for advancement in his profession, such a baronial residence, far more grand than Reynolds', with twenty-one feet of frontage on the street, would saddle him with enormous costs; the rates alone were £105 a year! To occupy these premises he doubtless resorted to some complicated financial arrangements. Once installed, by whatever drastic means, he again was hard-pressed for furnishings; Ozias Humphreys, another friendly artist whom he had painted for Boydell, this time came to his assistance. But no one who now saw Stuart's handsome establishment could doubt he had well and truly arrived.

VII

The Conquest of London

B Y THE latter part of 1784 it was obvious to all that Stuart's career had gathered new momentum. He had passed unscathed through the first precarious period when heavy mortality overtook London's aspiring neophytes, and he advanced despite the sudden rise and fall of John Opie, who in 1781 had found sudden clamorous success as the "Cornish Wonder," an untutored natural genius. Opie had impressed even Reynolds; "Ah, there is *such* a young man come out of Cornwall . . . like Caravaggio, but finer!" he exclaimed to his pupil James Northcote. "I must plant a cannon at my door to keep the multitude off," Opie himself exulted; but a year later he lamented: "They have deserted my house as if it was infected with the plague." If Stuart did not arouse quite the same wild clamoring, neither did his clients desert him. Though he presumably still knew periods of relative uncertainty, it is unquestionable that he was solidly established in the favor of a restricted public.

The trickle of naval officers he painted earlier now had become a steady flow to his house in New Burlington Street. The Service portrait was a recognized road to better things: "We have all the great families in the navy—ay, and all the best families, too," boasted Lord Mulgrave, who commissioned a portrait of his brother, General Phipps. Early in his own career Reynolds had returned to his native Plymouth, to profit from this special article of commerce. Now in London itself, Stuart's forceful, frank portraits of officers filled the need for an artist of caliber capable of painting men who looked manly and real. Reynolds was too costly and overworked;

Gainsborough too often conferred the air of a dancing master. Officer's trade in London had been going to George Romney, but increasingly that artist was harassed, overworked, and careless in finish. Stuart brought something of Romney's blunt approach, mingled with considerable Georgian elegance, and his likenesses were unequaled by any of his three major rivals. Not a favorite with the ladies, suddenly Stuart had become the painter for military and naval figures who wanted a likeness they could esteem a good picture.

The heights to which Stuart's reputation now climbed can be seen in a letter written from London to Benjamin Franklin by his grandson, Temple Franklin:

> London, November 9, 1784
>
> . . . my father expressed a great desire that I would sit to Stewart, who is esteemed by West and everybody the first portrait painter now living. He is moreover an American. I have seen several of his performances which appear to me very great indeed! He is astonishing for likenesses. I heard West say "that he *nails* the face to the canvas" by which he meant I believe to express not only that the resemblance of the person was perfect, but that his coloring did not change; a fault common to some of the first painters in this country, and particularly to Sir Joshua.
>
> I am to begin sitting tomorrow, and Stewart has promised to make all possible dispatch. He hopes to finish the principal parts [the head] by Monday. If so, the day following I shall endeavor to get away . . .

One might entertain doubt that Stuart still worked for West, did not the brevity of his slashing portraits give him more free time than other painters. Further evidence is found in the new large version of *Moses As The First Law-Giver*, dated 1785. Tucked away at left is Stuart's carefully wrought head of John Trumbull, awestruck at the spectacle of ready-made tablets handed down to Moses out of cloudy heavens. Stuart's own neat profile, painted from an earlier sketch employed elsewhere in West's works, appears at lower right of this same huge canvas.

And, though the Royal Academy exhibition had been held without his participation that spring, in the summer three of his portraits attracted attention at Alderman Boydell's gallery. In carved ovals, attached to the frame of Copley's *Death of Major Pierson*, Stuart's portraits of Copley, James Heath, and Josiah Boydell celebrated the trio responsible for painting and engraving the Alderman's print.

THE DEGREE of Stuart's success, the increasing numbers of his sitters, and his enlarging income urged him on to still greater extravagance. His time for play was passed in the environs of the Drury Lane Theater, where he drew friends from the orchestra and behind the curtain. Though he had a keen eye for the ladies, of flirtations or his acquaintance with the youthful star Mrs. Wilson we know nothing. His behavior in every other sense continued giddy. Of modest origin, and having passed through grim periods, he had neither the balanced judgment nor the coolness of head necessary successfully to emulate the brilliant, easy, dawdling figure of Sheridan. Yet this was the path he deliberately followed, and unlike Reynolds, whose cold inner ambition early directed him to lay the foundations of a fortune, Stuart proceeded on the gayer principle that exterior manifestations of his success would bring respect, a larger clientele, and an ever-increasing income. Enjoying his irresponsible romp, he persuaded himself it was beneficial.

His theory may have been correct, but to pursue such a dangerous policy required self-control, of which he was incapable. The cost, he admitted, "was more than I calculated on," if in fact he ever did calculate. A bachelor, alone in a fashionable house surrounded by friends eminently willing to share his food and wine, he required servants. One footman, at least, was necessary to open the door, serve dinner, and show interested parties through his gallery of portraits. A cook was essential; and, attracted to good food, he boasted that his was French. From Drury Lane he drew musicians to perform before his guests: there was a famous dinner for forty-two persons, which probably took place soon after he was installed in New Burlington Street, for later he admitted he found entertaining seven more comfortable.

"I tasked myself to six sitters a day," was his own statement. We must assume that at times a smaller number came nearer the truth, though even this, in the custom of the time, implied a working day from ten to four, roughly the same hours he had labored for Benjamin West. Such a day, however, subjected to the vanity and exactions of a stream of sitters, produced a severe nervous exhaustion, and Stuart's nerves were not so capable of bearing great tension. Liquid refreshment was required, and then, "these done, I flung down my palette and pencils, took my hat and ran about and around the park for an hour, then home, got ready for dinner, and approached my drawing-room with the certainty of meeting as clever men as could be found in society."

Gay, facetious, full of bantering humor and vain display, Stuart's affectation of speech became a new quirk, as he acquired the special accents of the upper classes. Desiring to be thought a scholar and a man of breeding, he blundered into the pretentiousness of a coxcomb. Only those few equipped with the learning to appreciate his depths saw Stuart at true worth, and the closest among these was now John Philip Kemble, younger brother of the celebrated Mrs. Siddons, who in 1783 had followed her from Dublin to the stage of Drury Lane. An unusual man for the theater, Kemble had been Jesuit-educated at Douai, and, except for a more levantine turn of feature, was considered to bear striking resemblance to Stuart, for whom he developed an "extravagant partiality." Drawing only five guineas a week from Drury Lane, Kemble shared a love for the fruit of the decanter, and their intimacy had grown over the wine Stuart's prosperity provided. Proximity to a thespian of more than ordinary consequence was a further influence on the painter, who admired Kemble's profound dignity off stage and on. He acquired something of the tragedian's weightiness in gesture, his bearing took on a swagger with definite histrionic overtones, and his speech likewise became marked by the arbitrary alteration of vowel sounds associated with the Deb's Delight. In the preciousness of his new mannerisms, Stuart's voice was pitched to the husky drawl of Kemble's, and he pronounced beard *"bird,"* hideous *"hijjus,"* infirmity *"infaremity,"* and virgin *"vargin."*

More damaging were the parallel alterations taking place in his essential character, for he now tried to adopt what he believed to be the code of a gentleman, as he saw it practiced, imperfectly, about him in London. Those primary manifestations he noted were kindness to inferiors, a certain sullen pride with all who were not intimates, and tediousness in matters reflecting on honor. A grotesque caricature of any genuine code, in this flush of his first success he wedded it to his own irritability and an arbitrary, capricious nature. The result was to make him even more awkward and difficult than previously. Sensitive to criticism, he refused to brook any: partly this was derived from applying too seriously advice from Lord Thurlow, the ever-angry Chief Justice; "If a man speaks disrespectfully of your art, give him battle, my boy, give him battle!" He did—with a torrent of scorn that turned patrons into enemies. The large group portrait ordered by William Bingham came to its desultory end in just this way. It was well under way, the attitudes established on the large canvas, to which heads already were copied, when Mrs. Bingham dared to make some remark. Whether or not his action was justifiable, Stuart refused to continue. It was rude, and worse, it gave gratuitous insult to a charming young woman who was a favorite with everyone: Thomas Jefferson, Abigail Adams, and John Jay all found her delightful. Stuart's portrait of Jay, the American Peace Commissioner, was abandoned too, whether as a separate example of bad judgment or because of the Bingham fiasco is unknown. Likewise his portrait of Temple Franklin, though finished, was never shipped to America.

An essential falseness, or, at the very least, a dichotomy between the lordly role he aspired to play and his own rude character, peeks out everywhere. The occasional checks and reverses he suffered can largely be traced to this, or to secondary manifestations that developed from this split in his personality. For as Stuart offended sitters and refused to complete works, he became established in London as a painter of men only, and generally on small bust-sized canvases. Too soon in his career he allowed the field of action to become restricted. In 1785, when Queen Caroline asked Benjamin West's advice on an artist to paint her three youngest daughters, that wise man proposed Copley. The Bostonian had shown far greater fertility with such works, and by his choice West evaded those twin dangers attached to any order given Stuart; failure to finish, and the possibility of an insult.

A snub administered to Mather Browne again reflected the duality of Stuart's conduct, for were his own curious code in operation, offense could not have been dealt so summarily to a younger artist who may, for a time, have acted as Stuart's assistant. Browne was observed about to call: the footman was instructed to say his master was out.

"Not at home?" repeated Browne in amazement. "Why, I saw him at the window."

"Yes, sir, and he saw you, sir, and he says he is not at home, sir," replied his jewel of a servant—if the account that Stuart maliciously repeated can be trusted.

Yet, deeper within himself than the strata where lay his misunderstood gentleman's code, exaggerated speech, or his compulsive extravagance, Stuart remained the uncertain lad who felt reverence for Benjamin West. And from this deeper being that was his true self the strengths of his art sprang. Impossible as it was for him to admit, his newfound familiarity with Reynolds had stirred a reverence. Like West, Reynolds had profound knowledge; his personality was expressive of certainties and complete assurance, and because his specialty was portraiture this wisdom lay closer to home. With an increased interest Stuart read over the notes Sir Joshua contributed to a translation of Dufresnoy's old verse treatise on art. Bound separately, after the text, were knowledgeable observations on the practices of Rubens, the Italian masters, and others of whom West also spoke, far less well. That the Venetian painters gave a prescribed proportion in their pictures to areas of light, dark, and half-tone was an interesting discovery to an artist who occasionally wondered whether a light or dark tone was preferable.

Much of what Reynolds wrote Stuart committed to a memory both capacious and facile. He viewed the President with increased respect, visited his private gallery, and acquired engravings after his works to assist study. In consequence his own art became more grave: the dashing, slashing first period suddenly halted.

STUART's portraits of naval and army officers painted early in 1785 were much altered from those done before. He now fixed on "three-quarter face," the view when both cheeks and nose outline are visible, as most typical of the human head, a standardization of practice earlier employed by Sir Peter Lely. Whether from right or left, Stuart adopted this single position in all his portraits. For a young man whose reputation was founded on likeness it was a useful but restricting move, that allowed him to proceed easily and with dispatch. But for the past year, every alteration of method had been a restriction narrowing down the field of his endeavors. Fewer poses, smaller canvases, a predominance of painted ovals, or oval frames fitted to bare spandrels, the resolute employment of three-quarter face; each in turn reduced his scope and increased his ease. Half the beauty of Stuart's work was found in its ease of accomplishment. The pictures of this period are the most accomplished in manner he ever produced; deftly modeled, clear of color, each touch carefully calculated, he never excelled them for beauty of style or grace of execution. From Reynolds he took the practice of adding burnt umber to his palette at the last sitting; gently washed over edges and into shadows, it gave softness, warmth, and strength. When painting draperies it permitted him also to add that shadow across the coat, as in Romney's recent works, that became the hallmark of a brief, distinguished period.

Now greater care is everywhere apparent. The hard-bitten expression of General Sir Richard Grenville is achieved with greater attention to finish; Admiral the Hon. Samuel Barrington is captured with a more literal, less stylized, realism, unkind to a snoutish English nose and bulging lower lip. Though better characterized than Reynolds' portraits, the solemn mood of Sir Joshua is present. Also notable is the absence of saber-thrusts that added brilliant skies to Stuart's earlier portraits of Copley and James Heath. Textures have become drier, the facture thinner, and soon, tracing alterations in his manner, we are aware of a double phenomenon. Competing fiercely in the world's most competitive portrait market, Stuart adopts in turn the newest mannerisms of his rivals. Like latter-day manufacturers, his eye was ever on his competitors, who were never allowed to get ahead of him. The second part of this curious orientation is that despite a rivalry that so constantly altered his externals, his personal qualities consistently become more pronounced: each portrait issuing from his studio appears more strongly grasped, more devastatingly characterized.

Captain Sir William Abdy, small, pudgy, notorious for attentions to venal ladies, captured with his odd tentativeness of expression, compounded of sulkiness and mixed inclinations, Stuart fixed to canvas by a short, choppy stroke that builds wonderfully rounded form. In one of his few non-service portraits, the same criss-cross of short strokes makes the Scot, Dugald Malcolm, a startling mound of flesh. Employment of small flat sable brushes led him to apply whites to officers' braid in steely hard beads that glisten high off the canvas. And an even greater force is given the heads. Defying convention, he showed heavy-rimmed spectacles masking the huge bulk of Admiral Peter Rainier, after whom an American mountain so rightly was named. Captain Richard Pierson scowls with a fierceness not employed when his *Serapis* came under the guns of John Paul Jones' *Bon Homme Richard*.

Experiments with sober backgrounds followed, and these are graded in tone to comply with the Venetian formulas written by

Reynolds. Asked to paint larger canvases at three-quarter length, Stuart carefully sought the best design. Among recent efforts in the three-quarter-length, the most successful was Reynolds' 1779 portrayal of Admiral Viscount Keppel, of which Copley, then living near Reynolds in Leicester Fields, helped to multiply copies. Derived from Van Dyck's standing portrait of *Charles I*, which surely had a more remote source, Reynolds' *Keppel* became Stuart's starting point for his own *Admiral Sir Edward Hughes;* he then painted *Admiral Lord Mulgrave* by reversing the same composition. He had graduated from the ranks of Captains to those of Admirals, and a period of new industry had overtaken him. After concentrating on bust portraits in ovals he was again producing larger canvases, among them a full-length of Captain John Gell, executed in his most searching manner; for a seascape behind this figure, he followed Reynolds' example by hiring a specialist to paint it.

PERHAPS flattered to be the inspiration of Stuart's latest efforts, possibly aware of the adoration now accorded him, or thinking the younger man sufficiently chastened, Reynolds must have signified that he would place no obstacles in Stuart's path should he wish once more to show at the Royal Academy. Though his participation in 1785 was only his second major appearance at Somerset House, yet it showed Stuart to be a well-established star in the constellation of London painters. Conforming to Reynolds' ambiguous attitude, he sent only three paintings. His pictures were well-treated, and William Dunlap, who visited the exhibition, noted that they were "occupying the best lights, and the most conspicuous places . . ." The principal work was his full-length of Captain John Gell, which was accompanied by bust portraits of Admiral Barrington and Lord Dartrey, the latter a patron of West's, who, married to William Penn's granddaughter, that very month was elevated to the new peerage of Viscount Cremorne.

Notably absent from the Academy was Gainsborough, whose withdrawal the year before had been final, as he then implied. Gainsborough never again submitted himself to Reynolds' indignities, but his career was passing through a difficult stage. The rise of Stuart had drawn off nearly all his male sitters, and since 1782 he had found himself specializing in women's portraits, his idle moments turned to poetic landscapes and idyllic subjects, for which he was slowly discovering a market. If one forgot the existence of George Romney, as visitors to the Academy exhibitions regularly did, there was a definite impression that Reynolds and Stuart were the only major portrait painters in London. That they shared honors alone at the Academy that year enhanced this view. While his own early promise slipped away, John Hoppner filled a critic's niche for the *Morning Post:* hurt and jealous, he seems to have disregarded the fact that Stuart was the cause of his troubles, and poured out his hatred on Copley's *The Three Princesses.* Perhaps his own less successful efforts with these same Princesses provided the obscure motive for his abuse of Copley's magnificent achievement. After employing Stuart's simplicity as a ram to batter Copley, he ended "we confess a partiality for young artists who aim at something."

To the ever-equivocal Reynolds Stuart's portrait of Captain Gell was sent soon after the exhibition, so the President might paint a portrait of Gell too, from Stuart's. The gesture was not pleasing, no more than the intimation that Reynolds' likenesses were less satisfactory than those caught by his younger rival. Sir Joshua did as asked, and pocketed his fee for a vigorous three-quarter-length of a much rejuvenated naval officer, evidently intended to overshadow Stuart's quieter effort; but Stuart never again showed at the Royal Academy. Aware his new break with Reynolds, like those between Reynolds and Romney and Gainsborough, was sired by Sir Joshua's intense competitive spirit, and therefore was final, Stuart for the first time displayed an awareness that he was practicing a narrow specialty. His sitters were exclusively men, and almost as exclusively they were men drawn from the services. His most recent display at the Academy had encouraged the notion of him as a specialist in service portraits, to offset which he made a concerted effort to attract women.

His naval portraits brought the first. The Earl of Sandwich, formerly a patron of Gainsborough, until the fall of Lord North's Ministry in 1782 had headed the Admiralty. At that time Lord Sandwich abandoned Gainsborough to have his younger brother, the Hon. John Montagu, painted by Stuart. Now he asked for a portrait of his natural daughter Augusta, a labor the artist undertook very seriously and conscientiously. Deftly he painted a head of much charm—its open-mouthed smile and gaily averted eyes unusual characteristics for a century with few other examples of teeth in portraiture. Quite unlike anything else in Stuart's own output, it gave him a fine start—but he had no model for the figure. Gainsborough had recently completed an attractive portrait of Kemble's sister, Mrs. Siddons; though his canvas was smaller, Stuart founded on his rival's portrait the general disposition of draperies, position for one arm, and a swath of cloth to cover an elbow. A black choker worn across the actress' throat was appropriated, and her tumbling coiffure blended with Marie Antoinette's, from whom a weak hand holding a letter also was adapted; a curiously pointing second hand he found in a work by Lely. Bows for the sleeves and bodice then were provided by an earlier Vigée-Lebrun portrait of the French Queen, and a fanciful white headdress came from another actress painted by Romney, *Mrs. "Perdita" Robinson.* Haphazard in construction and somewhat ineffectual in painting, rustling fabrics and a spritely look nonetheless developed a picture of very special charm, closer to French than English contemporaries.

Other sitters were provided by Drury Lane; Kemble already had been sketched in the slashing earlier manner, and Henderson, the ugly little tragedian who carried Shakespeare's great weight at Drury Lane, was essayed in a variety of his roles. Sheridan's father, Thomas Sheridan, sat, and soon, in the person of Eliza Farren, Drury Lane's leading star of fashionable light comedy, Stuart had another beauty on whom to try his skill. Little experienced with women's portraits, Stuart found Miss Farren difficult; he worked hard, eliminated all shadows, stressed her large dark eyes, and created a head that almost passed for pretty. Compared with his portraits of men, however, it remained a static performance, and lacking a model for the figure, again he was at an impasse. Two engravings after Vigée-Lebrun offered a partial answer; Marie Antoinette's double ruffle of lace, recently employed by Reynolds for *Lavinia, Countess Spencer with Her Son*, was painted over the shepherdess frock worn by the *Countess of Provence*. To a background of studio sky he added dark touches of foliage, a device he had not employed for five years; and then, because Miss Farren disliked any suggestion of bodily display, he added a white fichu that covered her from the bosom to the ears. Creditable, but undistinguished, and missing the comedienne's legerity, nothing about this performance recommended Stuart to women of fashion. Orders for ladies' portraits remained scarce, though the artist's own curious blend of personal charm and naivete should have been sufficient to bring them in droves. The discovery that one titled sitter (her identity unknown, unless she was "the Hon." Augusta Montagu) wore rouge on her cheeks put him in sullen temper. Without bidding he gave her to understand that she was quite lovely enough without artifice.

"Oh, Mr. Stuart, have you found me out?"

"Of course I have. Any one having knowledge of the human face knows there is a boundary to the color in every lady's cheek, and if you go beyond the line you certainly will be detected."

Not content, he demonstrated where nature would place color on a cheek formed like hers, which she took with good grace, and said she would remember.

"Pray do not do it; you do not *need* it," came his naively generous reply.

VIII

"At the Summit of His Profession"

S TUART'S extravagantly styled high, wide coiffure and cut-away coats showed that he had adopted the fashions of the Prince of Wales, acknowledged leader of the rakes and silly-set. But the artist had no personal association with this young Prince, and much of the sudden upward movement noted in his affairs during 1785 proceeded from the fact that Reynolds had blundered by identifying himself too closely with the Prince and Charles James Fox. To do so had been reasonable enough while the Shelburne Cabinet tottered and Fox, supported by the heir to the throne, was the strongest leader in opposition. When by a cynical arrangement with Lord North, Fox at last forced Shelburne to resign, the election of 1784 unexpectedly transferred power away from "Fox's martyrs." The King sent for a little-known son of Lord Chatham, who had served, despite his youth, in Shelburne's cabinet, and England was treated to the spectacle of an impassive youth of twenty-six forming a government. Few persons believed William Pitt could remain long in his new eminence, and Fox, seeking to outmaneuver his cold firm grasp, rapidly discredited himself.

To Reynolds, who yearly exhibited portraits of the Prince and of Fox, the blow was serious. He had shown too definite a partiality. Pitt now was firmly settled in power, and would remain there, almost as long as he lived.

For men of policy there was need of another painter; a need Stuart was ready and willing to fill. As the numbers of his portraits increased, so the political nature of his patronage became more pronounced. Many of these new sitters had served as senior officers in the American war, the assumed allegiance of Americans with the Whig party an ever-present assurance to them. The first, naturally, were drawn from the ranks of his naval patronage, though now the emphasis in his work was shifting, from service portraits to those of governmental personalities. Admiral Lord Hood had added the only illustrious page to the American war, by defeating de Grasse's French Squadron—after it had forced Cornwallis' surrender at Yorktown. His reward was an Irish peerage, and, in 1784, his was the glory of personally opposing Fox in the heatedly contested Westminster election. Weeks of rioting were seen, while Hood's sailors fought pitched battles in St. James's Street with Fox's hackney coachmen. Despite the intervention of the Duchess of Devonshire, who gave away guineas and kissed a shoemaker to obtain his vote for Fox, Hood received more votes than his opponent. Together with other American veterans such as Lord Rawdon and the Duke of Northumberland, both of whom had been present at Bunker Hill, Admiral Lord Hood joined the march of political leaders to Stuart. To their portraits he added one of the ex-Prime Minister, Lord Shelburne himself. His first meeting with this Earl, who for two decades and in three countries would influence his life and career profoundly, he recounted thus:

> When I was in good practice and some repute in London, a stranger called upon me, and finding me engaged with a sitter begged permission to look at my pictures, which was readily accorded. He passed some time in my exhibition room. From his shabby black dress, and respectful politeness, I concluded him to be some poet or author from Grub Street, and made up my mind that the chief purpose of the visit was to prepare some article as a puff for the next periodical.
>
> A few days after this I received a polite invitation to breakfast, from the Earl of ——— [Shelburne]. And you may judge of my surprise when I found in my host the supposed Grub Street scribbler. After breakfast the Earl complimented me, and expressed his satisfaction with what he had seen at my rooms. [He] . . . requested me to receive a commission from him, to paint a list of characters, whose

names I should find on the paper he then handed to me, the which he intended should decorate a new gallery he was constructing on his grounds. The list contained the names of the most distinguished personages of the day, in the political and literary world, and seldom has so splendid a denouement followed so unpromising a beginning.

The new impetus he felt freed Stuart of the self-consciousness evident in his previous work and stimulated him to give of his best. He worked harder, with more conviction, and was troubled less by superficial considerations of style, allowing his portraits to stand as simple, direct statements. So recently an imitator of other leading painters, suddenly he brought to the London scene a harsh new realism completely his own. Such relentless reportage and marvelously controlled integrity of vision had never before appeared in England, where no painter at the height of fashion ever before had been sufficiently flexible, amid the artifices of style, to put on canvas the physical appearance, expression, and mental state of his sitters. No other had possessed the requisite skill Stuart now unleashed; his ability to capture the flicker of mingled expressions made of portraiture a newer, more sensitive, revealing art. Beside Stuart, the best of Reynolds' works became mute effigies, carved from wood, and for any historic parallel of Stuart's achievement one must return a century and a half, to the prime of Frans Hals. Stuart's gift was no ordinary one; it has never been surpassed, rarely equaled, and is unique in the long annals of art.

London had to acknowledge it had a new master with no taste for dissembling, who revealed himself possessor of an incisiveness with the brush they did not dream existed. Shocked and intrigued, filled with a slightly uneasy sense of joy, the political minions of orthodox Whiggery followed Lord Shelburne, now created Marquis of Lansdowne, and the friends of Pitt to the New Burlington Street house of Gilbert Stuart. There, with a vitality unseen before in English painting, sometimes harsh, tempered more often by sympathy, filled with remarkable insight and a searching integrity of vision, Stuart painted portraits of the men who controlled the Empire. Such was his esteem that Thomas Jefferson, author of the American Declaration of Independence and Ambassador to France, when he arrived in England for a fortnight in April, felt too modest to approach Stuart, or pay his thirty guineas. His picture, and that of John Adams, was painted by Stuart's follower and imitator, Mather Browne.

THE PROMISE of Stuart's first success was now abundantly fulfilled. He was more sought after, and more prolific in his production, than any portraitist in London, and his connections were widespread through the theatrical, social, and political worlds.

Stuart still nourished a passion for music, which found him taking lessons, probably on the oboe, from a member of the King's Band. At his own musical parties he took a prominent part, playing well on a variety of instruments, and singing. He was remarkable for the extreme elegance of his dress and manners. Efforts at decorum and his constant intercourse with people of breeding had succeeded in polishing him. Indeed, his friend Gainsborough Dupont, nephew and assistant of the great artist, painted a stinging rebuke to Stuart's haughty appearance in elaborate coiffure and display of frills. The picture leaves a remarkably disagreeable taste, without any compensatory wit; it shows how closely Stuart ran the gauntlet of ridicule.

Little that he now wished in the world could have been denied him, and in a future still hidden, he could not be aware that those he was elbowing aside in the race for favor shortly would pass from the scene entirely. Gainsborough had only two years of life left to him; Reynolds hardly more, and Romney would cease the battle at almost the same moment. The future was Stuart's; and, at this proud moment, what he wanted most in the world was a wife.

For a man with a certain position and the promise of fame and fortune, he chose modestly. Charlotte Coates lived at Reading; she was the younger sister of one of his oldest friends, William Coates, whom he had met much earlier when at the suggestion of West he had attended the anatomical lectures of Dr. Cruikshank. Coates almost immediately had filled part of the void left in Stuart's life by the departure for Leyden of Benjamin Waterhouse. Visits to Reading followed, and there we must assume that Stuart first met his intended wife when she was a child of ten. William Coates already had passed the examination of the Surgeon's Company, to become a Surgeon's Mate in the Royal Navy; the flow of naval figures to populate Stuart's earliest London works must, to some extent, be attributable to his efforts in behalf of his friend.

Arrived now at a position of extraordinary eminence, thirty years old, and, despite the demanding nature of his profession, possibly lonely, it was this modest provincial family Gilbert Stuart chose to enter. The alliance could bring him no advantages; the eighteen-year-old daughter of Dr. Thomas Coates, a physician, Charlotte offered, despite her comfortable upbringing, no allurements of fortune or position. It is to Stuart's credit that at this dizzying moment he sought neither. Instead he suffered from the delusion that he was in love. The causes are obvious. We are assured that Charlotte was extremely pretty, and, for Stuart's sake, we trust this was so. English women take on a special glow at this age, when youthful innocence mingles with the softness of maturity and color kindles bright in their clear fresh skin. Charlotte's vocal gifts appear to have been an equal charm: to the music he played she brought a fine contralto voice, and something of its trained beauty carried over to her speech. Stuart's suit was pressed with all the force at his command: desire walked with opportunity, and neither was denied. In the urgency of his passion he pressed his demands on the parents of the willing girl, and there, despite the pride with which he offered himself, he was mortified to be dealt a summary rejection. Neither the brother, who was his friend, nor the father, both of whom expressed the greatest admiration for his genius, would countenance the marriage. Aware of his reckless habits and unstable nature, they recoiled before the obvious dangers; the elder Dr. Coates, fearful for his daughter, appears to have been particularly stubborn in his refusal, and to have antagonized the artist. Stuart began to call Charlotte, in her own moods of pique, "Tom," after her father. The estimate of the Coates family was just, and yet they relented; a proper respect for mathematics and its immutable laws implies that a danger of disgrace at last wrung from them their reluctant consent. The marriage was arranged, and solemnized by the Rev. Mr. Springate, May 10, 1786. The first child of this happy young couple was a boy.

What happiness marriage brought to Stuart we do not know. One expects the pleasures of requited love to sooth his disturbed nature and to bring him a new stability and maturity. Yet no change is visible. There was no lessening of his eccentricities or excesses. Had his young wife been older, one might have hoped for more, for no sign whatever is discernable of any influence she had over him. He continued in his own path so obstinately one wonders whether he was actually capable of a marriage, beyond the ordinary legal fact. Filled with the unique fire of his genius, he possessed in an extraordinary degree its characteristic defect. A devouring egotism, and a devotion entirely to himself, vitiated every finer element in his nature.

Alone, frightened, at the summit of a remarkable success, to him-self he was the unquestioned center of the universe, and he seemed unaware of any authority beyond his own inclinations. What he liked was right: what he disliked was wrong: and, as a man, this made him extraordinarily unpredictable. Stuart's self-absorption, in fact, had tainted his reactions. Like his letter to Benjamin West, all his feelings were *part* genuine, but also present was self-indulgent pleasure in emotion for its own sake; and much of his tantrum-in-clined, gay, and sulky nature was a means of self-glorification. It is questionable whether even his most intense affections and most exalted enthusiasms were not make-believe, for what portion of reality re-mained in the image he presented to the world? His career had been composed of a succession of theatrical performances, designed to achieve whatever aim he strove for at the moment. His entertainments, his musical parties, his brilliant dress and flashing wit, all were ex-cused as the necessities of his profession. Of this he had persuaded himself more fully than anyone else, and, in part, probably it was true; though West, Reynolds, and Romney lived more modestly, and Gainsborough's occasional extravagances were carefully hidden from a shrewish wife. Were not these indulgences to which Stuart drove himself desired really to exhibit to the world and to himself the brilliance of his own personality?

Comedy and tragedy came easily to him: they existed in the bare outlines of his life, though no one ever drew so much pleasure from their exaltation as Stuart himself. If she would join his life, Charlotte Coates Stuart would be assigned a supporting rôle, and required to give a perfect performance as dispensing goddess of arts, home, and fertility. While living his own rôle, he had come to believe in it. In that sense, the personality he had created for himself became his own; occasional lapses grew fewer, until those that remained were attributable mainly to his failure to grasp his rôle's real character. But no woman endowed with less genius than himself was capable of what he demanded, and even had she possessed those necessary qualities of urbanity, drama, and pathos, would they not then be a couple doubly unstable?

Some slight qualifications Charlotte brought to the part of his wife; but, though she was said to be pretty, it is immediately a wonder that her likeness is not known to have been preserved. Stuart, em-ployed throughout his life in setting down the images of others, was not averse to recording his own visage, in some present rôle: playing an imitation Benjamin West and a sparkling beau are the two early self-portraits with which we are familiar. It would be curious if he never painted a likeness of his own wife, and even more curious still if the vanity of an eighteen-year-old girl could not wring this homage from her husband, and lover. Yet, fortunately, we are able to see what attractions the young artist found so endearing, for Stuart employed his wife as a model for the portraits of others, and the partial portrait of herself, assembled from them, shows her to have been small of stature, with short neck, dainty waist, and high, deep bosom. Her delicate hands are equally well-known, the fingers slender, and short in proportion to the palm; to honor their vows, she wore a simple gold band.

The only further contributory fact is that very soon Stuart began to notice that his young wife was commonplace. Her resemblance, in nature, to her father, was confirmed so strikingly that "Tom" became his ordinary name for her.

CERTAIN realities always penetrated to Stuart, and at this juncture he was wise enough to realize that marriage forced him to take his career even more seriously. To remain at the top of the heap, he was obliged to compel admiration for his artistry, and in a world orientated as London was, early in 1786, that could only mean a great composition from history.

Added to the necessity of asserting himself was the realization that he could not continue to live at his extravagant pace by painting bust portraits alone. At this time he confided to a friend that he was earning £1500 a year; a goodly sum, though only half Romney's peak earnings, and a fifth those of Reynolds, a wise gentleman who concentrated on larger pictures. The figure nonetheless is bold; the reality may have been less so. Though his prices now equaled Gainsborough's at thirty, sixty, and one hundred guineas, for bust, half-length, and full-length portraits respectively, Stuart's concentration on smaller canvases require nearly fifty portraits a year to equal the income he claimed. The fact is, he did not paint that many. The historian is troubled by the disappearance of large numbers of Stuart's English works; even so, the lifetime pattern of his production belies this possibility. And the fact to be gleaned from examination is that caught between sums paid, expected, promised, received, owed, and *wished*, he probably was not certain himself of the extent of his annual income. As debts mounted, he lived in constant expectation that something would happen—some unknown, unforeseen, merciful occurrence, some stroke of marvelous luck—that would alter unfavorable balances.

He saw that no possible number of bust portraits could support the establishment he had created in New Burlington Street. Through long association with Alderman Boydell, he was aware the great print-seller was planning a new series of subjects from Shakespeare. To create a prestige-making major work, to produce the extra income, through engravings, that his economic circumstances demanded, became his object. He chose a subject which had been suggested to him the previous year; to be precise, on March 31, 1785, when John Phillip Kemble opened at the Drury Lane Theatre in *Macbeth*. To paint Kemble in the rôle and life-size was Stuart's original idea, far surpassing the abstract embodiments of drama for which Reynolds had previously utilized Garrick, Mrs. Abington, and Mrs. Siddons. Together Stuart and Kemble selected their moment from the fourth act, when Macbeth, crossing the moor, comes on the witches conjuring a charm over their cauldron and exclaims: "How now, you secret, black, and midnight hags! What is't you do?"

Begun in the winter of 1785–86, the picture immediately stirred interest through London. Such an effort had been long awaited from Stuart; by February, 1786, news of the picture's advancement was sought, and *The Morning Chronicle* was able unctuously to assure readers that Stuart, "who singularly excels in the great excellence of portrait painting, accuracy of similitude, has made a head of Kemble for Macbeth, marvelously exact."

Drunk with their own schemes, Stuart and Kemble, even before this work's completion, searched for further subjects from Shakespeare. The same newspaper shortly boasted of finding at Stuart's house a new portrait of Kemble, as *Richard III*. Soon *Macbeth* was completed, and though it was the first work to have taxed Stuart's imagination since he quit West, and as such was a break with his more perfunctory studio methods, the artist himself was singularly charmed with it. But Alderman Boydell, on whom all depended, disgraced himself by an unwillingness to accept the picture. A month after Stuart's marriage, Boydell went to Leicester Fields, proposing to Reynolds *Stuart's very subject.* Sir Joshua showed a lack of interest, on which Boydell pressed five hundred guineas into his hand, gaining a grudging acceptance from Sir Joshua. For consolation to Stuart, later that year Boydell exhibited at his gallery, now renamed *The Shakespeare Gallery,* all fifteen portraits of London artists executed for him by Stuart since 1781. But such a niggling gesture could not restore the dashed hopes of the artist.

Among those most impressed by Stuart's *Macbeth,* which remained in his house, was a handsome lad of seventeen, recently come to London. A child prodigy, intent upon maturing his talents, Thomas Lawrence one day would also paint Kemble in great tragic roles. Closer to Trumbull, beside whom he nightly sat as they drew at the Royal Academy School, Lawrence's pastel portraits were the principal support of his family. "I knew Stuart well," Lawrence later recalled, and his first exhibited works drew so heavily on Stuart and on Rigaud that they imply he had access to the painting-room. To Stuart, Lawrence's talent was clear; of his continued efforts in pastel he asked abruptly why he wasted his time on "such damned little things as these?" The abashed air of the boy stuck in his mind, and he never forgave himself this lapse into an unkind manner. Other aspiring younger men gathered about Stuart too, happy to clutch at his rising star; young William Beechey was struck by his superb talent and witty disposition. At the home of the engraver, John Raphael Smith, Stuart was first glimpsed by Fuseli, among whose eccentricities was a devotion to the "science" of physiognomy: Smith blandly enquired whether, by his appearance, he thought Stuart could paint. "I don't know but what he might," said the analytic Swiss, and, as a verifying note, "He has a *coot* leg"; a reference to the bony, fetlock-like extremity, left so exposed by eighteenth-century garb.

An increased income was becoming more urgent. In part it was supplied by full-length portraits such as that of Admiral Lord St. Vincent, with whom he became intimate and from whom he received numbers of recommendations to Lord Rodney and other senior naval commanders. Now cautious when faced by the full-length, and finding it necessary to fit such laborious undertakings into a busy schedule, he continued his practice of executing separate studies of the head, on small canvases. At leisure the figure was developed, then the head copied onto it before the whole was finished together. Painters were subjected to many inconveniences, and whether by choice or necessity, Lord St. Vincent's head was developed from an earlier portrait by Francis Cotes before it was completed from life.

From this successful endeavor he turned again to bolster the most forlorn. Since his marriage he had a model, and felt better able to cope with female sitters; again he made the effort to attract them by issuing invitations to prominent stage personalities. The singer Elizabeth Weichsel, who in 1783 married a double-bass player and henceforth was known as Mrs. Billington, held her renown as much for the beauty of her person as her singing. With his wide acquaintance in musical circles, Stuart probably had known her since the time of her marriage, and now invited her to be painted. Because Mrs. Siddons had been portrayed by every other artist in London, and Francis Twiss, the dramatic critic, who was married to Kemble's other sister, Frances, seemed desirous of a picture of his celebrated sister-in-law, he issued Mrs. Siddons the same invitation.

The Academy exhibition of 1786 opened and closed without him, though his *Macbeth* ought certainly to have been shown. Stuart's absence was significant enough to find comment in newspapers: "We were in hopes to have seen a picture at the Academy," wrote the *Morning Post*, "of that beautiful singer, Mrs. Billington, by Stuart, who from his well known abilities certainly could produce a charming picture from so beautiful a model." And in the *Advertiser:*

> But yet, more material, why is Stuart absent? Is he already so giddy at the summit of his profession as to overlook what is expected from him at the bottom—the example, the pecuniary aid which pupilage must perish in want of? His head of Colonel Barré would have counted largely in the exhibition in the sum total both of money and of skill . . .

At the summit of his profession: how good it must have been to find that acknowledgment in print. Intended to be opprobrious, the phrase found a ready ear and a happy heart.

IX

Collapse

AS WILLIAM PITT'S ministry became more securely entrenched, Stuart's position in London showed a parallel improvement. He was now firmly attached to a group influential at Westminster headed by Colonel Barré, Lord Rawdon, and the Duke of Northumberland, the last of whom soon shared with Lord Shelburne his place as the first among those patrons and champions who throughout Stuart's life did so much to shape his fame and fortunes. Northumberland was not popular with the King, who accused him, possibly with justice, of a "peevish temper." His irritability flowed equally from family pride and gout, yet few persons directed so much real influence, or were so courted by rival factions. Twelve years before troops under his command were "almost entirely cut to pieces" at Bunker Hill. In March 1776, without heart for the enterprise, he took command of 2,400 men who attacked General Washington at Dorchester Heights. Much valorous action followed, until in 1777 "Lord Percy" returned to England, disgusted by the conduct of the war. After his succession to the Dukedom, Northumberland controlled a bounty of rotten boroughs that spoke with his voice in the Commons: his adherence brought a block of votes to any cause, and he was himself vocal in the Lords. Angry that he received no reward for his services in America, and strongly critical of that wasteful struggle, Northumberland's weight contributed to the fall of Lord North, and the election of 1784 that established Pitt's unshakable majorities. A full general in the army, commander of the Second Horse Grenadiers, his influence was behind much that transpired in government.

One experiences a sense of intimate acquaintance across the centuries, rare in the portraitist's art, from the two portraits Stuart did of Northumberland. He also painted the Duke's chief henchmen, Lord Rawdon and Colonel Barré, and found himself as firmly established, socially and politically, as Reynolds had been.

Only a change of ministries could hurt Stuart now, and in the Commons William Pitt's icy candor daily made that eventuality more remote. The real threat rested in areas unseen by the public that admired Stuart's portraits more devotedly than ever. Daily the pressure of his debts was becoming more importunate; a larger income, or an additional source of funds, was urgently required. Hope of painting Kemble in Shakespearean roles had evaporated, and he remained equally unsuccessful attracting orders for female portraits. What woman was so bold that she dared face his vigorous realism while able to choose between Romney and Gainsborough?

Notorious for her vanity and a severe countenance, Mrs. Siddons had been a difficult, disapproving subject. By the middle of April, 1787, his first too-true effort, unfinished, was seen in his house by a journalist who considered it a work of "much spirit and delicacy," but in truth, this attempt to make a proverbially stiff-miened lady smile was slightly monstrous. Though the draperies were half-painted, Stuart realized his error and discarded the canvas. He began anew, softening Mrs. Siddons' features excessively, until nearly all anatomical detail had been brushed away. This second effort also remained incomplete, for his finances now reached a crisis and became his principal concern. Well could he envy the Parliamentary immunity that allowed Sheridan to act so gallantly before adversity.

From Mrs. Siddons, Stuart had doubtless heard that salaries were unpaid at Drury Lane, where Sheridan, penniless as Stuart, daily cleared out the treasury of receipts. Sheridan Mrs. Siddons described as "certainly the greatest phenomenon that Nature has provided for centuries. Our theater is going on, to the astonishment of everybody. Very few of the actors are paid, and all are vowing to withdraw themselves: yet still we go on . . ." To seek Sheridan at Drury Lane was to find Kemble waiting in the library, while other creditors were variously distributed according to their rank and intimacy: some tired the chairs in the parlors, while mere tradesmen lost their time in the hall, butler's room, or the scenic divisions of the premises.

A door opening above-stairs moved all to hopes, but when Sheridan came down his hair was freshly powdered for the day, and so cordial were his manners, his glance so masterly, that for the most part creditors seemed to forget their errands and went away as if they had come only to look at him. The worst consequence of his defaulting was spared Sheridan by his Parliamentary immunity; at least his creditors could not seize him. This marvelous exemption from the consequences of debt Stuart could not aspire to, though during the calls of creditors, his house may have begun to resemble the frantic arrangements more normal to Drury Lane.

The possibility of seizure and debtor's prison now added a new threat to Stuart's existence. Thomas Lawrence thought he was in fact seized, and though there is no record, the possibility of short periods in confinement cannot be entirely discounted. Small sums were always at his disposal, and a night's detention, followed by release in the morning gained by payment of overdue fees or by loans from those interested in his career, would not have affected his position, however unenviable the strain it placed on his nerves.

There is not much mystery about what Stuart had done with his money. He could never have squandered vast sums, for he never had vast sums to squander. In an age when gambling losses were often on an enormous scale, no such charge ever was laid to him; nor did he belong to any of the Clubs where such sums might be lost. The simplest analysis shows not that he had a great deal of money and wasted it, but that he did not have enough. Like Sheridan, he was discovering that for a man without a substantial fortune life is an unstable adventure, and if perhaps he did not attend assiduously to his accounts, it is because careful attention would have made no particular difference. The astonishing thing is that he should have been able to carry on as he did for three years, since the move to New Burlington Street. The magnificent gamble of those years had been repaid by his emergence as the leading portraitist of men; but fortune, though it was approaching, seemed to hesitate in its stride.

Rumor of his position began to circulate about London, based as much on fallacy as truth. His ostentatious use of snuff gave rise to gossip that he owed eighty pounds to Fribourg, the tobacconist in the Haymarket, into whose accounts his name had never entered! But money was owed to someone, and most likely it was for the simplest things; canvases and colors, rates on the house, groceries, wines, and the lavish clothing in which he walked abroad. Faced with incessant demands, and always calculating on greater receipts, he probably had already begun the habit of later times by borrowing only to find his notes called. His was an uncertain, casual, precarious mode of existence, in which his very position constantly presented him with temptation to spend after the means were exhausted. The gap, constantly recurring, however got over, was filled with anxieties, misgivings, mortifications, and deplorable embarrassments of every description.

Particularly disturbed by Stuart's threatened position was Lord St. Vincent, the distinguished Admiral, who calculated he had sent in excess of two thousand pounds' business Stuart's way. He spoke to Colonel Barré and the Duke of Northumberland, and together these three decided they must call on Stuart. The artist never forgot their ominous visit, for on entering his painting-room they locked the door behind them. From Stuart's own account of the occasion we can be certain only that he complained of unpaid fees, and that as sensible men of business they instructed him to insist on receiving half the price at the first sitting. They may also have offered some cash, which he claimed to have refused; probably he did so, for though in later years he was less ceremonious, it is not unlikely that delicacy about money was still a part of his code; and his curious sense of honor already had begun to operate persistently to his disadvantage. Each of his three callers already had sat for a portrait, and Lord Rawdon had purchased one of his earlier sketches of Thayendanegea, the Mohawk Indian, Northumberland the second. Now they may have requested replicas of their own pictures, and put down half the money: "They insisted on setting the example," Stuart recalled, "and I followed the practice ever after this delicate mode of showing their friendship."

An impressive consortium of power and influence, Barré, St. Vincent, and Northumberland appear to have appointed themselves informal guardians, and set other wheels in motion. On the eighteenth of April the London *World* carried an extraordinary eulogy dedicated to Stuart's works, headed *The Van Dyck of the Time*. Broadly calculated to drive new sitters to Stuart's house, the logic of this move implies that were he to accept a sufficiency of new orders, receiving half the price for each, he could still extricate himself from embarrassment. Shamelessly, the writer of this extrordinary piece praised Stuart above every painter in London, even casting a slur on Reynolds' colors which were apt to fade:

> In the most arduous and valuable achievements of portrait painting, *identity* and *duration*, Stuart takes the lead of every competitor.
>
> Those who wish to redress themselves of accident, and, independent of time and place as far as eyesight goes and eye service, to have before them the glowing fidelity of friendship and love, may here secure the perpetual presence of the charm they wish.
>
> Not only skin deep, and skimming superficially over complexion and contour, Stuart dives deep—less deep only than Sir Joshua, more deep than any other pencil—Stuart dives into *mind*, and brings up with him a conspicuous draught of character and characteristic thought—all as sensible to feeling and to sight as the most palpable projections on any feature of a face.

Mixed into these praises was a list of Stuart's more notable subjects, designed, all too obviously, to flaunt the nature of his high patronage. The Marquis of Lansdowne (Lord Shelburne) the Duke of Northumberland, and Lord Rawdon are listed in that order, as well they might be as the established powers of whiggery. Lord Porchester was another recent sitter, and to amplify the thunder of declamation the portrait of Lord Sydney was drawn from five years' obscurity; Caleb Whitefoord, Mrs. Siddons, and Colonel Barré are equally thrown before the public, with the final claim: ". . . the *first* head of Kemble, [for Macbeth] . . . as a characteristic portrait is ranked by the *World* with the two best portraits the world before could boast." (!)

Barré was enjoying great personal popularity; the Pennsylvania town of Wilkes-Barre had been half named in his honor, and further to stem the ebb of Stuart's financial tide, the engraver John Hall brought out a plate of Barré's portrait. Despite the alarm that filled the air, appearances were assiduously kept up. Fuseli was a frequent dinner guest, who pleased his friend's young bride by admiring her singing. New sitters were received with customary aplomb, and entertained to dinner, where they sat among musicians such as the oboist William Thomas Parke. Parke's older brother John, also an oboist and a composer for that instrument, from whom Stuart may have taken his lessons, had been painted some years before. The younger Parke now had joined the ranks of Stuart's sitters, and one evening, invited to dinner, he leaned back in his chair, his coat stretched tight across his torso. The movement caught his host's ever-observant eye; "Sit still,—don't stir for your life!" he rang out with great vehemence, then, in more subdued tones, explained to the astonished Parke, ". . . your drapery as you now sit is very effective. I wish to make a sketch of it before you move." This he did, and, transferred to canvas, it produced a picture unusual among his works.

The Sunday evening following this incident, Stuart gave another dinner at which John Hall, who commonly discharged a cannon in his garden to celebrate the completion of plates, was present with Parke and a Mr. Smith, who that day had given his last sitting for a portrait. The occasion was a jovial one, for Hall's presence probably marked the issuance of the Barré engraving. Parke, who had been with friends the night before at a Saturday Night Club, complained of a headache.

"I observe that on Sundays you generally have a headache," said Smith. "How happens that?"

"Oh," broke in their host. "I will tell you. If a man's head comes into contact with a club overnight, it may be expected that it will ache the next day."

WHILE her husband worked furiously, taking no rest even on Sundays, and as furiously pretended nonchalance in the face of crisis, Charlotte Coates Stuart, married little over a year, gave birth to a second child. This time the couple was blessed with a daughter, whom they named Agnes. Of the progress of their marriage otherwise nothing is known. Charlotte Stuart had sung at her husband's entertainments, and recalled with pride the praises of Fuseli. Yet so retiring or ill-suited was she to her rôle, either by forgetfulness or clemency she was passed unnoticed. Of the character of her husband, and the curious blend of naiveté with histrionics he spread wide, even Parke was aware: "He . . . was a little enthusiastical, or pretended to be so."

While persuading the world that all was well, he was the chief victim of his own pretense, and ceased to have an objective view of his affairs. From this grows the mystery and confusion surrounding the period. He needed time; time to finish more pictures, begin more pictures, collect more half-fees; time to make part payments to creditors and give excuses for the balance. Most of all he seemed to count on the arrival of some stroke of fortune that would save him, though what this could have been even he surely did not know. Meanwhile, time was running out. Soon the annual summer paralysis would creep on London. When Parliament prorogued gentlemen returned to their estates until autumn, and a portrait-painter's work ceased. Most alarmed was the Duke of Northumberland, who invited Stuart to Syon House, near Kew, on the banks of the Thames. There, far from the dangers facing him in London, beyond reach of sheriffs, Stuart found more time.

Northumberland seemed willing to throw his own great prestige into the balance for Stuart. No secret was made of where the artist was; the *World* reported that the artist was engaged on full-lengths of the Duke and Duchess. The Duke's picture may actually have been begun, for he had come equipped to work, accompanied by a cabinet of dry colors, oils, turpentine, varnish, probably an easel, and, of course, the portfolio of his engravings. Stuart's flight from London obviously was premeditated. His wife and his two children probably had sought shelter at Reading. Safe in temporary haven, enjoying the calm of a beautiful country house, Stuart turned to the most unusual picture of his career. The canvas normally employed for a full-length portrait was turned on its side, to serve for a group of the Duke's four children. One is amazed that while his world crumbled about him he was able to commence work of this unaccustomed sort. His host had a definite fancy about the arrangement of the picture. "I think my [oldest] girl has found out that she is very pretty, and her brother, who has also discovered it, like a true boy, is fond of teasing her . . ."

Schooled thoroughly by West in classic principles, Stuart formed three of the small figures into a triangle, the fourth, the oldest girl, standing alone. To paint four childish heads did not tax him; each morning he ground his own colors with oil and prepared his palette for the day's work. Then, after the heads were completed, his engravings were brought into play. The eldest daughter's robe, and a pointing hand for the baby, came from Reynolds' group of the *Marlborough Family*. Reynolds' *Angerstein Children* provided a skirt and ribbons for the second daughter, and probably the idea of a comical over-large hat for the vain prettiest. From somewhere Stuart produced a large dog and a landscape, then he finished the whole with the addition of stray draperies from Rigaud.

"Stuart has nearly finished the Duke of Northumberland's family picture. The children, Lady Elizabeth, Lady Agnes, Lady Julia, and Lord Percy, with a distant view of Syon in the background, form this agreeable work," announced the *World* in July. It had the gratifying sound of wealth, and as usual, little more than the sound; but worst, it was certain to stir up his creditors in London. In fact, the large canvas, as it stood completed on its easel at Syon, was more successful as portraits than a picture. It is no wonder that under such circumstances he did not rival Copley's *Three Princesses;* a certain quaint charm fills this canvas produced under trying circumstances by a man sorely troubled. July twenty-ninth the Duke of Northumberland wrote in his private accounts; "To Sundries for a Picture of the Children— £120.9.0," and Stuart returned to London.

What was he to do? He appears to have spoken of a return to America, the first intimation that he considered giving up the battle in London. His father's lands in Nova Scotia were mentioned, but if any clear plan were projected it too disappeared in obscurity and temporizing.

Northumberland had given him a respite and cash in hand, though the Duke had paid him no more than the fee of four bust portraits; a well-meant but possibly a minimal gesture, that gained time without other advantage. Possibly he objected to this compensation, or in some other way acted with his usual lack of tact. All is obscure, but he did something that deeply offended Lord St. Vincent, for this great Admiral stated openly in London that Stuart was an ingrate.

At the same time Benjamin West, perhaps confused by Stuart's air of confidence, believed the worst of Stuart's troubles were over. West had just completed his picture of the *Institution of the Order of the Garter* for King George. A year before, while it was in progress, he had sent for Stuart to don the robes of Charles I, and so struck was he by the resemblance that he called his students to see this "extraordinary likeness." West now made allusion to the King about his own English ancestry; to the sovereign's delight, the Marquis of Buckingham declared that the Wests of Long-Crendon, from whom the American branch had sprung, were undoubtedly the family of Lord Delaware, renowned in the wars of Edward III. August 3, 1787, the *Public Advertiser* reported the King's desire that West's own portrait be added to his picture, and that West, "properly studious of identity," had asked Stuart to do the work. If it was done, this was the final service Stuart rendered his master; and it was marred by treachery. His earlier portrait of West he begged to have returned, on the plea of some minor alteration, or for use in the *Garter* picture. It was sent to him; nothing further was heard of it until, to his surprise, West found his portrait at Boydell's Gallery, and was told the Alderman had purchased it from Stuart. West claimed his wife's property, and Boydell lost his money—for Stuart had disappeared.

REDUCED to last stratagems, Stuart had only one move left to him. It was planned, it was orderly, it was executed with all the precision and military discipline his erratic nature allowed. It was flight from his debts.

England had become untenable. His departure he considered to be a temporary expedient, similar to his stay at Syon: he merely planned to go elsewhere, recoup his fortunes, and return to London. He spoke of liberal offers from France, meanwhile having determined that his haven would be Ireland, where many of his closest patrons had connections. Lord Shelburne held extensive Irish estates on which he had been raised, and for which Copley's half brother, Henry Pelham, was agent. Barré, Rawdon, Kemble, and Sheridan all had a foot in Dublin, and could provide him with introductions. The Duke of Rutland, Lord Lieutenant of Ireland, who had so admired the *Skater* when it was exhibited at the Royal Academy, for two years had been inviting Reynolds to visit him in Dublin Castle. His continued loyalty to a painter who bore the Foxite label could be excused because of his absence from London, and a note from Northumberland might have caused him to extend the same invitation to Stuart. By whatever route, or however proposed, such an invitation did come to him. His wife Charlotte, nineteen years old, and burdened with two babes in arms, sinks into the murkiness of supposition: most likely she remained at Reading, while the artist dodged London creditors and matured his plans.

For a time false scents were laid; talk of America and France deliberately filled the air. Then it happened. The house in New Burlington Street—vanished; and its contents. Stuart never learned what had become of his *Macbeth;* like other furnishings, all the canvases that remained in his house presumably were seized by a sheriff. The month of September 1787 is a blank entirely; for coaches, country inns, and packet boats do not publish lists of their anonymous travelers. In October Gilbert Stuart appeared in Dublin.

X

The Ascendancy

STUART appeared in Dublin under the best possible circumstances. Equipped with letters of introduction to leaders of the Irish government, probably with much of Northumberland's money still in his pocket, he could examine the new scene of his endeavors with a greater sense of ease. He found Dublin's streets surveyed straight and proud, its principal houses clustered around parks and greens, and the whole presenting the aspect of a model city on the banks of the Liffey. At dead center stood the elaborate walls of Trinity College, and facing it, across a muddy green, the twin classic drums and joining pediment of the most beautiful building in Dublin, the Irish Parliament. Three minutes' walk up Castle Street stood Dublin Castle, stronghold of the Lord-Lieutenant, who represented England's Royal authority. Elsewhere, dotted through older labyrinthine streets, were the handsome town houses at which he called to present letters of introduction. Everywhere was a consciousness of the enormous chasm separating upper and governmental classes from the broad-brogued folk who on occasion drove their pigs across the College Green.

Principal among the persons Stuart expected to paint was the Duke of Rutland, Lord-Lieutenant of Ireland. Only thirty-six, and an intimate friend of Pitt, with whom he had served in the Shelburne cabinet, Rutland was exactly the enthusiastic, artistically inclined patron of whom Stuart might have expected most. At the moment of his arrival Rutland was absent from Dublin. His sudden return to town and death on October 24, 1787 was the most notable event of the next weeks. An enormous funeral pageant wound through the city a fortnight later to deliver his coffin for transport to England by sea. It was the greatest procession Ireland had ever seen: newspapers described the preparations and published diagrams of the line of march days in advance, then boasted of the spectacle for weeks; forever after Stuart associated it with his own arrival. Disappointed in this most immediate hope of high patronage, he remained resourceful, and was quickly at work. By his own admission, when he had been a month in Dublin he had painted three portraits; Luke White, the print-seller in Castle Street, Jonathan Fisher, one of the better topographic artists, and Henry Grattan.

"My name is Hill, Mr. Stuart: I am called Dr. Hill," said a gentleman who came to his door; Irish blather was new to Stuart, and it did not cease. "I am fond of painting, and had an early inclination to become an artist. I drew in pen and ink, and was considered eligible to become an engraver. I have called to ask the favor of viewing your works, of which I have heard such good report." Despite this door-speech, which seemed highly eccentric to Stuart, he bowed his assent, saying he had but few pictures to show. He placed one on his easel and the doctor evidently was pleased, observing that the artist must have two looking-glasses to get that view of the head, which he acknowledge to be "very like."

"Like who?" asked the puzzled artist.

"It is your own portrait, is it not?"

"No. It is Luke White."

"So it is,—and very like indeed; but the contour is not very different from yours."

"Here is another," Stuart broke in, replacing the picture on the easel.

"Oh,—aye—," said the doctor. "Had I seen this first I could not be mistaken. This is you, indeed."

"Jonathan Fisher," said Stuart.

"His very image!" cried Dr. Hill. "My good worthy little Jonathan. Good morning to you, Mr. Stuart; I'll call again when you have more, and I must get more perfect in my vision. I find I require *re-vision*."

A third picture Stuart had been preparing to show, an intention forestalled by the visitor's departure, was that of Henry Grattan; and that he had painted this most important member of the Irish

Parliament within a month of coming to Dublin indicates that he
was beginning at the very top. The people of Dublin had quickly
noted Stuart's enormous affectation in speech and dress, and those
who said he not only looked like Kemble but spoke like him he
found an especial delight. Like his thespian friend, whose early career
was passed before Dublin audiences, Stuart gave an appearance of
stiffness and difficulty of approach, which, however, quickly evaporated when his comic humors were felt.

His price for a bust portrait, thirty guineas, was nearly as much
as Robert Home, the leading Dublin artist, asked for a full-length;
yet such were his qualifications that in the first weeks he became
established as the foremost portraitist in Ireland. A contemporary
recalled:

> His portraits were so well reported by the cognoscenti that a rage
> to possess some specimen of his pencil took place, and a difficulty of
> obtaining a finished picture became universal, so fond was he of
> touching the half-price. . . . He was perfectly aware of his pre-
> eminence in painting; and he, by his manner, exhibited that self-
> opinion to his visitors. This gave him an air of a coxcomb, although
> he assumed an independence of mind which scarcely would be en-
> dured from another man.

He erupted on the artists of the community with the same force
as upon the patrons. By St. Luke's day, October 18, 1787, a fortnight preceding Rutland's death, he was sufficiently well known to
receive an invitation to the annual dinner of artists, held in their
Eustace Street hall. His London fame prompted the invitation, and
never at a loss for a word in company, he sat between James Dowling,
assistant to Robert Home, and Vincent de Waldre, an Italian artist
at work on ceiling decorations in Dublin Castle. Stuart was his usual
communicative self, until he found his voice drowned by that of another man who sat further up the table. Obliged to be a listener, he
listened, and sought an opportunity to avenge himself.

The story he heard concerned Sir Joshua Reynolds, as artists'
stories so frequently did. The speaker boasted of his intimacy with
the great man; an intimacy so great, he confided, that he had the
privilege of walking into Reynolds' private study. One day he entered to find Reynolds sketching a picture of the Holy Family.

". . . I have been puzzled with this design," Reynolds admitted.

"The foreshortening of the infant's thigh;—I must lay it by 'till I get a model."

"Sir Joshua, your eye is fatigued," his visitor told him. "Now, I come in with my fresh eye, and I think I can drawn the line you want. Will you permit me"—this in a softened, low voice—"to point out what strikes me?"

Reynolds handed him the chalk; "I think it should come in so . . ." he drew it as he explained. He went on to tell how Sir Joshua had thanked him, afterward revoking the freedom of his studio, as though irked by superior abilities. The admission of this motive, he implied, lay in the line, which remained a part of the finished picture.

Nothing about the tale is altogether incompatible with Reynolds' behavior, and such a picture as was described is now in the Tate Gallery. Stuart, who knew Reynolds better than most, nonetheless was fired with indignation at the doltish misunderstanding of the speaker, his effrontery to Reynolds, and his loud manner. He leaned to Waldre, at his side, and in what must have been a stage whisper, asked, "Who is that person relating these stories?"

"Mr. Pack."

"Pack, Pack," said Stuart. He sensed an opportunity. "Well, I have often heard of a pack of nonsense, but I never saw it before!"

An involuntary burst of laughter ran like a volley through the room: Pack fell mute.

This receptive audience now smiling at him, Stuart launched into a train of caprice which he professed to be an account of his own history. The sound of his voice gave him what inspiration he wanted, and it developed at considerable length. He had come from America, he said, with no certain aims, and was received by Mr. West as a member of his own family. At first he thought of being a musician, but the sight of West at work made him long to paint. (Doubtless Stuart was thinking of the famous account of Van Dyck's call on Frans Hals, and intended to conclude by adapting it to himself; after West had painted his portrait, he might have said, it appeared so easy he borrowed the master's palette and did a portrait of him. But this was too simple—the story continued to expand.) West derided the absurdity of his ambition because he could not draw. He told his genial audience how, undaunted, he then contrived to paint a head by placing the sitter between two mirrors!

Three or four reflections of the sitter appeared in gradations less perfect as they receded; he had only to paint the last reflection, working his way to the first. When that was reached he had a head as like the subject as any ever painted. West had not been able to believe it was his! Of course this fiction contained the same parallel he had frequently employed to explain the stages of painting to pupils. He recounted it now with a wealth of detail and extraneous impressions of the appearance of the work, which made it altogether persuasive as fact, and concluded by assuring his listeners he no longer found need for mirrors. He was now able to lay aside their use "as boys lay by corks when they have became familiar with the action of swimming."

"That night," remembered Dowling, who sat beside him, "was memorable for years to those who were present."

STUART was not without his own acquaintance in Ireland. In London he had already painted the Hon. William Burton Conyngham, and Viscount Cremorne, each of whom now ordered replicas of their earlier portraits. At that time Stuart was still too ill-arranged to provide a suitable chair, painting into these pictures a shabby substitute, hidden under a draped cloth. The retired Speaker of the Irish House of Commons, Edmund Sexton, Viscount Pery, sat at this time, and Stuart had a further applicant of considerable consequence in the Hon. John Beresford, a gobbler of sinecures, who, behind the scenes, operated as Pitt's confidential agent. In the patronage and family alliances of these personages Stuart already had the key to Ireland, and the country opened to him like Ali Baba's cave.

His English difficulties were common knowledge. "I saw Mr. Stuart in London; his likenesses were very striking, and had not his affairs obliged him to leave it, I was to have sat to him," appears in a letter of the time, passed to Stuart by the recipient. Through the summer of 1787, and the wet Irish winter, he did portraits prolifically. Those who at first had accepted him on reputation alone soon were drawn by his extraordinary skill. Then, in the dead of winter, on January 17, 1788, the Irish Parliament was called to order in its beautiful palace facing College Green. From distant counties the gentry had flocked to Dublin. For every official and man of prominence Stuart had met, now there were half a score adherents, younger sons, country magnates, and ambitious orators for him to put on canvas. The advice of

Barré, St.-Vincent, and Northumberland was remembered with pride, and he began all the portraits he could, extracting from each sitter half the price, while quoting by what exalted authority this was done.

By the spring a considerable sum had accumulated, which was matched by a considerable store of unfinished canvases. That Ireland could give him continued employment was obvious, but also that he would be unable, after finishing all his canvases, to accumulate funds sufficient to pay off London creditors. Even at the lower cost of living in Ireland the answer was plain: an artist could not exist on the scale he chose by painting bust portraits alone. Only by concentrating on the full-length, and subjects suitable for engraving, could a fortune be made. If he could not return to London immediately, perhaps one day the means would be found. That dream did not leave him. But, for the present, he was forced to act with moderation. For six months he had been alone in the Irish capital; it was now time to bring to Dublin his wife and children and find a home for them. The London *World*, which the previous November had spread the inspired report that he had departed for America, took note of his brief return, *after* he again had safely left England. Still in a friendly vein it announced, April 1, 1788:

> Stuart's last trip to Ireland so far answered perfectly, as to establish for his portraits in that kingdom, as in this, a pre-eminent fame for identity.

ON HIS second arrival in Dublin Stuart seemed a much chastened man. Many of his more blatant affectations and much of his old zest had departed in the definite dissolution of his London career. The house he now took for his family was far from the center of the city, in Pill Lane. Adversity had confirmed him in his ways, but also it had added a new grace to his inner self. The nobility of manner and sentiment that were adopted attitudes in London were now a true part of his character: the strength he demonstrated before an inimical fate was real, as was the taciturn hauteur of his appearance, and the polish of his manners. The enormous coiffure he affected in London was rejected; instead, his powdered white hair, which had receded from the temples, was combed back flatly, the ends gathered in a meager roll above his ears. The high bare forehead that was revealed accentuated an appearance decidedly older, for at thirty-three Stuart looked middle-aged. The bloating of drink was visible, and under the twin influences of alcohol and snuff his nose began to expand out of its neat contours. Heavier of face, deeper of chest, signs of sadness were discernible. Life had dealt him a blow.

To assist in the production of replicas, and to have that freedom that came when someone else daily prepared colors and cleaned brushes, he took on a pupil. To young Martin Archer-Shee he showed the gentler side of his nature reserved by his code for inferiors. Impressed by the youth's intelligence and abilities, Stuart urged him to seek the advantages to be found in London. Withdrawn, sad-eyed, his head held at the peculiar angle habitual to him while listening, Stuart allowed Archer-Shee to paint his portrait. His avuncular advice was accepted, and on June 24, 1788, the apprentice departed for London. There he made copies for Boydell, and picked up the threads of Stuart's acquaintances. "I have been introduced to Mr. Opie, who is in manners and appearance as great a clown and as stupid a looking fellow as ever I set my eyes on," he wrote soon after his arrival. Lawrence impressed him more favorably; "He is a very genteel, handsome young man, but rather effeminate in his manner . . . wonderfully laborious in his manner of painting, and has the most uncommon patience and perserverance . . . There is no young artist in London bids so fair to arrive at excellence . . ."

Though Stuart could exhibit a species of almost maternal kindness to those dependent upon him, another side of his nature appeared when he was less at his ease. Then either his coldness and formality grew impenetrable, or, on the contrary, his affectations became conspicuous when the necessity to be the center of every group found him the hero of purely imaginary tales, invented to set company in a roar, for the sake of a quibble, a point, or a pun. To his wife such habits were a repetition of annoyance, foolishness, and wanton waste: his self-absorption she answered with an intolerance that was going far to wreck their happy hopes. His joking moods, which she found incomprehensible, became a form of teasing she could not bear. And what drove them further apart was that exactly those things which exasperated his young wife made him attractive to the world at large.

His many involved tales, his odd bits of learning and man-of-the-world appearance, urbane, graciously mannered, cultivated, and well-read; his acquaintance with the great and famous, his constant recourse to humor, his delight in odd turns of phrase and homely

THE SKATER

Mellon Collection, The National Gallery of Art, Washington

GILBERT STUART
Self-portrait at the age of twenty-four

*The Redwood Library and Athenaeum,
Newport, Rhode Island*

A West design executed by Stuart for the
ceiling of the Royal Academy

Royal Academy of Arts, London

BENJAMIN WATERHOUSE

*The Metropolitan Museum of Art,
Bequest of Mary Stillman Harkness, 19*

HENRIETTA ELIZABETH FREDERICA VANE

Smith College Museum of Art

RICHARD BRINSLEY SHERIDAN

Witt Library, Courtauld Institute of Art

Portrait of Gilbert Stuart by
Gainsborough Dupont

*Reproduced by courtesy of the Trustees
of the Tate Gallery, London*

THE ENGRAVER, WILLIAM WOOLLET

Reproduced by courtesy of the Trustees of the Tate Gallery

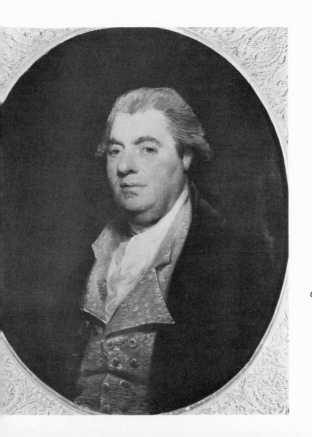

DUGALD MALCOLM

*Collection Colonel George Malcolm,
Scottish National Portrait Gallery*

JACOBUS BENIGNUS   BOSSUET EPISCOPUS

Meldensis Comes Consistorianus, antea Serenissimi Delphini   *præceptor, et primus Serenissimæ Ducis Burgundiæ Eleemo*
synarius natus 27ª Septembris an 1627 obiit 12ª Aprilis 1704   *synarius natus*

Hanc effigiem æternam amoris ac venerationis monumentum inedi curavit   *Jacobus Benignus Bossuet Episcopus Trecensis ex fratre nepos*

Engraving by Pierre Imbert Drevet after portrait of Bishop Bossuet
by Hyacinthe Rigaud

British Museum

BENJAMIN WEST

National Portrait Gallery, London

JOHN SINGLETON COPLEY

National Portrait Gallery, London

SIR JOSHUA REYNOLDS

*Mellon Collection, National
Gallery of Art, Washington*

JOHN PITT, SECOND EARL OF CHATHAM

Private Collection, Ireland

GEORGE MATCHAM

Mrs. Booth Tarkington

JAMES HEATH

Wadsworth Atheneum, Hartford

Engraving of the lost portrait of
Admiral Lord St. Vincent

British Museum

The family of the Duke of Northumberland

Country Life, London

JOHN FITZGIBBON, EARL OF CLARE

The Cleveland Museum of Art

LORD DARTREY

Montclair Museum

Engraving of the lost portrait
of Henry Grattan

National Gallery of Ireland

Stuart in 1788 by Archer-Shee

THE EARL OF CARYSFORT

Jocelyn Proby, Esq.

Sir William Barker

Major George Ponsonby

Lady Barker

CHARLES TOTTENHAM OF BALLYCURRY

Charles Tottenham, Esq.

Snuffbox given to Stuart by
the Bishop of Ossory

Boston Museum of Fine Arts

JOHN JAY
The National Gallery of Art, Washington.
Lent by Peter Jay

MATILDA STOUGHTON DE JAUDENES

The Metropolitan Museum of Art, Rogers Fund, 1907

MRS. RICHARD YATES

*The National Gallery of Art,
Washington*

GENERAL MATTHEW CLARKSON

*The Metropolitan Museum of Art,
Bequest of Helen Shelton Clarkson, 1938*

JOSEPH ANTHONY

Mellon Collection, National Gallery of Art, Washington

LAWRENCE YATES

RICHARD YATES

JOHN ADAMS

MRS. JOHN ADAMS

MRS. SAMUEL BLODGETT
Pennsylvania Academy of the Fine Arts

ANNE ALLSTON
Frick Art Reference Library

THOMAS JEFFERSON

Courtesy of the Bowdoin College Museum of Art

SARAH MORTON
Worcester Art Museum

JAMES MADISON
Colonial Williamsburg

The Athenaeum portrait of
Martha Washington

Museum of Fine Arts, Boston

Gilbert Stuart in Washington (1805)
by Charles Willson Peale and
Rembrandt Peale

New York Historical Society

JOHN RANDOLPH

*Mellon Collection, National
Gallery of Art, Washington*

MRS. STEPHEN PEABODY

Arizona State University

JARED SPARKS

New Britain Museum

JAMES MONROE
Pennsylvania Academy of the Fine Arts

RUSSELL STURGIS
Worcester Art Museum

similes, all made him good company and a person whose company was sought. Stuart was a man's man. The earliest of his Irish friends were an extraordinary mixture of artists and clergy, for whom he resumed the custom of entertaining at dinner. During one particularly riotous party, at which the guests included the Rev. Mr. Best, Dean Beatson, and possibly Kemble on a visit from England, a violent dispute arose over who possessed the truest eye. All trooped forth to test themselves with pistols on a mark placed in the garden. The exact state of affairs soon became apparent, and Stuart deliberately walked in front of the target.

"Stuart!" they shouted at him. "Stuart, what are you about? By heavens, you will be shot!"

"Oh, no," was his unconcerned reply. "From all appearances this is the safest place."

In this amiable way the first year in Ireland passed. Many portraits that were begun failed to reach completion, which for the first time encouraged a new subject of gossip. Shortly after Christmas this too reached the London *World*, whose columns were still friendly: on December 27, 1788, after an account of pictures seen at Reynolds' house, it added:

> Stuart, a portrait painter fit to be mentioned even with Sir Joshua, must wait for this account of his works—as for the works themselves all Dublin is in waiting.

And though he was possessed of a talent for procrastination to an unexampled degree, stronger reasons for his tardiness lay in the politics of the Emerald Isle.

THE MEANS of Stuart's introduction to Ireland had made him by implication, if not in fact, the adherent of a party. The nature of his patronage had made him the established painter of a political faction. Whether or not he ever gave more than nodding acquiescence to Whig principles, he had come to Ireland as a man sent from the Whigs, and was received by those the Whigs employed to rule Ireland. By painting them and consorting with them, he called attention to that association. His friendship with members of the clergy was itself a political act, because in Ireland association with Protestant clergy was tantamount to a declaration of allegiance to the system of power.

When Protestant England strengthened its ancient control and parceled out lands among loyal elements, the Roman Catholic clergy became the leaders of their flocks both socially and politically. The Roman Catholic faith was a part of Irish opposition to British overlords, though the two religions marked lines of antagonism of which they were not themselves the cause; the struggle was one of nationalities, not creeds. The *Ascendancy* had grown up in Ireland by time and by usage. To London it was essential that Ireland be pacified, and controlled, as a conquered land of rebellious tendencies needed to be controlled—by a Protestant church and state, and by an economy closely subordinated to that of England. To achieve this with a minimum of trouble the country for generations had been left to what James I described as "a kind of beasts called Undertakers." With these persons responsible government had struck a bargain. The Undertakers, or their deputies, undertook to keep the country quiet, to secure majorities in Parliament for necessary bills, and to see that revenue was collected. In return they distributed among themselves and their families and followers all the patronage, jobs, and emoluments that could be squeezed from government. The system was utterly corrupt and inefficient, but it worked to the satisfaction of London until the disaster of the American Revolution upset the Irish political scene.

The modest prosperity Ireland had enjoyed for half a century was abruptly altered by the loss of American markets. The cessation of flaxseed and potash imports from America ruined the linen trade; the militia withdrawn for American service left Ireland open to invasion from France. By superb oratory and cunning Henry Grattan, whose family long had figured among the Undertakers, found a means of exploiting the opportunities presented: with Lord Charlemont he organized the United Volunteers. Eighty thousand men were armed, organized, and drilled. They proclaimed their absolute loyalty to King George III, and their irrevocable determination to secure economic equality and an independent legislature for Ireland. At war with half of Europe, defeated in America, the government of Lord North was helpless to cope with the Volunteers. At every point the British gave way, until in 1783 Ireland had virtual independence. In effect this revolution delivered the country to the Protestant Undertakers, or the *Ascendancy*, who, though a small minority in their own land, were by education and background the only ruling class.

To counter this, England employed the normal methods of Irish politics. By judicious use of patronage, jobbing, and outright bribery, in two years the new independence was whittled away. When Stuart arrived in Dublin the autumn of 1787 and took Henry Grattan for his third sitter, he had before him a slight, intense, nervous man who was a national hero—and whose achievements already had vanished. A corrupt Irish Parliament had been bribed into acquiescence, and the country squires, the center of Protestant and therefore English interest, were again struggling between the upper and lower jaws of a vise.

This special society, the outpost of the Georgian world, already had on it the sign of death. Fundamentally it was a landed aristocracy of the same order that existed in England. English in orientation, its blood long had been mixed with that of Ireland, and many were the ancient High Kings and Clan Chieftains whose lineage had entered its ranks. Its special ingrown character was the product of isolation, like some vestigial growth in an alien climate that flourished perversely, even though in a miniature fashion. Thinly scattered across the country in their stately homes, each surrounded by an extensive acreage from which the true wealth of Ireland was derived, they lived as a gentle, educated, cultivated, gracious people, religious as all persecuted people tend to be, intolerant perhaps, embattled, but never embittered. The community was small, and its mark of recognition was cousinage, for in a limited society one was raised among cousins, and met no other to marry. Everyone who mattered was acquainted with everyone else, and probably related.

In January each year, when the real work of harvesting crops was finished, and men set to work cutting and caring for timber, Parliament was called. Only this brought the gentry to Dublin, and now what mattered was how many votes a peer or squire could muster in support of himself and his position. A man was assessed by his influence. If it were large he could trade it for concrete profits, places, and pensions, or jobs for his relatives and dependents. A secret report drawn up for Pitt in 1784 revealed that Lord Shannon controlled no fewer than sixteen members of the Commons, the Ponsonby family fourteen, Lord Hillsborough nine. Peerages were an especial reward for borough-owners who returned subservient members, and in this way both houses of the Parliament were simultaneously corrupted;

53 peers are said to have nominated 123 members of the Commons. The successful politician thus could one day expect to be a Baron, and every Baron hoped to be a Viscount or an Earl. Few had success to parallel the Fitzgerald family, whose blood was ancient Irish, and who burst forth in full magnificence as the Dukes of Leinster.

Willy-nilly, whether he fathomed its systems or approved its ways, this was the world to which Gilbert Stuart had been introduced by the patronage of Shelburne, Barré, and Northumberland. He would have to tread lightly, identify himself only with dominant elements within the Ascendancy, and make no serious enemies. In London he already had demonstrated his perfect capacity for such a task.

XI

The Dublin Monopoly

ALMOST at once Stuart's career in Ireland assumed the form it would retain. He had a virtual monopoly of all fashionable portraiture. But it was abundantly clear, however, that he would be dependent upon the short winter sessions of Parliament to bring his sitters to town. The abbreviated meeting of 1789, which began a month late and prorogued May twenty-fifth, indicated how precarious this dependence might be, for in large part his year's work was limited to the four months Parliament was in session. Then his income was good, from the numerous half-fees he collected. Through summer and autumn he slowly completed these canvases; his earnings in those months were sporadic. With luck, the eight months of the year when Dublin was quiet could yield only as much as the four gay winter months when the city was crowded with gentry; entertainments and balls were continuous, and he was solidly booked with sitters. During the greater part of each year, therefore, funds had to be stretched until the next meeting of Parliament. It was soon obvious that he would be seriously in debt before each meeting of that august body.

Appointive officials, Bishops, holders of posts in government agencies and the courts, more permanently established in the capital, might be expected to patronize him during the slower seasons. They were a small consolation. So long as he was politically secure, however, he could keep Ireland his own private artistic domain. Then, suddenly, even that was not certain, for hardly had he brought over his wife and children, than, in November 1788, a most unexpected threat to Pitt's control arose.

King George III descended from his carriage in Windsor Great Forest and peevishly addressed an oak tree as the King of Prussia. The King's insanity brought new hope to the followers of Charles James Fox. A Regency was surely in order, and no one could doubt that were the monarchy turned over to the Prince of Wales he would ask Fox, his friend, advisor, and drinking companion, to head the government. Pitt temporized and prevaricated, gambling on the King's recovery. Dr. Richard Warren, whom Stuart had painted four years earlier, gave it as his opinion that His Majesty was incurably afflicted. Fox planned his cabinet. For Lord-Lieutenant of Ireland he selected the Duke of Northumberland: Stuart was safe in favor. The War Ministry Fox offered to Lord Rawdon, another palpable hit for Stuart, who already had committed this military peer to canvas. Rawdon was a bad enemy; recently he had noted his officers' interest in John Trumbull's splendid picture of the British Victory at Gibraltar. Rawdon remembered only Trumbull's imprisonment in 1780. "Gentlemen, nothing done by that man ought ever to be patronized by officers of the British army," were words which effectively negated Trumbull's deliberately conciliatory gesture.

While Fox exulted over his list of ministers and expected to take office, the King gradually recovered and met with Pitt; the latter had prevailed. His loyalty holding him more securely in power than before, Pitt formed an alliance with a brilliant, vitriolic, arrogant man, who under his Premiership for the balance of the century became the real ruler of Ireland. John, Lord Fitzgibbon, was an eminent lawyer and Member of Parliament who had wagered his abilities against preferment for himself and his family. An earlier Lord-Lieutenant complained of him, "Fitzgibbon . . . asks a bishopric for Lord Tyrone's brother, who married his daughter, and although this gentleman is not qualified by Canon Law to take a bishopric on account of his youth . . . Fitzgibbon . . . makes it a reason for opposing government with great rancour and vehemence." Great rancor and vehemence, in fact, were the twin pillars of Fitzgibbon's strength. A man of many enemies whose public character was not a pleasant one, he was reckless in his assertions, and seemed, if his pistol-shot words missed the mark, to knock down his opponents with the butt. Associated at first with Henry Grattan, for the greater part of his career it was Fitzgibbon's duty to oppose that patriot in behalf of

England. As Lord Chancellor, Fitzgibbon ordered Stuart's first major work in Ireland, a full-length portrait; and that this was begun as soon as the King recovered again demonstrates the forces at work.

Few invitations to Fitzgibbon's home in Ely Place were refused, and Stuart appears to have been a frequent guest. To be among the associates of the all-powerful Lord Chancellor was advantageous, for this now was the center of patronage and real power. Just as the cloth was removed after dinner one evening a gentleman came in, looking rather confused from not being on time. Lord Fitzgibbon ordered a servant to place a small table on one side and provide him with dinner.

"You must try and make the best of it," he explained. "It was your own fault; we waited half an hour."

To the artist, seated beside him, Lord Fitzgibbon said, "Now, Stuart, you are so accustomed to look all men in the face who come before you—you must be a good judge of character. Do you know that gentleman at the side table?"

"No, my lord, I never saw him before."

"Well, now tell me what sort of man he is in disposition."

"Is he a friend?"

"No."

"Then I may speak frankly?"

"Yes."

"Why then, my lord, if the Almighty ever wrote a legible hand, he is the greatest rascal that ever disgraced society."

Lord Fitzgibbon laughed his immoderate appreciation and explained to Stuart how right he had been.

Stuart's alliance to Lord Fitzgibbon was fruitful. It cleared away the hint of irregularity that might have existed because of his original association with Henry Grattan; it led him to the newer and inner sources of influence; and in more direct fashion, it produced the most impressive of his achievements in Ireland. An official portrait, wrapped in robes and emblems of office, the Lord Chancellor's picture was the first of that difficult genre Stuart ever had undertaken. West's training had prepared him for every eventuality, and he acquitted himself of unfamiliar problems with tremendous aplomb. The necessary classic allusion, a torso and legs from Van Dyck's *Prince d'Arenberg*, again are topped off by an akimbo arm from the Fleming's *Duke of Bedford*. The Chancellor's heavy brocaded gown follows the cloak Van

Dyck draped from the arm of his Duke, and, in an extraordinary revelation of his retentive memory, Stuart transformed the armor at the foot of Van Dyck's figure into a further section of drapery, as West had done for his own portrait of Queen Charlotte. His agility is well demonstrated by how easily his brush changed shining steel into an upturned edge of cloth lining, though the impetuosity of his attack occasioned minor difficulties; a gloved hand from Van Dyck, painted without its glove, as had already been done for Sheridan's picture, did not succeed. Nearby, Van Dyck's carefully varied edge of velvet risked worrisome collision with the frame; his decision to lose this troublesome contour in obscurity created the weakest portion of the picture. Pointedly it recalls that unlike his Georgian brethren Stuart never had studied landscape, except as it appeared behind portraits: where Gainsborough worked his way out of difficulty by the addition of a tree from Claude, Stuart had no landscape engravings in his portfolio.

Continued psychological reliance upon West is revealed again by Stuart's reference to Rigaud for the further elements of column, drape, and sky with which his picture was finished. Though himself a far greater exponent of portraiture than his master, and despite his successes with large canvases, which actually are the happiest part of his production, his self-assurance still required to be bolstered, for the elements of insecurity were fixed within him. Even so, Stuart was not the first artist who failed to realize his own strength, and when completed, the portrait of *Lord Fitzgibbon* was a work beyond the capacities of any living contemporary. Simple, direct, forceful, elegant, firm in drawing, psychologically revealing, and painted with a downright fury, it was a unique masterpiece of Georgian art.

Lord Fitzgibbon's portrait put the seal of official approval on Stuart, and as time passed, his Dublin monopoly grew more complete. From humble country squires and younger sons who yearly sat in Parliament to the magnificence of the mightiest petitioner of all, the Duke of Leinster, the whole of the Ascendancy flocked to Stuart. The Lords, the Bishops, the Parliamentarians, appeared in turn. For lower members of this set, the Deans, he employed canvases slightly smaller than normal bust size, paring his price accordingly. "Mr. Stewart, an English gentleman lately arrived in this metropolis, excels in his delicacy of coloring and graceful attitudes," noted the Dublin *Evening Herald*. His children's group painted for the Duke of Northumberland was known, for the journal added, "He paints portraits in groups and has a happy method of disposing his figures and at the same time preserving a strong resemblance." His grasp on patronage grew so strong there was no hope of competing with him; previously established Dublin portraitists began to drift away. Thomas Hickey departed for India, returned, then joined Lord Macartney's mission to China. Even so able a practitioner as Robert Home in 1789 gave up the unequal contest. His assistant, James Dowling, came to work for Stuart, bringing much of his former master's hard enameled surface to "replicas" of his new master's more fashionable works.

Whatever the development of his fame and fashion in Ireland, or his apparent prosperity, to Stuart Dublin remained a place of exile, from which he followed the situation developing in London. Thomas Gainsborough, after sitting in a draft at the trial of Warren Hastings, listening to the most famous speech of Sheridan's career, took to his bed. For several weeks he wasted away, then, brooding over his relations with Reynolds, he sent the President a note, by which a warm though possibly cynical deathbed reconciliation took place. Gainsborough died August 2, 1788, and Reynolds carefully covered his tracks with a "Discourse" delivered at the Royal Academy, devoted almost entirely to his deceased rival. A fair and impartial view, that struck an appropriate pose before history, Reynolds was left little time to exult; in July, 1789, while at work on a portrait, he was struck blind.

Of three great masters who for half a century were the glories of British painting, only George Romney remained. The path now seemed open for Stuart to reclaim his rightful heritage. His recollections of Beechey, Hoppner, and Lawrence, the triumvirate vaulting into prominence, admitted none of them into his own category. The most promising, Thomas Lawrence, was, curiously, given by Viscount Cremorne Stuart portraits of himself and his wife from which to develop full-length portraits. Employing Rigaud to strengthen his hand, Lawrence's success with this unhappy task was complete. So pleased was Lady Cremorne she persuaded Queen Charlotte to invite the twenty-year-old boy to Windsor, to paint a Royal portrait, which again he developed with the addition of draperies added to the skirt from Stuart's French source.

The path to fortune now trod by Lawrence was the one marked out by Stuart for himself; yet, for the moment, Stuart was still the principal master of the Georgian mode, and the time had come for him to re-assert himself in London. The leading exponent of British art must not remain painting provincials in a provincial capital. That he kept up his London contacts, despite a certain repugnance for letters, was well known; on occasion he provided introductions for persons going over, and a request for one came from Dean Beatson:

> You recollect you were so obliging as to promise me a bottle of varnish, for our pictures, which indeed mine seems to want, and it is a pity so capital a performance should not have every advantage. I should be obliged to you therefore, if you would order that bottle to be left at Mr. Sam. Roberts, attorney, who lodges in Castle Street, opposite almost Latouche's Bank . . .
>
> I am so particularly anxious for it now as the [effaced] who was to make use of it is soon going to London. He is a native of this town, an ingenious artist in the landscape line—was never out of the kingdom, and is going to London to study. If you could favor him with a letter of introduction to any artist you think would be of service to him, you will oblige me, and I am confident he will not disgrace your recommendation.

No TIME was more propitious for Stuart's return to London: the death of his older rivals had left the field to him, and as an established name, with a definite following, he could easily best younger men. It would be wise of him to do so before they grew in maturity, skill, and patronage. There is no question his mind had returned that way, and he appears to have promised he would paint a few portraits when he again came to London. The only obstacle to such a move remained in the profoundly complicated question of his debts.

His first necessity was to force more money from Dublin to pay off English creditors, and the distinguished nature of his Irish patronage at last provided a means, for his portrait of Lord Fitzgibbon was worthy of engraving. In 1790 Charles Howard Hodges, a highly skilled engraver, made the journey from London, evidently in response to Stuart's invitation. In the new mezzotint process that more readily reproduced the texture of a painted surface, he made a large and striking plate of Fitzgibbon. Published in Dublin and London simultaneously, in September 1790, it brought profit to all concerned. An engraving of *The Hon. John Beresford* followed almost immediately, on November first, and the natural sequel to these successes was a series of plates commemorating the leading Irish political figures of the day.

The new funds from these prints were most welcome, for Stuart was again deeply in debt. Various of his whimsical tales, artfully told for effect, have been construed to mean he was actually imprisoned. Clues point to a date of 1790, and this may have been what prompted subsequent generosity from the Earl of Carysfort; but no record survives, and one cannot help distrusting Dowling's too waggish account: "Don't you know that I have been some time in confinement?" Stuart is said to have remarked.

"No, I never heard of it."

"I have been, and you will be surprised when I tell you I painted myself out of jail."

"How did you paint yourself out?"

"Why, I painted the jailor and his wife, and he was so penetrated at the honor I had done him, that he was glad of an opening that offered for my escape. It was thus:—One Lord-Lieutenant left the Castle, with his suite, to make way for a newly appointed Viceroy, who was waiting at Howth, until they had a meeting and conference. Then the new Lord came to town, and took his place at the Castle, and was sworn in agreeably to the usage of this great official regal establishment. I knew so much law, that, from the abdication of one, to the investiture of the other, although it took in process but a few hours, the government of the country slept until the great work was accomplished. I therefore demanded my liberty. The jailor knew that I was born out in my demand, and opened the door, permitting me to depart . . ."

That Stuart had cultivated his own Irish waggery can be seen from the context, if it is authentically his, and not some later fabrication by Dowling himself. The only change of Lord-Lieutenants during Stuart's Irish career took place in 1790, when his debts had become pressing. His position in Ireland had become compromised, and though to abandon debts, as he had in England, was in the nature of his character, he could not hope to return to England without honoring his indebtednesses there. One place or the other he now had music to face, had a new champion not appeared on the scene.

Though the Earl of Carysfort was among Sir Joshua Reynolds' most conspicuous patrons, his own fine taste, and Reynolds' blindness, were sufficient reason for him to ask his portrait of Stuart in Dublin. Lord Carysfort did not normally spend long periods in Ireland; his true home was at Elton Hall, Peterborough, but from his mother he inherited extensive Irish estates, which, together with his own Irish peerage, made him active in Dublin's affairs. A friend of Pitt, who entrusted him with diplomatic missions, Lord Carysfort was in a position to assess Stuart even before he fled from London, and as an enlightened patron he too was on the lookout for Reynolds' successor.

Early in 1790, his position rapidly deteriorating, Stuart appears to have placed himself under Carysfort's "protection," and was settled on a small holding of eight acres on that Lord's Stillorgan estate, four miles south of Dublin. Because of his debts, from which Lord Carysfort wished to give him a measure of protection, a lease was executed March 5, 1790, to an unknown party, possibly fictitious, named Richard Sinclair, who then sublet to Stuart in an unrecorded transaction. Stuart thus became the occupant of a modest, newly erected house, surrounded by gardens and land enough to keep a few cattle. To the sense of security that came to him again from the earth was added the assurance that this shelter for himself, and his growing family, was a safe one, not subject to seizure.

The move to Stillorgan was a happy one. Stuart's little home constituted a corner newly carved from Lord Carysfort's enormous *Stillorgan Deer Park*. On the boundary of this little property an obelisk, erected many years before, soared into the heavens: deer grazed lazily past or gamboled up its base of rough-hewn boulders, and during late autumn their deep and horrifying cries echoed miles away. Far below in the distance spread a panorama of Dublin Harbor and Kingstown; time could be measured by the appearance across the horizon of packet boats, beating their way in from England. The area was fertile and productive, and Stuart, elated to find himself again in contact with the earth, quickly acquired a stock of pigs. A mature apple orchard was on the property, which annually bore an abundance of fruit, some of which he stored away to feed his pigs through the winter months, a plan that pleased him by its exuberant caprice. But though he remained whimsical and volatile by turns, farming, the experience of his most secure youthful years, once again had its tonic effect, calming the tensions that struggled within him. Flowers were an equal joy, and not content with a mere garden plot, Stuart lined his paths with potted plants. His skill with this miniature eight-acre estate became a source of infinite vanity, and every visitor was marched about to be shown the garden, neatly tended by his own hands, and the pigs, fattened so voluptuously on apples.

Life at Stillorgan brought Stuart into a new, closer contact with Ireland; but of the further heart of the country, the long bare valleys, magnificent corridors walled with mountains, roofed with mists, and lit by shafts of sunlight, he saw nothing. The real country existed in regions he did not penetrate, for Stuart remained planted at Stillorgan, surrounded by a countryside carved into great estates, and dotted by splendid houses. To these nearer folk his conviviality was welcome. They became his friends, with whom his leisure was passed in the prevalent occupation of downing French, Spanish, and Portuguese wines, the consumption of which astonished even English visitors. From these neighbors he learned of the divisions that rent the luckless land; of peasantry which gave smiling service that masked generations of inspired resentment; of gentry, isolated by their religion and education, family-proud, and frustrated by their small numbers, who existed as outposts of cultivated society.

From Stuart's front gate a narrow country lane descended into the village of Black Rock. Daily his heavy leather heels clattered over this uneven surface, then below, at the Inn, he waited for a horse-drawn coach, which, in good weather and bad, careened noisily to the city along the perimeter of Dublin Bay. Since his removal to Lord Carysfort's Stillorgan estate Stuart retained a "painting-room" in town; the address is unknown, and descriptions tell us only that it was on the second floor. Any of the attractive Georgian residences then rising in blocks, constructed as speculations by the great land-owning families of Lords Spencer, Pembroke, Shelburne, Fitzwilliam, or Mountjoy, would have served admirably for Stuart's purpose; their characteristic large windows and the spacious high-ceilinged rooms were eminently suited to an artist's needs. Here he kept a servant, who probably was caretaker as well, and lived in the mews behind.

MORNING and evening in his busier season Stuart made the four-mile coach journey along the Black Rock road. Frequently in the early darkness of his busy winter he remained in town to take dinner with clients. He became attached to his assistant, James Dowling, and sometimes when invited to a great house he dined instead with Dowling and his family, for the strain of serious company had begun to show on him. He preferred the companionship of simpler folk, who treated him with deference and thought him a gentleman. With Dowling he spoke at length of the masters, and took the long walks to which his infirmity of limb had habituated him. Dowling proposed to introduce Stuart to his own first teacher, who, by coincidence, was named West: "Pray, have you heard of the West, of Ireland?"

"No; what of it? Is there anything extraordinary to be seen there?"

"Oh, I mean a man, not a district: West, an artist of celebrity."

"Yes; a master of the Dublin Society's Drawing School. Ha! that is a curious circumstance,—West, of England, and West, of Ireland, artists. Well, how does he rank in the art?"

"Oh! a very clever draftsman! so far he keeps pace with the great West of England."

"Pray introduce me to him. I should like to know him, that I might add to the name another master."

"Let us see; how long will you remain in town before you return to Stillorgan?"

"About an hour."

"That will do. Get your hat and come with me to West's house; it's not far, and you shall see the great little man, then judge for yourself."

On their arrival the two were shown into a parlor, and when West appeared, instead of greeting his guests he continued to glide about the room, settling drawings that hung awry.

"Mr. West," Dowling began, "I have brought Mr. Stuart to visit you."

"I am greatly obliged to you. Mr. Stuart, I am glad to see you, sir; I have never seen you, but in your works, which have afforded me great pleasure. Your pictures have the merit of being like, a great requisite in a portrait. I perceive you finish your head, nearly, before you put in the eyes, that gives you a great advantage in disarming criticism; and thereby saves you from remarks that might mislead, for no one could censure a head without eyes; then you ascertain the exact spot where the eyes should be placed, and are able to paint them at once, without the trouble of shifting or amending them. Your eyes are, by this plan, vivid and good and clear and bright; they remind me of Van Dyck, the king of portrait painters. I saw a picture of his at Hampton Court, of Charles I on a white horse, and a finer picture I never beheld."

Stuart was restless under this stream of verbiage, with its never-ending Irish twang, but, asked by Dowling if he had seen this picture, he answered courteously; "Oh, yes; often. It is admirable! There's a stream of light that comes trickling down, from the head of the man, to the hoof of the horse, that gives it not only relief, but reality."

"A stream of light trickling down!" West burst forth: "That's an apt phrase. I never heard it before, but I understand it. What a pleasure to hear a person converse upon art that understands it, and can exemplify."

But West's monologues already were too much for Stuart, whose irritability was never far beneath the surface; he distracted himself by looking at a drawing on the wall, to which West's eye followed him.

"That's a drawing by my father, Mr. Stuart, of the Roman Soldier, —the muscles in the back are correctly drawn; my father was a pupil under Carlo Van Loo, and he got the silver pallette for that drawing; he beat his master out of the field. That's a portrait of my brother John; he's gone out; he's not at home, or you could perceive it is like. That's a head of O'Keefe, considered clever; he has turned author and left off drawing, his eyes having failed. That's Mrs. Abington, the celebrated actress, praised by our critics, from it being so like a mezzo-tinto print; that is reversing criticism . . ."

West never looked at Stuart during his extended speeches, and at length, to relieve himself of such a bore, Stuart stole out of the room, Dowling following. "I perceived Stuart walking fast, so I had to run before I could join him . . ."

"You seem in haste, sir," he said, as he reached Stuart's rapidly retreating figure.

"I am. I should prefer your playing practical jokes on others."

"What, you don't like the West of Ireland; another visit will give you a knowledge of his character!"

"Had you not compared him with my friend, Benjamin West, I might have listened to him with some patience."

"Yes; but I meant all in due proportion, as Ireland bears to England; and I am sure you cannot be angry with him, for he gave you great credit for your works, as a brother brush!"

"Brother John gone out; damn his brother John! Let him *stay* out! What have I to do with him? Then, Carlo Van Loo, his father's master, and the Roman Soldier; they may all go to blazes . . . I never saw your dear friend's face, though he spoke half a volume at me, addressing the wall."

To DOWLING it was all mere whimsy, and he admitted surprise at Stuart's affection for him. At the same time he noted "the equalizing spirit of the American," or so it was interpreted, for how else could he understand the wonderful contempt with which his employer looked upon titled rank? Nor could Dowling fathom a man who would be rude to the Archbishop of Dublin, when one day he called at the studio. A message was carried in that His Grace was below in his carriage, and wished a word. Construed by Stuart as an air of superiority, this haughty summons was sufficient to disturb him, and he sent word down that he was not accustomed to waiting on carriages.

Archbishop Fowler was reduced to returning a message that it was the gout that prevented him from mounting Stuart's steps. This aroused the painter to mischief, and he sent his servant back yet again to say he was sorry to hear of the Archbishop's sufferings, as he had the rheumatism himself: as an accommodation he suggested they meet half way, on the landing. His heel pulled out of his shoe, a silk handkerchief wrapped around his foot, Stuart walked to the landing where he awaited the Archbishop painfully limping up.

"Well," said Archbishop Fowler, "I have contrived to hobble up, you see, Mr. Stuart. Sorry to see your foot tied up."

"Ha! Oh, dear!" exclaimed Stuart.

"Do you suffer very much with your foot?"

"Oh, very much, my lord."

"Well, Mr. Stuart," proceeded the Archbishop, "I came about my daughter's portrait. I am not quite reconciled to the picture. Now, she is not a bad subject, and I expected she would have made an interesting picture. Now, all these portraits, so far as I know the originals, are not only striking likenesses, but pleasing pictures. I candidly own, I cannot say so much for my daughter's picture."

Unknowingly the prelate had touched on a sore point in Stuart's art, for his portraits of women, and those young and attractive in particular, had not the same success as male likenesses. The silent artist was stung; he led the way to the studio, where he placed the picture on an easel, and with a large brush began to lay a dark neutral color across the background of sky. He continued until he had covered to the edges of the head—then he covered that too.

"Now what are you doing?" remonstrated the Archbishop. "Are you painting it out?"

"Yes, I am putting your Grace out of pain, as much as I can. I shall return the half-price, and am sorry I could not please your Grace."

"I wished you to alter the face," said the outraged prelate.

But Stuart was stuck hard on a point of vanity and pride. "That I could not," he replied. "I make it a rule never to alter, but to rub out."

"*But I don't wish it rubbed out,*" was the annoyed response.

"Oh, don't you. I have then only to restore it,"—and he dipped tow in turpentine to wipe the fresh color away.

Vanquished, the Archbishop asked that Stuart send the picture home at three o'clock, remarking he was the first painter to refuse altering a picture. Stuart resorted to homilies and platitudes. "That's not to be done! And I have long since proved that point, which made me adopt as a rule . . . painting from my own vision and conception. A dress-maker may alter a dress, a milliner a cap. But a painter may give up his art if he attempts to alter to please. It cannot be done."

Archbishop Fowler bowed obsequiously, and hobbled down the steps. Stuart attended him half way, and bowing low, returned to his painting-room in full enjoyment of pyrrhic victory. Immediately he asked Dowling how he had enjoyed the scene, for an audience had to be savored. Dowling told him he could not have believed it had he not been a witness. Perhaps to capitalize on this amazement, Stuart gave an order to his servant to deliver the picture at the appointed time; "and get fifteen guineas, or bring the picture back."

IN PRIDE and ego Stuart served harsh masters. Under whatever accumulated hurt he labored, objection still can be taken to his impertinent actions on grounds of propriety. Many people surely did; and one is obliged to question the character of a man who willingly gave pain for the sake of a joke. More worrisome is that such peccadilloes were a part of larger behavior patterns, for the decidedly unpleasant substrata that always had existed in his character was more in evidence, and as his judgment deteriorated his work followed the same path. A first indication had appeared in "replicas" made when he arrived in Dublin. Compared with the London originals, these portraits, and especially *The Hon. William Burton Conyngham*, had lost all bite. Eyes that had fixed one sharply were made a bland and pretty blue; brows that had been satanically arched fell level. At every point in the replica the conviction of the original is lacking, not because of the copying process, but because he elected to soften and weaken the youthful audacity of his former vision. Though on occasion he fought back and defied by stealth even so notable a personage as an Archbishop, these exceptions became more rare, as a new, more bland, character slowly spread through his Irish work. Some few pictures were superbly hard-hitting, as only he could paint them. But more lacked the depth of perception, the lurid asides, of his London period, substituting the gracious empty mask of the Georgian age. The demands of these less sophisticated clients were chiefly responsible; like Archbishop Fowler, they wished pictures to be pleasing, unaware of any deeper artistic merit a man of Stuart's caliber was capable of giving them. The ultimate result was a loss of interest in his work. Devoid of the ambitions that had motivated him in London, aware that he could not remain long in Ireland, working for bread alone and careless of the quality of his product, he accepted the limitations imposed by ephemeral circumstances. And the knowledge of what he did, for it was not hidden from him, added further to his sense of futility.

The elements of his art remained in place, and his perception was still acute beyond belief. Tied to the model, he brushed a portrait of Lord Carysfort from which, two centuries later, the kidney ailment that produced blue discolorations about the eyes can be diagnosed. Yet, strong as he remained in some departments of his art, it was equally true that limitations were asserting themselves with greater insistence. The predilection for three-quarter face became absolute, and, as variety went out of his work, the zest vanished too. Fortunately, good professional that he was, an absent enthusiasm was replaced by technical simulation; but the bravura that had captivated London less than a decade before was as lost as his own spontaneous flow of spirit.

Early in his independent career his ability with flesh tints had been a marvel. To press his advantage further he took a step that forever set him apart from English rivals: he ceased entirely to employ brown as a component of his pictures. The innovation was greater than can immediately be understood, for it was counter to the trend of British art. He adopted instead the contemporary French practice by painting all parts of his pictures in clear colors—gray, blue, green, rose, ochre, red—but *never* brown, which though present on his palette, was used only as a final wash for flesh tones and to soften passages of drapery. This formula of coloring, too, now became set; as did the use of small canvases, painted ovals, and ovals whose spandrels are left unpainted under fitted frames.

Finally, his pictures began to bear a family likeness to each other. Five and six of the heads painted during winter sessions of Parliament later were finished together in sets. Once a design was arrived at, with a happy disposition of form and color, the white ruffles of the chemise carefully balanced on an axis of the head, he adopted it for the group of pictures. After the vast scope of his last years with West, it is disappointing to note the rapid closing down of his field. One finds him playing on a smaller stage, with smaller ideas, smaller dreams, smaller pretentions. From the world of Royal command, sublime subjects and the dread mood of their creation, he was too quickly transported to an existence of bust portraits in three-quarter face. Only occasional works, like the picture of Lord Fitzgibbon, still gave evidence that the divine fire had not been entirely extinguished. His extraordinary abilities remained. The degeneration was moral, a sickening process that had eaten deeper into his substance than could yet be seen.

XII

Breakdown

REMOVED from London and the world he had aspired to conquer, Stuart's career in Ireland was without pleasure, and coupled with a sense of frustration. The loss of his youthful ambitions left him without any sense of accomplishment. The dream of a return to England was slipping away, and neither in his professional nor his personal life had he other compensating satisfactions. In a circle of convivial friends the temptation grew strong to raise his spirits up by pouring spirits down.

The instability which spread everywhere through his earlier years now began to settle and gain possession of him in drunken neurotic complications. Anything capable of rousing the now almost somnolent artist within him still brought forth overwhelming proof of how extravagantly he was endowed. In a drunken frenzy he brushed a tomato-red portrait of Charles Tottenham of Ballycurry; never had small flat sable brushes cross-cut their own strokings so furiously, nor had he more trenchantly caught the alarm of a sitter.

From the artist's Valhalla Frans Hals doffed his hat, whispering warnings of peril ahead. They were heard, and Stuart rarely faced a client except in a state of entire down-hearted sobriety. Sir William Barker's request for two slightly larger-than-usual seated compositions produced once more the obvious interest required to evoke better work. Sir William was painted with scrupulous care, seated behind the plans of his new County Tipperary house. Brussels lace, nine years old, is proudly introduced, and everywhere is the delightful touch of a spirited artist scattering pure pigment to form curtain, cloud-wafted skies, and a view of the ruined Kilcooley Abbey, whose name Sir William appropriated for his newer residence. The earnestness of this effort was replaced by charm and a graceful dexterity when Stuart turned to Lady Barker. His first wholly successful female portrait, a part of its special attraction is attributable to the stressed epicanthic folds of her eyes, which bring an elfin quality to the half-smile of a woman of advanced years. But its chief delight lies in swirls of creamy pigment that dance across her skirt, to echo in the abstract beauty of the sky, while a hitherto unseen gift for still-life is disclosed by the tambour frame, covered in luscious heavy silk, into which Lady Barker sews designs.

On occasion, when moods inexplicably relented, he scattered pigment with this altogether joyous ease, and with obvious satisfaction. The success of Lord Fitzgibbon's picture had brought him greater confidence, until, early in 1791, with an unaccustomed self-assurance he began a full-length portrait of the Hon. John Foster, Speaker of the Irish House of Commons. A man who by his position in the Parliament represented one of the pinnacles of Stuart's patronage, Foster's picture appears to have been intended as part of a series, wherein notable Parliamentarians were to be seen in some act typifying their careers. It was a natural consummation of Stuart's special relationship with the Parliament. He had, in fact, blundered in advance of his time into a genre that would not see fruition until the Romantic Period he now foreshadowed was at its height, and portraits were created as memorials of specific historic events. Henry Grattan also gave sittings for the third in this series of large works, and in April, while Parliament was in session, and Foster's picture probably no more than a head high up on a bare canvas, *Saunders Newsletter* announced an engraving "from the capital whole-length picture now painting of him by Mr. Stuart."

For attitude Stuart adopted one of Reynolds' last productions, a portrait of Lord Rawdon, whose switch to the camp of Fox at the Regency crisis had returned him to the lists of Sir Joshua's patrons. Stuart's choice was uncongenial to the task in hand, and one can only attribute it to his excessive admiration for Reynolds. No official portrait could be other than ludicrous if built on the swivel-hipped posture of Rawdon. Bad judgment was followed by a poor transfer to canvas; the figure he drew was too short and narrow, while a vacant stare marred the head, copied from a separate study. Soon this work, undertaken so easily as part of a larger scheme, became the most unredeemed failure among his larger efforts. No other full-length figure from Stuart's brush stands so badly, nor is any stricken by the same false relation between a torso twisting stodgily back and legs of uneven length. Shoulders do not materialize to support the gown, and one gesturing hand fits its wrist unwillingly, while the other, taken from Reynolds' late portrait of Sheridan, has lost its desired elegance with the removal of a glove.

Unhappy choice of a setting added insult to so much injury. Stuart's scheme required a composition suggestive of the actual interior of the Commons, for Foster was to be shown addressing the body over which he presided. Stuart's training, with the rigid mental set it imposed, here was at odds with his purpose. To picture the interior of the Commons he felt the need of an engraving; if unable to work according to this predetermined understanding of materials he was uneasy or ineffectual. To examine that accessible chamber itself, or execute drawings on the spot, was utterly foreign to his attitude, and the only engraving of the interior he found in Dublin was an old one by Mazell. Less a scene or view of the chamber than an architect's cross-section, it provided no appropriate features for his picture. To salvage his idea Stuart adapted from this engraving the screen of columns that ringed the second-floor visitor's gallery. Speaker Foster's already unhappy figure thus was elevated to an imaginary rostrum, suspended in mid-air, fifteen feet above the floor! Even a curtain brushed behind the first column, for which, surprisingly, he failed to employ Rigaud, operates ineptly in the general chaos. This lamentable performance was engraved by Hodges, as planned.

That Stuart permitted such a plate to be issued is less astonishing than at first appears, for, always subject to sudden and devastating crises of emotion, the effect of this picture was so grievous he was almost beyond caring. This was the last full-length, save his Washingtons, that Stuart ever completed; he had tried, and he had failed. The Lettsom portrait and earlier experiences of failure arose to plague him; the collapse of the fragile structure of his confidence left him shattered. From this moment the possibility of greater things always inherent in him vanished, and forever after, a psychological cripple, obsessed by fears of his weaknesses, he was an artist in full retreat. In Ireland, showered with orders and praises, he became needlessly an artist of smaller scale and lesser achievement. He was aware of the fact, and it infuriated him; for a time it agitated him violently; it did everything but what it should have done—drive him on to greater effort. Of that he seemed no longer capable.

The moral decline thus spread deep into his art, and with the inherent sense of insecurity that was his, Stuart's decline found disagreeable expression. Praise and acclaim were a drug to him, quieting a gnawing fear of artistic failure. He posed and preened, and threw thunderbolts of invective at anyone doubting him in the slightest degree.

THE PERIOD that followed was one of sudden and complete degeneration. He became careless and cynical. Anything was quite good enough; no longer is there a clear distinction in his work between what he did for himself and Dowling did for him. The full-length of Henry Grattan, its body successfully completed, was abandoned; this historic picture, intended to show Grattan moving his *Bill of Rights* in the Commons, dressed in the red coat of the Volunteers, was beyond his suddenly contracted capacities. With the Grattan painting died the entire scheme of such portraits, that would have been a monument to his own place in Irish history. His utmost efforts were bust portraits, and even these now show a curiously uneven approach; a new fluid impasto, hastily applied, is jarring against the pasteboard edges and savage harshness. The portrait of Mrs. William Colvill has draperies dashed in at breakneck speed, lace jaggedly defined; the line of the shoulder is a dreadful error, and the brush so savagely gouged at the hands it dug rows of trenchlike incisions in the paint.

He reserved for all women a brutal resentment; Lady Harriet Ponsonby's uncomely features were underscored to an unparalleled degree—a needless insolence to a young woman whom a year before he would have viewed sympathetically.

Broken in his profession, a new shock afflicted him. Fast, unstable, at times unbalanced by passengers who clung inside and out, the Black Rock coach was a part of his world: "I happened to be travelling in a dark night," he recalled, "when coachee contrived to overturn us all—or as they say in New York—*dump us*—in a ditch. We scrambled up, felt our legs and arms . . . and finding on examination that inside and outside passengers were tolerably whole (on the whole) some one thought of the poor devil who was shut up with the baggage in the basket. He was found apparently senseless, and his neck twisted awry. One of the passengers, who had heard that any dislocation might be remedied, if promptly attended to, seized on the corpse, with a determination to untwist the man's neck, and set his head straight on his shoulders. Accordingly, with an iron grasp he clutched him by the head, and began pulling and twisting by main force. He appeared to have succeeded miraculously in restoring life; for the dead man no sooner experienced the first wrench than he roared vociferously, 'Let me alone! Let me alone! I'm not hurt—I was born so!' "

Stuart's own injuries had no such light resolution. On arriving home he discovered that his painful right arm was indeed fractured. The doctor who attended him was so unskillful that after setting the bone, the arm became inflamed and swollen. The clumsy surgeon then spoke of amputation. Stuart was confronted by the specter of losing the arm by which he existed. Fortunately, he was called on, at first unprofessionally, by a young Dublin physician, who was struck by Stuart's despondency. Dr. Haughton had studied at Edinburgh, where treatment of infection was a specialty. The arm answered to a therapy of bathings in cold water, and eventually Stuart was able to work again. The long confinement, however, after the shock of Foster's picture, furthered the progress of his mental and spiritual malaise.

UNWILLING to trust himself again to the coach, which, with typical reaction, he now refused to face altogether, Stuart purchased a horse, on which he daily rode the four miles to Dublin. By day the animal was well stabled in the mews behind his painting-room. Exercise was a tonic and an antidote to an inclination towards corpulence; it also stirred him from a disposition to melancholy. But his work interested him very little, and consequently suffered. Stuart's sensual love of pigment, so apparent in earlier works, and even in those so recent as the Barker portraits, left him entirely, a loss for which again no compensating replacement was provided. The heads he now put on canvas were created of pigment flatly rubbed into the cloth; yet slowly he began to get himself in order. Soon pictures painted in this strange super-thin manner, a remarkable parallel to Van Dyck's final works, were more seriously considered than those just before. One sees again the commencement of an artistic integrity.

Stuart's economic situation had deteriorated seriously during his long convalescence. Dowling had continued to turn out "replicas," even while his master was absent. A small income was assured from the sale of engravings; and association with miniature painters like John Comerford, and Walter Robertson, who copied his portraits on chips of ivory, brought him a trickle of guineas. Small sums were also realized from the frames he put on each portrait, supplied from an ever-replenished stock. This last source alone may have brought him an extra hundred pounds each year, from the thirty or more portraits and replicas that left his studio. Even so, large sums were owing, and the Dublin bailiffs, acquainted with Stuart's dislike for the inside of their lock-ups, developed a habit of posting themselves outside his studio door. On threat of an execution it was easy for them to bilk him of a guinea, with which tribute they departed until he was again ripe for extortion. He became sufficiently acquainted with these persons to recognize them on sight, and one evening, returning from a walk with Dowling, he performed the astonishing feat of recognizing from behind a group preparing to snare him.

"Do you see three men there going before us?" he asked.

"Yes, I do."

"What are they, think you?"

"Let me see their faces."

". . . Cross the way—get on quickly—recross and return to me—you will then be able to see these characters," he instructed.

On his return Dowling guessed them to be bailiffs.

"You are right," Stuart agreed. "You shall assist me to avoid their clutches; they are now going to wait my departure."

"Then can't you return, and go in another direction?"

"No. They won't appear until I am mounting my horse. Then they will mulct me of a guinea or more. Now, if you act well you'll be amused with character; you'll see natural feeling and character worthy of Hogarth's pencil, and I shall save my guinea. Mind these directions—we first shall enter; in due time you turn out at the front door, as if waiting for me. Occasionally look into the hall, and call out 'Stuart, are you coming?' I, meantime, will mount at the stable door, and ride to the corner. Then I'll call on you to know why you stay there,—then bid you goodbye. You'll then behold their disappointment, and we shall triumph over the rascals."

Everything worked "as he had foretold, and it was truly entertaining to see their maneuvers preparing for him." But Stuart, appearing on his horse at the end of the street, was so bubbling with his escapade he could not forebear a show of bravado. He called aloud, asking Dowling "if those gentlemen were my friends. Then, clapping spurs to his horse and dashing away. . . . Deplorable looks in every face of the three wretched ruffians. They had some low converse, and sauntered away."

By the repetition of such indignities his tendency to preen became more aggravated. Like his father before him, he stiffened his pride in adversity; dignity, to be treated as a gentleman deserved, and as a social equal by noble patrons, became matters of the first importance. Nor could he resist an audience, switching in a blink from the lordly austerity of his outward self to an over-amiable taleteller; for every occasion he produced a lengthy story, sometimes two or three, frequently fictitious and always amusing until his untruthfulness became too plain, and his slow Kemble-like drawl a bore. The Hon. William Beresford, Lord Bishop of Ossory, was among those most aware of his deterioration and the obvious psychological disturbances that plagued him. A brother of the Hon. John Beresford, who had been among the first Irish patrons, a brother also of the Marquis of Waterford, for whom Stuart made numerous portraits, Ossory was married to a sister of Lord Fitzgibbon, and was father-in-law to Bishop Preston, whom Stuart had painted earlier. He was thus at the very heart of Stuart's Irish patronage, and an amiable, warm-hearted subject, who, as befits a bishop, tried to use his sittings to solve the artist's dilemma.

The religious turn Ossory gave conversation was an annoyance to a short-tempered artist. Early uprooted from a community, exposed in turn to strong Quaker and Catholic influences, Stuart never felt any of the religious urge that is a part of community life. Properly respectful to belief in others, he felt little himself, nor was he disposed to dwell on it, even for the Lord Bishop of Ossory. Not caring to be lectured any longer, when he came to the lower part of the face he bowed politely and said, "Will your Lordship please close your mouth." The Bishop complied, as an amused expression passed over his handsome round countenance. Notwithstanding the nature of the rebuff, he presented the arrogant, rude American with a delicately engraved silver and tortoise-shell snuffbox.

XIII

Desperation

BY THE early part of 1792 the disenchantment of Stuart's once-proud dream of the future was complete. His abilities had partly deserted him, and his prospects in Ireland were nothing but dim: each of his schemes to enlarge his earning capacities had failed; to continue in his path was to walk to ruin through debt, and he had no hope of expanding a practice that was already a monopoly. Before the debacle of London repeated itself he would be wise to move on—to where? Zoffany and Ozias Humphreys had gone to India; Robert Home, whom Stuart earlier had flushed out of Dublin, was likewise in India, appointed court painter to the Nawab of Oude. Thomas Hickey for a second time was en route to the east, now attached to the Earl of Macartney's diplomatic mission to China. The real object of his hopes still remained London, and circumstances conspired to rivet his attention there.

In February 1792 his landlord and "protector," the Earl of Carysfort, was a pallbearer at the interment of Sir Joshua Reynolds. The extraordinary pomp of a funeral at St. Paul's was fitting tribute to the man who had created Georgian art and guided it to unique eminence. Reynolds' passing cleared the way for others; soon the Royal Academy elected the less dictatorially inclined Benjamin West its new President. The position of Principal Painter to the sovereign also falling vacant by Reynolds' death, with much pleasure King George conferred it on twenty-three-year-old Thomas Lawrence, who now in every respect had stepped forward to reap the harvest once intended for Stuart.

His Royal appointment brought Lawrence new honor and security, in return for official portraits which were multiplied by assistants. Soon Lawrence had raised the standard of Royal portraits to new heights, and the modest stability that was his reward was sadly lacking in the career of his older friend, with now thinning hair and sad eyes, who consumed quantities of port and madeira in his Irish exile. A lengthy absence from the London scene and Lawrence's unexpectedly brilliant development conspired to push Stuart aside entirely; he was all but forgotten in London, where Reynolds' unquestioned successor was Lawrence. Older and unhappy, overlooked at thirty-six, confined to a provincial role in Dublin, and no longer certain he was capable of the exactions required of London painters, Stuart's career had passed its zenith and now only lingered in the descent.

At this same time he could not fail to notice that every newspaper he picked up in Dublin bore mention of American affairs. Ireland was closely interested in the fortunes of those more successful revolutionaries beyond the Atlantic, where a stable government had appeared, at the head of which was a President. Though his election was a polite fiction, and his prestige derived from military victories leading American rabble and French regulars against the English, George Washington was the most famous man in the world. A successful revolutionary, a gentleman and an aristocrat, his achievements appealed to every level of Irish thought; no personage on earth was watched so eagerly, nor so adored, and Washington's every utterance, even mundane businesslike addresses to Congress, were reported in entirety by Dublin newspapers.

In fact, it was evident that America now had both a sovereign and a court. Whatever Washington's chosen title, his worldwide acclaim was such that a portrait of him, treated like the official portraits of British monarchs, then multiplied and engraved, might be as lucrative to the painter as ever they had been to Reynolds. And to what court did Stuart, by his own American birth, more rightly belong? To his fertile brain, attuned to the exigencies of scheming, the scene across the broad Atlantic presented possibilities. Eighteen years had passed since he left his native land. Probably he never expected to return; but in those years America had grown from wilderness colonies to a united nation presenting institutions of new sophistication, and a practical governmental approach to philosophic concepts; did this mean also that an artist of his caliber would be made welcome? But it was only idle speculation, for to cross an ocean with no certain prospects, encumbered by young children and a wife who would pine for the land of her birth, required more courage than Stuart ever had demonstrated. Even the idea of a brief raid, such as Cosmo Alexander had so lucratively carried out, was unattractive to an artist whose ideal was the steady practice of Reynolds.

How much easier to think of paying off English debts and returning to London, where he would dispute the succession with Lawrence! An American raid might assist this bigger project, even if his sedentary habits made its prospect remote. Perhaps it was all a dream, for since the nineteenth of January, 1792, the Irish Parliament had been in session. Dublin was thronged, entertainments were frequent, sitters came regularly to his painting room, and life ground along in its disenchanted way, until unexpectedly, on the seventeenth of March, Parliament suspended business for nine days. Members drifted away to their country homes; on the appointed day the Parliament met again only to adjourn to April eighteenth, when it prorogued.

Desperation forced him to a decision for America.

THE LOSS of his brief season had made worse Stuart's already deplorable financial circumstances. However desperate the choice seemed, or how much his wife objected, to cross the Atlantic at least was possible; a return to England was not. To leave Ireland he would be forced to adopt stratagems and trickery, abandon his debts, and decamp in secrecy. Only some few people closely associated with him were told of his intention, though even to them doubtless his full plan remained hidden. From Dr. Haughton, who had successfully treated his arm, he probably asked for letters to his relatives in New York. Walter Robertson, the gentleman miniaturist, entirely dependent on Stuart to feed him work and experiencing the prolonged agonies of a bankruptcy in which he lost property in Great Britain Street and Cavendish Row, elected to accompany Stuart to America. However uncertain that gamble, Robertson's faith in Stuart was so strong that it seemed infinitely preferable to face even an unknown future attached to his star.

The only occasion on which Dowling was invited to pass a night at Stillorgan was for the purpose of breaking the news of Stuart's plan. On a Sunday morning, late in the autumn of 1792, he descended from the coach at Black Rock. ". . . As I walked up a narrow road . . . I saw some very pretty pigs; it struck me, at one moment's view, that they belonged to Stuart, and that I could not be distant from his house. To try that I was right in my conjecture I took up some little pebbles and threw them at them. They ran on, and I followed. They led me to a gate, into which they entered. It lay open, and before the house I saw Stuart tending some flower-pots.

"Ha," said he, "you are come."

"Yes, please the pigs."

"Then I told him," Dowling recalled, "how they had led me. He was delighted at my recital, and more complimented than at anything I could say in praise of his works."

"You shall taste pork of their kind, and you will acknowledge my plan to be a good one for feeding."

"He then took me to his garden, which was well cropped, all by his own hands, walked me over his grounds, and pointed out his skill in farming. He valued himself more on these points than on painting. I candidly confessed I should rather see his works in the painting-room, that I was ignorant of farming, gardening, or feeding of pigs. He pitied me very much, observing what a loss I sustained by not attending to the cultivation of that on which mankind were supported and rendered wealthy and powerful. We then got back to the house, and dinner was served. I ate of the apple-fed pork, and I was greatly pleased with it. I praised it, and he felt vain on the subject. After dinner he entertained me with anecdote . . ."

The stories Stuart told revolved about his ability to judge character, a subject on which, like his pigs, he showed childish vanity. Nor did he stop short of prodding agreement: "You may form some notion, or opinion, from this one example, that I have been expert at developing character," said he.

Dowling was equal to the jibe; "Your works should have proved the point had I any doubt. But what dealings should you have with bailiffs? You are not in debt in this country, I hope."

"My good friend, you are mistaken. I am deeply in debt."

"Well, great patronage, then, is less productive than I thought for; I have had, in my humble practice, but a moderate share of patronage, and I never incurred a debt of one pound."

"Well, I have to learn that art," joked Stuart. But he was aware of his faults, and admitted them with objectivity. "So silly am I, and so careless of keeping out of debt, it has cost me more to bailiffs for my liberty than would pay the debt for which they were to arrest me. I confess my folly in feeling proud of such feats . . . I am unwilling to be locked up . . . so submit to be plucked by these vultures—the bailiffs. Now, sir, answer me—have I not made some advances in the arts?"

"Yes; but not the fine arts, you'll allow."

"Well," said Stuart, "I mean to begin."

To Dowling he explained his intention when shortly the new Parliament met in Dublin. "I'll get some of my first sittings finished; and when I can net a sum sufficient to take me to America, I shall be off to my native soil. There I expect to make a fortune by Washington alone. I calculate upon making a plurality of his portraits, whole-lengths, that will enable me to realize. And if I should be fortunate I will repay my English and Irish creditors. To Ireland and England I shall bid adieu."

But Dowling was troubled by the dishonesty of the proceeding, which Stuart appeared to overlook. "And what will you do with your aggregate of unfinished works?" he asked.

Stuart's answer was gay. "The artists of Dublin will get employment in finishing them. You may reckon on making something handsome by it; and I shan't regret my default, when a friend is benefited by it in the end. The possessors will be well off. The likeness is there, and the finishing may be better than I should have made it."

"As your friend, the West of Ireland, says," Dowling sarcastically added, " 'Likeness is a requisite in a portrait.' "

"Es, es, no doubt," replied Stuart, in astringent imitation of the Dublin accent. That the perversions of logic that had stilled his own conscience failed to satisfy Dowling did not please him.

On the tenth of January, 1793, the Irish Parliament was called to order in its beautiful Dublin palace. The city took on its accustomed wintertime luster, the usual entertainments broke out, and at his painting-room Stuart received members and their wives for a new series of portraits he had no intention of completing. His plans, and the fascinating devilment he was embarked on, raised his spirits; he was in better form artistically than he had been for the two years previous. His new thin technique, the paint a mere breath on the canvas, was of the utmost flexibility, and obviously he was making a serious effort to lick himself into condition for the American campaign ahead. To the Viscountess Northlands' portrait he imparted a delicacy of finish, not unmixed with perception, that was the start of a new phase in his work.

His original intention must have been to leave Ireland at the end of May, when Parliament adjourned. He would then have painted the maximum number of heads for the maximum number of half-fees, and could depart without further ado. But history intervened, for on February first, France declared war on England, the commencement of an onslaught that would last two decades, until the final defeat of Napoleon. War upset Stuart's calculations by posing a new threat; no better blow could be delivered against England than for the French to land an army in the west of Ireland, where a Catholic peasantry would welcome it and perhaps rise up itself. A battleground such as it was certain Ireland shortly would become was no place for an artist. Memories were evoked of Bunker Hill, the dislocation of his family, and the loss of every tie in Rhode Island. Now it was essential to depart immediately, before his great scheme was negated by the imposition of embargoes, the closing of ports, or the movement of troops.

Few ships dared venture out into the Atlantic at that uncertain moment when Ireland held fast and awaited the blow. By good fortune he found at dock in Dublin, preparing to make the long crossing to New York, a large vessel called the *Draper*, under command of Captain Collins, an enterprising native of Cobh. At the start of March, accompanied by his wife and children and Walter Robertson, a portable cabinet of colors, portfolios of engravings, and the large agate slab on which he ground his colors, Stuart embarked. Would they ever reach America, or would they be caught up by a hostile French fleet? The risk had to be taken, and had been taken before, for he was returning to America under precisely the same conditions he had left it in 1775—through the lines of a hostile fleet.

His FOURTH and final crossing of the Atlantic found Stuart crowded into close quarters with his family. Uncertain, anxious, unoccupied, he drank to excess and inclined to be irritable; Robertson became the butt of his insults; one day at dinner he treated the Irishman with gross abuse. After imbibing his own share of the wine, the miniaturist went to his cabin, from whence he returned with a brace of pistols loaded and primed, insisting on an apology or shots across the table. Captain Collins' good offices were required to prevent a duel, and so hot-headed were the two that only by reminding them of their present danger at sea and promising a further opportunity *if* they landed in America, was harmony restored.

Stuart's ungentlemanly departure from Dublin received only laconic comment in the *Dublin Chronicle* of March 19, 1793. "Mr. Stewart's quitting this kingdom for America gives a fair opening to the abilities of Mr. Pack, who now stands unrivalled as a portrait painter." Behind Stuart lay an abysmal confusion. Unfinished pictures, some of them begun two years earlier, were claimed from his abandoned rooms, to be finished by Dowling, Robert Woodburn, Thomas Hickey, and others unworthy to touch a canvas Stuart had begun. The full-length of Henry Grattan was taken away by the sitter, to wait forty years for an inappropriate background added by Nicholas Kenny.

As in England, so too in Ireland, the exfoliation of Stuart's vast oeuvre had begun. His pictures, in common with those of his contemporaries, were not signed. Recollection of him lingered a while; thirty years after his departure Chester Harding was told by the miniaturist John Comerford that he owed more to Stuart than "to all the world besides." "Ah, no one could paint a head like our Irish Stuart," was heard by Washington Allston. Then, in the twilight of that ampler, more gracious age, and the growing wonder of a Victorian world, memory of Stuart's brief, cryptic career vanished. When a new generation arose, twice removed from that Stuart served, it knew only the few English names of Reynolds, Gainsborough, and Romney, which it assigned to the fine portraits of grandparents. Stuart had vanished; his works became the works of others, to be searched for, and one day wrested back from oblivion.

WHATEVER his unworthy moods as he crossed the Atlantic, Gilbert Stuart had been plucked from provincial obscurity to take a special place at the center of the world's stage. A beneficent destiny had selected him for a second opportunity at greatness; he was not temperamentally suited to the role, nor had he the strength of character to fill it with proper dignity; yet he was a man of extraordinary gifts, whose career in Ireland had set a clear pattern for what lay ahead.

PART TWO

Return of the Prodigal

XIV

A Third Beginning

FOR MORE than fifty days the *Draper* plowed its way westward; March became April, and April turned May before the gray shores of Long Island gave Charlotte Stuart a first glimpse of her husband's native land. A pilot took the ship into the harbor; Gravesend and the wooded slopes of Brooklyn gave way to a view of the small, windswept city of New York, crowded on the tip of its island. On May sixth, the long voyage was over, American accents rang fresh from the wharf, and Stuart faced a landing barren of prospects.

With the notable absence of anything so magnificent as the Dublin Customs House, or the Irish Parliament Building, New York presented the familiar collection of houses in the English provincial taste; in character it was not unlike the places from which he had come. The few ships that had preceded them across the wintry Atlantic already had carried news to Charleston and New York that Louis XVI was dead, guillotined on a public square in Paris. New York was hungry for information about Europe, and divided in its sympathies, for it had suffered long years of military occupation by the English. In only ten years since the red-coated troops had been evacuated, the population had doubled, and New York served briefly as the national Capital. Then the National Government departed for Philadelphia, and now New York's importance lay not in a mercantile population of forty thousand, less than Dublin, but in the fact that, settled by Dutch landed proprietors, it had always been the center of opposition to British rule. Now, too, it was the home of two persuasive personalities, Alexander Hamilton and John Jay, who, with James Madison of Virginia, had written the Constitution, forced its adoption, and built the Federalist Party controlling a government presided over by the victorious general, George Washington.

To Stuart, fresh from Ireland, absent during eighteen years of internal strife and revolution, the atmosphere had vastly changed; this, now, was topsy-turvy land. Gone was the element most aristocratic, cultivated, and learned, the same that had been Stuart's patronage in Ireland, and to whom he would most naturally have looked. It did not bode well for an artist that the classes who were his natural patrons were gone; nor was it in his favor that he was without any family connection in New York. Even casual reference to his former American friends might be taken ill by the new classes that supplanted them. The political tact he so long employed in England and Ireland again came to his rescue.

In a strange new land, foreign in thought and manner; despite his birth, almost unknown; and probably lacking funds from the start, Stuart was in the most difficult position of his life, burdened by his wife, four children, and Robertson. He seems to have forgotten his personal dramas, as though the sea had cleared his mind of the flagrant absurdities and strident antipathies that marred his path through Dublin. Faced with grim reality, he acted with a courage and determination that cloaked him in new dignity. Quarters were found at 63 Stone Street, near William Street, close by the site of what is now Chatham Square. In the shop of Thomas Barrow, a British collaborator during the occupation now turned merchant, he discovered he could obtain, imported from England, the same fine canvas he was accustomed to paint on. Pigments were available too, though probably he found it necessary to make use of native American oils and turpentine. Only at one point did his acute anxiety become visible; his London and Dublin price for a bust portrait was the equivalent of over 120 United States dollars, a sum monstrously large in a land short of ready money. Though his materials were proportionally more costly, he began by asking fifty dollars. News of this derogating change reached London, where Joseph Farington, librarian of the Royal Academy, noted in his diary:

The arts are likely to be encouraged in America. Stuart is now at New York employed. His prices are not so great as he had in England, but his expenses are proportionally more reasonable.

UNLIKE his earlier arrival in Dublin, Stuart found that in New York he had few contacts through whom to find work. The most prominent prospect with whom he was acquainted was John Jay, Chief Justice of the Supreme Court; unfortunately Jay was more often at Philadelphia, seat of the Federal Government. Nearer to hand was John Shaw, the wine merchant and ship-owner, whose affairs left him free only on Sunday to sit for the portrait Stuart painted, probably in payment for his transportation across the Atlantic. It is probable too, that Stuart carried from Dublin a letter to George Pollock, Dr. Hartigan's Irish-born brother-in-law. From these few contacts his infinite resource made a start. Other recommendations, less useful in short term, were what he would finally depend on. To the discerning, to those who had traveled abroad, or had an extra long memory, he was the man who had electrified the Royal Academy a decade before, and whose triumph had been noted in American journals. More substantial recommendations lay in the sheafs of engravings after his principal works: the rank and importance of the European sitters alone excited interest.

And decidedly in his favor was his appearance, for at thirty-eight he was a fine-looking man, possessed of an air of breeding and a lordly austerity that was no longer feigned. Athletic, broad-shouldered, deep of chest, his height better than average, he commanded respect. Probably the powder now had been combed out of his hair, leaving raven locks to contrast with his bright complexion; and he was also a figure of great fashion. He brought from Dublin modes that seemed extravagantly elegant in New York, however threadbare they already had become; the beautifully tailored dark blue coat, its collar cut to stand high about his ears; a coat of striped silk, and another of black velvet with notched lapels—all were as remarkable to American eyes as his complementing collections of waistcoats and cravats.

These first impressions were supported by an overcultivated accent, echoing Drury Lane and intimacy with haughty society, a fine deep voice rising sonorously from his chest, and eyes that twinkled with merriment. Within limits he put himself on terms of confidence with each person who came his way, and appeared to confer an honor by permitting this intercourse that belied the coldness of his correct, upright exterior self. Each acquaintance felt himself an especial friend, perhaps not noting he also allowed no intrusion into his private affairs and feelings. Then an endless store of anecdote poured forth, spiced by sly illustration and earthy humor, and his elaborate manners were seen to mask simple reactions, as when he spoke, with too evident pride, of Dukes, Lords, and Bishops, the celebrated artists of London, statesmen, orators, and eminent jurors whom he had known and painted. Some had entertained him at their estates, others gave him gifts he flourished; if he stretched the point by saying he had painted King George and the Queen, the discrepancy seemed only an inadvertence, and his claim to membership in the Royal Academy may have been mere playfulness.

Talents that had been unique in London and Dublin seemed overwhelming to New York, where nothing comparable had ever been seen, and his first works testify with what composure Stuart viewed his own lofty accomplishment. Asked for a kit-kat of a woman, he answered with one almost identical with Mrs. Samuel Dick, among his last completed Irish works. Except for the greater care given hands, this portrait of a Hoboken matron, Mrs. John Stevens, had nothing to distinguish it from the last Irish efforts. He felt no need to stir his long torpid industry.

Apparently within some months of his arrival in New York, Stuart took himself off to Philadelphia, alone, to visit his uncle. Joseph Anthony, after weathering the Revolution, had returned to his mercantile pursuits and grown rich. A portrait was begun of this large rubicund relative, but Stuart was disappointed to learn that Anthony was not of the Presidential circle; and though the government was located in Philadelphia, his uncle could not assist with introductions to Washington, nor those about him. Without completing more than the head, Stuart returned to New York, determined to use his old acquaintance with John Jay for an introduction to the President. In the new burst of family feeling his sudden visit had inspired, his aunt and cousin Marthe followed from Philadelphia, eager to meet the wife their preposterous kin had brought from England.

Then, back in New York, the magic worked. Just as had happened in Dublin, Stuart found himself besieged with sitters. At first they were merchants, attracted by Shaw, and the Pollock family, simple direct people, who kept warehouses, and labored over ledgers. It was not the high patronage Stuart enjoyed in England and Ireland, but he did not refuse and under the pressure of circumstances he labored at more literal representation. It was expedient to paint them at their desks, seated in chairs they recognized, quill in hand, or within reach. Copley could have told him what differences of attitude he would encounter working in America and England; in America he could not be literal enough and in England literalness was an abhorrence. In reverse order, Stuart ran hard on the same problems. Hands he now painted from life, in casual attitudes; less graceful or studied, lacking the classical allusion, they satisfied his new clients. Quickly these unwigged merchants of New York forced a harsher realism from a man whose training had been that of a court painter. It would have been unlike Stuart not to protest his exertions, and at first he twisted the literalness of Americans into a tactful compliment: "In England my efforts were compared with those of Van Dyck, Titian, and other great painters—here they are compared with the works of the Almighty!"

THE PRESSURES that forced Stuart to adapt his work to the unformed tastes of New York merchants caused him to flounder, though he accepted the people themselves, and made them friends. From Dr. Hartigan sprang an intimacy with Hugh Pollock, to whom he attested himself "indebted for more civilities than to the world besides . . ." Portraits also grew from this fertile relationship, as he painted George Pollock, his wife Catherine, and the Yates family, associated merchants. Heads were executed in his accustomed way, but to finish portraits of Catherine Pollock and Matilda Caroline Cruger, he added awkward, uninteresting door paneling, from Copley's portrait of Mrs. Seymour Fort. Rarely had works by Stuart been so maladroit as these unhappy creations; where, or how, he had come on this work from Copley's brilliant English period eludes research, but slowly Copley's masterwork played a decisive role in Stuart's American orientation.

Aged, small-boned, lean, her shoulders narrow and bent, Mrs. Richard Yates called at the studio in Stone Street. Time-worn and fragile, she was a sitter to strike terror in the heart of any London painter, her face distinguished by an eyelid drooped low behind the bony ridge of her nose, a pouting mouth, and fallen-away chin. But the literal transcription Stuart put on canvas owed no debt to European contemporaries or predecessors, nor even to his own previous manner. New impulses were being stirred within his art; the exacting head he painted, its thin tissue of skin drawn tight over the skull, was journalism at its best, though to paint such a person objectively was itself a more roughhewn interpretation than artistic tradition countenanced. And more than his accustomed skill was expended on Mrs. Yates' figure. A plain white fichu modestly garbed the flat swath of chest; on the head he sketched the white Irish cap employed earlier in Dublin. Next he indicated where two hands were to be painted in the act of sewing—another emulation of Mrs. Fort. The left hand he took direct from Copley; in the other he wished a needle, and for that his wife was pressed into service. Draperies and cap then were painted off in tones of gray and silver, after which his brush, full-charged with white, picked out lacy details to frame the face, hit heavily across the forehead, and returned to perform pirouettes along the fastening. Similar treatment was given the fichu, its values held more in check, before his virtuosity exploded again on sleeves and broke into a jig-step about the finger-tips, where a muslin cloth miraculously materialized. To create a better silhouette he swept the background tone down over a sketched chair-back, then improvised a silver drapery to lop off a disagreeably pointed elbow.

A dazzling success had come from the new impulses stirring within him. *Mrs. Yates* is a portrait unequaled in art; by clarity of insight, the utmost restraint, and new fertility of invention, all touched in by a sparkling witty brush, he brought himself to a further maturity, and created a masterpiece whose flavor is distinctly American. The trend to a closing-down of his scope and abilities, so apparent in Ireland, is sharply reversed; and the same happy strength came again as he painted Mrs. Yates' son, Lawrence, making him an essay in baroque angles and edges. By showing his subject leaning attentively forward in a modest Captain's chair, his large, dangling cravat the only excuse for virtuoso pyrotechnics, Stuart scored again, brilliantly.

A SAD-EYED gentleman of fashion now appeared in the Stone Street painting-room, his high complexion evidence of a recent sea voyage.

Colonel William S. Smith, former aide-de-camp to Washington and son-in-law of Vice-President John Adams, had returned to New York from Paris, as confidential agent of the French Directory. With him came the report that a new French Minister, Edmond Genêt, was en route, empowered to purchase American provisions for a military and naval venture in the Caribbean. On his own credence Smith expected to receive payments from the American debt to France, for application to this campaign! While two portraits of Colonel Smith advanced, the full fury of international intrigue burst on America. Smith's announced counterpart, Citizen Genêt, unexpectedly materialized at Charleston, put ashore from a French man-of-war. Before presenting his credentials to President Washington, he sent four privateers to sea from Charleston. The arrival in port of their prizes created convulsions of outraged passion.

At Philadelphia President Washington maintained a cautious silence; except for Secretary of State Thomas Jefferson, his administration was aghast. Alexander Hamilton, Secretary of the Treasury, ridiculed Jefferson's "womanish attachment to France and womanish resentment against Great Britain." Next to Hamilton, whose proud brilliance aroused the greatest hatred on the American political scene, Chief Justice John Jay was the least popular man in government. Though he declined Washington's offer of the post of Secretary of State when Jefferson's resignation made it vacant, it remains difficult to understand how at this juncture John Jay found time to give Stuart sittings. Probably it was during the epidemic of yellow fever that emptied Philadelphia of the government in September 1793, that the portrait was begun in New York.

Jay's portrait was only a step in Stuart's larger scheme, but that he was able to bring such a figure before his easel within four months of his arrival in America in large part explains his rapid success. If the Chief Justice had taken umbrage a decade before, in London, he appeared to bear Stuart no enmity over that earlier unfinished picture. After Stuart's flight from London, the canvas had been discovered by John Trumbull, who completed it, to his own ideas. But Jay had not forgot Stuart's London reputation, and, again, he wished the same three-quarter-length portrait. The artistic problem was complicated by the Chief Justice's lack of teeth, which gave his face an unsightly wobble. Only when pressed firmly shut did his lips take shape, or draw attention from the marked hollow beneath his nose.

By raising the chin high, to stress the line of the jaw, Stuart created a pattern of singular distinction; again, too, he was demonstrating a new fertility of invention, for a century would pass before such high-chinned patterning of features became the common usage of portraiture.

Sittings progressed in amiable fashion; an invitation followed, to breakfast at the Jay home, the first American social acknowledgment Stuart received; and indications are that it was there that talk first took place about Stuart painting President Washington. Jay, who had the unequaled confidence of Washington, and knew, at first hand, Stuart's great London acclaim, could see the justness of his wish to paint the President. Jay was also the obvious person to make tactful arrangements. History is tantalizingly silent on what form the suggestion took; but in time Jay informed Stuart that Washington would give him sittings at Philadelphia in the autumn when he returned from Virginia to meet with Congress.

Provocations meantime were being multipled by Edmond Genêt, who charged about the United States impetuously issuing proclamations; and older dissatisfactions with England became simultaneously more aggravated. Hamilton suggested a special mission to London by Jay, "the only man in whose qualifications for success there would be thorough confidence." After a conference with Washington and a private visit from Hamilton, in company with four influential senators, Jay agreed to go. He left behind his portrait, unfinished except for the head, surrounded by a six-inch patch of color. New York was much smitten with the new honor done its Chief Justice, a member of whose circle, Mrs. Gabriel Manigault, noted in her diary:

> I have been writing to my brother, [in England] . . . by Mr. Jay.
> It was pleasant to see that worthy man rewarded for leaving his wife
> and children to serve his country, by a concourse of the most respect-
> able men in N.Y. who followed him to his vessel.

Since that short period when New York had been host to the Federal government, and Washington frequented the Jay home, Mrs. Jay's salon was the most notable in the city, and from its habitués came a stream of sitters for Stuart. Eleven days after the Chief Justice's leave-taking, Mrs. Manigault noted further in her diary; "I accompanied Mr. M[anigault] into town, and left him at Stewart's," where, in fact, Mrs. Jay herself also made frequent appearances, to urge completion of her husband's picture. Delightful though she was in society, she was perhaps not a person to win her way easily with the painter; "his little sharp-faced, grinning wife," as Mrs. Jay is recorded in Mrs. Manigault's diary, where her humors were further analyzed:

> Those sweet smiles which are evidently a mask for company must appear highly ridiculous to one who has frequently seen that face deformed by anger. Whenever I observe that unnatural, fixed grin on a countenance, I take pleasure in pulling the features apart, and I imagine how this face appears to the husband, who sees it often without this affected grin.

However she appeared to Stuart, who, with his trained eye and pride in his perception, was no less observant than Mrs. Manigault, in Mrs. Jay and her connections Stuart had found the first American center from which to pluck his patronage; through the ranks of her friends he strode his lordly, austere, talkative way.

XV

The Summons

S TUART . . . is a very entertaining well-informed man. He diverts us with droll anecdotes all the time that we pass with him. He had it seems a passion for old books. He picked one up entitled *Characters* by Sir Thomas Overbury, one whole chapter of which he recited, and this is it. '*Character of the man who disgraceth his ancestry. He resembleth a potato, the better part whereof is underground.*' I like the picture he is doing of me much"; recorded Mrs. Manigault, Saturday, March 5, 1794. His charm and the depth of his personal resource quickly added to Stuart's growing reputation in New York. His comical scowl as he sat before his easel, his look of quiet philosophy when listening, his anecdotes that made him all snarls and winks, on easy acquaintance covered over his often uproarious villainy. Though he was not accepted socially, and rarely, if ever, was received at sitters' homes, he was well-launched on the most prolific period of his career.

For the first time he came to grips with his lack of diligence, and successfully overcame it. Couched in terms of the self-effacing flattery he adopted, this came through in conversation with sitters: "I can answer for him that he took great pains, for he is desirous that you should not think he has fallen off, and he says that this is one of his best pictures," Gabriel Manigault wrote to his brother Joseph, who had known Stuart and been painted by him in London. The succession of pictures he executed for this family indicated the paths by which his patronage was widening. A Charleston merchant, married to Margaret de Lancy Izard, Gabriel Manigault carried on the business of his family in New York. His sittings, and those of his communicative wife, were arranged at intervals, interspersed by others from landowners and heroes of the revolution. Generals Matthew Clarkson and Horatio Gates, brilliant in their buff and blue uniforms, decorated by the *Order of the Cincinnati*, became military portraits equal to any; Clarkson handsome and assured, executed with marvelous certainty; Gates elderly and shrewd, an ambiguous hero; and both men seen against stirring expanses of sky.

With a new sharp tang, this was the portraiture of London, at its best, being produced in New York. Stuart was in better form than since the decade before, and represented, in his extraordinary gifts, a startling phenomenon to a provincial society; but the force and felicity of his portraits were only half of his breathtaking skill, for he was working with centuries of knowledge, stored in the studios of Europe. The heritage Van Dyck had brought to England, Lely intensified, West, Reynolds, and Romney distilled in their own Italian studies, Stuart, for the first time, displayed with his own remarkable ease in the dusty confines of New York.

The numbers of portraits asked by Manigault continued to multiply, as he intimated to his brother, at Charleston:

> New York, 13th March, 1794
> It is now a long time since I promised you my picture, if I should ever meet with a good painter. You know that no opportunity ever offered for performing my promise. At last one very good, and as unexpected, has occurred. No other man than the very Stuart who drew yours, eight or nine years ago.
>
> You will receive by [Captain] Sheffield a likeness he has taken of me. I hope you will find it a good one. I am told that it is so . . . I must inform you that this is his second attempt, and that his first failure was owing to my meddling too much in the business, which induced him to bargain with me that if I would leave him entirely to himself he would produce a good picture.

But Manigault purchased both efforts, and his wife recorded how the picture promised to Charleston, with her own, was loaded aboard Captain Sheffield's coastal packet, March seventeenth. Two days later she began to sit for her second portrait, and now Anne Izard, her fourteen-year-old sister, had joined her. The younger girl evoked solicitous treatment of large soft eyes and cupid's-bow mouth; and five such portraits for Gabriel Manigault were not sufficient. Before paying Stuart a balance for three pictures, on April 23, 1794 (at fifty dollars each; a total price of £35 sterling), the South Carolina Society of Charleston, to whom an elder Manigault had left five thousand pounds, wrote for permission to have his portrait, by Jeremiah Theus, copied. The reply received from New York ran thus:

> New York, 18th April, 1794
>
> I would advise that the copy should be taken by a painter now in New York. His name is Stuart, he is a pupil of West, and is certainly the best portrait painter who has even been in America. I am warranted in saying this of him as Mr. Trumbull the painter has told me it is his opinion. If Dr. Poinsett thinks that it would be agreeable to the Sa. Ca. Society that he should be employed, it would give me great pleasure to assist in having it done and the picture can be sent here for that purpose. They will then have such a picture as I am sure they will approve of.

Instructions for shipping the Theus picture were cautious: the extent of French intentions in America were not yet clear, nor whether the United States was obliged to join in hostilities beside her ally. A sea-captain was named to

> . . . bring it the next time he comes, but should America be at war before that, I would by no means have it sent at all, as I would not run any risk of losing it.

When the Theus portrait arrived at New York, Stuart quickly constructed, from this head and shoulders, a posthumous three-quarter-length of the merchant seated at his desk, dressed in brown coat and breeches. By August his task was completed, and Stuart received his fee of one hundred forty dollars: a like sum could be expected for his portrait of John Jay, but that picture, begun nearly a year before, lay unfinished. The numbers of his orders left him short of time, but also, out of sight was out of mind. The haste and the quantities of work he had in hand were pressing him again to arbitrary studio usages: to a marvelously firm, intense portrait of William Bayard, son of a hated Royalist, who, despite the confiscation of his family property, now was rising again as a merchant, Stuart gave the same hands attributed to General Gates. Manigault noted another example of his freedom with accessories; "I am not altogether pleased about the coat. I should have preferred it plain (I think a spotted coat too youthful). But it is Stuart's choice, and I promised him that I would leave everything to him."

Among the pleasanter aspects of New York were the wigs, still worn by conservative persons, who lagged far behind the fashions of Europe. Stuart's best stylistic element thus was handed back to him, and he found opportunity to indulge its use, for the upper parts of society were now the larger proportion of his patronage, though merchants from their counters and ledgers took their places with heroes of the revolution, upstate landowners, and older London contacts like Manigault and Jay. More conspicuous were Dutch patricians named Stuyvesant, Roosevelt, and Gansevoort, whose unfinished canvases mingled with those of later English rivals bearing the names of Cooper and Livingston. The German accent was added by John Jacob Astor, his countenance betraying neither piety nor wit when he expressed displeasure at the oval of a keen, incisive, characterization. That he was shown garbed in Stuart's stylish coat and polka-dotted waistcoat, decorated by the flowing tissue of an enormous cravat that previously had graced a Ponsonby in far off Ireland, did not trouble him. He insisted that his picture be made square, and then, unhappy still, requested the busy artist to make a second effort, adding hands.

Bright spring became hot New York summer, and by dusty coach that followed the Hudson, Stuart answered a call to the Van Rensselaer Manor, near Albany, to paint the holder of that hereditary Dutch land grant. A head boldly executed on his blank canvas, he returned to Stone Street, where great landowners came in turn once more, among them the famous Chancellor, Robert R. Livingston, who had administered an oath of office to President Washington. Canvases of Livingston, Bayard, and Judge William Cooper, father of the novelist James Fenimore Cooper, were finished together, each receiving one of General Gates' hands. The least compromising of many stirring performances was a robust Halsian study of the Chancellor's mother, Mrs. Robert R. Livingston. A Beekman, she had the good sense to marry New York's greatest landed proprietor. Age and good health had made of her an enormous Rabelaisian character, whose bulk transformed the Irish cap, so crisp and capacious on the head of Mrs. Yates, into a witch's bonnet.

THE SAD NEWS that his father, that elder, gentle, equally improvident Gilbert Stuart, had died at Halifax, the previous November, 1793, reached Stuart in New York. Like his Pretender Prince, the elder

Stuart had, at last, got "over the sea to Skye." Consistent to the end of his seventy-five years, he left behind debts. In lieu of £800, his Nova Scotia lands came "unwillingly" into the hands of three Mc-Masters brothers. It was the sad history of Rhode Island repeated, for, after moving into the city of Halifax, Gilbert Stuart had returned to his old trade of snuff-grinder, for which he ran a wind-powered mill on what became known as "Windmill Hill." Whether the astonishing renown of his son ever penetrated to him is doubtful; but, nearer to home, his daughter, Anne, when past thirty, had made an advantageous marriage with Henry Newton, a twice-married man with grown sons, who was Collector of Customs at Halifax, a position held since 1731 by his father before him. Like the parallel sinecure enjoyed in Dublin by the Hon. John Beresford, such posts were a sign of influence and a source of wealth. Anne Newton's position was one of some comfort, in which her widowed mother now joined her. These tidings had the effect of re-opening communications, and soon Stuart was joined in New York by his sister Anne's younger stepson, who came for a lengthy visit, with much news of those kin at Halifax. Doubtless, too, the Newtons were pleased to learn of the remarkable roots their artist relation already had planted in the young republic.

The international crises that drove his sitters Smith and Jay across the Atlantic had a newly direct effect on Stuart. Never before habituated to the fall of court favorites, he was equally unaccustomed to having his subjects whisk across the ocean for negotiations, and to the sudden dizzying heights of popularity, followed by intense hatred, experienced by those he now painted. In Philadelphia, Washington himself underwent a succession of blows that altered popular views of his achievement. Late that summer of 1794 the President donned again his buff and blue uniform to join an army of 12,000 militia, gathered to suppress revolt in western Pennsylvania. Whether he would return to meet with Congress and give Stuart promised sittings lay in the balance. Plundering and kidnaping by Indians broke out on the Georgia border, surely the work of Corondolet, Spanish governor of Louisiana, whose emissaries offered arms to the savages. Spain's two Commissioners at Philadelphia, Viar and Josef de Jaudenes y Nebot inferred that punitive action by the United States would be found disagreeable by their country; their insolence increased, and they charged that Washington had incited Chickasaw

Indians against the tribes friendly to Spain.

On the morrow of these unsavory events, Don Josef de Jaudenes y Nebot, small, elegant, swarthy Spanish provocateur, journeyed to Boston, where he married Matilda Stoughton, the rose-petals-and-cream, sixteen-year-old daughter of the American who had been appointed Spanish consul. Jaudenes brought his young wife to New York. "We went afterwards to Mrs. Jay's," noted the assiduous Mrs. Manigault, July 3, 1794. "Mr. and Mrs. Jaudenes were there, as fine as little dolls." But at Stone Street, where Jaudenes next conducted his bride, for three-quarter-length portraits, feelings were more complicated. Sympathetic as he found any bright-cheeked child, to Stuart's eye something cruel appeared in the Spaniard's heavily-colored jaw and lips. As with John Jay, he painted heads of this husband and wife, each near to the center of a large canvas and balanced slightly to one side, to allow for flights of fancy. These portraits too were then put aside with Jay's, to be finished at a propitious moment, but, amidst the convivial animated bustle of many sittings, neither the mood nor the opportunity came quickly.

His delays at this period can, in part, be excused, for all work ceased when Stuart fell ill with fever. Slowly he recovered, but his strength did not return quickly. Mrs. Jay visited him during his illness and in rotund phrasing urged the completion of the Chief Justice's year-old canvas. Mr. Jay had wished to appear in his robes, the sort of formal composition Reynolds had excelled in and Stuart infrequently attempted. A grave, monumental effort, like Titian's portrait of old *Pope Paul III*, was required. Roughly, from an engraving of this, he marked outlines on the canvas during the rainy, hot New York summer of 1794.

To advance the work, Mrs. Jay arranged for her husband's nephew, Peter Jay Munro, to wear the Justice's gorgeous silk robes, but when he assumed the pose indicated, his hands did not fall naturally into their pre-ordained positions. His voluminous gown entirely covered the chair, an essential part of Titian's design, and everything seemed wrong. Unaccustomed to the exigencies of a model from outside his family, Stuart proceeded with vexation, his colors flying onto the canvas in thick patches. Restrained preparation was cast aside, as he plunged onward recklessly. The brush skidded and jumped, occasionally lost its way, or left crude, hard edges where it had passed. Jay's farther hand, intended to rest on the chair-arm.

was lost beneath the gown. This he scraped away: into its soggy patch he flushed charged strokes to form a baize-covered table taken from a Raphael Pope, then hastily he painted a Bossuet hand holding a Bossuet book. Another Rigaud portrait, a seated three-quarter-length of François Gigot de Lapeyronnie, may have influenced his plans too. That he had referred to the works of Rigaud intimates that he momentarily felt uneasy and required security; but the alarm passed. Held high before the Chief Justice, the hand and book, happily improvised, brought perfect monumental squareness: the rapid execution had left hard edges which he ignored, to draw wild ribbons of pigment across the area where an arm would later be supplied. Too edgy, broad, and in places undefined, his extraordinary violence of execution carried startling immediacy!

While the canvas dried in this half-finished state, he received another visit from Mrs. Jay, who, August second, reported to her husband in London:

> Would you believe that Stuart has not yet sent me your picture? I call on him often. I have not hesitated telling him that it is in his power to contribute infinitely to my gratification, by indulging me with your portrait; he has at length resumed the pencil, and your nephew has been sitting with your robe for him; it is now nearly done, and is your very self. It is an *inimitable picture*, and I am all impatience to have it to myself. He begged me to remind you of the promise you made him the day he breakfasted with you. There is an excellent engraver in New York, and Stuart has been solicited to permit him to copy that portrait of yours by a very respectable number of citizens, for which reason he has asked and obtained my consent.

His brush dipped in turpentine, Stuart swished dull tones across the top of Jay's portrait, then formed a piece of Bossuet's curtain, and, to grip the frame at right, his column. Sable brushes slid dexterously in the wet mixture; the column materialized loose and crooked, and the curtain, continuing a line of the robe, was comprised of scarcely a dozen clean, loaded strokes cut into his rough scrubbing. Areas of alteration remained obvious, parts required more labor, and the arm was never painted, but he now felt himself done; and, in fact, nothing could detract from this victory of temperament over matter, impatience, and the sticky heat of New York. All likeness to Titian had vanished from a work dignified, solid, and stable, wherein fundamental Georgian principles were exultantly vindicated.

This same fierce brilliance flared forth again, when Dr. Samuel Johnson, President of Columbia College, came for his sittings. An eminent legal mind, equally famed as an orator, Dr. Johnson's sharp-eyed look lent itself to acute portraiture. To create a picture of him challenged Stuart's newly restless spirit; he recalled how Copley had pored over Titian's *Pesaro Altar-Piece;* majestically, St. Peter leaned forward, at heaven's gate, over his volume of records. The very gesture required! Portions of Titian's slope-shouldered Saint were taken whole, contours were transferred with only slight alterations and changes in perspective, the hand taken direct, only Stuart's own long thumb added. The fire in his soul overcame him again, as the same impetuous energy that drove him through Jay's picture guided his brush in prodigies of robust virtuosity, forcing a monumental renaissance conception to become an expression of baroque audacity.

The new qualities that now dominated Stuart were an astonishing phenomenon, from a man who had seemed settled into the routine mechanics of face-painting. At thirty-eight, celestial fire had touched him a second time, turning him to new paths, assured, confident, master of himself and his craft. Fortified by his mood of absolute assurance, during August of 1794 he put on his easel again the large canvases of Jaudenes and his young wife. Immediately his mind went back to Sir William and Lady Barker, painted in Ireland: a successful plan always seemed worthy of repetition. Sir William had been seated to one side of his canvas, his farther arm extended to the plans of his house. Arrogant little Jaudenes, with his unsavory look, could be treated in the same way, the required legs adapted from Reynolds' *Percival Pot:* and his own Brussels lace cravat and ruffles would add to Jaudenes' éclat of brilliant scarlet and blue, embroidered in silver. Mrs. Jaudenes was contemplated in much the same mood, seated like Lady Barker, a fan in place of the tambour frame—and all resemblance ended there. It is difficult to overstress how much a year in New York had shaken Stuart. His temperament and patterns of action had altered; his artistic sense had new fertility, and deliberately he now turned his back on easy solutions when halfway down the road to them. His eye had been caught by another engraving after Vigée-Lebrun; an actress playing a role, all startled motion—her bosom heaving and knees alluringly pressed through skirts tucked across the picture's corner. He would have this exciting outline!

Now again his brush began to move, firm and sure as never before; transferred to his canvas, the actress' neck, her proffered breast, and revealing knees sprang to life. Sixteen-year-old Madame Jaudenes became all luscious flesh, immodestly protruding; hands were painted from Mrs. Stuart, a hint of whose heavy arm he failed to eliminate. A chair was introduced, to poke its carved and gilded arm through gorgeous rustles of fabric, painted in creamy strokes thrown off a carefully charged brush. Jewels, pendants, chains were touched in by a magic facility, sable brushes swiveling by a turn of the wrist. Long hours of intense, slow concentration piled up an astonishing performance; he knew it, and continued with elaborations; frills about the neck in paraphrase of those worn by the actress, blended with another larger portrait of Marie Antoinette; an elaborate seed-pearl choker, earrings, short, hard strokes to indicate curls in the hair, heavy clasps of jewels, a fabulous headgear, and to crown all, plumes from the portrait of Marie Antoinette!

Behind Madame Jaudenes the swing of a curtain was expected to answer that in the Commissioner's picture, welding the two into a pair: Raphael's covered table and books would complete the ensemble, until here too, his miraculous brilliance burst out to transform everything. Trees from behind Vigée-Lebrun's actress became scintillating dabs of cloud scudding across an infinity of sky, books objects of beauty—a few broad sweeps formed a Bishop's curtain. Lo! Matilda Stoughton de Jaudenes y Nebot had become his supreme example of style, a picture such as few painters achieve, possessed of an elegance worthy of Versailles, and a perfection rarely achieved in those halls where fire of execution was extinguished by protocol. Her popinjay husband was finished with equal perfection, comma-shaped strokes falling with precisioned grace, leaving steely-hard, glistening ridges of pigment to pick out the beauty of his costume.

If art with a decorative intent beyond its incisive portrait content can be admitted to the categories of immortal achievement, Gilbert Stuart had created two of the world's masterworks. He suspected as much, for partly in pride and partly because he had falsely represented that he belonged to the Royal Academy, a curious inscription was given each canvas: *G. Stuart, R.A., New York, Sept. 8, 1794:* for even at his finest moments, the temptation to be roguish still was strong.

SUMMER heat soon gave way to the scarlet and yellow cooler days of autumn, that season of natural splendor, so different in New York from the lesser display Stuart had known in England and Ireland. Washington's brilliantly uniformed little army progressed through western Pennsylvania until, at the end of October, the President delegated command to General Lee and Alexander Hamilton before returning to Philadelphia to meet with Congress. Five days after Washington's return Stuart made preparations for travel. Hugh Pollock, leaving for Philadelphia on business, carried a letter to Joseph Anthony, written with rather less cohesion than prolixity.

New York, Novbr 2, 1794
My dear Uncle

I should have been with you before this time had not a smart attack of the fever and ague prevented me. Fortunately for me I feel myself so well recovered as to be able to promise myself that pleasure while the weather is fine, perhaps in less than three weeks. The object of my journey is only to secure a picture of the President, & finish yours. My other engagements are such as totally precludes the possibility of my encouraging the most distant idea that any other application can have any effect at present.

Mr. Newton, the second son of our relation in Halifax has been some time here. He gives a very pleasant account of our friends there—I am particularly delighted with him & lament very much when my aunt & cousin were here that they could not make it convenient to meet him at my house— . . .

With respect & affection give my duty to my aunt—love to Marthe & cousins

Dear Sir
Your obliged nephew
G. Stuart

Further to prepare for his absence from New York, Stuart delivered John Jay's picture, a drawing of it having been prepared for an engraving. In the chill and early darkness of a mid-November evening he carried it to Jay's residence, facing the Battery. In good humor after Mrs. Jay's praises, he lapsed into waggery, boasting that he would do another, better portrait, if the absent Chief Justice sent him a plaster cast of his face! Immediately an account went off to London:

November 15, 1794

Just as I laid aside my pen to take tea, Mr. Stuart arrived with your picture. He insisted on my promising it should be destroyed when he presented me with a better one, which he said he certainly would, if you would be so obliging as to have a mask made for him. In ten days he is to go to Philadelphia, to take a likeness of the President.

Though Stuart habitually dawdled, one suspects the fatigue of a President faced simultaneously with the suppression of revolt, exactions of Congress, and negotiations with London, Paris, Madrid, and Indian tribes, made Washington delay and frustrated Stuart's immediate expectation. Washington was an important subject, Stuart's trip to America had been more or less predicated on painting him, and as his words to his uncle implied, he wished "to secure" this portrait, one that Washington had not ordered from him. It was a venture for which Stuart felt it was worth being at some inconvenience. John Jay, still in London during the anxious period Stuart awaited a summons from Washington, observed the climate on that side of the ocean: "It may seem strange, and yet I am convinced that next to the King, our President is more popular in this country than any man in it."

Weeks of waiting became months. Stuart's sister Anne's husband, Henry Newton, requested him to come to Nova Scotia to paint Prince Edward, the Duke of Kent, who, in 1794 had taken up the post of British Commander-in-Chief in North America, with headquarters at Halifax. A warship was mentioned as available for his transport, and the order for a royal portrait was perhaps tempting— the first notice he had received from the family of George III—but, alas, it had come too late. The loss of months, for a single picture, could not be borne. He declined, possibly giving his intention to paint President Washington as his excuse. In time, Walter Robertson, wearying of the long wait, went on ahead to Philadelphia, where he met Charles Willson Peale, adding his name to the founding members of Peale's *Columbianum Association*. Still in New York, Stuart remained fully occupied, ready to depart when called. Apart from the flow of fresh sitters, he executed replicas for the Yates family, Van Rensselaer, Mrs. Livingston, and John Jay. The last portrait, one of his noblest achievements, continued to give pleasure; "Your picture," wrote Mrs. Jay, in December, "hangs in the dining-room, where the little prints used to hang, and you cannot imagine how much I am gratified in having it."

Though the persons who passed through the Jay home formed the bulk of Stuart's patronage, by his own tact the artist successfully avoided identification with Jay's politics. Among his last efforts in the city was the eleven-year-old daughter of Senator Aaron Burr, leader of the faction allied with Jefferson, that opposed the "premiership" of Alexander Hamilton. To this adored child, Burr wrote:

> Jan. 25, 1795
>
> Your picture is really like you; still it does not quite please me. It has a pensive, sentimental air, that of a love-sick maid. Stuart has probably meant to anticipate what you may be at sixteen, but even in that I think he has missed it.

More of Burr than Stuart is found in these comments, which misread for pensiveness the childish boredom experienced in the artist's painting-room. Burr had also noted that Stuart took young John Vanderlyn, a lad from behind the counter in Thomas Barrow's shop, and put him into his studio, where he gave him instruction, even allowing him to copy a portrait of Judge Egbert Benson. Stuart's kindness to the impecunious young man showed a trait of character Burr remembered warmly. But all was drawing to an end. Like Vanderlyn, the first of Stuart's American apprentices, and Stuart himself, Burr was unaware that this fertile period neared its close. In less than two years, in excess of thirty-five portraits had been created, among them four of his American masterpieces; Jaudenes and his wife, John Jay, and Mrs. Yates—these alone are a claim to fame among the world's great portraits. That they flowed from Stuart's brush in such rapid profusion is startling illustration of the sudden flaming of genius. But, finally, towards March, 1795, the summons from Washington came: Gilbert Stuart left New York for Philadelphia and an appointment with destiny.

XVI

George Washington

HE STATELY residences of English and Irish grandees had not prepared Stuart for Washington's modest red brick house on High Street, Philadelphia. Nothing about its exterior indicated the occupant's rank, and next to it was the establishment of a hair-dresser. When he was admitted to the house Stuart's limited view surveyed a narrow stair, neatly carpeted in the center, and nowhere either pictures or ornaments: the President of the Republic appeared to have undistinguished taste in his surroundings.

Stuart left his card, and assuming it would be some few days before the President would acknowledge his courtesy, he made a quick journey into the country. On his return he was alarmed to find waiting for him a note from Bartholomew Dandridge, the President's secretary, inviting him to a gathering—that very evening! Hastily prepared and ill at ease, on his arrival again at High Street he found himself being shown up the neat little steps to what he presumed to be an antechamber, where persons milled about talking. As he stood, waiting to be escorted further, to his surprise the enormous figure of Washington detached itself from the throng, came forward, and addressed him by name. The suddenness and unexpected nature of this meeting robbed Stuart of his composure; momentarily he was flustered, then, after a faulty start, regained control and entered into conversation.

Washington proved to be a man of enormous size and bulk, itself intimidating to the artist, who felt unexpectedly diminutive; deliberate speech and slow Virginia courtesy added to an impression of majesty Stuart never had known among King George's nobles. His own reaction astonished him, and contributed to persistent discomfort, for he was not accustomed to being impressed. The President expected shortly to depart for Mount Vernon; probably he wished to know how much time this artist, more renowned than the scores he had faced before, would require. Himself anxious to proceed, Stuart was pleased to learn that Washington would grant him sittings almost immediately. Dandridge, the secretary, could arrange for the receipt of his easel, canvas, and portable cabinet of colors at the President's house.

The discomposure Stuart felt when so suddenly thrust into the presence of Washington returned when sittings were begun. More analytic now, he noted the General's hands and feet were large, as was his head; his shoulders appeared too high and narrow, and his enormous bulk was unattractively exaggerated by a fashionable tight waistcoat. The entire appearance conveyed a sense of force held in restraint, while deliberate movements of a six-foot-two frame, and the care of his speech, made him an even more formidable presence, before whom Stuart continued to feel insignificant. As it was at first, so it remained; Washington's appearance and remoteness cut Stuart to his heart, no matter with what consideration he was treated.

At the first sitting Washington was placed so that light fell on him from the left, approximating the effect of a better-arranged painting-room, and his chair probably was raised, to bring his head above Stuart's own where he sat before the easel. The experienced artist noted that delicacy would be required to render a pink-and-ivory complexion, then directed his subject to assume the three-quarter-face position. At the center of his canvas Stuart drew an oval; no need this time to risk an off-balance placement. A simple, direct head was all he required.

The absorbing nature of his task must have made Stuart more at ease. He spread a thin coat of pigment within the oval, keeping it clear and white, almost girlish in tone. His brush marked large half-tone areas into which the President's eyes were set, then roughed a shadow to locate the further limit of the nose and made a red smudge for the mouth. Except half-tones on far contour of cheek, lip and chin, only the cheek's high pink would be useful to shape three-dimensional form, and, fortunately, this hue offset the clarity of gray-blue eyes; the President's leonine beauty would look well on canvas.

Fortunately too, Stuart's technique in the flexibility of its normal components had perfect solutions for each problem encountered. His method of reserving strongest accents to the eyes, with a shadow of secondary strength beneath the nose, distracted from distortions where Washington's bulky false teeth forced out his lower lip, leaving a second unsightly protrusion nearer the chin. A deep pale ridge across his nose, where spectacles rested for long hours each day, could also be caught in nuances that escaped prominence.

Despite his own uneasiness and the tension apparent in the President's silent, resigned demeanor, Stuart made a pretense of going about his task with accustomed ease. Each morning that Washington appointed he arrived early at the President's house, to grind his colors with oil on the agate slab. And after each session the wet canvas was taken from the easel, and stood with its face to the wall. The President then departed, to wrestle with problems created by John Jay's treaty, negotiated, at last, in London. The night of April second, with Mrs. Washington, he was host at a dinner of the diplomatic corps, at which a more amiable Jaudenes and his blooming wife were present; April ninth, the Presidential couple attended the wedding of Robert Morris' daughter. Each morning Washington suffered the boredom he found most difficult to endure: sitting for an artist. Stuart proceeded with all signs of ease, the head, against a rub of dark background, floating in the center of his canvas. At least once, aware of his haste to arrive early, Washington sent a note inviting Stuart to take breakfast with him and Mrs. Washington.

One morning as he approached the President's house, Stuart noted that a manservant had opened the front door, and left it so, after sweeping. An inner door stood open also, allowing his eye to run direct to the parlor that he had made a studio. As he was about to ascend the steps he saw Washington seize his servant by the collar, then violently thrust him, broom and all, across the room. Embarrassed, Stuart walked on a short distance, then turned and retraced his steps, to find the President sitting composedly in a chair. After normal greetings Washington betrayed his agitation: he pointed to the canvas standing against the wall, its face exposed. "When I came into the room this morning the face was turned outward, as you see it, the doors were open, and here was a fellow raising a dust with a broom, and I know not but that the picture is ruined!" Fortunately the damage Stuart found was slight, and work proceeded;

but something of the restrained ferocity of the President's act made its way onto the canvas.

When the President's sittings ended Stuart took away the completed head to add draperies, and, impressed by the extreme simplicity of Washington's dress, he painted no more than a plain white neckcloth and ruffle, with his own black velvet Irish coat. The neutral background tone he had worked against was brushed over with scarlet, to throw into stronger relief the ivory-and-pink complexion. That he was painting Washington had become general knowledge in Philadelphia, and considering how many pictures of the President by American artists already existed, the anxiety to see this new work was remarkable. So persistent were requests that Stuart arranged a public exhibition, a rare instance in his life, and the acclaim of the general public who thronged to see it was the most notable triumph of his career. His plaudits were well-deserved, for only in the thousands of pages written about Washington can one find portraiture so positive and perceptive; the remoteness, the majesty, the sense of restrained violence and tension prove Stuart's extraordinary sensitivity. That they are present without any effort to dramatize or underscore them is further credit, both to his delicacy of perception and the essential rightness of technical means at his command. To those who knew Washington it was the man as nothing else could be; to those who did not, it was a symbol of a most imposing sort.

Never since his Royal Academy exhibition of 1782 had any work from Stuart's brush met with such universal approbation, and when it became known that the President had not ordered the portrait, he was overwhelmed with requests for it. Curiously, he did not allow the price to rise astronomically, as was Reynolds' habit with popular works, but promised each applicant a copy made by his own hand, at one hundred dollars; double his New York price. By April 20, 1795, to aid his memory of multiple orders and payments, Stuart drew up a paper ostentatiously headed:

> *A list of gentlemen who are to have copies of the*
> *portrait of the President of the United States.*

J. Watson, Esq.	1	B. West, Esq., P.R.A.	1
Don. Jos. de Jaudenes	5	Messrs. Pollock, N.Y. 100	2
Marquis of Lansdowne	1	J. Vaughan, Esq. 200	2
Lord Viscount Cremorne	1	Col. Burr, N.Y. 100	1

—— Mead, Esq.	1	Mrs. Holmes 100	1
M. T. Barrow, N.Y.	1	Mr. Fitzsimons 100	1
John Craig, Esq. 100	1	Mr. Necklin	1
John Stoughton, Esq.	1	Gen. Lee	1
Kearny Wharton	1	Mr. Crammond	2
Casaubon, Esq. 153 M.J.	1	J. Swan, Esq.	1
Meredith, Esq.	1	—— Smith, Esq., S.C.	1
Blodget, Esq.	1	—— Crammond, Esq.	1
Greenleaf, Esq.	1	Doctor Stevens	1
Wm. Hamilton, Esq.	1	—— Scott, Esq., Lancaster	1
Mr. Chief-Justice Jay	1	Grant, Esq., Susqueha'a	1
Col. Read	1	Wm. Ludwell Lee, Green-spring, Va.	1

Most of the persons can be identified, and perhaps it is only Stuart's consistent indebtedness that brought Thomas Barrow onto this list, doubtless to wipe out a debt for unpaid materials. At least four of the persons, Pollock, John Jay, Burr, and Jaudenes, were recent patrons in New York, though none quite matched the exuberance of the Spanish Commissioner, who ordered five copies without offering the artist any advance! Madame Jaudenes' father, John Stoughton, is also present, but one presumes that when rumor of Jaudenes' extensive debts soon circulated through Philadelphia, Stuart did not give him preference. Others, like General Lee, were close friends of the President, shortly to follow him onto Stuart's canvas. Vaughan, Burr, Greenleaf, Swan, and Blodgett also would wish to be painted by the artist who so marvelously rendered Washington. Persons far away in England and Ireland were listed too. These must have communicated their desire in the months while the artist waited in New York, otherwise Benjamin West in London could not have given this token of esteem for a pupil, nor could word have come from old patrons like Viscount Cremorne and Lord Lansdowne. John Jay, who arranged the President's sittings, had doubtless bespoke his own copy before departing for London.

Even by working on two replicas together, painting an hour on each, in two mornings, a habit acquired while finishing "sets" of pictures with the same accessories, he would require months of drudgery to deliver the copies ordered. The hysteria to possess these pictures was remarkable, and the tumult in that quaint old Quaker town pressed new orders on the startled artist while he yet struggled with the old; it was a clamorous success such as few artists anywhere have known. He found time to complete the head begun of Joseph Anthony a year before, for which he reverted to his crisp New York merchant style, showing his uncle seated in his specially constructed writing-desk chair. His cousin Joseph Anthony, Jr., his cousin's handsome wife, and Bishop White, Chaplain of the Congress, soon were dashed in too, the latter a stunning performance that renewed his joy at impasting creamy whites on clerical garments. Robert Morris, financier and land speculator friend of the President, pressed the artist and was painted in a most uncompromising style of realism. Mrs. Morris was begun, also her two daughters; other brilliant heads were hastily brushed on canvas, then set aside, to await a slackening in the demand for Washington replicas.

In a way he had never dreamed, Stuart had touched the very wellsprings of American patronage. If originally he had planned to return forthwith to New York, where so shortly before he thought his engagements precluded "the possibility of my encouraging the most distant idea that any other application can have effect at present"— how uncle Joseph Anthony might smile at that verbiage now—the acclaim he received surely held him a prisoner at Philadelphia. In one stroke he had put all America at his feet, proving that even where patterns of patronage did not previously exist, an artist of his importance could create demand for his own work. And what was more natural than to locate himself in Philadelphia, capital of the nation? London and Dublin both had been capitals; only there did an artist find sufficient scope, for by painting people famous to their countrymen a portrait painter established himself securely. An argument equally puissant was that in Philadelphia *all* his portraits now brought twice what they had in New York.

Whether at this juncture he returned to New York for his family and possessions is not recorded, though past and future patterns suggest that he did, whisking into the city and away without notice. If he returned to Philadelphia encumbered with unfinished New York canvases, another likelihood, these only added to the pandemonium awaiting him. A house was found and rented on the southeast corner of Chestnut and Fifth Streets; here Stuart continued to produce replicas of his *Washington*, while devoting himself increasingly to sittings with new subjects.

These mornings frequently were passed with intimates of the Presi-

dent, who familiarized him further with the thought and habits of
the remote Chief Executive. Washington himself recorded no observations on Stuart, whose loose tongue made him seem a man whom
one took lightly, aside from obvious professional ability. Too many
elements of buffoonery existed even in the more chaste behavior of
this untroubled period; his impudence was evident, and in its humorous phases this sometimes rebounded on the sensitive President. Fresh
from his own sittings, at breakfast with the President General Henry
Lee remarked, "I saw your portrait the other day—a capital likeness
—but Stuart says you have a tremendous temper."

"Upon my word; Mr. Stuart takes a great deal on himself to make
such a remark," broke in Mrs. Washington, coloring.

"But stay, my dear lady," continued Lee; "he added that the President had it under wonderful control."

With something like a smile Washington acknowledged, "He is
right."

The President was unaware of the incident that gave rise to Stuart's
observation, and the artist himself, still childishly vain of his ability
to perceive character, gained the ever-desired reputation for insight.
But only surly applause and implied admiration was granted by the
Presidential couple, for reasons soon apparent. Charles Willson Peale,
an older pupil of West, and until the appearance of Stuart the leading
portraitist in America, pressed his artistic nemesis to look in at the
State House while *he* painted Washington. Stuart went along, and
again sent shivers through propriety. He found the President faced
not by Peale alone, but surrounded as well by the table of James
Peale, the miniaturist brother, and easels behind which worked sons
Rembrandt and Raphael Peale. The comedy of the situation was too
much, and the impertinent wit of his Irish years flashed again; "They
were *peeling* him," he punned in recounting the scene, and one fears
he may similarly have made mock in Washington's presence. "As I
went away I met Mrs. Washington. 'Madam,' said I, 'the General's
in a perilous situation.'

" 'How, sir?'

"He is beset, Madam. No less than five upon him at once. One
aims at his eye; another at his nose; another is busy with his hair;
his mouth is attacked by the fourth; and the fifth has him by the button. In short, Madam, there are five painters at him, and you who
know how much he suffered when only attended by one, can judge

of the horrors of his situation.' "

Of such a man the President could not think highly; one suspects his silence was calculated generosity to a great talent. The minor events of this period nonetheless demonstrate how secure was Stuart's pre-eminence. Not wishing to find him outside their fold, the American Academy, in New York, elected him a member. He acknowledged his election the ninth of May, from Philadelphia, in very proper sentiments: "It is particularly flattering to be thought worthy of choice in any society among my countrymen, but more especially when that society is formed of artists. Permit me, gentlemen, to thank you, and assure you that my best endeavors shall not be wanting to promote the interest and honor of that society."

In June a minor embarrassment was eased when Senator Aaron Burr arranged for John Vanderlyn, who briefly assisted in New York, to come to Philadelphia. A letter of Burr's explains:

> Phila., June 21, 1795
> I understand that young Mr. Van Der Lyn, who lived a short time with Stuart the painter, left him for want of means of suitable support. You must persuade him to allow me to remove that objection. . . . He may draw on J. B. Provost, New York, for any sum which may be necessary for his outfit, and on his arrival in this city, where Mr. Stuart now lives, he will find a letter from me addressed to him pointing out the channel of his future supplies, the source of which will never be known except to himself.

A separate note explained further, "He is to live in the house with Stuart. I have settled all necessary arrangements. He had better come on without loss of time."

Stuart's studio burdens were eased, and from his work came considerable prosperity. But weeks spent copying the image of Washington were not congenial. The least diligent of men, he suffered severely from the enforced application, and soon wearied of the President's face. In the mood of dejection that seized him, despite the greatest clamor he had ever experienced, he came to despise this picture. Comparison with other famous official portraits, frequently repeated by their authors, Rigaud's *Louis XIV*, Reynolds' *George III*, and Lawrence's sumptuous *George IV*, demonstrates what is evident, that Stuart had not the temperament for such repetitious work, and, isolated in America, the skilled assistance available to Rigaud, Reynolds, and Lawrence was unavailable to him. Employing experienced studio helpers, no other painter permitted variation in the features of his subject. But Washington experienced subtle changes, imperceptible swellings and shrinkages; eyes grew narrow or wide, his chins multiplied or diminished; his expression is now majestic, more often sneering, simpering, or angry. A virtuoso painter, the very instrument Stuart used for his task of mechanical duplication was inappropriate. Never could he restrain the extra flourish, nor cover the beauties superficial and alluring his brush accidentally created.

It is equally true that no painter of his subtlety and extreme sensitivity ever submitted himself to the abuse of his delicate gifts as did Stuart while copying his Washington. In the weeks of mechanical duplication something of the divine spark that had come to him in New York began to fade. When, at length, he again was free to devote himself more fully to living models, his style had lost the hard tang, and become the softer manner for which he is better known in Philadelphia. The burden of *beginning* the Washington copies now had been transferred to Vanderlyn. "I have not made any copy of the President for myself yet, but will ask his [Stuart's] consent . . ." the youth wrote in April, 1796. The sheer drudgery lessened, Stuart made efforts to improve the quality of the replicas. Gentlemen had been begging for the merest sketch, and too many had been nothing more; pictures of which everyone was glad, and nobody was proud. Now they became painfully earnest, dressed in a variety of costumes, a curtain behind—but it did not help. He had looked at Washington so much his eye no longer perceived harshness of expression, nor occasional flatness of nose and grimness of mouth.

Other sitters found him strong in the habit of storing their heads away, then after frequent angry demands for their completion, finishing the canvases in lots. The curtain device notable in later Washingtons, and used also in portraits of other men, is matched by similarities among the women. His cousin's wife, Mrs. Joseph Anthony, Jr., was completed together with Mrs. Greenleaf, and a third woman whose identity has been lost: all three received the shapely contour of Marie Antoinette, and a hint of her swelling breast, charms to which, now that fashion revealed them, Stuart betrayed great sensitivity. Feminine awareness was a new feature of his art, and unfortunately, of the forty-year-old artist himself. Never before a favorite of the ladies, he was delighted at last to receive their patronage and attention. Versailles had much of the allurements he interested himself in, and increasingly he turned to its art. Each lady of Philadelphia who gave him sittings had bestowed on her a paraphrase of curls that tumbled seductively to the neck of an ill-starred Queen, whose elaborate head-dress he fashioned into charming ribbons and dangling bows.

XVII

Washington Sits Again

FEW MEN were more sensitive to questions of their own prestige than President George Washington. If dominant motives existed in his life, surely they were found in his acquisitiveness and ambition, qualities that led him from obscure landed origins in Virginia to the heights he scaled leading his country. When he returned from Mount Vernon on May second, doubtless Washington was gratified to learn that the exhibition of Stuart's portrait had brought forth a demonstration of personal popularity. It was well, for a most difficult period lay ahead. The treaty John Jay had negotiated caused widespread dissatisfaction, and much agitation was felt among Stuart's new friends and patrons in Philadelphia. The house of George Hammond, British Minister, was treated to violence by a mob that stoned its windows and burned a copy of the treaty on the doorstep—most ungracious treatment of a man who had ordered a three-quarter-length portrait of himself and a bust of his Vice-Consul, Edward Thornton. For his English partiality William Bingham, with whom Stuart had renewed the London acquaintance cut short by refusal to complete the family group, received similar insults.

Stuart had chanced on the most complex period of Washington's administration, when, caught in the struggle of emerging parties, the government was being wracked with a new ferocity. That August the President unexpectedly was summoned again to Philadelphia, to be faced by the charge that his friend and fellow Virginian, Edmund Randolph, Secretary of State since the resignation of Thomas Jefferson, had treasonable communications with France. The accusing evidence was nothing more than the French Minister's letters, too garrulously written, which, intercepted by the British navy and seen to be susceptible of misinterpretation, were passed back by Hammond. Washington, hurt by the seeming infidelity of a friend, failed to treat the accusation with proper caution; Randolph hotly resigned, to gather together the full story, which he published, the lengthy *Vindication*.

Notwithstanding the personal popularity he maintained, Washington was subjected to a deluge of abuse few public men ever before had suffered. Betrayed, Edmund Randolph wrote that the President had "a temper which, under the exterior of cool and slow deliberation, rapidly catches a prejudice and with difficulty abandons it . . ." A newspaper scoffed, "His modesty is conformable with his abilities," while another described "Saint Washington" as distinguished only by "the seclusion of a monk and the supercilious distance of a tyrant." The President was mocked by offers of a crown, damned for "dark schemes of ambition," and branded a "usurper." Even his military reputation was negated, and he was declared to have been raised to the Presidency because of his "insipid uniformity of a mind." The cruelest insult came from the Philadelphia *Aurora*, which declared that the President was overdrawing his salary!

Violent attacks on Washington continued through November, until Stuart began to notice a lessening interest in delivery of the President's portrait. Despite his exertions and complaints, and even with the assistance of Vanderlyn, of the thirty-nine orders from thirty-two persons he listed in April, only seventeen canvases have survived; very few more seem to have been executed, and as winter fell on Philadelphia the great clamor for them died. Still the painter of the hour, Stuart turned his full attention to fresh sitters who were awaiting him. Factions who favored and opposed Washington agreed only in offering him their patronage, and he was without rival. It was the Dublin monopoly again, but on a larger scale, and without the troublesome seasonal problem.

Unpredictable in even the best of times, Stuart quarreled with Robertson, whose use of his name and dependence on him had grown irksome. After executing miniatures of Washington the talented Irishman, whose suave, bland style had great influence in America, left the scene, to be heard of next in India. The completion of most portraits still was accompanied by a request for miniature copies, and

Robertson's place quickly was filled by Benjamin Trott, a boy still in his teens. On January thirtieth the Chief Justice of Pennsylvania, Edward Shippen, whose glowering portrait displayed Brussels lace, wrote to his daughter, Mrs. Benedict Arnold, in London: "I have lately got my picture taken by one Mr. Stewart who is said to have been eminent in London. I have therefore employed a Mr. Trot, a young man of talent in that way, to take a copy in miniature."

SINCE he left the frustrations of Ireland Stuart's quixotic temperament had partly abated, leaving him more settled, with less violence in the alternations of his moods. He had girded his loins, for the personal failings that contributed to his two disastrous flights were not hidden from him, and the increased artistic power that came to him in New York was the corollary of a less troubled spirit. Whatever the petty storms that blew up in his path, for his inclinations to drink, dream, quarrel, and despair were ever-present, he had a stronger hold on himself, and that winter of 1795–96 he must have felt the world was good. Receiving now the full equivalent of Romney's London prices, he was the established quasi-official artist of the new republic. The factional disputes that destroyed the burdensome boom in Washington portraits left him as dominant as ever he had been in Dublin, and his nostalgia for the elegance and free-flowing wine of Irish hospitality was partly assuaged by the gaiety of Philadelphia, where he won the personal acceptance that had been denied him in New York. Almost nightly he moved, always alone, through assemblages where his sarcastic raillery, a pleasant singing voice, and much skill with the harpsichord were as creditable to him as his brush.

The most influential of his new hosts was William Bingham, grown to his full stature as Senator, banker, presidential advisor, and land speculator on a scale of magnificence. The large canvas of his family that Stuart had abandoned eleven years before had been rescued from London and brought to Philadelphia, together with its preparatory sketches, and perhaps in hopes he could persuade the reluctant artist to complete it, Bingham relieved their fresh encounters of old embarrassments. That he did so was advantageous, for Mansion House, the residence Bingham had built on his return from Europe, by enlarging the plan of the Duke of Manchester's palace in London, was the scene of Philadelphia's most extravagant entertainments; amuse-

ment was general at the long line of servants who hurtled the names
of arriving guests across the sidewalks, up the stairs, and along the
corridors. Wealth, position, and the charm of his remarkable wife
extended Bingham's interests beyond mere banking, diplomacy, and
politics to oil, the construction of the Philadelphia and Lancaster
Turnpike, and the world of the Bingham Patent, on the Susquehanna
River, where Binghamton shortly rose.

Largely assisted by the wiles of his wife, Bingham had become
an intimate of President Washington, in itself a strange all-embracing
accomplishment, for the Senator's English interests were a well-
known secret, and the presence in his second household at Lansdowne, outside the city, of a reputed French spy named Volney,
implied some magnificent double game. Yet the aging President was
dazzled by Mrs. Bingham, who assumed, as though by right, social
leadership of the republic: even at quiet evening gatherings held by
Mrs. Washington, it was Mrs. Bingham who shone most brightly.
Abigail Adams, wife of the Vice-President, noted her role:

> The room became full before I left, and the circle very brilliant.
> How could it be otherwise, when the dazzling Mrs. Bingham and her
> beautiful sisters were there; the Misses Allen and Misses Chew; in
> short, a constellation of beauties? I am serious when I say so, for I
> really think them what I describe them. *Mrs. Bingham has certainly
> given laws to the ladies here, in fashion and elegance;* their manners
> and appearance are superior to what I have seen.

Though Mrs. Bingham had a generous natural endowment of the
charm and the perspicacity necessary for her unique position, its creation must be credited to her husband, a courtier of genius whose record is a blending of cunning and ruthlessness, neither of which
thwarted his accomplishments in the arts of flattery and manipulation. The sinister element marking Bingham's progress through life
was exactly such manipulation of women; it was notable again in
1798, when his sixteen-year-old daughter Anne Louisa was given in
marriage to a member of the Baring family, the English financial
house into which her older sister already had married, and to whom
the Senator thereupon sold in excess of a million acres of the State
of Maine. Lest it be thought so much good fortune was a consequence
of purely feminine desires, one must recall the Senator's cold reply
to Louis Philippe, exiled Duke of Orleans, who one day reigned as

King of France, when he also presumed to ask the hand of a Bingham: "Should you be restored to your hereditary position you will be too great a match for my daughter; otherwise she is too great a match for you."

Stuart entered Bingham's schemes that winter of 1795–1796 as a relatively inexpensive Beau Geste. Earlier the Senator had joined the rush for Washington replicas; what better proof of his continued affection for the President than were he now to wish a new portrait, uniquely his own? His ideas took a more particular form because engravings of John Jay's three-quarter-length, published in London, now were becoming available in Philadelphia. Jaudenes, the lavish, impulsive little Spanish Minister, had brought his two sparkling portraits to Philadelphia, where their brilliance, seen glowing over frequent entertainments, helped to consolidate Stuart's position. A seated portrait like these was what Bingham suggested. Stuart, unhappy with his first effort, and after copying it so often, unable to see its very real merits, proved willing, provided the President could be induced to sit.

At Chestnut Street Stuart was then receiving members of the President's family, which was to his advantage. In February, 1796, Martha Washington marked the engagement of her granddaughter, Betsey Custis, to Lawrence Law, by ordering portraits of the young couple. Impressed by prints that reached Philadelphia of Jacques Louis David's *La Tricoteuse*, a gem-hard portrayal of revolutionary womanhood, Stuart, with remarkable ease, adapted its cross-armed posture to his own more gracious purpose; a notable success, to which he added a softening background of the sort Romney dreamed. Gratified by this lovely portrait and possibly assured that Stuart's farcical wit had charm without malice, when subjected to the force of Mrs. Bingham's coquetry Washington agreed to face Stuart again. It was a form of valedictory, for on March 25th he informed John Adams that he intended to retire from the Presidency at the conclusion of his term.

A day before his sittings were to begin, the President's namesake, George Washington Lafayette, son of the French nobleman who had distinguished himself in the American Revolution, arrived at Philadelphia with his tutor, to stay with Washington. Entertainments were provided for this youthful guest whose presence, politically embarrassing, was made poignant because his father then languished in a prison of the Emperor Frederick. Washington wrote confidentially to Hamilton that the tutor might stay indefinitely, and become "a troublesome guest amongst us"; a prescient thought confirmed that very night, when Washington was presented with a plan of intervention with the Emperor. That same evening the President was further inconvenienced by the disappearance of Dandridge, his secretary; uncertain about his appointment with Stuart, he wrote a note in his own hand.

Sir,

I am under promise to Mrs. Bingham, to set for you tomorrow at nine oclock; and wishing to know if it be convenient to you that I should do so, and whether it shall be at your house, (as she talked of the State House) I send this note to you, to ask information.

I am Sir
Your Obedient Servt
G. Washington

Monday evening 11th Apl 1796

As Washington entered the hall door of the Chestnut Street house the following morning, the painter's wife, who caught her first glimpse of the President, thought him the most superb-looking person she had ever seen. None of the sense of majesty his presence inspired had abated, but, as he entered the painting-room, Stuart's own sharper eye noted the President was a changed man; the attacks he had sustained so long had hurt him deeply, and his sudden lack of vigor made him appear heavy and older than his years. Unaccountably he had grown sideburns; naturally white, matching his wig, they made their way nearly to his jaw. Stuart had prepared a half-length canvas, sufficiently large for the seated portrait Senator Bingham had specified. Because his first effort showed the right side of Washington's face, he now asked the President to turn the other. Less intimidated than formerly, he made conversation while his rapid motions laid a thin film of color on the canvas, into which he began to trace areas of tone. Resigned, on guard against the tricky artist, Washington sat like patience on a monument, a quiet, weary man.

Visits from General Knox, Washington's old chief of artillery, and General Henry Lee, enlivened the sessions; Betsey Custis, grown fond of the painter's chatter, frequently made her merry presence felt, to the delight of her grandfather, who suggested that her friend Harriet Chew come too. Whether on order from the Binghams, which seems unlikely, or through his own desire, Stuart suggested a parallel portrait of Mrs. Washington; its purpose is obscure, as is why this patrician lady risked an impudence that so obviously troubled her. One can only surmise Stuart's reputation stood so high it over-balanced all eccentricities. Mrs. Washington sat, surrounded by close friends, a tiny round figure of a woman with no claim to beauty. Despite her lack of schooling and despite grammar that was never dependable, the President's lady had captivated generations of Americans by her kindly good humor. Her bright eyes and gay manner seemed to invite Stuart's sympathy, and he easily caught her twinkling look, indicating the mobile mouth.

The General's sittings prospered less. Surrounded by distinguished soldiers, Stuart attempted to dispel the settled gloom of his countenance by talk of military history, great battles, and heroes of antiquity. No improvement was seen, nor did Washington betray interest, for he had determined that remoteness alone would preserve decorum. One morning the door burst open and Stuart's eight-year-old son Charles came rushing in; the painter instructed the child to leave, when, unbelievably, something in Washington's cold exterior gave way, to reveal a gentler nature. He took little Charles on his knee, where he held him, President and infant entering into an amiable chat, and seeming much pleased with each other. Public life, however, had made an accomplished actor of Washington, who afterward reverted to his role of cold impassiveness.

Accustomed by long habit to cast forth words as he worked, Stuart continued to do so, until at length his idle tongue fell on the hoary tale of how King James I, on a progression through his kingdom, was presented with a testimonial by a baker. As village mayor this worthy fellow, expected to treat the King with perfect aplomb, startled his neighbors by becoming speechless. One wonders whether in the recesses of Stuart's mind some association did not exist with his own first meeting with Washington: that *this* tale straggled forth was remarkably revealing, though a bored President seemed oblivious, until Stuart recounted how the baker, told in a whisper *"hold up your head and look like a man!"* repeated this admonition to the King. A sudden quake of laughter shook Washington; then, as quickly, he reverted to the granite-faced Chief of State. Stuart spoke of horses, and noted a quickening interest; country life and agriculture came under review, and perhaps Stuart touched on his own farming experiences at the Carysfort estate in Stillorgan. Actual knowledge of European farming methods was what Washington thirsted for; he might even have been told about "apple-fed pork."

Fresh tones the painter applied each day to his background to provide wet edges against which to model the head, are still visible, which indicates that Washington came three times to Stuart's house in Chestnut Street. And everything that had passed in the studio is equally apparent in his remarkable portrait. The rugged vitality of the first picture is replaced by thinner cheeks, and silent weariness. Washington's unwillingness to become involved with Stuart's personality is writ large, and technically, this second effort is a marvel of simple direct reportage, journalism accomplished with the utmost economy, dexterity, grace, and delicacy. The secrets it imparts are different from those of the first portrait, but equally revealing.

XVIII

The Lansdowne Portrait

DAILY THE Chestnut Street painting-room was thronged by the young Republic's most notable persons. Some were sitters, and more were prospective sitters, but with them too came an elegant, powdered, rustling, silk-and-bewigged society of aristocrats, gentry, merchants, and high government officials, to flutter like captivated moths around the incandescent wit and astonishing skill of an artistic and social sensation. "These idle people do not consider that my time is worth five guineas an hour," cried an irate Sir Joshua Reynolds under parallel circumstances. Stuart was less resolute in the face of admiration, and his new valedictory study of Washington, still floating unfinished in the center of its canvas, was a major attraction. Only then did Senator Bingham express his preference for a picture of even larger dimensions.

For the first time since the failure of Foster's picture in Dublin, five years before, Stuart agreed to talk of a full-length portrait. That most dreaded of his professional chores still exercised its special awe; but he was stronger nervously, accumulated successes gave him unbounded confidence, prosperity removed other anxieties, and the time had come to hurl back with scorn the limitations too long clamped on his genius. His first necessity, before undertaking this large work, was to move the household; Chestnut Street perhaps had been a temporary expedient, adopted to attract crowds, when it had seemed appropriate to live fashionably in the center of Philadelphia. The cost of fashion, as previously in London, was high, and now he sought, and leased, a less costly house in Germantown, a suburb. Behind it stood a two-story barn that he soon had converted to a workshop of suitable proportions, where, with vexation and with fear, he began his fateful struggle with the architecture of a standing figure.

Faced again by a canvas of large proportions, Stuart was thrown back on the unhappy experiences of his past. The shock that had withered his self-confidence never really had disappeared; now it hit him again, with staggering effect. Well-trained Georgian artist that he was, he reached for his portfolio of engravings. His own achievements were represented there in Hodges' fine mezzotints of his Dublin works, and earlier prints that recalled London life, fast and gay, when pictures tripped so easily from his dancing brush. Sir Peter Lely, Titian, Raphael, Van Dyck, Vigée-Lebrun, Gainsborough, and Reynolds were present too, and the favorite of them all, Drevet's engraving after Rigaud's *Bishop Bossuet*. Stuart's best figures had been evolved from Van Dyck's beautifully draped *Duke of Bedford*, from which Gainsborough earlier had fashioned his famous *Blue Boy*; but use of this was eliminated now, because the American President wore no gown of office. Instead Stuart turned to the body he had employed for Sheridan and Henry Grattan, Van Dyck's *Prince d'Arenberg*. Its graceful posture, balanced forward on the balls of the feet, was admirably suited to the President's massive frame and easy carriage, and when inverted, as was done for Grattan's picture, it would join smoothly onto the new head of Washington.

On his high oblong of stretched white canvas Stuart sketched outlines, slightly to right of center. Unlike smaller works, he conceived full-length portraits in a special romantic vein; like those once planned in Dublin, each was a scene from a drama; Washington must be shown addressing the Congress, his gesture counterbalancing the figure itself. A self-torturing man, Stuart was consciously re-fighting the Foster picture's failure. From Bossuet he formed an arm, foreshortened and below shoulder level, held as though emphasizing unspoken words. It was an error of taste: the gesture belonged too fully to the vanished rhetorical world of his engraving portfolio. But he was satisfied, and began to copy, high up on the canvas, the head for which Washington had recently sat. This hateful work fatigued him before he half started. Shadows that lay beside Washington's high-colored cheek lost their delicacy; the mouth, its nuances perfectly rendered from life, became hard and thin when he searched for its exact shape, and the nose became even more a vulture's beak. Arbitrarily he decided to avoid direct address between Washington and the spectator, a mannerism consistent in his larger works. Following Rigaud, he averted the eyes left, involving himself in dubious approximations of anatomy, whereby he lost the steady gaze that had been Washington's own. And the gravest error was not apparent until later, for he had made the head too large.

Impressment was practiced on studio visitors, who unceremoniously were dragooned into position for parts of Washington's figure, sketched on the huge canvas. Alderman Keppelle and a man named Smith, with whom Stuart lodged when at first he was in Philadelphia alone, each contributed sections of their persons. Trott, the miniaturist, was thrust into service; the buckled shoes, previously given to Henry Grattan, possibly were Stuart's, though this fails to explain why they appear in portraits by Gainsborough. The Brussels lace was his, as was the outstretched right hand, its position studied from Reynolds' *Omai*, and painted from a wax cast, prepared with help from Charles Willson Peale. A sword, held as Henry Grattan held his, was supplied by Viscount de Noailles, Lafayette's exiled brother-in-law, a veteran of Yorktown, whose superb silver-mounted rapier was finer than anything Washington possessed. Pleased by his own generosity and the picture in which his weapon took prominent part, Noailles insisted Stuart keep his splendid sword.

Distracted by the gradual growth of individual parts, Stuart had allowed Washington's figure to become an amorphous mass of extremities, innocent of central structure or torso, for which, in fact, he had used no model. Further embarrassment was found in limbs ridiculously short for so large a head; and in the appalling state his tensions produced, he retained neither freshness of vision nor the sureness of judgment to recognize his errors. Nor did Senator Bingham's effort to hasten him lessen the toll. The Senator's exhortations brought him down in an attack of nerves that for a time rendered him unable to work.

When able again, his mornings were given over to those who pressed him for portraits; persons distinguished in government, their wives, and wealthy Philadelphians, who came the eight miles to Germantown. More than ever at ease with simple bust portraits, he continued to execute heads; then, after a number were stored away, to add figures, draperies, and backgrounds, transforming his reportage into pictures. Thought was required to juggle the few elements of position and costume available to him; however strained he felt before the enormous *Washington*, within the smaller confines of these bust portraits he was a greater master than ever; the best qualities of his Irish portraits were augmented by a new refinement and grace. The new austerity of his approach relieved these canvases of those devices that had added luster to his London works, yet he was distinguishing them with a surprising decorative brilliance, added to telling characterization.

Charles Lee, invited to become Attorney General, hardly arrived at Philadelphia before taking up his post before Stuart's easel. Alexander James Dallas, notable for his role in the tortuous Genêt affair, now concluded by that Minister's dismissal, was recorded, handsome, spirited, and troubled, at the same time as the bland merchant John Vaughan. Each canvas received Stuart's handsomely tailored London coat of blue, set off by the gorgeously indulged whites of his large-bowed, lace-edged cravat, first seen in the portrait of Sheridan; the extravagance of that other day had been a profitable speculation, undimmed by fourteen years and three thousand miles. A third work they graced represented William Kerin Constable, Dublin-born New York merchant and friend of Washington, Hamilton, and Jay, who earlier had served on Lafayette's staff. Placed within an oval, like Vaughan, Constable's picture was a new ultimate, its execution suggesting Louis XV delicacy.

An intimate of the President and a merchant of wealth and connections, Constable evinced great interest in the unfinished standing portrait he saw in the studio-barn; he requested a similar picture, and, Stuart agreeing, Constable elicited a promise that the two canvases would be advanced by alternate work, giving neither the advantage as an original. His problems thus doubled before him, Stuart worked on; however uncongenial the task, Bingham's picture would realize five hundred dollars, equivalent to the sum he recalled Reynolds had demanded in London. At last he saw himself rivaling the prices of a deceased painter he knew in another vanished career; and a second five hundred dollars would be realized from Constable's duplicate. In fact, he had been presented with a second opportunity to make his fortune by portraits of Washington, and in the form long before envisioned; an official image, on heroic lines, paralleling the English royal portraits.

Nothing could be permitted to impair the success of these works, and as always when in a crisis of self-assurance, he took shelter in the brutal grandeur of Rigaud. Somewhere in the intricacies of that painter's *Bishop Bossuet* lay solutions to all that troubled him; poring over its marvelous clutter he could wrest some detail, that, transferred to his own canvas, gave him a sense of security. And at this critical stage, aware of the lofty rewards awaiting this work, and seized with nervous anxieties, he showed himself more completely crushed than ever; for now he elected no longer to improvise from Rigaud's portrait, but to copy it whole. His skilled hands gave a new quiet reticence to Rigaud's noisy clatter of stuffs; nor was he lacking in powers of invention. The heavy chair behind the French Bishop he turned to face the figure of Washington (as Rigaud himself had done in his portrait of Louis XIV); covered with patterns of giltwork and the five-pointed stars of the republic, on its terminal he traced a deeply carved national crest. The marvelous Bishop's cloak, pouring wildly through the center of Rigaud's composition, he eliminated, except where it ran, torrentlike, across the table; changed by deft brushing to a soft velvet, it hung over the gleam of a Federal table-leg of eagles and fasces. The Bishop's untidy volumes of church lore remained stacked in their corner, altered to bright new volumes in chaste bindings: the clutter of his table remained too, and his quill pen, protruding now from a gleaming silver inkwell before the President's emblematic black-cockaded hat, a miniature masterpiece of still-life.

Daniel McCormick, another New York merchant, who came to Philadelphia with William Kerin Constable, one day found Stuart making his way home to Germantown laden by an opulent Turkish carpet. Prodded to explain, the artist replied, cautiously, that it was for his studio.

"You extravagant dog!" bantered McCormick. "Why did you not buy a Kidderminster for your studio? It would have answered as well."

"Some day, McCormick, you will say I have done right," was the evasive reply.

But the fact was that this acquisition had been inspired by recollections of the carpet Benjamin West, so long before, had painted into his portrait of Queen Charlotte. At Germantown it became a last laborious addition to a picture now as overwrought as its painter. In his own way Stuart had spared no pains with this curious work, yet, too clearly, it was the effort of a psychologic invalid, and by throwing

him back into tortures and anxieties, it undid the healthy advances
of three years in America. Minor failings, such as faults of perspective
in the carpet, chair leg, and table, show him lured into problems he
lacked the will to solve. His Van Dyck figure, composed of extremities, fails to achieve a spacial relationship with its surroundings; Washington stands isolated, a stodgy pigmy, his contours hard against
empty space, his hand gesturing above furnishings he does not see.
Objective criticisms, however, must not obscure that the young United
States never had known anything so dazzling as this mighty image;
the adulation Stuart received never had been greater, and in large
measure it was deserved, for works of far lesser caliber regularly
were acclaimed at the Royal Academy.

Twice Constable came to Philadelphia in his coach-and-four to
watch progress, and in November, 1796, he carried away a bust of
Washington: "hundred dollar bills" the artist now called these too-
numerous replicas. Finally, he brought McCormick, whom Stuart
nudged familiarly with his elbow; "Well, McCormick, what do you
say to my rug?"

"You have done right."

Enormously pleased, Constable next asked Stuart for a seated half-
length of Washington, such as Bingham originally ordered, as a gift
for Alexander Hamilton. This, and *all* replicas, now were executed
from the second head of Washington. Vanderlyn had left Philadelphia, and again Stuart painted unending heads of the President, two
at a time, in the intervals of his sittings, from which further requests
for "hundred dollar bills" frequently came. Colonel Chesnut and
Chief-Justice Shippen added to the demand; but in large and small,
Washington portraits again had taken their fearful toll. Stuart no
longer functioned properly, and in his shattered state he parted with
the original of his first Washington, which, probably sent to fill Viscount Cremorne's order, appeared in Ireland.

The Marquis of Lansdowne had received his bust of Washington
too. Senator Bingham, who outdid Contable by inducing Stuart to
sign *his* full-length, then intimated he wished to send Lord Lansdowne
a full-length like his own. The gesture was remarkable; the more so
because Bingham was not well-acquainted with Lord Lansdowne,
whom he had met only recently, through John Vaughan. That winter,
while Vaughan again was in England, Senator Bingham, desiring to
plant a garden on the street side of Mansion House, asked Vaughan

for a London design. Lord Lansdowne, with the sudden enthusiasms that distinguished him, proposed to make the plan himself. "I am setting about some sketches for Philadelphia," he wrote Vaughan, and shortly, drawings executed by a servant from the Marquis' ideas were dispatched. Bingham's characteristic opportunism required that he capitalize on this service from a former Prime Minister, who, though long out of office, retained an influence in British politics. Stuart, familiar with Lord Lansdowne's convoluted character, mentioned the indelicacy of forcing on this fastidious nobleman a personal obligation he might resent. Based on his considerable familiarity with the former Lord Shelburne, Stuart's objection gave Bingham pause. To remove any appearance of motivated imposition the Senator resorted to his classic maneuver; the gift became one *from Mrs. Bingham* to Lord Lansdowne, and when the Senator pressed him, Stuart acceded, commencing a third version.

Few painters receive such an opportunity to paint their most famous work a third time, nor did Stuart fail to correct earlier faults. He worked, in fact, with an enthusiasm even Bingham noted, for the English destination opened greater possibilities; if he were to have a well-known engraver make a large-scale print, the sale in America might be enormous. Dublin sales of Hodges' prints could easily be exceeded, for the fame of Washington and demand for his likeness were the phenomenon of the age. He explained carefully to Mrs. Bingham, who acted for her husband with the temperamental artist, that he reserved engraving rights to Lord Lansdowne's picture; it was essential to inform the Marquis. That done, Stuart himself put arrangements for his engraving in the hands of Benjamin West, to whom he dispatched a letter. The picture was completed in happy expectation of the fortune it would realize. In every way superior to his first double effort, at last worthy of him, it was framed and packed, then, in October, put on a ship. Senator Bingham wrote to Rufus King, American Minister in London:

[Philadelphia, October 29, 1796]

I have sent by the present opportunity a full length portrait of the President. It is executed by Stewart (who is well known in London) with a great deal of enthusiasm and in his best manner, and does credit to the American artist. It is intended as a present on the part of Mrs. Bingham to Lord Lansdowne. As a warm friend of the United

States and a great admirer of Washington it cannot have a better destination.

The frame that accompanies it is manufactured at Philadelphia with much taste and elegance. It has been suggested that some difficulties may exist relative to its admission, in which case I must request your interference to obviate them.

At last, after frustrated careers in three lands, Stuart was relieved to know he would have rewards commensurate with his abilities. It was none too soon; he was forty-one, the father of six children, and his clothing, purchased years before in London and Dublin, showed wear. But Benjamin West and Senator Bingham were busy men.

XIX

Washington and Adams

AT THE New Year Philadelphians called on the President en
masse to pay their respects, and following his custom, he
received them and gave refreshment. State business occupied
Washington less than usual, and during the first freezing days of 1797,
he went with Mrs. Washington by carriage to Germantown, to see
the much spoken-of full-length portrait. This, the ninth time Washington braved Stuart's intimacies, was the artist's last meeting with
the man whose name is entwined inextricably with his own. How
the simplicity-loving first President felt on seeing himself enshrined
in exuberant grandeur is not recorded: as with his sentiments towards the artist, Washington observed a tactful silence, though as
an intimation of how posterity would view him, Stuart's lofty image
surely gave a tickle of surreptitious delight.

The first faulty versions of this picture, prepared for Bingham
and Constable, probably were what the President and Mrs. Washington found in the studio-barn. Lord Lansdowne's much improved canvas already was on the wintry Atlantic, and still in progress in the
barn was its twin, ordered for presentation to the French Directory
by the new American Minister, General Charles Cotesworth Pinckney. Washington's invitation to Pinckney to go to France had been accepted the previous July, and he arrived in Philadelphia September
twelfth, for his instructions and credentials. In a whirlwind of activ-
ity, both Pinckney and his fellow South Carolinian, Congressman
William Loughton Smith, gave sittings, and like others who saw the
first pair of full-lengths advancing that autumn, Pinckney was

tempted. When he departed for France, he left Smith in charge of the sumptuous gift, work on which proceeded amidst distractions.

In March the Lansdowne portrait, with slight damage to the coat, arrived in London, where the reception awaiting it in every way justified Stuart's hopes. Lord Lansdowne was delighted, and March 5, 1797, he passed to the American Minister, Rufus King, letters of thanks, to be forwarded to America. His covering note, addressed to King, read:

> I have received the picture, which is in every way worthy of the original. I consider it as a magnificent compliment, and the respect I have for Mr. and Mrs. Bingham will always enhance the value of it to me and my family.

To Major Jackson, Washington's secretary and husband of Mrs. Bingham's sister, he added graciously, "If I were not too old I would go to Virginia to do him homage." Nathaniel Dance, who had forgot neither Stuart nor his youthful work in London, was so impressed he suggested to Joseph Farington, Librarian of the Royal Academy, the propriety of applying "to Lord Lansdowne for Stuart's portrait of General Washington to exhibit." The subject was perhaps thought inappropriate for the King's Academy, and though this ultimate tribute, which might again have stressed Stuart's claim to leadership in the British school, failed to materialize, in July, back at Philadelphia, the generous praises of London journals reached Stuart:

> The portrait presented . . . to the Marquis of Lansdowne is one of the finest pictures we have seen since the death of Reynolds. Stuart painted it, who, if he had done nothing more, established a first-rate fame by his picture of Kemble [as Macbeth].

But, when he glanced further down this flattering report, terror struck him: "The liberality of his Lordship has consigned it to the graver"; what did this cryptic statement mean?

The letter Stuart had dispatched to Benjamin West, nine months before, was still unanswered. Had his old master arranged for the engraving, and failed to inform him? Or was some other person making off with his expressly reserved rights? Fear of the latter was strong, and he communicated it to Senator Bingham, who placated the uneasy artist by writing to London. Not wishing to cause annoyance to Lord Lansdowne, he addressed Rufus King, and, by his tone, he did not seem persuaded of any urgency.

Phila July 10, 1797

Dear Sir,

I received your letter of April 26th, with several enclosures from the Marquis of Lansdowne, who, I am pleased to find, is much gratified with the portrait of the President.

Stewart has been much disappointed in his hopes relative to profits which he expected to receive from this picture. He had wrote to his friend West requesting him to engage an able artist to execute an engraving therefrom, which, from the general admiration which the picture attracted, might have been disposed of to great advantage in this country. He has not heard from Mr. West, and he is fearful that Lord Lansdowne's obliging character may induce him to permit some other artist to take off the impression. . . .

Yours, etc.

Wm. Bingham

Such a letter was not the forthright assistance Stuart might have expected; it contained no suggestion that King enquire of West, or Lord Lansdowne, nor even a request for information. In his own pusillanimous way Senator Bingham could truthfully tell the anxious artist he had written to London "fully," satisfying himself by a half-measure, hesitantly taken.

Whatever the well-founded fears that surged inside Stuart, he remained at work, and more than ever it appeared that the major events of the world were contiguous with the flow of sitters to his Germantown barn. Philadelphia soon was treated to the sensational disclosure that General Pinckney had been *refused* by the French Directory; and what of his picture, advancing in the studio? The country experienced a sudden alarm, magnified by Washington's entire determination to retire from the Presidency. The Constitution so definitely was written around him as Chief Executive, it was commonly thought the union itself was in danger. Ambitious persons now arose to challenge the succession. John Adams, dull, cantankerous, intellectual Vice-President, after serving an eight-year apprenticeship, seemed matched in qualifications by Thomas Jefferson. Warm supporters flocked to each, and, in fear of a deadlock, John Jay's name was advanced.

Had the attacks of the previous year created doubt of Washington's true popularity, an enormous fête, organized on the occasion of his birthday, February 22, ushered in by the ringing of bells and firing of cannon, set all minds at ease. Schools were excused, servants given liberty, uniformed militia marched through the streets, the artillery paraded to fire a mid-day salute. Colors flown from ships in the harbor were matched by buntings on the houses. Under escort of Grenadiers and Light Infantry, Congress, Governor McKean of Pennsylvania, and the Legislature, accompanied by the Society of the Cincinnati, presented themselves to Washington with a formal address. Until after midnight the President and his lady were entertained to supper at Rickett's Amphitheater, from which a door was cut to Oeller's Hotel, to allow guests to circulate. Mrs. Washington was seen in tears, and though the President appeared in fine spirits, at times his emotions made speech difficult.

A fortnight later, March 3, the last evening of his Presidency, Washington gave a dinner to his associates; "Ladies and Gentlemen, this is the last time I drink your health as a public man. I do it with sincerity, and wishing you all possible happiness!" he toasted, and suddenly all gaiety was gone. Bishop White, who glanced at Mrs. Robert Liston, wife of the British Minister, saw tears roll down her cheeks.

John Adams' inauguration as second President, the following noon, is best described by himself: "A solemn scene it was indeed, and it was made affecting to me by the presence of the General, whose countenance was as serene and unclouded as the day. He seemed to be enjoying a triumph over me. Methought I heard him say, 'Ay! I am fairly out and you fairly in! See which of us will be the happiest!'" In a letter to his wife, he added, "I believe there was scarcely a dry eye but Washington's"; nor is it any less significant to future generations that all the major actors in these dramas of the young Republic were painted by Stuart.

CONSTABLE did not receive his copy of Senator Bingham's full-length until July 1797, when its usefulness in the studio for advancing the Pinckney version was ended. With it he received also the seated Washington destined for Alexander Hamilton, who, though himself in Philadelphia, failed to make the trip to Stuart's painting-room. His country lacks a persuasive likeness of this brilliant man, the only distinguished figure to escape the mantle of Stuart's special immor-

tality. Nine days after Constable received his picture through
Vaughan, Stuart received payment for Constable's three pictures of
Washington. Not including the portrait of Constable himself, of
which a duplicate was executed for his daughter, it came to the ap-
preciable sum of $850, and, punctiliously, Stuart gave an itemized
receipt. Or was the caution of these merchants responsible for the
numerous careful receipts he now wrote? He did not always err
in his own favor, as Robert Hare discovered when he received the
elaborate picture of himself and his small daughter; the artist declined
payment, remarking it had already been made. Painfully, Hare pressed
him: "Excuse me for contradicting, Mr. Stuart, but it has not, I assure
you."

Since Stuart established himself in Philadelphia he had steadily
received large sums. The only limit to his practice and remunerations
lay in dilatory habits, despite which this was the most prosperous
period of his career. Later that July another large sum was paid him,
which Adams' Secretary of State reported to General Pinckney, still
in France, where he hopefully awaited recognition.

Sir,   July 22, 1797
    This morning I paid Gilbert Stuart five hundred dollars, agreeable
to your verbal order, for the copy of the full length portrait of General Washington which you gave Mr. Stuart orders to make for you.
The picture remains with him, agreeable to the advice of William
Smith, Esq., subject to your orders. The frame is unfinished because
Mr. Stuart says the gilding will get tarnished before it can be called
for, if laid on at this time. The frame he says will cost 150 or 160
dollars more. I enclose a duplicate of Mr. Stuart's receipt for the
five hundred dollars, which I charge to your account as Minister
Plenipotentiary of the U. States to the French Republic.

> I have the honor to be
> very respectfully, dear sir,
> Your obt. servant
> T. Pickering

So occupied was he, Stuart doubtless failed to notice the end of other
diplomatic moves; two days later, Jaudenes, having failed to win appointment as Ambassador, and supplanted by the Marques D'Yrujo as
Minister, sailed out of Philadelphia with Stuart's portraits—leaving
behind memories of splendid entertainments, much extravagance, and
a sizable debt.

In Philadelphia Stuart discovered he was a profoundly unhappy man, and this intriguing revelation delighted and absorbed him. As the objectivity of his earlier work had mellowed through design and chance and the vicissitudes of life, from a specialist in male portraiture Stuart had become an equal success with women. For the first time surrounded by women young, attractive, admiring, intelligent, wearing the revealing gowns in vogue, he felt a new consciousness of their charms, and recorded them with emotional impact. More than ever before he was introduced to the pleasure of feminine companionship, and this, especially, altered his perspectives.

His return to America had given him a fresh hold on himself. He experienced a moral resurgence; but that ability to conquer his indolence, and even the sudden creative fertility displayed in New York, were negated by his overwhelming Philadelphia vogue, and the torments of the Washington full-length. Amusing socially, flashing a pleasant, witty personality and glib charm, his polished surface concealed an enlarging strain of morbidity. Relieved by his relative prosperity of real exterior problems, his mind free to wander, his association with women of fashion upset relations with a commonplace, tedious, English wife. It was not that familiarity and many pregnancies had bred contempt; his pattern of living made him the frequent guest at homes of his sitters, where he went, always, unaccompanied. The voice that had pleased Fuseli is heard no more, except when raised in rancour; even in that former life Charlotte took little part, and if she ornamented her husband's table, her presence never was mentioned. Now he discovered women who were equal to men in talents and charm, and who were partners in a brilliant society. One further insight allowed us is that frequently, when Charlotte was required to go to the studio-barn to pose female figures for the greater numbers of such canvases her husband produced, she still wore the white muslins acquired across the Atlantic.

The crushing effect of his huge Washington and its infinite reverberations on him had arrested the promise of Stuart's third career. But few, if any, of the persons who knew Stuart in Philadelphia were aware that a great door had finally closed. Women, especially, expressed their unconditional approval of its grandiose treatment, which satisfied their love of display and sensuous fabrics. He was so impressed by their reaction to the Washington portrait that he made a new effort to give even his smallest pictures something of its sumptuous quality. A group of women's portraits lay many months unfinished in the studio. From his wife as model, Mrs. Philip Nicklin, Mrs. James Chesnut, and Mrs. John Travis were provided with the same bodies and identical hands. Then Sarah Anne Peirce, who faced the opposite direction, received this treatment in reverse. The arrangement was a commonplace one he had employed in Ireland for Mrs. William Colvill, a simple unimaginative plan, the skirt fanned out across the frame's lower member, thus lending the solidity required by monumental compositions. It came back to him now, when in the same state of distress. His wife's gown as she sat in the studio-barn was the same too; altered by the addition of a fichu and bows, he made it seem high fashion again.

Each of these canvases carried some minor variation; Miss Peirce and Mrs. Travis had a tight lacy ruffle about the neck, giving an Elizabethan air, Mrs. Chesnut and Mrs. Nicklin open bosoms, that new danger. Mrs. Chesnut was given a lacy border, worthy of the French Queen from whose neck it was plucked. Except for the care he lavished on these slow creations, each built like a pastry-cook's masterpiece, to this point he had followed his own routine procedures. The departure came when he brought out his engraving of Rigaud's Bishop. Columns and draperies were rubbed behind Mrs. Young; painted months before, the attitude of her head was too uncompromising—the picture's elements remained dissociated, despite his introduction of a unifying chair arm. Next he tried the sweep of an enormous canopy behind Mrs. Travis—a recollection of Augusta Montagu, painted in London. His effort met with failure again; Mrs. Travis appeared sunk to the neck in this prodigious seat. To paint the fripperies of Rigaud into a bust portrait was no easy matter, as Stuart might have known had he ever seen the simplicity of Rigaud's own bust portraits.

Mrs. Nicklin's head had been executed later than the others, boldly and more blandly; it took elaboration better. Satisfied with the arrangement, he reversed it exactly for Miss Peirce, substituting different chair arms. For Mrs. Chesnut, whose smaller face and apprehensive look when she faced him had brought out his best efforts from the start, he achieved a better solution; a curtain that dipped gracefully against the sky, then passed behind a column. Artistically it was the single success of this group, but Philadelphia was enchanted by them all!

One wishes it had been otherwise, for by spreading the contamination of the Rigaud, now become the feeble talisman of his psychologic abnormality, he spread the area of his decline. The malady, previously localized to his rare full-scale efforts, was now seeping into the heart of his art.

YELLOW FEVER, in epidemic proportions, struck Philadelphia with the August heat of 1797. President Adams was in Massachusetts, and in his absence government officials and their families promptly fled the city. For a few short weeks Stuart was free to advance old portraits in the comparative safety of Germantown. Then, with his wife and children, he moved further from the center of infection to the Falls of the Schuylkill, where he stayed with Dr. William Smith, Aberdeen-born cleric and former Provost of Philadelphia College. More than a thousand victims of the sudden plague had been buried when the spread of disease was halted by the autumn's frosts, and in November with the returning population Stuart was launched on a new round of sittings.

The curious quasi-official position he occupied in the republic was recognized by a request from the Massachusetts Legislature for a full-length of Washington, and, in addition, a full-length of President John Adams. Here was an opportunity to fulfill the hope he once entertained of a place comparable with that of an appointed court painter. But Stuart had retreated into himself and had ceased to dream such mighty dreams. Aware what prestige accrued from the portrayal of public figures, he hastened to sketch heads of President Adams and his wife Abigail. The discerning second President posed and, like his predecessor, evidently held private views on Stuart, for the impertinent look he fixed on the artist was recorded with clinical accuracy. "Look at him—it is the very like of him, is it not?" Stuart remarked proudly of this effort. "Do you know what he is going to do? He is just going to sneeze!"

But Adams' stubby figure, so successfully treated by Copley in London a dozen years before, did not have Van Dyckian proportions. Reynolds' final great full-length of Keppel might have provided a suitable starting point, or even Rigaud's *Louis XIV*, but Stuart could not now bring himself before another large canvas. He made no effort to prepare a full-length; the second President's head was finished on its little bust-sized canvas, with the same black coat previously given Washington. Mrs. Adams' picture, begun twice, was put aside like that of Martha Washington. The President's son, John Quincy Adams, expressed the family's attitude; "Mr. Stuart thinks it the prerogative of genius to disdain the performance of his engagements," a sentiment against which he would have expostulated warmly, despite its obvious justice.

For the fact is undeniable that Stuart, broken, and preoccupied with his inner turmoils, had lost the capacity to cope with his career, or to alter the direction it had taken. A towering, turbulent, enigmatic figure of unique importance in the young country, his long reputation for dilatoriness and eccentric behavior became a familiar joke. Some orders he ignored entirely, for, lacking trained assistants, unable or unwilling to bring them from London or train them himself in Philadelphia, unable to develop a functioning studio capable, like Reynolds', of meeting the enormous demand, he abdicated his own aspirations. Stuart's inability to organize his affairs lies at the root of his needless snubs that destroyed his place in a nation anxious to make him the government's portrait bureau. An apt illustration is the Indian Chief who one day called on him, bearing a letter from the Secretary of War:

Sir:—   War Office, 14th February, 1798
    The Little Turtle, who will deliver you this, is an Indian Chief of great consequence. I am desirous of having an expressive likeness of him, at half length, taken by a painter of eminence.
    Your professional abilities have induced me to apply to you for this purpose in order that, if it suits your convenience, and will not interfere with your engagements, no time may be lost in beginning and finishing such picture as soon as possible.
    I am with much respect, sir, your obedient servant,
                                             James McHenry

Stuart's conveniences were *not* suited, however, nor was this flattering request complied with; and, as he rarely wrote letters, and was inclined to evade questions, he spread incivility after disobligeance. The surliness of approbations grew more common, and from the President's entourage were heard courteous, cautious insinuations.

Requests for changes, dealt with so charmingly in New York, again met with a shrill refusal, or the same rude treatment accorded to Dublin's Archbishop. To Benjamin Trott, he burst out; "That picture has just been returned to me with the grievous complaint that the muslin of the cravat is too coarse! Now, sir," he continued, with increasing indignation, "I am determined to buy a piece of the finest texture, have it glued on the part that offends their exquisite judgment, and send it back again!" Discriminating people had an air of permanent irritation with him, while Philadelphia learned to rely little on assurances Stuart afterwards seemed disinclined to keep. Indispensable, without peer in his profession, entirely dominating the field, he was hopeless; but if he seemed to remain impenitently himself, it was only the illusory appearance of a man suffering the undignified ravages of decay.

XX

The New Washington

WITH REGRET, with resignation, steeped in wine, Gilbert Stuart saw the century of his birth slip away. To be the principal painter of his homeland was the same joyless disillusionment he had found life itself; return to London was as impossible as ever, there seemed nothing worth looking at in the future, and his private life ran the same unprofitable course. An abusive wife, the squawling of infants, the expense of older children entering their 'teens, made his home less than a haven. At forty-three, his figure grown more thick, his nose larger, and red dappling on his cheeks, his nerves now permanently in chaos, he required peace: neither professionally nor personally could he find it. Irascible, brilliant, frequently drunk, filled with an illusory gaiety, intellectual pretensions became his newest refuge from aching realities. He became intimate with the man who should have been his greatest antagonist, Charles Willson Peale, the portraitist most in vogue until Stuart's arrival ended his sway.

Fourteen years older than Stuart, in that age when professional boundaries were less fixed, Peale was more than a mere painter. A natural craftsman, he was first trained as a saddle-maker; he repaired watches and clocks, then became a silversmith and brass-founder, before trading a saddle to colonial limner John Hesselius for instruction in painting. At Boston, Copley early loaned Peale a picture to copy, and in London for two years (1767–1769) Benjamin West gave him the instruction he later gave Stuart. Even during the revolution Peale painted colonial portraits, pictures lacking the technical understanding of Stuart's, but telling likenesses with an acute feeling for character. Peale developed a gallery where these historic portraits might be seen, and later he added to it a museum of Natural History. By 1794 the collection had grown so large it was transferred to Philadelphia's Philosophical Hall, and finally, in 1802, to the upper floor of the State House.

Stuart's establishment in Philadelphia channeled Peale's energies into the growth of his museum; his collection was arranged to show the entire order of nature, according to the best knowledge of the time, and it included the disputed bones of a mastodon Peale himself had unearthed. The immensities of the past became an opening perspective, and to Stuart's burgeoning intellect, it was accentuated by familiarity with another scientist of importance. At Lansdowne, the Bingham estate outside Philadelphia, lived the reputed French spy Constantin François Volney. Before the French Revolution Volney spent four years in Syria and Egypt, where he made the first significant scientific explorations into antiquity; he discovered clues to civilizations previously unknown. Scholarly prestige won him a place in the Estates General and the Constituent Assembly, beside Jacques Louis David. Then, in 1791, on the eve of disaster and his expulsion from France, his greatest achievement, *Ruins, Or Meditations on Revolutions and Empires*, appeared, in which an impassioned eloquence suggested the awe-inspiring panorama of entire civilizations dead, vanished, and swept away on the stream of time.

From Lansdowne Volney could walk to Stuart's studio-barn at Germantown, to sit for a portrait probably ordered by Senator Bingham. Exposure to his persuasive intensity, added to the enthusiasm of Peale to demonstrate the un-Godly proposition that entire orders of animals had been lost in the earth's evolution, gave Stuart a new sense of intellectual stimulation. He became increasingly conscious of his mental powers. The conglomerate knowledge Stuart acquired as a part of social intercourse, to confound an occasional sitter, or from a wide curiosity—for he had read Gibbon and Hume, and was acquainted with orthodox historical thought—he now mistook for part of an organized scheme. Reynolds and West had been *thinkers*, though of no high order; with a sullen pride Stuart smiled to recognize the superior caliber of his own understanding.

Introduction of a third distinguished man of learning contributed further to this belief. Joseph Priestley early found fame in England for his experiments that isolated oxygen and other gases, as a Non-conformist Minister, and by political tracts favoring the American colonies at a moment inopportune for King George III. He accepted a position as literary companion to Stuart's London patron, Lord Shelburne (now Marquis of Lansdowne), from whom he received a small pension after fleeing to America. Though Priestley felt it necessary to issue an explosive tract answering Volney, his own connection with Lord Lansdowne undoubtedly brought him to the attention of Senator Bingham. Washington earlier tried out both men; Priestley was asked to dinner in Philadelphia, with John Adams and young Lafayette; Volney passed a night at Mount Vernon, after the first President's retirement. At the request of Jonathan Williams, who wished the portrait for the Philosophical Society, of which Priestley was so distinguished an ornament, Stuart began sittings with Priestley.

Nourished by wine, the painter's intellect flourished, as intimations of a misspent life became more urgent and distinct. He attacked dinner and the wine flask as though they were the key to all imaginable pleasures. Now with wild and wayward eye he recalled the aberrant genius of his youth, recounting to all and sundry the flashing joy of a London career, while to his solemn neighbors in a Philadelphia suburb he seemed the very son of Belial. What an unimaginative wife thought as his personality markedly deteriorated is not recorded. Antagonistic she remained, nor was this calculated to bring her closer to the mysterious amalgam that was her husband.

A PART OF his trouble was that the new century had started off too busy and agitated. Robert Liston, the well-liked British Minister, whose wife had shown such emotion at Washington's farewell dinner, resigned, and as Mrs. Liston explained in May: "Mr. Liston and I, busy as we are at this moment, have consented to everybody's advice, and are sitting for our pictures to Mr. Stewart, an artist of great fame, but remarkable for being dilatory. I am endeavoring to persuade him to finish them soon . . ." but persuasion meant little against the frenzy of his nerves, an unorganized studio, and the inundation of demands for Washington's image. The first President's unexpected death on December 14, 1799, as the country again placed its confidence in his military leadership, passed him direct into immortality. Few persons make so immediate a transition, for, though

GEORGE WASHINGTON
The first life portrait

Mellon Collection, National Gallery of Art, Washington

GEORGE WASHINGTON
The second life portrait

Museum of Fine Arts, Boston

Washington's letter of April 11,
1796 to Gilbert Stuart

The Earl of Rosebery

The Bingham full-length portrait of Washington

Pennsylvania Academy of the Fine Arts

The Lansdowne portrait of Washington

The Earl of Rosebery

Heath's pirated engraving of the Lansdowne portrait

British Museum

The final great full-length portrait of Washington

New York Public Library

Washington had been canonized while alive, his last years were embittered by factional disputes.

Unprecedented numbers of requests rained down on Stuart, whose patent was secure as the one man who could provide a living image of America's hero. Individual orders soon were drowned under those from Institutions and legislatures; fifteen days after Washington's death the American Philosophical Society voted to purchase a Washington portrait; the State of Connecticut followed suit, asking a full-length; and Peter Jay Munro, who had posed in New York for John Jay's robes, added his own desire for a full-length to the demand. Stuart's wild eye viewed it all with vexation, for since the end of 1798 his Germantown studio had been barren of those large canvases. The full-length requested by the Massachusetts Legislature was never executed, for lack of a picture from which it could be copied. Now Stuart realized that new orders would oblige him to produce freshly, even if from the same sources, a full-length portrait of Washington. There is a pathos to see him stagger beneath this fearful new necessity; the promise of his youth a flickering candle, his middle years dominated by the portrait of George Washington, which, finding him young and in his best stride, would leave him old and shattered.

As he drew himself up to face this obsessive task, Stuart was floored by a blow from an unexpected quarter. In May, while the Listons still gave sittings, on one of his regular visits to Dobson's bookstore in Second Street, Stuart was present when a box of engravings was opened. To his utter dismay, he saw a print of his Lansdowne portrait of Washington, from a plate cut by his former London acquaintance, James Heath. He must have hesitated, for Washington's face was so poorly rendered it was not recognizable, though the picture unquestionably was his sumptuous Rigaud-inspired composition, and its legend identified both subject and artist, stating, even more boldly, that the original belonged to Lord Lansdowne.

Thunderstruck, then overcome by rage, he was unable to answer Dobson's questions concerning the engraving; he did not long forbear to express himself however, and summoned his most baroque language.

"Sir, the work is as infamous in its execution as the motive that led to it."

"What!" replied Dobson. "Have you the feelings of an American? Do you not respect the man here represented . . . What would Mr.

Stuart say if he heard you speak thus?"

"It has been my custom," replied Stuart, or so he later recounted it, "to speak the language of plainness and truth whenever the character and fortunes of any man are thus jeopardized. By this act the family of the painter is ruined. My name is Stuart; I am the painter and have a right to speak."

Whether his words actually had such dignity and hindsight, the discovery was truly a sad one. Posterity, that inexorable tribunal, must question why he allowed three years to pass without himself producing an engraving. The single letter he addressed to Benjamin West is hardly sufficient, and, in fact, it was only an instance of others stepping in to supply his own deficiencies. His anger made Stuart, at last, the active person he should have been earlier. Unfortunately he adopted the unprofitable course of a call on Senator Bingham, whom he furiously reminded of an express stipulation regarding the engraving. It was not denied; the enraged painter then asked how the Senator proposed to compensate him for the injury sustained. Poor misguided artist, despite his years in elevated circles he seemed to know little of the arts of the plausible smiling courtier. Bingham merely asked, "Have you anything to show for it?" a gently dishonorable maneuver Stuart found deeply offensive. He departed abruptly, as though Bingham were unclean, and by his intemperance had alienated one of his most important patrons.

He thrashed about in the same furious vein until he hit upon the plan of writing direct to Lord Lansdowne. A letter was prepared in the prolix style he considered appropriate to communications of weight, then re-copied; it began with a recollection of their London acquaintance:

My Lord
    The liberality with which you have uniformly patronized the arts, and a grateful recollection of my personal obligation for your approbation and countenance have inspired a hope that your Lordship will receive with indulgence the representations of an injury, to which I have recently been exposed under the apparent sanction of your name.
    As a resource to rescue myself from pecuniary embarrassment, and to provide for a numerous family at the close of an anxious life, I had counted upon the emoluments that might arise from a portrait of George Washington, engraved by an artist of talent. It was, there-

fore, with peculiar pleasure, that I found myself invited by Mr. Bingham to take the portrait of President Washington, to be presented to your Lordship; as I knew of no one in whose hands it could be placed with more propriety and advantage, nor on whom I could more confidently rely to secure the rights and promote the interests of the artist.

I complied immediately with Mr. Bingham's request, but expressly stipulated with his agent in the transaction, that no copy should be taken of the picture, nor should any engraving be allowed but with my consent, and for my benefit. Scarcely, however, had the picture been received by your Lordship, when I had the mortification to find an engraving promised to the public; and soon afterward, at a moment when the sensibility of Europe, as well as of America, was keenly excited by the death of General Washington, the print was published in England and in the United States; executed by Mr. Heath, for the emolument of himself and Mr. Barry, of New-York; and stated to be taken "from the original picture, by Gilbert Stuart, in the collection of the Marquis of Lansdowne."

Thus, without my privilege and participation, despoiled of the fair fruits of an important work, and defeated in the great object of my professional pursuit, your Lordship will readily allow me the privilege to complain. There is something due to my feelings as a man, and to my character as an artist; and to repel, as far as is practicable, the wrong that has been committed, I have issued proposals for a superior engraving, from a portrait intended to be fixed at Mount Vernon, and I address myself respectfully to your Lordship, to enquire into the source of my misfortune.

It is obvious that to you, sir, there cannot have been communication of the right which I reserved (for even my letter on the subject must, I presume, have miscarried), nor am I willing to impute to Mr. Bingham the suppression of so important a fact; I can only, therefore, at present, suppose that some improper artifice has been employed by the person immediately interested in the engraving, and I pray your Lordship to honor me with an explanation of the means by which so unprecedented and warrantable a violation of the right of property has been accomplished.

Legal phrasing, introduced into a letter that elsewhere has the authentic ring of Stuart's style and self-pity, can be explained by his consultations with Horace Binney, under whose guidance he tried to lead Lord Lansdowne into some declaration that would provide grounds for proceedings against Senator Bingham or James

Heath. The Marquis' response, if he made one (for such may have occasioned Stuart's call, demanding compensation, on Senator Bingham), is unknown; but the announcement of Stuart's own engraving, mentioned in this letter, had indeed taken place, inserted in the Philadelphia *Aurora*, June 12, 1800; a date which demonstrates how soon after the arrival of Heath's engraving Stuart acted.

> Gilbert Stuart having been appointed by the Legislatures of Massachusetts & Rhode Island to prepare full length portraits of the late General Washington, takes this mode to apprize the citizens of the United States of his intention to publish engravings of General Washington, from the Mount Vernon Portrait, executed, upon a large scale, by an eminent artist.

That he had neither fixed on an engraver for this work, nor completed the *Mount Vernon Portrait*, as he had christened his new full-length, from which he proposed to have it done, is symptomatic of the entwined fantasies in which he lived. Lest someone suspect his motives in making this sudden announcement, a parenthetic untruth next sought to dispel adversions:

> This advertisement (which has been suspended from motives of delicacy towards the afflicted family of Mount Vernon), is deemed to be peculiarly necessary, as Mr. Stuart has the mortification to observe, that without regard to his property, or feelings, as an artist, an engraving has recently been published in England; and is now offered for sale in America, copied from one of his portraits of General Washington.
>
> Though Mr. Stuart cannot but complain of this invasion of his copyright (a right always held sacred to the artist, and expressly reserved on this occasion, as a provision for a numerous family) he derives some consolation from remarking, that the manner of executing Mr. Heath's engraving, cannot satisfy or supersede the public claim, for a correct representation of the American patriot.

Good taste twice offended, by mock deference to the Washington family, and his reflection on Heath's work, however well founded, Stuart next proceeded to turn this extraordinary public display into a solicitation!

> He therefore respectfully solicits the assistance of the public on the following conditions:

1. That a full length engraving of General Washington, shall be delivered to each subscriber at the price of twenty dollars.
2. That towards defraying the expenses of the work, each subscriber shall pay in advance the sum of ten dollars, and the remainder of the price on the delivery of the print.

Subscription papers, containing a description of the print and the size intended, will be ready in a few days.
Adams & Jefferson.

Mr. Stuart informs the public that engravings from his portraits of the President and Vice-President are likewise preparing, under his immediate direction, and will be published in the course of a few weeks.

And, in his sudden haste to preserve a market that for three years he had ignored, Stuart neglects to give an address!

One doubts that many persons rushed to entrust the notoriously dilatory Stuart with half the price of an engraving, the very size of which had not been decided. The immediate and obvious purpose of this remarkable solicitation was to cut off sales of Heath's engraving; its further plots and counterplots, bolstered by untruths and so revealing of the artist's moral state, were secondary. In pursuit of his foremost aim he wrote to Mr. Barry, the New York print-dealer who imported Heath's work. The tactics of a bully were adopted here, using implied threats where actual resort to law would have been useless:

Sir,

When the portrait of General Washington was undertaken for Mr. Bingham, it was on the express condition that I should retain the exclusive right of making an engraving from it. It had, indeed, been the object of the most valuable years of my life to obtain the portrait, with a view to such a right; and surely, sir, you, who have endeavored to deprive me of it for your own emolument, could not have been ignorant of its value, when you employed Mr. Heath on the occasion.

I know not on what terms Mr. Bingham presented the picture to the Marquis of Lansdowne, but I am persuaded that nobleman has either been imposed upon by some misrepresentation, or has never received the letter which I addressed to him on the subject. I shall, however, endeavor speedily and fully to develop all the circumstances of so cruel an outrage upon the property of an artist (and the chief hope of a numerous family), and, in the meantime, as far as it is practicable, the injury that is meditated to my fortune; and I may add, from a view of Mr. Heath's print, to my professional reputation.

THE EXTRAORDINARY cause of so much commotion was that Stuart's portrait of Washington had developed into the most sought-after image the world had known. Not even the duplication of monarchial effigies, carried on in many eighteenth-century studios by groups of assistants, matched the demand for this picture; and as his need for a well-organized studio progressively grew more exigent, the artist revealed himself alarmingly out of his depth. His situation was quite beyond him; he was unable to comprehend or deal with such unparalleled demand, and as he lost grip on his affairs, his existence became a succession of forestalling actions against those too willing to supplement his deficiencies. The engraving rights already lost to the unfastidious James Heath, spurious portraits now appeared on every side, while Stuart was forced constantly to defend his proprietary interest against the shoddiest of plots. He recounted another: "When I lived in Germantown a little pert young man called on me, and addressed me thus:

" 'You are Mr. Stuart, sir, the great painter?'

" 'My name is Stuart, sir.'

" 'My name is Winstanley, sir; you must have heard of me.'

" 'Not that I recollect, sir.'

" 'No! Well, Mr. Stuart, I have been copying your full-length of Washington; I have made a number of copies; I have now six that I have brought on to Philadelphia; I have got a room in the State House, and I have put them up; but before I show them to the public, and offer them for sale, I have a proposal to make to you.'

" 'Go on, sir.'

" 'It would enhance their value, you know, if I could say that you have given them the last touch. Now, sir, all you have to do is ride to town and give each of them a tap, you know, with your riding-switch—just this, you know, and we will share the amount of the sale.'

" 'Did you ever hear that I was a swindler?'

" 'Sir—oh, you mistake, you know—.'

" 'You will please to walk downstairs, sir, very quickly, or I shall throw you out at the window.' "

His deceptive gaiety when he retold such tales belied the drain they were on his emotional resources. Untoward events troubled him profoundly, and magnified until he conceived himself to be the most transgressed-against of the world's creatures. Two-thirds of his professional life was passed quietly finishing portraits begun in the pleasant intercourse of sittings. Without the beguilement of his own talk, his mind too easily slipped back to all that ached within him; he felt aversion for these sickening hours, and the habit of procrastination, with its accompanying lassitudes, so well-rooted in his earliest beginnings, took firmer hold of him. An exaggerated loquaciousness made him the bane of anyone eager to get on, and no inducement was required for him to call at Horace Binney's law office in Front Street, talk over problems real and imaginary, take snuff, jest, pun, and satirize.

"I was always entertained by his conversation, and endeavored to enter into his peculiar vein," Binney recalled; aware of Stuart's genius, and tormented soul, he perhaps pretended that he "relished his wit and character" more than the exhausting visits allowed. "Binney has the length of my foot better than anyone I know of," Stuart acknowledged; and later that summer of 1800 he again sought his assistance to enjoin the sale of copies from his Washington, painted on glass in China!

DESPITE her persuasion, it was October 8th before Mrs. Liston could report, with obvious pleasure, "The pictures, for they really are pictures as well as portraits, are nearly finished, but paint dries so slowly in this climate that the artist says they must not be sent home [to Scotland] immediately. We, therefore, propose taking them along with us in a box formed as frames, to be opened occasionally for air . . ." And as the autumn advanced, Horace Binney sat for his own portrait at Germantown, probably as payment of his many services. A canvas was ready on the easel when he arrived.

"How do you wish me to sit?" enquired the young attorney. "Must I be grave? Must I look at you?"

"No, sit just as you like, look whichever way you choose; talk, laugh, move about, walk about the room if you please."

Binney did not act on this too literally, for the picture was accomplished with dispatch, while artist and model led off in a merry vein. After his first session Binney found the head excellent, except that the eyes were not indicated; when he came again Stuart gave special attention to this particular.

"What do you consider the most characteristic feature of the face?" the lawyer asked. "You have already shown me that the eyes are not . . ."

Occupied by his work, Stuart just pressed a brush handle against the tip of his nose, distorting it oddly.

"Ah, I see, I see," exclaimed Binney.

Whether through predetermination, or because of his carefree instructions, when it came time to dress this head into a picture, Stuart found it awkward; none of his normal shoulder arrangements fitted the tilted position. Among his engravings he found it approximated by Reynolds' *Josiah Wedgwood*, from which he proceeded, painting the coat an arbitrary claret color he had used at intervals since London. Unhappy still with the eccentric balance, as always when now he found himself in a quandary, Stuart referred to Rigaud. Bossuet's hand, holding his book, was plucked, and, its thumb altered to the new perspective, he painted it into Binney's portrait—a recollection of James Barry's self-portrait perhaps also contributing. So careless had he become that while copying folds into the coat before his mirror, Stuart neglected to reverse the buttons.

"By the way," said Binney, when he, artist, and picture, were again together, "do you know that someone has remarked that you have put the buttons on the wrong side of the coat."

"Have I?" said Stuart, with obvious annoyance. "Well, thank God, I am no tailor."

But immediately he took up his brushes, and with a few touches he added a lapel to the collar of the coat, on the nearer side.

"Now," said he, "it is a double-breasted coat, and all is right, only the buttons on the other side not being seen."

But the arbitrary arrangement of the picture, and its wide-staring eyes, mark it as one of an increasing number of unsuccessful works.

ONLY James Heath's engraving and his own anger brought Stuart new life that autumn, for, when, towards winter, he finally attacked the new full-length of Washington, it was with an intention to astonish. Stung, his aroused energies were evocative of abilities one might have doubted he still possessed. He would not be so foolish as to alter the essential character of the full-length, but he made deliberate efforts to throw the Lansdowne picture into a secondary category.

A new body was fashioned, more in the character of Washington's commanding physique. From what source he secured it is a mystery; only the legs, several times employed by Gainsborough, suggest that the source was one well known. He sketched it on canvas well, the proportions long, suitable to Washington's frame, with an ample chest and powerful shoulders. The outstretched hand of his earlier efforts, rhetorically false, was brought down onto the table, and the second hand, with de Noailles' sword, made less prominent. As his scheme advanced he brought out the second life-head of Washington, never far away in the studio, reduced its scale slightly to fit properly, and copied it onto this new body, retaining Washington's own direct gaze.

Despite moments of nervous exasperation when he scrubbed under-tones, and furious outbursts as with a fully charged brush he picked out details of drapery, the new Washington developed into a remark-able success. Each critical fault found in earlier versions was elimi-nated; the fine dignified figure had all the majesty of Washington himself, and though not painted from the General, surely is a recol-lection of him. The Rigaud cornice, that had cut awkwardly, was lowered to elbow height, altering a flat area of wall into opening vistas of sky which flooded the picture with a new, lighter atmosphere. Highlights were dashed about, and heavy curtains assumed a flutter and rustle whose staccato counterpoint is pure music. Even the de-structive detail of the once-proud carpet is eliminated, Rigaud's marble floor re-asserting itself in proper harmony. Such elegant virtuosity and marked temperament in a controlled facture were unequaled since the death of Rigaud himself.

Pushed to an extremity, for the last time Gilbert Stuart rose bril-liantly to meet the challenge, producing one of the supreme master-pieces of Georgian art; a lavish pyrotechnical display-piece filled with incongruous quiet dignity. This, his third separate effort to create a full-length portrait of George Washington, takes its place among the world's most distinguished full-length portraits: nor must one overlook that within the purely biographical frame of reference, it was a manifestation of extraordinary heroism.

XXI

"Next to the Beauty of Virtue"

THE REMOVAL of the United States capital from Philadelphia to the new federal city of Washington did not at first affect Stuart. Philadelphia, the nearest metropolis to the array of vacant sites and "water lots" quartering President Adams' government, remained the center of America, its greatest and most important city. In Germantown Stuart functioned as though no change had been made, and his masterpiece of Washington, ushering in a new period of affluence, came after John Adams had led his cabinet into bivouac on the Potomac's swampy shore. Nor did Thomas Jefferson's inauguration to the Presidency, on March 4, 1801, alter Stuart's position: the third Chief Executive whose portrait stood to Stuart's credit, Jefferson had been painted while serving as Vice-President to John Adams. At the time of his inauguration the artist was engaged in a familiar task: extracting payment for a *Washington*. To Jonathan Trumbull, who had placed the order in behalf of Connecticut, he wrote in formal style:

Sir   Germantown February 16, 1801
    The portrait of General Washington, which was engaged by you for the State of Connecticut, is completed, together with the frame. It will perhaps be necessary that you should designate some agent here to receive it.

Permit me to intimate to you that it will be peculiarly convenient to me to receive the stipulated compensation by the first of March (the time agreed upon for the completion of it) as I have made a purchase of a small farm for my family, for which payment will then become due.

> I am, respectfully,
> Sir,
> Your Obedient
> Humble Servant
> G. Stuart

Three repetitions of this, his most brilliant *Washington*, already had appeared in his studio, two of them requested by his native Rhode Island, and intended to hang in the State Houses in Newport and Providence. Official confirmation of that order came in May, after which, in rapid strides, both pictures were completed, probably from the finest version of all, destined for Peter Jay Munro of New York. Rhode Island's pictures Stuart confided to his uncle, Joseph Anthony, who shipped them by water in the sloop *Eagle;* their display at Newport that October drew crowds for weeks.

Each of these masterly works brought Stuart six hundred dollars, an advance over the price of his earlier full-lengths, justified by their quality and induced by the new hope he cherished. Little is known about the farm mentioned in his letter to Jonathan Trumbull, except that as a man of the eighteenth century, it was natural for Stuart to invest in land the funds flowing from his labors in greater quantities. Recollections of Stillorgan and its peace may have been a further motivation and a step in the right direction, for he was wound dangerously tight. In a lesser, more meager way than he had hoped, his Washington portraits at last had provided funds. The entire proceeds from these, his finest full-lengths, and every excess dollar he earned at this prolific moment, was put into his farm, stocked with imported Durham cows. Whatever the mischief of James Heath, Stuart felt his labors on Washington had made provision for his family.

The sums he withdrew from current income for further payments on the farm left Stuart's finances precariously balanced; but had he brought to fruition his scheme to engrave the new Washington, and followed it with plates of Adams and Jefferson, unquestionably he could have consolidated a position of considerable promise and security. Unless one thought back to Rubens in Flanders, or Van Dyck's brief years in England, few artists had ever so entirely dominated any country; perhaps, too, Stuart was newly aware how wise his coming to America had proved, for angry currents were buffeting the artistic circles in Dublin and London. For one last bribe of uncommon munificence, in August 1800 the Irish Parliament had voted *itself* out of existence! To achieve this goal Pitt had created twenty-two Irish peers; five peers received English titles in addition; and twenty peers were granted higher titles. It was an ignominy of avarice, but to Stuart it was an utter disaster he had escaped; the very catalyst of his trade, the Parliament that had brought country magnates to Dublin each winter, had ceased to exist.

Nor was the news from London any more encouraging. Except for toothless old Benjamin West, bowed with age and cut off from his friend the King, the great men Stuart had known had passed from the scene. Copley grew old painting portraits in a studio crowded with unsold historical pictures, while that talented chameleon, Hoppner, disputed the supremacy with Lawrence, as earlier Gainsborough and Romney had with Reynolds, and with as little effect. Britain had girded herself for a death struggle with Napoleon, with little means left for other pursuits. Even Lawrence, leader of the English portrait painters, had nothing like the assured prosperity of Reynolds.

Instead of purchasing land in America, it might have been possible, at last, for Stuart to return to England. War, and unpropitious conditions in London, surely deterred any such thought, and now that he was the father of nine children, the oldest a girl of fourteen, it is doubtful whether he actually was capable of uprooting himself again. His lethargy alone might have determined that final fateful throw with America. Whatever the cause, his money was invested in the soil of his native land, and he continued the greatest prosperity of his career. For a time he was in top form again, as demonstrated by his portrait of Frances Cadwalader, who recently had married a British consul, the Hon. David Montague Erskine. Stuart alone seemed capable of the clear, graceful, and untroubled surfaces of his beautifully accomplished works; qualities as uniquely his own as the brusque truth of his male portraits. More than ever dedicated to the tasteful embellishment of devastatingly frank heads, he had groped closer to the art of Versailles than seems possible for an artist working in isolation. He had never seen those magnificent halls, now abandoned and swept clear of furnishings: probably he never saw a portrait by

Quentin de la Tour, Roslin, Perroneau, Tocqué, or Danlou, to whose spirit he was most closely related. Early in 1801, again in top form, he stood at the apex of twenty years' development.

But the world had not stood still. The rude sound of drum and bugle and the shattering clang of the guillotine had severed the present world from that of his youth. The death of a King, revolution, war, and military despotism sent a new shiver of horror across Europe. In Ireland while Stuart was struggling with himself, his younger friend, Lawrence, had felt the new impulses of the times, adding dramatic emphasis to portraits that heralded the romantic sweep he would champion against the classicism of a coldly re-oriented France. In the new century Lawrence hammered home a vigorous, romantically lighted portraiture; while far off in his own corner of the world, Stuart battled his private ghosts to perfect a gentle Georgian art—unaware that the Georgian world had passed.

THE SHORT cycles of energy and prosperity, with a notable improvement in the quality of his work, always present in Stuart's life, now became more marked, each followed by a trough of recession. The death of Mrs. Washington in 1802 ended his scheme, if, indeed, it ever had been broached to her, to create the "Mount Vernon portrait"; nor was its angrily promised engraving ever issued. And, though for a short time he surpassed himself, it is disappointing to note that the average of his Philadelphia work had been declining for some years. As always, he was himself aware of the fact, for late in the nineties he began to make arbitrary shifts in his style. Elizabeth Beale Bordley, a school friend of Nelly Custis and a sparkling intimate of that now sadly decimated older Presidential circle, he painted in an effort to emulate his own English portraits. Large bland surfaces, and a background primitively suggestive of sky and foliage, recall the previous decade; larger patterns of hair and the frank texture of the brush bring to mind George Romney, whose portrait of *Mrs. Jeremiah Milles* he recently had studied in an engraving. When finishing his own portrait of *Mrs. John Bullus* he all but copied it direct.

His latitude with details in finishing portraits, once he was induced to do so, left sitters in a state of equivocal amusement; Miss Bordley dubbed her own picture "The Rural Lady," and put her reflections into verse for the friend to whom she presented it:

> You'll now receive the 'Rural Lady':
> I fear you'll think her face too shady;
> But that's the fancy of the painter,—
>   A very good one, by the bye,—
> For if the shade were any fainter,
>   The wrinkles would appear,—O fye!

For a time the new texture is constant in his work, and everywhere one is conscious of a luscious pigment, performing its tasks without loss of identity. One is conscious, too, that frequently these pictures are successful in direct proportion to their modesty. His simplest works succeed far better than more pretentious efforts at composition, and for this his patronage, which urged him to flights of fancy, must bear a share of the blame. At times he still met the brilliant Lawrence on even terms, as in his study of Mrs. Blodgett, where purity of line and strength of drawing, freely brushed, are a marvel of painter's skill. But Lawrence, like Rigaud, had the wisdom to keep small pictures simple, reserving effects of grandeur for canvases whose scale gave scope; Stuart, on the contrary, flung himself headlong into fantastic compositions on bust-sized canvases. In meretricious portraits of the Barry sisters, essays in rosy vacuity, one including an amorphous dog whose cuteness derives from Reynolds, he descended to a new low. His former occasional use of chair-backs grew into an obsession, peeking into every picture, transforming brilliant virtuoso heads into efforts at formal portraiture for which there was not space. A natural result was to further the progress of poor proportions that were destroying him. And the brilliance of some efforts, cheek by jowl with others demonstrating a marked decline, is the best indication of his chronic instability.

A FURTHER manifestation of his moral decline is that the darker side of his nature had begun to predominate. Once a lordly, austere individual, and still so to outward appearances when sober, his personal excesses had become as widely remarked as his professional abilities. Good eating and drinking were well-known indulgences, as was his addiction to snuff, taken in immoderate quantities that filled his nose, already grotesquely large and red. He was noted for "a much inflamed face, and much recklessness in his actions when excited by his drink.

In this he dealt in a wholesale way, buying his wine, brandy, and gin by the cask. On one occasion he was seen kicking a large piece of beef across the street from his house to Diehl's, his butcher, and tumbling it into his premises, as if to say such beef was not only unfit for his table but too bad to be handled. On another occasion he took a fancy to paint for Riter's tavern a finely executed sign of the King of Prussia on horseback (the painter to be unknown) . . ." Portraits of his wine merchant, Philip Wager, and his wife, worth two hundred dollars, were executed in settlement of a debt; and some who knew Stuart claimed the debt had been larger still, and the balance in favor of the merchant, when accounts were reviewed.

Exasperating though he was, and nervously ill, among patrons and friends faith in him remained secure. When his large earnings were too much committed to the purchase of his farm, Colonel Isaac Franks came forward with a loan; pasted to the back of his portrait is a paper reading, "Presented to friend Isaac Franks as a token of regard by Gilbert Stuart, Germantown, Oct. 1st 1802." And, as in Ireland, the clergy felt high regard for his erudition. Dr. William Smith, Provost of Philadelphia College, sent a touching note, not unmindful of his need for cash:

> My dear sir;—   February 28th, 1803
>   By Dr. Rush's order, I am now wholly confined to my bed-chamber, and the Doctor, my brother, and my friends who have any regard for me, or business with me, visit me here. I grow every day weaker, but, thank God, he keeps my mind sound and my intellect not much impaired.
>   I beg the pleasure and comfort of a short visit from you in a day or two. My son in two or three weeks will embark for England; I shall never see him again as I believe. He has consented to sit to you for his picture before he goes. I shall pay you cash down, as we may agree. An answer per bearer is requested, by your affectionate,
>   Wm. Smith
> Gilbert Stuart, Esq.

Though always hard pressed, this picture is another he failed to execute; and for those he did undertake, everything depended on the harassment, exhaustion, anxiety, depression, vehemence, or fury he felt when before the easel.

Larger patterns appear too, and, since his breakdown in Ireland,

Stuart never had experienced so extended a nervous attack. Its duration is attributable in part to new factors, and the deleterious effects of many secondary manifestations, as they heaped pressures on him: for now, when agitated and careless, and heedless of his own welfare, the fates pursued him. While out exercising one day on a horse, a measure taken for his health, he passed a crowd attracted by a man beating his slave. Stuart's sympathies were aroused, especially when he recognized the victim as the son-in-law of an old woman slave owned by his mother. Out of compassion he decided to buy the poor creature; but, possessed of no ready money, and asked an outrageous price of near five hundred dollars, he signed a note, and rode on. Probably he thought no more about his generous deed, until the note, which had been discounted, was presented for payment.

Inattentive, and seeing no need for haste, he dawdled. To his horror, the debt was given for collection to a sheriff, who attached his household furnishings, his pictures, and even those of his eleven-year-old son Charles! General alarm followed. Stuart found himself unable to raise the five hundred dollars, and appealing to a friend named Helmbold, found him equally unable, though willing to attempt a general subscription. Philadelphia cared nothing for the drunken and disobliging Stuart in his plight; no money was raised, and on May 12, 1801, the sheriff seized Stuart's entire furnishings. Mrs. Stuart and their nine children were taken to live with a friend; the morning of the sale, in a last desperate effort, Helmbold wrote to President Thomas Jefferson:

> [Stuart's] household furniture, little specimens of genius exhibited by his son, nay, even the last bed has been attached by the Sheriff and will in all human probability be sold this very day. . . . To you sir, as an acknowledged patron of genius I appeal in behalf of Mr. Stuart, and I assure you it is done without his knowledge. I would not have troubled you, already incessantly surrounded by the affairs of State, with a perusal of these few lines had it been in my power to have obtained the money on credit. If your excellency should think proper to consider the case of Mr. Stuart, and grant him relief . . .

The sale did not take place, and, though nothing more is recorded, it is possible that Jefferson's intercession was responsible. Dazed by the combination of circumstances, Stuart eventually re-assembled his household, and, in time, returned to work.

Then worse followed. Despite his familiarity with men of law, who should have given him sage advice, he had failed to see that his farm was properly made over to him. The money was paid out as he received it, frequently with adverse effect on his financial equilibrium; only the fact that Connecticut's payment was credited to this purchase exposed Stuart to the seizure of his furniture. But, before all was concluded, and the deed properly registered, the party from whom he purchased the property died; and among his papers and books no trace was found of the transaction. Everything for which Stuart had worked and deprived himself, a total he sadly concluded was $3,442, was *lost*. This new shock settled him into a mood of misery that haunted him forever after.

TWENTY-FIVE years of unceasing labor had earned him only a morbid disillusionment. Nothing in life had been as he hoped; every ambition had either eluded him or had its fruits plucked away. A bitter taste filled his mouth, his temples throbbed, and he ceased to do battle against destiny. Wine rather than work, despair rather than diligence, consumed his days, a reputation for indolence and needless prevarication spreading as the normal attributes of his name. Exhausted emotions and compulsive actions make no clear pattern, as, fulsome in contradictions, laughing, smirking, and leering, the balding Stuart sank deep into what modern terminology calls a nervous breakdown.

Among a hard-working populace, spiritual desolation and nervous collapse seemed the whim of an impulsive or even dangerous eccentric. Daily variations in his strength and mood, as he sought to control himself and work to mend his ruined fortunes, then through utter incapacity failed to complete or even begin what he undertook, escaped the comprehension and destroyed the sympathy of those closest to him. His uncle Joseph Anthony, aware of sharply declining fortunes, penned astringent words to John Trumbull in London: "Stuart is still here in very indigent circumstances; never works but when compelled to it by necessity, although the applications to him are so numerous that he might in a very short time make himself independent." Trumbull's reply equally lacked comprehension of the disaster that had overwhelmed Stuart:

> I am sorry to hear that Stewart still continues to be so great an enemy to himself. With his talents, poverty is a crime, as it can only be the consequence of idleness.

I expect to return to America early next spring and I shall offer my services to my fellow countrymen as a portrait painter. If I am fortunate enough to have any business offered me, my friends may be assured I will not neglect to do it. And I hope I may even serve Stuart by rousing his vanity.

Vanity, in fact, might have roused him, but adverse fortune now flowed from other external sources, and to these he showed some reaction. The effects of the government's move to Washington now were felt at Germantown, where fewer persons appeared for portraits. The eight miles seemed a deterrent; like a wounded lion, Stuart lifted his head to open a painting-room in Philadelphia, at 392 North Front Street, not far from the law office of Horace Binney. He worked there and at Germantown, traveling by coach to Philadelphia for sittings or when apprized by his wife that the domestic treasury was empty. At the halfway point a tavern was the scheduled stop, and there one day, he discovered in his pocketbook an unsuspected fifty-dollar note. "You may go on; I mean to wait for the return coach," he called impulsively to the driver.

The frequency of his punning, satirizing, snuff-taking calls on Horace Binney imply the new location was not a success; and also that after his lunchtime wine he ceased to function as an artist. However, one new sitter, the poet Mrs. Perez Morton, took interest in his fortunes, the nostalgic anecdotage of his European career, and the sad ignominy to which he had fallen. This beautiful woman's sympathy, and the comfort he derived from it, had a therapeutic effect; her sittings were prolonged, as she allowed him to employ her long, slender, tapering hands in portraits of *Mrs. William Rawle* and others. The resulting greater ease of mind brought a firmer determination to mend his fortunes, and the sad realization this no longer was possible in Philadelphia. For three years he had parried an inexorable move after the government; the delay had been costly and futile, and by the summer of 1803 it was imperative that he follow. Haltingly, he put a plan into operation. Each previous move, whether to Dublin or Philadelphia, had been undertaken alone: when prospects seemed to warrant it, he had returned, to bring out his wife and family. Except for the first flight to Dublin, when for six months he had worked alone, separations were not lengthy, which underscores how at this moment, when Mrs. Perez Morton loomed large in his recovery, he chose to send his family far away.

THE SCANDAL of boudoir intrigue has never touched Gilbert Stuart, nor have his relations with Mrs. Morton been examined. Necessary documents, the indiscreet notes on which such histories are built, are lacking, as much through his habitual distaste for writing as through any skill in concealment; both were foolish enough to make public, though veiled, declarations, for neither found it possible to observe the restrained behavior of the inveterate intriguer. Mrs. Morton's conscience fought her a hard battle for chastity: "Goodness is often known to exist without HAPPINESS; but never did the angel of felicity illumine the features of the wicked," she penned during their earliest acquaintance. Such almost Victorian morality might be credited, had she not prefaced it with the more equivocal passage:

> Next to the beauty of virtue is that of Happiness; causing the eye to speak unutterable things, the complexion to bloom, and the countenance to open and brighten, and harmonize with that look of heaven which stamps the human face divine.

—too frank and convincing a description of romantic exultation to require further argument. Noted previously for her poise and restraint, she now had reason to learn again how the complexion of even a matron will bloom, and to express herself in schoolgirl rapture, as charming as it is anomalous.

Love, awakened at middle life, is an overwhelming experience, and Sarah Wentworth Apthorp was only four years younger than Stuart, or nearly a decade older than his wife. She had married Perez Morton in 1781, and bore him five children, while establishing a fashionable reputation as a poet. Well educated, a woman of great distinction and considerable beauty, her cultivation was very noticeable to a man of Stuart's attainments. Poised, confident, moving easily in the same circles, and sympathetic to the artist's cares, two portraits of her were begun during this period of his greatest instability. Unlike the woman he had married, Mrs. Morton was able to discern his problems, and treat him with a flattery the more acceptable for its apparent sincerity. "Enough for me that *she* extends the meed, Whose approbation is applause indeed," he wrote of her, in his only known poetic effort. But beneath her glacial beauty and cultivated manner, Stuart also had learned that Sarah Wentworth Apthorp Morton concealed much sorrow. Her earthly existence was overcast by one of New England's most famous scarlet tragedies, for, as a snobbish

young bride in Boston's rarefied circles, many years before she had
brought her younger sister, Frances Theodora Apthorp, to live with
her. After the birth of two children, in the summer of 1788, her home
was rent by the appalling discovery that her sister Frances, too, had
borne a child by Perez Morton. Confident of her safety from detec-
tion, Frances afterward had boldly returned to the Morton home,
resuming clandestine relations with her sister's husband; and there,
when she was discovered, and mocking rebukes and confrontation
by her father threatened, she took poison.

Such dramatic events made a coroner's inquest mandatory, and
thus it was publicly determined that Frances had met death by deliberate suicide; nor was any hesitation felt about implicating Morton.
To avoid the public disgrace, two influential friends, John Adams
and James Bowdoin, the former Governor of Massachusetts, undertook a private investigation, the verdict of which they published in
October, 1788. Their calm effort to set aside the sworn findings of a
coroner's jury was ill-advised; heated and sarcastic comment produced
an excess of acrimony, and though Mrs. Morton pursued the noble
course of taking her husband's side throughout, the blow was a crushing one to her domestic happiness. Ardent and eloquent, Perez Morton
could bring no happiness to the woman he had married, conscious
though she remained of the other women he pleased. She bore him
three more children, but what passions she knew were reserved for
her poetry and her friendship with John Trumbull, who during the
early nineties directed her reading. Perez Morton continued a successful career in politics, until in the winter of 1802–1803 he brought
his wife to Philadelphia and Washington, where he represented the
Boston Proprietors of the Yazoo Purchase. Mrs. Morton's personal
beauty and literary gifts sparked an enormous social success.

Able to move in the same circles as Stuart, to understand his impulses, and the pressures that drove him near to ruin, Mrs. Morton
opened new worlds to a man who had grown to enjoy the Byronic
agony of his unhappiness. His own marriage was an uneasy stalemate;
his wife, like his children, lived in dread of his violent tempers, and
the views of Charlotte Stuart, too, must be explored, for her brilliant,
irresponsible husband, a handsome beau when first she yielded girlish
embraces, had led her a merry chase from intemperance and debt
through England, Ireland, and America. Rarely had she understood
the problems of his work, or the social demands attendant on it. He

went everywhere alone, and even Washington, with whom her husband's name already had found its eternal linkage, she only glimpsed as he chanced to pass through the hall. To her the charming flamboyant figure of Gilbert Stuart was reduced to different terms; he was a violent, tormented, irascible, brooding man, whom too often she received at home, drunk and unhappy, to soothe by what pathetic arts she could, until she was worn out by child-bearing. After seventeen angry years of marriage, her tenuous hold on him was shattered.

William Dunlap, who found Mrs. Morton possessed of the reputation of "an amiable domestic woman," also heard Boston's laughter because after his wine her husband spoke only of himself. Later, Dunlap discovered that an appointment book Stuart kept at Germantown contained the frequent notation, "Today quarrelled with Tom," and he observed himself that Stuart was "Undoubtedly an imprudent man, a bad husband and father," with which, as an observation of superficialities, there is no disagreement. Imprudence was at the bottom of his problems, and it proceeded from an instability which his marriage had appeared to aggravate. All brilliance and sensibility, the height of fashion when they were joined, he quickly had come undone in London, in Dublin, and again in Philadelphia. Whatever the intensity of his nature, the delights of fulfilled love never soothed for long his disordered nerves, and each catastrophe was still felt at home, where he needed to be insulated from the pain of the world.

The summer of 1803, when in the presence of Mrs. Morton, Stuart contemplated yet another removal, to Washington. Never in his professional life had he been so long in one place or one house; his habit of signing notes added to a confusion compounded of outstanding accounts from grocers and merchants and private loans from such well-wishing Philadelphians as Isaac Franks. The tangled skein of unfinished and even unpainted portraits, for many of which he had been paid, and all of which he had sincerely promised, defied unraveling. And in the midst of all, with the assistance of another friend, Edward Stow, who, like Sarah Morton, was from Massachusetts, Stuart came to an understanding with his wife. With the children she would go to Bordentown, New Jersey; he undertook to supply her with funds, to the extent of about eighty dollars a month, sent direct from Washington, where he proceeded, alone. Little more might be thought of this, did not Sarah Morton, America's outstanding woman poet, burst out in song:

Stuart, thy portrait speaks with skill divine:
Round the light Graces flows the waving line,
Expression in its finest utterance lives,
And a new language to creation gives.

Ordinary flattery was not her object; the next lines show how clearly
she had perceived the types of male sitters he painted; the second
surely Washington himself:

Each varying trait the gifted artist shows,
Wisdom majestic in his bending brows;
The warrior's open front, his eye of fire,
As when the charms of bashful youth retire;
Or patient plodding, and with wealth content,
The man of commerce counts his cent. per cent.
'Tis *character* that breaths, 'tis *soul* that twines
Round the rich canvas, trac'd in living lines,

Thoughts traceable to the sonnets of Shakespeare were prettily expressed when she came to speak of his preserving beauty.

Still on her cheek the rose of beauty blows,
Her lips full tint its breathing sweetness shows:
Like a magician's wand, thy pencil gives
Its potent charm, and every feature lives;

Nor had she failed to note how rapidly he worked, and with what
unusual effect:

Quick as the powerful eye's transcending ray
Steals its soft glance, and bids the heart obey,
Thy fine perceptions flow, by heaven design'd,
To reach the thought, and pierce the unfolded mind:
Through its swift course the rapid feeling trace,
And stamp the sovereign Passion on the face.

As her poem ran towards its end her woman's heart became more apparent in its formal tones. Sarah Morton had confided to Stuart the
unhappiness of her existence, just as she had learned of his. Their common understanding was part of a bond, and, in womanly fashion, she
felt it pressing forward for a hint of mention.

> E'en me, by no enlivened grace array'd,
> Me, born to linger in affliction's shade,
> Hast thou, kind artist, with attraction drest,
> With all that Nature in my soul express'd.

She ends with a message, and an exhortation to the artist; he must *go on,* without fear of what lay ahead. He could be consoled by his glory, the brilliance of his achievements, and sustained by the pride they must bring him. And always, he could count on her, the poet; "The Friend of Genius must remain thy friend," even though "sordid minds with impious touch" (could this be a reference to the ever-angry wife?) seek to ruin him.

> Go on—and may reward thy cares attend,
> The Friend of Genius must remain thy friend;
> Though sordid minds with impious touch presume
> To blend thy laurels with the cypress gloom,
> With tears of grief its shining leaves to fade,
> Its fair hopes withering in the cheerless shade,
> The well-earn'd meed with sparing hand deny,
> And on thy talents gaze with dubious eye.

> Genius is Sorrow's child, to Want allied,
> Consol'd by Glory and sustain'd by Pride;
> Unknown—unfelt—unsheltered—uncaress'd—
> In walks of life where worldly passions rest.

"Uncaressed—in walks of life where worldly passions rest"; what hint was Sarah Morton throwing out by these words? Stuart understood their mystery, as has no person since.

Stuart replied, and his less womanish verses are filled with fewer half-hidden secrets. Yet, clearly, he had been touched and pleased, as his casual words betrayed:

> Who would not glory in the wreath of praise,
> Which M----n offers in her polished lays?
> I feel their cheering influence at my heart,
> And more complacent I review my art;
> Yet, ah, with Poesy, that gift divine,
> Compar'd, how poor, how impotent is mine!

The comparison of their arts is driven home, like a well-enjoyed compliment, through twelve lines, when, launching on a reply to her praises of his portrait, painted of her, Stuart breaks into gentler words in a different mood.

> No wonder, if in tracing charms like thine,
> Thought and expression blend a rich design:
> 'Twas heaven itself that blended in thy face,
> The lines of Reason with the lines of Grace;
> 'Twas heaven that bade the swift idea rise,
> Paint thy soft cheek and sparkle in thine eyes:

How often have lovers' words echoed the sentiments here so lightly obscured by the pretext of a portrait? "The lines of Reason with the lines of Grace," her intelligence, sympathy, and understanding, coupled with great beauty. Stuart too ends on a personal note, reflecting on the happiness brought him by the poem, or perhaps, by similar sentiments expressed by the poet. The reference to "sordid minds with impious touch" he compresses into the single word *vulgar*, which points like an accusing finger to the same quarter.

> Mid varied scenes of life, howe'er deprest,
> This blest reflection still shall sooth my breast;
> M----n commends—and this alike outweighs
> The *vulgar's censure*, or the *vulgar's praise*.

He ends, evidently wishing to say no more, with his own reflection of a Shakespeare sonnet:

> With such distinction, wrapt in proud content,
> No more my adverse fortune I lament:
> Enough for me that *she* extends the meed,
> Whose approbation is applause indeed.

XXII

The Poetic Muse

STUART found Washington a haphazard conglomeration of half-constructed government buildings, accentuated in its disorder by a Capitol and a barnlike Presidential palace. To this center, from the far corners of the nation, came much the same collection of country worthies and their dusty henchmen that each year had flocked to Dublin. His wife sent away, free from nine children, the artist proceeded to find bachelor lodgings. Then, at the corner of F Street, near Seventh, he opened a painting-room, filled with his unfinished canvases brought from Philadelphia and the second life-portrait of George Washington, calculated to exert its attraction. Doubtless he hoped for the best; quietness would sooth and relax him, release from accumulated tensions would have its tonic effect, and he could count on the Friend of Genius.

A part of his calculations proved accurate, for immediately he became the fashion; portraits in a heightened and perfected Rigaud manner came from his easel, and that satisfaction, against the stimulating background of a new city, and its gay camping-out atmosphere, eased his emotional tensions. For the moment a new vigor came to him; but every stimulus now had the further effect of fatiguing him, while he grew more irascible and careless in dress. He forgot himself only in the concentration of his work, and when he did, any interruption infuriated him; he showed himself ill-tempered, angry, and impatient, and if unable to surmount the forces that drove him from the easel, he refused to finish.

Prince Jerome Bonaparte, spoiled youngest brother of the newly crowned French Emperor, was just such a party to infuriate him. Probably at the recommendation of the Marquis D'Yrujo, a Spanish Minister who like his predecessor found consolation in marriage with an American heiress, the adenoidal Prince Jerome arrived with his own eighteen-year-old Baltimore bride, Elizabeth Patterson. Himself only nineteen, young Bonaparte required the sponsorship of Spain, for vast sums melted at an alarming rate, as the couple paraded America on an extended honeymoon, scandalizing society by the brevity of modes Prince Jerome imported for his wife from Paris. "All that Madame Bonaparte wore I could put in my pocket," wrote one who saw her at a ball, and her animal pleasure in herself is equally attested by the bare-breasted portrait of her later painted in England by Vigée-Lebrun. Like Philadelphia and Baltimore, Washington derived a season's diversion from adoring this childish couple, while a philosopher President penned avuncular recommendations of the Patterson family to Napoleon. Well he might, for the Princely darling of social America remained among them contrary to his imperious brother's wish, and had married without the Emperor's consent. The recipient of Jefferson's epistolary effort was too preoccupied to reply. After his coronation at Notre Dame, Napoleon turned his back on a glowering Britain to defeat the combined armies of Russia and Austria at Austerlitz. When he had rested, Napoleon declared his brother's marriage invalid, and informed an unhappy Pope it had been performed not by the Bishop of Maryland but an ignorant Spanish priest. Meanwhile, young love knew its delights, and the French Minister, forbidden to advance Prince Jerome funds, found his cards played by a more accommodating D'Yrujo, who conducted the star-crossed lovers to Stuart's painting-room.

Young women, and their early ripeness, often before had evoked responsive portraiture from the aging cynic, but the effect of Elizabeth Patterson on Stuart was instantaneous; never before had he ventured to paint three heads on one canvas—an idealized front-face, deep-cut Grecian profile, and tip-tilted three-quarter face, each conveying the clear girlish skin, pink lips, white neck, and curiously elfin eyes of his radiant subject. His sketches delighted him, and were finished not as portraits, with the addition of three separate draperies, but to represent angelic heads floating in cloudy heavens; the very last Royal Academy he had seen, in 1787, included a canvas of five such little childish heads by Reynolds. After this most eloquent of compliments, and a silken show of courtesy, Stuart found the arrogant French Prince delighted him less. Soon Jerome suggested his wife might have been provided clothing, convulsing the artist's delicate emotional balance. "That you can buy at any milliner's shop in the city," he barked; and, having revealed himself the captious cross-grained fellow he was, he refused to touch Bonaparte's picture further, or deliver *either*.

A SUCCESSION of incidents such as would ruin a lesser man left unaffected the steady flow of sitters to his room; not that every portrait failed to show some mark of his state. Unmoved by the fine intellectual head of Vice-President Aaron Burr despite that gentleman's previous courtesies to him in providing the paid services of Vanderlyn in Philadelphia, he merely fell back on the resources of style. The Secretary of the Treasury, Albert Gallatin, Swiss by birth, and speaking with a colorful trace of his native tongue, became more of a success, only because his bald dome induced the artist to try for its luster. James Madison, Secretary of State, seemed strangely vacuous when Stuart had done with him; but an ebullient Dolly Madison shook the roguish artist to responsive performance. Eyes narrowed with suppressed mirth, her mouth mutely grinning, though she did not inspire his greatest brilliance the opaque expression and flaccid surfaces of too many recent efforts were overcome. Chattering as sweetly by letter as in person, Dolly Madison noted, June 3, 1804: "Stuart has taken an admirable likeness of Mr. Madison; both his and mine are finished." Two days later, she added: ". . . Dr. & Mrs. Thornton sat yesterday for the last time to Stuart," but these pictures, when he came to finish them, suffered excessively from nerves, lack of interest, and ennui.

The delightful Dolly Madison was among guests at Dr. Thornton's when Stuart came to dinner with the Secretary of State, and there, too, he discovered Charles Willson Peale, an attentive guest as Mrs. Thornton played to the assembled company, singing songs in her native French, then English and Italian. Peale called at Stuart's painting-room, and with a slyness his visitor did not relish, Stuart enquired whether he had a good room for painting in Philadelphia, intimating he might return, to paint a picture improving on Peale's self-portraits:

I told him I had not a good room, nor was it worth while for him to take it. He replied that he believed he would paint a better portrait of me than yet was done—that we do not know our own faces, alluding, I suppose that altho' . . . [I] had often essayed to take my own likeness, yet that done by another artist would give a more faithful expression.

I thanked him for [the] intention, and passed it by . . .

Though he still appeared to dawdle, and his lunchtime wine prevented afternoon work, the quantities of pictures he executed were burdensome. To sitters it was quite clear that he was ill; that summer Dolly Madison heard from a friend: "I can tell you nothing new. Stuart is all the rage. He is almost worked to death and everyone is afraid they will be the last to be finished. He says: 'The ladies come to me and say: *Dear* Mr. Stuart, I'm afraid you must be very tired. You really must rest when *my* picture is done.'" And Peale noted variations in quality:

This morning in viewing Mr. Gabriel Stuwarts paintings, amongst them was a very excellent portrait of the Marquis Casa d'Yrujo (Minister of Spain) and his lady. The latter was a very handsome picture but not so strikingly like as that of the Marquis.

By fits and starts, at best, he worked on, a resentful tyrant, ever prepared to hurl studied incivilities. A lady who broke into his concentration by rising from her seat, to look over his shoulder, was given a text from St. James: "A man beholdeth his natural face in a glass and goeth his way, and straightway forgetteth what manner of man he was"; but voluble amiability quickly vanished. "Excuse me, madam, I cannot paint by direction," he announced, as he strode across the room, rang for his servant, and ordered the picture taken away. Floods of tears could not save it. He painted a rich but unlovely wife twice without pleasing her husband. The request that he try a third time was dodged with a hint of Elizabethan bawdiness, Stuart observing wives seldom were pleased with pictures of their husbands, unless they were living ones; the cause he advanced for husbands being as seldom pleased was considered too colorful for preservation. Its rudeness found the men bawling at each other, until Stuart jumped from his chair, laid down his palette, and took a large pinch of snuff: "What damned business is this of a portrait painter," he exclaimed, "you bring him a potato and expect he will paint you a peach!"

NOR HAD personal pressures on him abated. A censorious wife was heard loud and clear from afar. Her needs, and those of the children, added to his own requirements in Washington, and debts that awaited payment in Philadelphia. To meet demands, his present income continued to be augmented by the sale of bust-portraits of Washington; after waiting three years, the American Philosophical Society had received its replica shortly before he quit Philadelphia; another, he brought with him to Washington, where it was quickly sold to Colonel John Tayloe for the famous Octagon House, designed for him by Dr. Thornton. William Rawle and Edward Pennington, in whose families he found sitters, purchased Washingtons, and yet his money melted away, while his wife's angry attacks pursued him.

The previous Christmas, Edward Stow, struggling to untangle Stuart's Philadelphia debts, received a note from the fourteen-year-old son, Charles Gilbert:

> [Dec. 22, 1803]
> Send me the gun as soon as you can, as vacation has commenced, which is only one week, and the greatest service you can do me would be to send me some powder and shot, be it ever so little, as Mama's circumstances are such at present as to be unable to let me have any money.

Still without funds, after Christmas Mrs. Stuart accused Stow of withholding her money, and the angry charge rang through to Washington, where it was heard with a towering indignation; "a being so base and impudent" Stuart termed her, his tone reverberating with rage:

> Nothing could give me more surprise and concern than to find that any censure should reach so sincere and disinterested a friend as I have on all occasions found you. But I feel the utmost indignation that should be found a being so base and impudent as to attack the character of my friend in the most tender point, and to make me an instrument for such a purpose. Truth, my dear friend, is simple but powerful, and I know no way to repel so infamous an attack as by stating it.
>
> First then—I never did until the present moment direct to you or to your care any letters containing money for the use of my family nor for any other purpose. . . . That there were three letters, of which I obtained no account, containing money—forty dollars each. They were directed to Mrs. Stuart at Bordentown, but they never

reached the post office, which is about two miles from my lodging. The weather being severe, the idle rascal who I had entrusted them to had concealed them in his own box. Thus, sir, I hope I have removed entirely anything that could give either of us uneasiness.

One hundred dollars were enclosed, and Stuart promised to send another hundred the day following, and still another the day after that, to return a loan from Isaac Franks, and meet a grocery bill, long overdue:

> This sum is more than sufficient for these debts, as I must insist on the deducting one hundred dollars, which is the price of the head of Washington which has been spoiled by Franks making a hole through it. Should any difficulty arise on the subject, Mr. Dallas or Mr. Hopkinson will, I am certain, give you their advice cheerfully on my account. I must beg you to make my best thanks to Messrs. Boller and Jordan for their kind indulgence to me.

Through the spring Stow arranged what was requested of him, but found his reports to Washington unanswered. Reply to a repeated letter was splendid and specious:

> Dear Sir   Washington 15th of May, 1804
>   I received yours of the first of May. I did not answer it because I am unwilling to give you the trouble and expense of an idle letter. Allow me now however to express my warmest thanks for the prompt and kind manner with which you performed my request.
>   I beg premission to subscribe myself with unshaken extreme affection your most obliged
>   Friend
>   Gilbert Stuart

In fact, the artist's mind was elsewhere, for Sarah Morton's loyalty to an erring husband, her habit of self-examination, and her religious views had induced an acute sense of guilt. She herself described "the early morning and late evening, given to the question of her own faults, many mistakes, and continued afflictions," which must have become centered about Stuart. These uncertainties had made their relations less a comfort and more of a continued strain than they might have been; and now, after two years, Perez Morton had wound up his business in Washington. Accompanied by his wife, he returned to Boston; filled with anxieties, love of family, and pride in her husband, Mrs. Morton departed, not without wishing Stuart to follow. Alone in the Capital and now with nothing to hide, Stuart was joined by his son Charles Gilbert, to whom he assigned the duties of assistant and apprentice.

UNEXPECTEDLY, departure of the Friend of Genius lessened the strain on Stuart. As personal torments perceptibly eased, his natural resilience again worked magically. He had painted pictures that were pretentious and slipshod and others lacking even the perception frequently distinguishing his least-inspired works. Now, again, he caught hold of himself, and soon was finding new compositions, new angles, and even, strange for him, new effects of light. A more romantic atmosphere made a tentative appearance; Anne Allston became a sumptuous, well-knit example of his Rigaud manner, and a picture of Congressman John Randolph, built around a hand from Reynolds' *Mrs. Abington,* was enlivened by a new spirit. Much the same Byronic mood found its way into a similar composition surrounding the distinctly romantic head of Mrs. Lawrence Lewis, who before her marriage was Nelly Parke Custis, Martha Washington's granddaughter. His art had begun to move ahead once more, and the returned sympathy of these works marks the start of a healthier phase.

Lack of any resident model forced him to depend more heavily, in Washington, on the person who gave sittings. Figures were more fully developed from the subject at sittings, amply verified by the rough sketch left from his abortive sessions with Prince Jerome; a head, not yet completed, already has a well-characterized body. His women lose the sameness of that familiar short-necked, high- and full-bosomed figure. The Marchioness d'Yrujo is portrayed as her own remarkable mound of flesh, an uncomeliness new to the tradition of English portraiture, which distinctly foreshadows a native American school. The flimsy tissues other of his female sitters wore over corsetless bodies played a part in awakening him; obvious delight is present in his painting of the proffered bosoms in their clutter of satins and laces, and equally often he conveys the weight of a bust pressing through its meager covering. In portraits of Mrs. Thomas Bartlett and Mrs. Richard Cutts, he also roused himself to more dashing arrangements of the now familiar curtain and drape. The decorative element that only gradually had become a part of his work began to predominate in portraits of women.

"So! You have come to take off a few heads of the members of Congress, and give them a brush, which is much wanting," he bantered, when with his son Rembrandt, Charles Willson Peale appeared again in the summer of 1805. ". . . We spent the greater part of this morning in Mr. Stuart's painting room; Rembrandt is not discouraged by what he saw there," Peale categorically noted. The egotism of the one painter was very well matched by that of the other. An energetic, enthusiastic organizer, earnest bumbling old Peale, with his clutter of ideas and projects and his enormous seriousness, never failed to strike Stuart as faintly ridiculous; for his part, Peale judged Stuart "an indolent thoughtless being." Cheerfully, and with an unflattering joviality, Stuart explained technical procedures to young Rembrandt Peale, nor could he miss sight of the grave-demeanored father, who, hovering about, bore the air of an apostle observing the mysteries. To him every gesture was implicit with profound significance: "I have observed that Mr. Stuart used to rub his pictures with a silk handerchief," Peale wrote of a habit probably acquired through contact with Irish patrons. "This might give a small polish to the surface if wax was in his pigments. This may be deserving of experiment."

The patronizing offer made the previous year of a portrait by which posterity could remember Peale had acted like a challenge. Working in tandem with his son Rembrandt, Peale now exerted himself on a picture of Stuart, to take its place in his collection of distinguished men exhibited in Philadelphia. Vain Stuart pulled his few black hairs forward over his brow where they hung in disorder, while he volubly entertained his painters. His pleasure in being *peeled* was diminished by the shock of their portrait, for when he looked he found an ogre fixed to their canvas. The handsome, distinguished youth who in London had suggested the swagger of King Charles had become a hard-faced, bulbous, red extrovert, time-ravaged and replete with uncouth, leering expression. Accustomed to this less-scrubbed view of his father, young Charles Gilbert volunteered it was the best likeness he had seen; but the sitter pretended no pleasure he did not feel, laughing at the image of "an awkward clown." One suspects he was further annoyed to find this highly unflattering work celebrated in *The Portfolio*, by a poem, presumably from the pen of the distant Sarah Morton:

To Mr. G. Stuart

Though thy fame like a current extend its force
No less pure, though still deeper and wider its course;
Yet a debt still remains to posterity due,
As thy name filled the ear that thy form should the view—

Now 'tis done—and each lover of nature and art
Will ever revere what so touches his heart;
Nor shall Fame its proportion to Peale e'er deny,
For united with Stuart's it can never die.

"Each lover of nature and art, Will ever revere what so touches his heart"; like every utterance of Sarah Morton's, this too contained veiled hints; it was *nature*, not art, that had touched her heart.

PEALE's Philadelphia museum and other institutions of the sort were becoming places of fashionable congregation, where people met in an atmosphere polite, entertaining, and instructive. It was essentially an extension of the artist's painting-room, with its visitors, but arranged so that troublesome interruptions of productivity were kept at minimum. The idea, centering on a man of knowledge and artistic achievement, appealed to Stuart's resurgent egotism; and the comparison of Peale's crude portrait with his own works possibly suggested the formation of a similar collection of historical portraits. What could be more natural? The great figures of the age had passed before his easel: he had only to retain replicas of their likenesses. Already he had painted three Presidents, and a fourth, for whom that elevation was hidden still in the recesses of time. More than Peale, Stuart was creating the unique visual record of United States history.

Despite his vogue, he felt dissatisfied with Washington, where again he had found the seasonal element of short Congressional sessions; and pressures natural in his relations with the Friend of Genius urged him to follow north, where, he recollected, Copley had established the greatest of previous American portrait practices. He listened now with increased interest to entreaties from Senator Mason of Massachusetts, who held out promises. Probably Sarah Morton, with her kinship through the fabric of Boston, could be an equally significant contact. And further convenient reasons were found in his mother and sister, who after long exile in Halifax had returned to Massachusetts: Henry Newton, his sister Anne's husband, had died in 1802, and the following year, with the artist's mother the elder Mrs. Gilbert Stuart, and her own children, Anne Stuart Newton had opened a school for girls at Medford.

To toy with the idea of moving north, where he would find fresh patronage and fresh credit, was increasingly attractive. Would he go to Boston or remain in Washington to found a museum? Not a simple museum, of course, for a man of his soaring intellect could present *all* fields of learning; what did Peale know of books, or men of literature with whom he had rubbed shoulders in London and Dublin? Had there not been a balloon ascent at Dublin, and had he not a classic turn? The age was one of classic terminology—grandiose ideals were worthy of classic names: a house where all the arts were represented was naturally a home of the Muses, or *museum*. Grecian standards of pure knowledge were what it pleased Stuart to contemplate: the sciences mingled with the arts in a new Athens on American shores; an *Athenaeum*, or a mere *Temple*—it was delightful to contemplate. While he talked with Senator Mason concerning his future in Boston, he divulged to the elite of Washington what more elevated project he was embarked upon. His confusion was quite apparent;

"He . . . says he means to go directly to Boston," wrote Dolly Madison, ever anxious to report what she knew, "but that is what he has been saying these two years; being a man of genius of course [he] does things differently from other people. I hope he will be here next winter as he has bought a square to build a 'Temple' upon . . ."

PART THREE

The Mask Is Lifted

XXIII

A Squalid Meandering

S TUART had never recovered from the nervous condition that had seized him in Philadelphia. How far he was relieved from it at any subsequent moment in his history requires a fine point of judgment, for never again was he really normal. An equally delicate question is to what extent he now wandered lost among his own fantasies; for his disintegration had been more grave than at first was seen. Though he was able to work again, with considerable effect, his imagination was wildly out of control. Did he really consider himself capable of building an Athenaeum, such as he proposed? Was this a flight of fancy from which eventually, on some devastating gray morning, he recovered? Or did he deliberately spread a fallacy behind which to indulge in the land speculation so prevalent in the new capital? Had he actually gone so far as to purchase land, one of the carefully surveyed "squares" into which the city was divided —a transaction of which the Washington Deed Registers are innocent? Or had he entertained himself and the President's wife by inventing a lie? We shall perhaps never know, and are permitted to doubt whether Stuart himself, the first to be persuaded of every tale he told, was any more certain.

His existence had settled down to a course of lies and hypocrisies, each eventually leading him to some act of outright dishonesty. No longer sure of the difference between right and wrong and impatient of such awkward distinctions, he reeled about, dazed but smiling, taking his snuff, and playing on the sympathies of those who recognized his undoubted genius. Sober, he was an alliance of anxieties and nervous compulsions; drunk, he lacked all judgment, all self-control. He was a victim of his own frailties, and a bully, a liar, and a cheat. Florid of face, a little careworn and dusty-looking, a bit thin on top, his nose packed with quantities of brown snuff from the ever-present box, he threaded his devious path to oblivion. His humor and personal charm were debased to the level of deception, carefully employed for dishonest motives, and behind the still-sparkling façade of the charm stood the grim fact of moral collapse.

From an artist of genius, the greatest head-painter of his day, he had degenerated into an unscrupulous adventurer, whose most devious side was reserved for the Presidents of his native land. Washington never had received anything but a replica of his second portrait. Far away in Massachusetts, retired in defeat, John Adams mused, "Stuart has taken a portrait of me, and intends, I suppose, to have it engraved. In that case—but nothing can be depended on. His health and motives are so precarious. This is a Bagatelle; I can't be serious about it." News of Stuart's latest triumphs at Washington caused Adams sulkily to repeat himself: "I know nothing of Stuart's success. I sat to him, at the request of our Massachusetts Legislature; but have never seen anything of the picture but the first sketch." Adams had not mentioned, as he might, that Stuart had failed equally to deliver the portrait of his wife; but then, the second President had lost no money, which kept him ahead of his successor.

To Thomas Jefferson the artist was obliged for that which he found most offensive of all, a great favor done him in 1801, when Jefferson had prevented the sale of his household furnishings. Earlier Jefferson had sat to Stuart as Vice-President in the Adams administration, while the government was still located in Philadelphia. The greater surprise would have been if he had not, for years before, in London, Jefferson had been witness to Stuart's first great vogue, and had modestly been painted in an imitative manner by Mather Brown. John Adams did the same, and the two men exchanged pictures. When opportunity presented itself in Philadelphia, Jefferson naturally wanted a portrait by Stuart himself, and the payment was recorded in his account book; one hundred dollars, paid May 12, 1800. No picture ever was received by Jefferson. The fact that an engraving of it appeared in London the August following (1801) leads to speculation that Stuart carried into operation at least part of his advertised scheme. How he did so remains a mystery; had he, with his usual lack of honor, sent Jefferson's portrait to London to be engraved, without the owner's knowledge? Whatever the answer to this neat question of propriety, it is dwarfed by the revelation that when he moved to Washington, Stuart sold this picture, *paid for by Jefferson*, to Senator Smith of Pennsylvania! A receipt, in his own script, has been preserved:

> Received 22 Dec. 1803 from S. Smith fifty Dollars in part payment of a Portrait of Mr. Thomas Jefferson to be delivered in six weeks.
>
> Gilbert Stuart

In legal terms, Stuart was guilty of fraudulent conversion; he had sold property that belonged to President Jefferson, and the ignoble fact to be faced is that it had become an habitual practice.

The full-length portrait of Washington, seen at Germantown by the retiring first President, New Year's day of 1797, had been ordered by General Charles Cotesworth Pinckney. In behalf of General Pinckney, Timothy Pickering paid Stuart from State Department funds on July 22, 1797: the picture remained with Stuart, pending instructions for shipment to Paris. In the confusion surrounding the French Directory's refusal to receive General Pinckney, Stuart profited; he sold this work a second time, to Gardiner Baker, proprietor of a New York museum. Seven years later General Pinckney recollected his order and the payment made in his behalf; he pressed the artist, who, impatient with just demands, failed to reply. Timothy Pickering then wrote most explicitly to William Loughton Smith:

> City of Washington, Decr. 13, 1804
>
> Dear Sir,
>
> You will recollect that General Pinckney, prior to his going to France, engaged Stuart to paint for him a full length portrait of Gen. Washington. Gen. P. desired me to pay the price, $500. for which he has Stuart's receipt. The General not being received by the French Directory, the picture was not sent to him—indeed I never saw it. But it lays in my mind that you went to Stuart's when in Germantown, on purpose to see it; and I presume the portrait was actually made. General Pinckney has lately written to Mr. Lowndes on the subject, stating that he has *repeatedly* written to Stuart on the subject, but cannot even get an *answer;* & therefore desires Mr. Lowndes & me to call on him, and endeavor to obtain the picture . . .
>
> I am dear Sir
Your obedt. servt.
T. Pickering

Brave men who risked the trumpet of Stuart's wrath, they failed in their purpose; and perhaps they too, like so many others, came away sympathizing with the artist's proud sorrows. Despite a trail of bad faith, deceit, and dishonesty, there were still persons who were willing to believe in him, and who made an effort to assist the strange, feverish man they found. These people fared less well at Stuart's hands than his outright enemies, for they were the objects of his tricks of confidence. He had grown fond of his treacheries and dazzled everyone as he deceived them by telling his own story with persuasive intensity. An extraordinary instance had developed around the portrait of Joseph Priestley, which probably he never had intended to finish. The canvas, abandoned seven years before, when Stuart fled the yellow fever epidemic in Philadelphia, had been carried to Washington; Priestley died, and the Philosophical Society, for which the picture was destined, became more anxious to possess his image. John Vaughan, one of the portrait's two sponsors, wrote to the other, Jonathan Williams:

> Dear Sir,   Phila. Feb. 9, 1804
> I received your letter and in consequence prepared to go to Bordentown, when I learned through D. Stephens that Mr. Stewart was at Washington. I have just written a *friendly* pressing expostulating letter and got D. Stephens to enclose it to Dr. Thornton, with a view to get the portrait, and have offered even to take it unfinished . . .
>   Yours in haste,
>   John Vaughan
> as soon as I hear, I will write again

Other parties became involved too, and when he recorded his own mission in his diary, Charles Willson Peale obviously did not suspect Stuart had tricked him into carrying an expedient account back to Philadelphia:

> His picture of Dr. Priestley for the Philosophical Society very like, though quite an unfinished picture . . . I was desired by several of the members of the society to urge Mr. Stewart to finish this picture, and he promised me he would have it done in about 3 weeks . . . [he wished] to have a print made by Edwin from it, and had stipulated to give the society their choice of purchasing a print for each resident member, and such number as they might to present to the societies in Europe with whom our society holds correspondence— and that after this the plate to be the property of Edwin and himself, to make what profit they would with the sale to strangers.

His engaging optimism over an engraving was Stuart's inspiration of the moment, designed to assist his deception. Another year passed, and eventually Dr. Thornton, to whom Vaughan had written, gave bond for the artist's performance; a benevolent interest that suffered extinction when Stuart blithely defaulted. He preferred to sell his pictures twice, and the portrait, hastily completed, was carried away by T. B. Barclay of Liverpool, an English relative of the subject.

LIVING by his wits, no longer interested in the steady flow of work, with which his experience had proved him incapable of dealing, in his fiftieth year Gilbert Stuart was content to proceed from one mire of deceit to another. The intensity of his personality and the force of each lie, backed by his international reputation as an artist, made him a confidence trickster of remarkable gifts; and by the early part of 1805, his sheer love of deceit had wound him into the depths of a hundred dishonorable circumstances. Exulting in them as though they were triumphs of ingenuity, he also felt an overwhelming terror of being found out. Now, as in London and Dublin, he was so awkwardly involved he had lost his way, and the only relief he could envision was flight.

Such a plan appealed to him; and as he considered the means by which he could escape the many claims on him—claims of honor and duty and integrity, those qualities he finally had eschewed entirely—certain facts stood out to form a useful pattern. Mrs. Morton had urged him to follow her to Boston. That had seemed impossible, until, on Christmas day, 1804, former Senator Mason of Massachusetts, a man of considerable wealth and prominence and a member of Sarah Morton's circle, had arrived in Washington with his family. Though he could not prolong his visit more than a fortnight, the Senator had the temerity to ask Stuart for portraits of two daughters. Further, by enlisting the assistance of Joseph Russell and Dr. William Eustis, he mounted pressures that induced Stuart to complete both heads before the Senator's departure, on January third. An achievement of no small order, it was further enhanced by an exceptional likeness of Miriam Mason, whose heaven-bent eyes exerted that special charm Stuart found in young girls. The Senator was highly gratified, and wishing portraits of himself and his wife, he invited Stuart to Boston, where he promised to find other patronage.

What the Senator proposed probably was only a visit, the sort of reconnaissance in force that would allow Stuart to survey Copley's pre-revolutionary hunting ground. To Stuart, the matter was different; were he to go, he would use Senator Mason's services more fully than they had been offered. To Sarah Morton this invitation, extended by a friend and member of her circle, had an especial fascination. Her earlier liaison with the artist had escaped notice. Now returned to the solemn respectability of her life in Boston, where as a living martyr to her husband she had the most sympathetic position any community could offer, she yearned again for the thrill of adventure. Her gentle hand, deftly suggesting, arranging, and informing, can be detected behind the succession of events that preceded Stuart's flight to rejoin her. President Jefferson had just appointed her friend, James Bowdoin, Ambassador to Spain. This old member of the Morton inner circle who in 1788, with John Adams, had attempted to spare Perez Morton the odium of his turpitude, suddenly desired to carry to Madrid portraits of the President and Secretary of State. So clearly a parallel to Pinckney's proposed gesture of 1797, then again attracting attention, surely it was Sarah Morton who acted as its catalytic agent. On March 25, 1805, Bowdoin contacted Henry Dearborn, the Secretary of War:

> I shall be much obliged to you to procure me the portraits of Mr. Jefferson and Mr. Madison if a good painter can be found in Washington, and they should be willing to take the trouble of sittings therefore. I should like to have them done by Stuart, could he be induced to execute them, as well he is able. They need not be framed, as I can procure more fashionable frames and better frames in Europe. Please to let yᵉ pictures be half length and of a size to match each other . . .

Duly transmitted to Stuart, Bowdoin's order became both an embarrassment and a facility to further treachery. Though vacuous, his head of James Madison, painted the previous year, would provide the basis for a half-length; but of President Jefferson he now possessed no likeness, and that would require delicate handling, lest Jefferson demand an explanation of his failure to deliver the earlier portrait. An experienced and persuasive liar, Stuart blithely informed the President he was dissatisfied with the first picture: "and [he] therefore begged me to sit again, and he drew another which he was to deliver to me instead of the first, but begged permission to keep it until he could get an engraving from it." Jefferson therefore was not told

Stuart's real motivation was the Bowdoin order, though it was executed for the man he had just appointed Ambassador to Spain, and
was transmitted to Stuart by Henry Dearborn, a member of the
cabinet: and to top this chicanery, after proposing a new portrait to
the President, to replace that done earlier, Stuart did not deliver this
picture either, on the same hoary grounds of desiring an engraving!

By June 27th, Henry Dearborn in Washington reported to Boston:
"I engaged Mr. Stuart to take a half-length portrait of the President
of the U. S. and one of Mr. Madison. Mr. Stuart has nearly completed them . . ." But dealing with *Stuart* was not so simple! To
obtain the sittings, he promised Jefferson this new 25 by 30 inch
study, painted from life; neither Jefferson nor Bowdoin would see
their pictures too soon. And at these same sittings, in June, Jefferson
asked Stuart to do a medallion head, simulating low relief, of the sort
he had seen decorating French salons. A rare effort at profile, done
in a manner he had never before essayed, in an aqueous medium on
paper, Stuart achieved the desired result to perfection, and Jefferson
paid him again, as though it were a formal portrait:

> June 18, 1805
> Mr. Jefferson presents his compliments to Mr. Stewart, and begs leave
> to send him the enclosed for the trouble he gave him in taking the
> head à la antique. Mr. Stewart seemed to contemplate having an en-
> graving made either from that or the first portrait; he is free to use
> either the one or the other at his choice; the one not proposed to be
> used I will be glad to receive at Mr. Stewart's convenience; the other
> when he shall be done with it.

How DELIBERATE were Stuart's acts shall always remain open to
question. Circumspection demands the acceptance of an area of doubt,
and the assertion that he was an improviser, reacting to events, always
eager to profit from another's gentility or default—finding advantage
where it was provided, with but little thought for the morrow. His
final decision to accept Senator Mason's invitation to come to Boston
can hardly be understood in any other context. It was a lure, at a
moment when his duplicity, in Philadelphia and Washington, had
created an atmosphere of falsehood and stratagem in which he was
suffocating. For how long could he deceive President Jefferson, General Pinckney, the Philosophical Society, and all those other worthy
and gullible persons he had made his dupes, without each discovering

what he had done with the others? How many of his sordid triumphs of double-dealing were so successful they have defied, to this day, the then too-evident danger of their discovery? Where in Europe he had given himself the character of a coxcomb, now he persisted, only half-willfully perhaps, but by inclination and for its unnatural joy, in the role of unscrupulous adventurer, plucking pennies by pathetically dishonest practices, while those greater rewards that could so easily have answered to his superb skills went begging.

Sometime in the late winter he informed Senator Mason of his resolve to come north. He also made a visit to his family at Bordentown. His only known interview with his wife during eighteen months of intense bitterness, this call was the occasion for a portrait of Anne Pennington, whose awkwardly constructed likeness, assembled without reference to his usual engraved sources, he inscribed, "G. Stuart, Bordentown, 1805." Aside from obvious paternal affection for a succession of little daughters, doubtless the new adventure he had determined on and its complications made this visit necessary; but if he hoped for any amelioration of domestic circumstances, the only certainty he brought back from Bordentown was that he would travel to Boston unaccompanied.

Meanwhile, John Trumbull had returned from England, and early in 1805 he appeared with his English wife in Boston, where he was received with kindness and cordiality. Soon, however, he observed that whenever he alluded to the idea of settling, as a portrait-painter, "a cloud seemed to pass over and chill the conversation. I could not, for a long time, account for this, but at length I learned that my old friend and fellow student, Stewart . . . had lately received an invitation from Mr. Jonathan Mason . . . to come and settle in Boston. He had been promised the patronage of Mr. Mason and his friends, who were the rich and fashionable of the city, and Mr. Stewart having accordingly accepted the invitation, was preparing to quit Washington and to establish himself in Boston. This was enough. Boston was then a small town . . . I therefore returned immediately to New York . . ." But though Boston preparations to receive Stuart had advanced to the point of discouraging Trumbull, in Washington Charles Willson Peale, who passed most of the morning of June 11, 1805, in Stuart's painting-room, came away with no hint that his host was on the brink of departure. It would not do to draw the Philosophical Society down on him while he was in transit!

The careful preparation that had preceded earlier flights now became obvious. Until the last moment, no one in Washington was told. He would bring with him to Boston the two unfinished half-lengths of President Jefferson and James Madison. These, when completed after his arrival, were to be his showpieces in the new city, and would provide necessary coin. Matters were accordingly arranged with Dearborn, who, on June 27, 1805, wrote to Thomas L. Winthrop in Boston: "Mr. Stuart . . . will take [the two uncompleted portraits] . . . with his other effects to Boston, and when completed there will deliver them to you, to be forwarded to Mr. Bowdoin, and as Mr. Bowdoin requested me to draw on you for the expense of the two portraits, I shall take the liberty of requesting you to pay Mr. Stuart the amount of his bills when presented." For further insurance, Stuart also carried with him to Boston the unfinished portraits of Senator Mason's daughters, which, after completion, would add further to the capital he required to bridge the gap.

Haste and lack of interest are apparent in the last of those works he finished in the sultry heat of July, before abandoning Washington. Among them, Mrs. Anthony Merry, wife of the British Envoy, held a heterogeneous dog whose obscene grin mocked its mistress. Awkward and ill-considered, it was delivered, together with the Envoy's own picture, and payment for both ($200) was graciously dispatched:

> Mr. Merry presents his compliments to Mr. Stuart, and begs leave to accompany the enclosed notes with his acknowledgements, for the valuable portrait of Mrs. Merry, on which Mr. Stuart has had the goodness to exert his known talents with so much success.
> Washington, July 3d, 1805

Among final courtesies, he sent a brief note to Mrs. Cutts, Dolly Madison's sister, with a humorous reference to her portrait's snapping baroque curtain, whose outline he thought resembled his own profile. His joke was not flattery, for, suggestive really of a purse-lipped satyr, the curtain resembled more closely Stuart's warped psyche than his crumbling Georgian exterior. This dominating darker side of his nature was defeating him utterly, for, in an absurdity of unnecessary flight, he was about to waltz himself off the center of the world's stage. A rash, improvident act, it served to demonstrate that he had grown so enamored of running his head against walls, at last he was building them expressly for the purpose.

XXIV

The Long Twilight

M R. STUART, the celebrated painter, who has immortalized his fame by his masterly portrait of our deceased Washington, is now on a visit to this town from Philadelphia," noted Boston's *Columbian Centinel*, July 31, 1805. Preparations for this "visit" had been admirable; he roused himself to an exertion of the charm that elsewhere had served him so well, and began painting in rooms at Champotin's Hotel, in Summer Street. Many reunions awaited him, though that with his aged mother, now living with his sister, Anne Newton, both of whom he had not seen since departing Newport, thirty years before, has escaped record. It is unfortunate that it did, for much about the man would have been learned, and one is curious to know by what shuffling prevarications he explained the absence of his English wife and children, whom his mother never had seen. Benjamin Waterhouse, by then a distinguished physician and Harvard Professor, after a quarter of a century welcomed the friend of his youth, whom he was shocked to find "a much-altered man. He had, it seemed, relished Irish society, particularly their conviviality . . ." and to those imbibing habits, strong as they were, Waterhouse chastely ascribed the horrifying degeneration his professional eye saw. His loyalty never was more touchingly expressed.

Mornings were passed in the painting-room arranged at Stuart's hotel, "and too much of the remainder of the day" at the dinner table. Quickly overwhelmed by applications and permanently incapable of organizing studio assistance, he soon heard murmurings of disapproval over accumulations of unfinished pictures. But those who complained were the more fortunate, for others waited months before they were granted the appointment at which he began to sketch their heads. In these less frantic times, devoted to slow routine, his nervous disabilities were eased, and Charles Fraser, who looked in on his painting-room, came away with the impression he was "painting very industriously . . . [with] all the beauty and talents of Boston under his pencil."

The calm of these first months, his industry, and his genial charm to sitters, shrouded but did not conceal his talent to cull the plots of best advantages, which, early in 1806, found its first opportunity to score. In March Samuel Parkman proposed to give the rebuilt Faneuil Hall one of the Winstanley copies after Stuart's Lansdowne *Washington*. Anxious to prevent this imposition, Stuart appears to have exposed the picture's shabby history to Joseph Batson, a stucco worker, who, in the fashion of that time, was an artist of considerable skill, creating the arabesques of low-relief sculpture that were so beautiful a part of interiors. Batson spoke at the town meeting, where the picture was to be presented, and despite much oral abuse and crude threats from leading Bostonians, his intervention effectively raised doubt concerning the desirability of so tainted a gift. Two weeks later, a letter from Batson appeared in the *Columbian Centinel*, again stressing Boston's shame, when "the celebrated Mr. Stuart who is at this time in this town . . . is the only man who ever took a correct likeness of Washington." This disruptive tactic, one more in a succession of those Stuart had employed to retain his patent as the sole painter of Washington, was a complete success. Shielded behind Batson's name and pugnacity, the maneuver forced Parkman to order a new full-length, to replace the offending Winstanley copy.

Unable to face the injured artist, Parkman appointed friends to negotiate, and they found Stuart obviously enjoying a businesslike pose.

"Certainly, gentlemen," he responded to their enquiries.

"Will you do it immediately?"

"Immediately."

"The price?"

"Six hundred dollars."

"Six and five are eleven," Parkman later mused, counting what the Winstanley picture had cost him. His need to save face, however, urged a haste to which the artist was little accustomed. Still enjoying his charade, he exhibited an uncharacteristic cooperativeness, which Boston itself could not equal—no canvas of full-length proportions was available, and, as an alternative, as he had done on occasion over the previous four years, Stuart had a large wood panel constructed.

Why he chose to begin afresh, without reference to his earlier successful portraits of Washington, and to represent the hero in an entirely new attitude, as a General in battle, remains obscure. The most obvious suggestion is that Parkman feared it might be said that Stuart had merely retouched the Winstanley copy. And, too, the new concept was consistent with Stuart's vision of a full-length as a piece out of drama, commemorating some special event. *The Battle of Dorchester Heights,* at which Washington had commanded personally, was the incident selected. A compliment tendered to Boston, outside which the action had taken place, only Stuart was aware of the paradox that in London he had been sponsored by, had twice painted, and ultimately, to escape his debtors, had stayed at Syon House with the very "Lord Percy" (later Duke of Northumberland) who on that day had charged his troops at Washington. This delicious jest he savored in silence, then began the work, which throughout was more a joyful deceit than a frightening full-length portrait. All his life he had suffered from a mechanism triggered by the apparition of any full-length portrait on his easel. Always he was thrown back to the horror of his first dreadful failures, and at Newport, Dublin, and Philadelphia, this had brought neurotic complications of a devastating nature. Now, amused by the order's origin and its paradoxical nature, cynically enjoying the gratifications of his cunning, he treated this effort with a bravado of contempt.

Parkman wanted haste, and would have it, for such a joke was too good to be kept back! With proper Georgian spirit he selected sources from among his engravings: the figure was constructed of elements chopped from Van Dyck's *Duke of Bedford,* whose widespread legs and long, trailing hand holding a headgear are easily recognized. His second life-portrait of Washington had accompanied him to Boston; he copied it onto the figure, eyes averted left, in poor approximations of anatomy that bestowed a sleep-walker's air. This image of a solemn, withdrawn, defensive Chief Executive, on guard against Stuart's own troublesome personality and seen at the end of his Presidency, was hardly appropriate to the picture of an active General, twenty years

younger. Stuart was not disturbed. From an engraving after Rubens'
Decius Mus Sends Back the Lictors, he took a horse, the first he had
ever attempted. The animal's lower jaw was lost behind a shoulder
in Rubens' picture, an omission repaired by Stuart's invention of a
slightly fishlike substitute; he carried over, as well, engraver's exag-
gerations of eye and nostril, and inappropriate leopard-skin girths
and saddle-cloths. At the end of nine days, when the entire composition had been filled in, he viewed his rapidity with considerable pride.

Though the thickened torso given the great hero was Stuart's own,
and the horse was the most wooden since Troy, Samuel Parkman was
equally delighted by what he saw, and importuned the artist to show
this unfinished work prematurely, at Faneuil Hall's annual Fourth of
July dinner. Stuart himself was present, and a toast was drunk to his
talents: "Mr. Gilbert Stuart, now a resident in this town, who painted
it, and who is at present engaged on several portraits of equal magni-
tude, to be placed, we understood, in the State House." Of such further works history remains uninstructive, unless hopes were entertained that the portrait of General Henry Knox, recently begun,
might be so honored. After a brief return to the painting-room, the
portrait of Washington was re-hung in August, its character unchanged, for it remained a problem boldly met rather than one overcome. The artist, however, found other solaces, and pleased himself
by savoring his ironies to the last: ". . . and the merchant [Parkman]
paid me in under-current bank notes, which I had to send to a broker
to be exchanged, I paying the discount," he happily concluded his
recitals of the tale.

STUART was not forgotten on that greater stage he had only so recently vacated. From Virginia President Jefferson sent a gold watch,
the case engraved *Gilbert Stuart, Esq., with compliments of Thomas
Jefferson, 1806;* a gracious note accompanied it:

Dear Sir   Monticello, May 30, '06
    Please accept this mark of my esteem. May you wear it with the
pleasure of knowing it is presented to you from a friend who appreciated your great talent and the success you had with such a very
poor subject. A few sketches such as need not take you a moment,
will greatly oblige me.
    I salute you with friendship
                                                        Th: Jefferson

A handsome gesture, it was made to a man who had taken his money and swindled him of both portraits for which he had posed. Yet, if the important eras of Stuart's career had passed, a new distinction remained to it, for the quality of those works he produced at Boston, in the years between 1805 and 1811, transforms this period into one that glows like a long autumn twilight. His career, previously so marked by unevenness, gained a final sustained luster. Because in large measure the persons he now painted were of no national importance, their portraits ceased to be sought by others; a circumstance that effectively ended his most joyous and damaging episodes of double-dealing. The atmosphere at Boston was saved that particular pollution, and the relative peace of this city and the lesser preoccupation with his manipulations reduced his feeling of harassment, permitting him to work with better effect. Whether his striking new successes, in fact, flowed from a more tranquil spirit or amiability and constraint flowed from his successes makes a fine point: a final coming to grips with himself may share the responsibility, for, except in the Parkman episode, Boston at first saw none of those qualities that had been dominating his nature. His new sitters were delighted and fascinated, as Elizabeth Temple Winthrop hastened to inform her aunt, Mrs. James Bowdoin:

> [Boston, November 26, 1806]
> Stuart has just finished her picture [Lady Temple's] which is an excellent likeness. His is also copying my father's, and my mother gives them to me, to take the place of those by Copley. I have sat three times for mine, and my mother is determined to have all her children taken by him. He is a very pleasant companion, and promises himself much pleasure in conversing with my uncle [James Bowdoin] when he returns . . . I asked him if he can alter the drapery of the one which he took of you, which he can with much ease when you return.

A glowing profile portrait of this young woman, a rare essay in his work, reflecting Reynolds' *Duchess of Ancaster*, shows Stuart's keen pleasure in her lovely, intelligent presence. The seated three-quarter-length of her mother, Lady Temple, was cast in his best vein of high-Rigaud swoosh.

Executed on wood, a rapidly brushed likeness of General Henry Knox was of an entirely different nature; an authentic new masterpiece, its force and depth outdistanced the noblest of Reynolds' less subtle achievements.

"I wish I could induce him to paint a portrait, or at least a head of myself . . . possibly it may, with some patience, be accomplished," wrote one applicant in 1807, and an offer of fifteen hundred dollars for a full-length of Washington, nearly thrice his usual fee, did not command the civility of a reply to the Pennsylvania Academy.

Thomas Sully, a young, talented, and aspiring artist, on his first pilgrimage from Philadelphia, was permitted to watch over Stuart's shoulder while he painted the British Consul. So occupied was Stuart that Senator Mason himself, who had extended the invitation to Boston, was unpainted until 1808—while the lovely picture of his daughter Miriam, pleasingly begun at Washington, *never* reached completion! A mellower tone seen in these years is well expressed when he presented to Isaac P. Davis a smaller version of the Dorchester Heights Washington:

> Dear Sir:
>   It is with great pleasure that I have in my possession something that will be agreeable to you. Accept if you please the small whole length portrait of Washington which you seemed so much pleased with the other day, as a small token of the gratitude I feel for the uniform kindness I have received from you since my arrival in Boston. Since I had intended it for you I have retouched the whole with care.
>
> G. Stuart
>
> Boston, Jan. 7, 1807
> To Isaac P. Davis

The buccaneering spirit of former times had abated, as though maturity had come to him too late. His discreetly guarded relations with Mrs. Morton perhaps also reflected this creditable phenomenon; one notes greater dignity in a new version of her portrait. Simpler patterns of pomaded hair frame the face softly, replacing the wilder array of his first effort. Eliminated is the device of fastening a locket to her wrist: seemingly too explicit a part of their earlier intrigue, the same locket had appeared in another Philadelphia portrait, *Mrs. Alexander James Dallas*, and may have signified nothing. Since Stuart's appearance in Boston Mrs. Morton had indeed made herself useful to him. Through her contact with General Knox that portrait had been arranged, and the head, at least, must have been completed before Knox's death, in October, 1806. Later, in 1808, when Sarah Morton's daughter was married, Stuart painted both bride and groom. Their relations obviously had been resumed, though it was a resumption on the part of slightly older people, and, with time, Sarah Morton had fallen more under the spell of religion. A strong influence in her life was the Reverend John Sylvester John Gardiner, Rector of Trinity Church, the literary mentor to whom she entrusted the revision of her poems.

The tragedy of Sarah Morton was her inability to make up her mind; unable to take any definitive position on the issues of her existence, she lived ever in a conflict of intentions. The deleterious effects felt by Stuart in Washington might have visited him again, did he not avoid them by a firm stand. The summer of 1807 brought a new domestic arrangement, and Stuart was joined in Boston by his wife and children. His last portrait of Mrs. Morton, in progress at this time, showed her veiled, half-retiring under an enveloping lace shawl. This masterwork, fascinating in its psychological overtones, was left unfinished. To shelter his newly reunited family he secured a house in Washington Place, then importuned Thomas Winthrop for payment on the large and hastily completed portraits of Jefferson and Madison, brought from Washington two years before. Patterned once more on his Irish portrait of Sir William Barker and finished with much sonorous coloring and impetuosity of brush, Jefferson's portrait expressed his ultimate capacities with the monumental. So successful was it, one willingly overlooked the awkwardness of James Madison's less satisfactory likeness: ". . . the pictures . . . remain with Mr. Stuart; you have omitted to give any directions respecting them," Winthrop reported to James Bowdoin, August 4, 1807—and though previously there would have been danger in leaving such attractive works to the duplicitous artist, now he modestly disdained plots.

Like any professional man forced to keep multitudes of daily appointments, probably Stuart, like Reynolds, always had kept a journal; one was seen at Germantown; but only a single sheet, torn from his book for 1808, has been preserved to confirm the practice. From it we learn that two months prior to her June wedding, on the 25th of April, 1808, Sarah Morton's daughter Charlotte already was coming for sittings; and that on this Monday morning she disappointed him. He noted the fact, then passed his empty hours preparing the backgrounds on portraits of Mrs. Howard, Mrs. Bussy, and Col.

Davis. Senator Mason's daughter Anna, accompanied by her new husband, Patrick Grant, called on him later that day, to arrange a picture of Grant begun shortly after; the name of a New York couple, who accompanied the Grants, Stuart failed to hear. Later that afternoon, at Seymour's warehouse, he was caught by rain, and the downpour continued through the night to Tuesday morning, when at nine o'clock the dyspeptic Mr. Hollowell arrived for his sitting, accompanied by I. P. Davis, who had become the artist's devoted friend. "Thunder, rain, and my room leaking like the devil," Stuart noted petulantly; these he did not consider propitious circumstances in which to work, and he was further annoyed when his eleven o'clock sitter, Mr. Appleton, altered his appointment for Thursday. "Mr. Townsend read over the correspondence between me and Bingham," was the final note of that day, implying that this twenty-four-year-old sitter, an attorney, was prodded into the same niche previously occupied by Horace Binney. Both the sparkling Mrs. Bingham and her less admirable husband had died since Stuart left Philadelphia, but Stuart was still seeking means of redressing his grievances against the dead.

"First salmon," he noted capriciously, on the Wednesday, a happy springlike observation sufficiently important to win a place in his business proceedings. That same busy day he recorded seeing Mrs. Morton and the British Consul, who came by with an English officer; he made a visit to State Street, took a walk in the Mall with Henry Sargent, and received an evening visit from the man who tuned his harpsichord. Each morning was given over to one or two sittings; in the afternoons he received numerous callers; payments are scattered about, recorded helter-skelter as received. It is the prosperous, even pattern of a well-established artist, whose life is taken up by his craft: his position seemed so secure that at Philadelphia, Peale, with his ear to the ground, recorded exaggerated accounts: "Mr. Stewart is at Boston full of business at 200 $ pr. head."

However tempered the pace, or sedate and respectable the appearance, Stuart remained disturbed by many things; among them was the Rev. Gardiner's ascendance over Sarah Morton. The many pictures he painted of her family and friends provided meetings that were not secluded; his long afternoon walks possibly cloaked others. One fine summer morning, seeing his family of many girls, and his son Charles Gilbert, prepare to accompany their mother to Trinity

Church, to the astonishment of everyone, he said, "Well, I think I will go." Mrs. Stuart showed her delight; "Oh, do go!" she urged; and in the church he leaned over the pew when everyone else was seated, took snuff, and was very much at his ease; but to the sermon, preached by Dr. Gardiner, he paid an especial attention. After his service the Doctor came down the aisle and shook his hand with expressions of delight. All seemed to have gone particularly well, and Charlotte Stuart doubtless hoped her unchurchly husband had been the object of a miracle, when he remarked, "Well, I do not think I shall go to church again."

"Why?" enquired his daughter Anne.

"Oh," said he; "I do not like the idea of a man getting up in a box and having all the conversation to himself."

EACH NEW part of the world in which Stuart found himself had acted as a fresh stimulus to his creative powers, and Boston, the last, was no exception. The practiced eye already detected how much his work had declined in the decade since his great days in New York; its character had softened, diffused, become less trenchant and more banal. They had not been years of drift, even so, for remarkable studies of character occurred too. In Washington and Boston he perfected a composition uniquely his own, in which ladies were shown seated halfway down in the frame, arms cut by the lower member, leaving only swirls of drapery, a few fingers, or half a hand, to add a sense of greater spaciousness than existed. Inspired by Rigaud, though as frequently organized with elements found elsewhere, these compositions were a happy evolution of thought. They carried him deep into the camp of painting with decorative intent. The formula was so strong that Mrs. John Gore, who sat to him wearing a high-buttoned riding habit, found herself portrayed in a low-cut empire mode, a shawl entwining her bare arms.

Originally devoted to male heads, powerfully characterized, Stuart had evolved into a master decorator, with a passion for decoration; but his downright indifference to the truth made him irritable were the new beauties of his works praised: "I don't want people to look at my pictures and say how beautiful the drapery is—the face is what I care about!" he rudely remonstrated. Though he rarely allowed sumptuous patterning to affect telling characterizations, and felt a special sympathy for older persons, whose decline is viewed with lofty dignity, Stuart's portraits of women had become his most satisfying works. And frequently too, in a kind of emotional transference, they are his most compelling; in the same set with *Mrs. John Gore* was an intriguing likeness of the dark, mysterious face and alluringly proffered bosom of *Mrs. Solomon Moses,* the impact of whose physical presence is such that it is difficult to realize that her provocative charms are derived from those of Marie Antoinette.

The change of hair style that had taken place while he was in Washington finally had rid Stuart of Vigée-Lebrun's high coiffures and trailing curls. In an unpowdered, glistening, and pomaded age, he sought newer models imported from England, and, in particular, those of Thomas Lawrence. Here high, soft coiffures revealed the new landscape of ears, constituting a frightening challenge to artists who recalled that when last they were seen, Sir Joshua himself had not been clever in their rendering. At Boston Stuart made a special effort, his loaded brush touching crisply drawn twirled patterns, treated dexterously, like so much complicated drapery. Pale pink and coral ears became a dazzling new beauty in his work, and one he came to indulge and at times to exaggerate. For a few years he painted them better than anyone except Lawrence, who, far away in London, was caught up in the same challenge, and acquitted himself with equal credit, if not the same gusto.

And whereas the first works Stuart completed in Boston were a mere continuation of his efforts in Washington, slowly their monumental simplicity became more pronounced, their quality improved, and he learned to sustain their level of excellence. Possessed still by illnesses of deep-rooted nervous and mental character, never entirely unharassed or able to live as other people did, the slow even tenor of his life at Boston and perhaps the renewed acquaintance of a mother, older sister, and the Friend of Genius brought him, in the late afternoon of his life, an unexpected stability. To that degree the move to Boston was salutary. In every other respect it had been a step of ponderous inadvertence. Thirty-five years had passed since Copley had sailed out of Boston, leaving behind his scores of portraits, and in those years, though the nature of Boston had remained constant, the balance of the young nation had shifted south. In a city of diminishing importance, which still proudly labeled itself a *town,* Stuart found himself faced by sitters who were the rich sons or wives of generations of shrewd Yankees; a comfortable, aristocratic society, British-oriented, and ready to welcome him for what he had been, rather than the ruin he was. He was an artist who had known greatness, and those able to get finished works from him still accredited his genius, as well they might. But never before had he set up his easel so far from the real power of a nation, and, though his employment continued, the days when he was a part of history had ended. Stuart had tricked himself into a back stream, where, leering and balding, equipped with a grotesquely accurate Drury Lane accent in which to recount his fictitious intimacy with Washington, he played out the last anticlimactic scenes of his existence.

XXV

The Cage

EMPLOYED as fully as his lack of organization permitted, in good circumstances, and with little of substance to trouble him, Stuart's abnormalities grew more prominent. Boston he found pleasant but dull; its restrictions he categorized as "blue laws," but actually, what he missed was the exhilaration of his own former less fastidious behavior. Boston provided no scope for his scoundrelly capacities. Though doggedly he trod the line between right and wrong, his removal from the center of the nation inevitably had separated him from those vaster schemes and delightful duplicities he enjoyed. Unamused, he imagined himself in bad health, complained of gout and the severe winters, and seems generally to have slandered heaven and earth for his bootless state as an honest and prosperous man. Even the charms of Sarah Morton waned, or perhaps her conscience and Dr. Gardiner had made infidelity even more boring than virtue. Benjamin Waterhouse found Stuart amenable to long visits at Cambridge, away from his family, until his snuff ran out, when nothing could prevent him from returning immediately to Boston; and in September 1808, on a visit to Philadelphia, Waterhouse told Charles Willson Peale that Stuart "now wants to leave Boston; that it is too cold a climate for his constitution." The desire was a vain one, for, since London, an unwritten law had operated in Stuart's affairs to prevent him from returning to any place where he once had been. Just as it had been impossible for him to take up again his career in London, so he would never return to Dublin, New York, Philadelphia, or Washington. At Boston he had reached the end of the line: though frequently blown about on the whirlwinds of his own vituperative rhetoric, he had no place further to go.

Boston was his cage; this knowledge acted as an added irritant on Stuart, whose ill-temper became less concealed, even for purposes of business. The caution of his first two years was forgotten, and Henry Sargent, who frequently walked with him, found it expedient never to dispute *anything*, "for he was a vain, proud man, and withal, quick-tempered. I chose rather to preserve his friendship as an artist . . . I told him once a story that was very interesting and original, at which he laughed immoderately, and on meeting me the next morning, he said he had a good thing to tell me. What was my surprise when he told me my own story! Knowing his peculiar temper, I let it pass, and we both laughed heartily, but we were laughing at very different views of the subject."

Difficulties over dealing with him grew more common. Bostonians adopted the habit of asking the intercession of Isaac P. Davis, one of those few men of tact Stuart respected. Robert Gilmor, the distinguished Baltimore collector, in 1807 attempted to secure delivery of the lovely triple portrait of Elizabeth Patterson Bonaparte, and thought he had succeeded. "Stuart has hitherto remained inexorable to all our solicitations, and his prompt acquiescence to your demand affords a proof of the estimation in which you are held by this distinguished artist," the subject wrote to Gilmor; but years later the picture still languished in Stuart's garret. When accidentally he trod on the companion study of Prince Jerome, lying without a stretcher on the floor of Stuart's lumber room, Thomas Sully, returned to Boston as Stuart's most recent pupil-apprentice, feared his master's violent reaction. "You needn't mind," came an unexpectedly quiet call: "it's only a damned French barber." Continued requests for the picture of Jerome's American bride found Stuart threatening, "if he were bothered any more about it he would put rings through the nose, and send it to any tavern-keeper who would hang it up. He would have done it, too," added Sully, "for he was not a man to flinch from anything of that kind."

To his sitters too he forgot the charm at first employed. Frequently his manner become directly insolent: in scathing sallies he objected to any observation they made, and he was irrefutable, because dexterously he took either side of any argument that ensued, and often both. He even objected to their personal appearance. Dr. Warren's elabo-

rate toilet was carefully surveyed, then he seated himself, to commence a series of those narratives for which he was famous. To in-
terrupt the irascible artist seemed dangerous, but eventually the young
doctor remarked, "Mr. Stuart, this is very entertaining, but you must
be unaware my time is precious. I feel very uncomfortable."

"I am glad of it. I have felt so ever since you entered my studio."
"Why?"
"Because you look like a fool. Disarrange that fixed-up costume,
and I will go to work!"

And when another pert coxcomb remarked, at the end of a first
sitting, "Why—it has no eyes!" he shot back, "It is not nine days old
yet."

THE THREE-YEAR cycle so pronounced in his life, during which his
neurotic pattern underwent change accompanied by gradual deteri-
orations and sudden improvements in the quality of his portraits, again
was operating to his detriment. Boston had palled on him, but it is
the distinction of this long twilight that external factors intervened
to preserve the high quality of his Boston work. In December, 1807,
President Jefferson's embargo, which held American ships in harbor
to prevent involvement in Napoleon's wars, stopped the importation
of canvas. The wood panels he previously had employed through
occasional necessity were pressed into regular use. Beneath his brush
their unyielding surface presented a new problem; paint too thinly
applied did not cover, heads could not be rubbed in with his accustomed dexterity, and the well-charged brush now threw off comma-
shaped strokes that sat high up off the flat panel. The new challenge
each work presented unexpectedly refreshed him, and, responding,
he found pleasure in technical tribulations. Voluntarily or otherwise,
his solutions altered his manner of painting. An evolution of style appeared, more original than anything previously essayed, as he grasped
for pragmatic, personal answers, and drifted away from the Georgian
convention he had practiced so long.

Frequently he was annoyed to find a picture on which he had expended hours of labor ruined by the splitting of wood improperly
dried. On one occasion a cabinet-maker said he could join such a panel
perfectly; "but judge of Stuart's anger and astonishment, when it
was returned, to find that the edges had been planed down and glued
together,—a process that ran nostrils into one, brought the corners

of the mouth nearly together, and did away wholly with the bridge of the nose,—a treatment so ludicrous as to cause the artist to laugh at the absurdity of the thing, while he swore at the stupidity of the fellow." A collection of these imperfect panels lay heaped together; and in time, Ruggles, a cabinet-maker on Winter Street, supplied him with more satisfactory wood. Complaints of the excessive smoothness of the surface then followed, for he found it difficult to coat, and also, he was accustomed to feel the uneven ripple of canvas beneath his brush. By dressing the wood face with a dull plane, whose finely serrated edge was passed over at one oblique angle, then crossed at another, Ruggles successfully simulated the texture of English twill canvas. Brilliant portraits of the Lenox sisters, where vivacious dancing strokes lay on clear tones of white, lavender, and pale green, acquired a special beauty attributable to the perfection of this new material.

The long twilight of his powers retained its sweet and melancholy glow, a seemingly unending phenomenon, while, as in previous years, the artist himself deteriorated, presaging what lay ahead. His irritability grew so proverbial that the presence of a preliminary effort at General Knox's portrait over a mushroom bed near his stable was assumed by Bostonians to be an expression of rage rather than the resourceful employment of a panel that had prematurely split. Women, especially those young and attractive, when they dared, were able to tame this terror, aged more than his fifty-three years; the methods of Mrs. Charles Davis were rudimentary:

> 13 October 1809
>
> The day before yesterday I called to see Mr. Stewart—found him in one of his happiest humors, and with a little flattery, which we all like at times, [and] a song Catherine had copied for him, we made him promise to have my father's portrait finished in a month from this time. I told him I should pursue him like his own shadow until he completed it . . .

Six days later, she reported further:

> I have been again to Mr. Stuart's, he has promised me my father's portrait shall be finished by your return. It is the very image of himself . . .

Mrs. Davis' own portrait, which fails to suggest her insouciant approach, in its emphasis on her extended bosom provides the added explanation that he had found her personally pleasing. Increasingly, however, women, especially younger ones, felt apprehensive about facing the scowling, leather-lunged painter, so wrinkled and uncouth in appearance, whose entire complexion seemed a red blotch, and who, with compulsive movements, tucked immoderate wads of snuff into his nostrils. So clearly marked in pictures like *Maria Cornelia Durant*, their apprehension added another delicacy to the acuteness of his perceptions. His patronage, however, diminished sharply; "Mr. Stuart painted some pictures after his arrival: but I believe his employment is now pretty much on the decline . . ." wrote two Boston matrons to their nephew, Mather Brown, still living in London. Continual movements about the city, to new addresses, was another indication of his reduced fortunes, and in May, while finishing his portrait of John Derby, he parted with President Jefferson's gold watch:

> Dear Mr. Derby: Boston, May 6, 1809
>   I acknowledge to have received the loan from you of one hundred dollars on the President's gift to me. I shall discharge it promptly.
>   G. Stuart

Seven days later he received a further one hundred and twenty dollars from Derby, in payment for the portrait and its frame; but Jefferson's gift was never reclaimed.

THE AUTUMNAL touch in Stuart, so long in the air, now grows stronger, suggestive not so much of mellow maturity as the bleak approaches of winter. One senses that the decline in his personal restraints soon will affect his art, as it had his patronage, then is astonished to see him working with greater effect than ever. He could still paint an excellent portrait, but the sitters he too long had treated as vulgar and irrelevant intruders had lost patience with him, and the sands of his fortunes ran out at a quickened pace. His first response, as always, was to move to a suburb; in the winter of 1809 he took a house at Roxbury, belonging to Mrs. Swan, where, in an L-shaped studio, all things continued as before. Bostonians, bred to caution and Yankee economy, carefully took receipts for money given him, and these are notable for the irregularity of his once beautiful script, and such evasive phrases as "to be delivered when finished"; one such scrawled note, written in November 1809, concerned a picture not delivered until 1815. All criticism brought fits of a startlingly ambivalent vexation; those who praised his draperies, painted with an even greater attention and charm, were directed to regard the faces; those who complained of carelessness with draperies were told, curtly, "I copy the works of God, and leave clothes to tailors and mantua-makers." Anyone who ventured to examine too closely was raked by, "Well, sir, does it *smell* good?" On completion of his portrait of James Sullivan, Governor of Massachusetts, two relatives called. "Is not the nose a *little* one-sided?" they ventured to enquire.

"Yes, but you see the portrait is taken in three-quarter view," he replied, "and it is, as with the Governor, less seen on this side than on the other."

"Isn't one eye a little larger than the other?"

"Yes, it should be on account of the perspective."

"I don't remember to have seen those white spots on the Governor's eyes"—a reference to the highlights.

He began to fume, walking rapidly up and down the room; fortunately the parties had left before he exploded: "Confound . . . [them], they've married and intermarried so often, that, if you were to scrape together the brains of the whole family, and throw them into a cock-sparrow's eye, it wouldn't make him wink."

So belligerent was his reputation and his appearance that the pleasant moods that punctuated many of his sittings were a surprise. In good temper he still made an effort to be entertaining, and when he wished, his attentions were invariably winning. His manner of speaking itself recalled another age, ampler, more gracious, less threadbare than that of Jeffersonian embargoes; the elegance of his periods, the high-flown loftiness of his sentiments, even his shafts of wit and carefully calculated commentaries on mutual acquaintances, gave each person the agreeable sensation of having been singled out for the honor of intimate acquaintance. It was all a deception now, but each ritualistic encounter was brilliantly carried out, according to the long-established pattern. As he thumped with words, his principal interests in life seemed to be the observation of persons around him and the sound of his own voice. Even the shyest of sitters, though frightened, responded warmly: "Mr. Stewart was very polite, appeared sensible, and entertaining; but I did not say a word to him about the price, as you desired me not to," Mrs. Stephen Peabody reported to her son. ". . . I felt so disagreeably to set down and be looked at, and to look up in a stranger's face, that I fear little of my true lineaments will be seen," she added, some days later.

Mrs. Peabody's shyness, discomfort, and the uneasy looks she gave him, stimulated the artist to more accurate, less stylized, rendering than had been his practice. An authentic masterpiece of Americana, her image paralleled his earlier superb accomplishments among New York merchants, with a more distinct native flavor and a suggestion of the homespun idiom previously absent from his fundamentally European art. In a time of personal and professional eclipse, turned inward on himself, he began to make more profound statements, and entered a deeper vein.

Removed from the center of American power and politics, no longer the delineator of history, even in his shabby condition Stuart brought eminence to Boston, as the artistic center he dominated. Washington Allston, who in 1810 returned to Boston from London, where he had applied his talents on narrative and monumental works and an artistic ideal that paralleled West's, had the clarity to appreciate the supreme skill of Stuart in his own severely restricted field. Allston declared Stuart's portraits better than any at the Royal Academy, and whether or not this was literally true, they did stand in a unique category of excellence. Stuart was sought out by aspiring artists from all parts of America; to them he retained his essential kindness, a part of the London code that made a gentleman indulgent to those less fortunate. Thomas Sully, who that same year had passed his six months as pupil-apprentice, *after* a period in London, noted how his own efforts were praised publicly, their defects noted in private. Sully saw too that Stuart's days of riotous drunkenness were over, and that his sleepy, semi-inebriated afternoons altered his personality but little, though they curtailed his productivity: "he was a very capricious man, and would never paint unless he was in the humor; although the way is to begin, and the humor will come afterwards." Jacob Eicholtz was another who made the long journey to Boston, where he received "sound lectures, and hope." Boston had adopted Stuart as a part of itself; among its people the application of his name to a picture assured its merit, and one instance that made its way into print concerned a gentleman who praised a picture in a shop, then traded his admiration for denigration on discovering he had mistaken the artist's identity!

Such adulation made more palatable, though it could not disguise, his reduced fortunes; and it is curious to note that while he had lost all direction, in a career now forever fixed in relative obscurity, far away in London dim recollections of him stirred. An engraving after his portrait of the Duke of Northumberland induced a critic to recall that "having a very correct eye, he gave the human figure exactly as he saw it. . . . He was, however, so well grounded in his profession that had not his eccentricities led him to quit this country he would have corrected his errors and figured very high in his art . . . We may safely add," continued the same critic, four years later, "that in point of distinct and characteristic resemblance, it will not be easy to find portraits by any other artist of this country that can be put before them."

At almost the same time, Francis James "Copenhagen" Jackson, newly appointed British Minister to the United States, called on an elderly and bowed Benjamin West, to say his farewells.

"Where are you going?" asked West.

"To the United States."

"Then, sir, you will find the best portrait painter in the world, and his name is Gilbert Stuart."

THOUGH West's loyalty did credit to his long memory, no one who had known Stuart's dashing, stylized London portraits would now recognize the images that issued slowly and at irregular intervals, from his Boston painting-room. For a few years, after the turn of the century, he had remained an island of Georgian thought in a world rapidly transformed into a revolutionary camp, peopled by bourgeois "Greeks." His enforced adoption of wood panels had altered the technical qualities of his work; soon the Yankee nature of his sitters interested him more, and his portraits were transformed into statements of authentic Americana. An instinctive approach was at work, as the old man, ill and declining, faced by a changing world, truthfully recorded its visual characteristics. Rembrandt Peale had returned from study in France, where David's classicism, of which Stuart had made use as early as 1796, in his portrait of Betsy Custis, ruled supreme. Isolated at Boston, only the engravings that arrived from Europe kept Stuart aware of trends beyond the Atlantic; yet, occasionally, his arrangements of stuffs, especially his lace shawl, which found its way into nearly every feminine picture, echoed the cascading brilliance of canvases by David and Ingres, with an approach to their hard classicism. The whole clattering Georgian impedimenta had been abandoned: skies and trees, broad draperies, and velvet-cushioned chair-arms, even the deliberately ovoid eyes of Vigée-Lebrun, are replaced by flat architectural pilasters, his lace shawl, the half-curves of Empire furniture, and an exacting Copleyesque rendering of faces.

New and equally arbitrary elements flourished, notably silken curls, softly brushed into the final wet surfaces of paint, to play about and shadow women's eyes, as romantic reflections of Lawrence. One becomes aware, too, that the artist is restudying the elements of his art, for a systematic tonal division becomes obvious. "The whole theory of shadow may be taught by a billiard ball—the simplest object I can think of. Lay it on a table and draw it," he explained to the young daughter of a sitter. "You first sketch a circle; you then look at it, and see there is one light, one shadow, and one transparent reflection; on the gradation of these all painting depends. My rule for a portrait is, one-third light, one-third dark, and one-third demi-tint." One wonders if he was aware he recited the formula written by Sir Joshua Reynolds, in his notes to Du Fresnoy's treatise?

Except for eccentricities of proportion, more pronounced as he forced too much into each small frame, he was, in fact, painting better than ever. And largely this was due to instinct, as he came to grips with the harsher stuff of Yankee character. Davidian elements such as interlaced fingers found in that painter's *Marquise D'Orvilliers* (and Reynolds' *Countess of Dartmouth*) became a feature of every picture, on which flashing comma-shaped whites were gracefully impasted. The native flavor of his work was pronounced. He reacted strongly to individuals, his interpretations tempered occasionally by darting sympathies or true malice. *Miss Lydia Smith* is seen sketching, her portfolio before her, in an arrangement unrelated to previous formulas, that meets her youthful charm with a freshness of its own. *Mrs. Samuel Parkman* is viewed with a trenchancy residing in her pretentiously held head and unlovely, simpering mouth; another authentic masterpiece of native art, that, with a kind of violent abandon, has wriggled free of the limits imposed on Copley by his natural restraint and gentility. The most devastating portraiture yet practiced anywhere began to flood forth from an irascible, uncontrollable Stuart. It overwhelmed even the limiting factors imposed by his own newly restudied compositional ideas, for that equalizing formula of thirds gave his pictures a flat lighting that drained them of the grandeur once residing in dramatic oppositions of dark and light. Only his still more meager and intimidated patronage prevented him from creating a fierce new approach to the art.

International politics, once the natural commodity of his painting-room, now had no place in Stuart's life. Thomas Jefferson's retirement, quoting the fortuitous precedent of Washington, and James Madison's elevation to the Presidency, though it added a fourth to the numbers of Presidents Stuart had painted, made no other alteration in his fortunes. Portraits of these Chief Executives were not multiplied as those of Washington had been, and, in any case, since he had "forgetfully" sold to James Madison his second life-portrait of Jefferson, Stuart possessed no likeness of either President from which to supply replicas. Removed from the center of the nation, his days with the mighty were finished; even the entry into another war with England in 1812 caused hardly a ripple in his life. That September the New York Common Council asked Commodore Isaac Hull, the first naval hero to emerge from the conflict, after winning his single-combat of the *Constitution* against the *Guerrière*, to sit to Stuart for his portrait. A head of Captain James Lawrence he earlier had painted also became a matter of note, when, commanding the *Chesapeake*, in June, 1813, Captain Lawrence lost his life in combat with the British *Shannon*.

To engrave Stuart's portraits of these two heroes, David Edwin came to Boston, traveling with John Wesley Jarvis, that somewhat bohemian artist who resembled a younger Stuart, and may briefly have served a Philadelphia apprenticeship to the master whose position he viewed enviously.

"I knew you were in Boston," Stuart greeted Edwin, when he called, alone.

"I only came last evening, sir, and this is the first time I have been out."

"I saw you—you came to town like a criminal going to the gallows—back foremost;" and Edwin acknowledged that he had indeed been riding in the front seat of the coach. Stuart's aversion to Jarvis was well known, and, not wishing to prejudice his project of engraving the Lawrence and Hull portraits, Edwin carefully dissociated himself from his traveling companion. Jarvis called on Stuart separately.

". . . He came to see me *in his buffs*. He had buff gloves; buff jacket; buff waistcoat and trousers, and buff shoes," Stuart complained. After hearing the report from Edwin, Jarvis, when he visited Stuart again, wore a less offensive black. "So! I caused him to put his buff in mourning," Stuart laughed heartily, clapping his hands, when next he saw Edwin. A third outfit Jarvis wore, consisting of a short coatee with large pockets, Stuart gleefully characterized as "all inexpressibles and pockets."

Invited to lunch, Edwin arrived early one day, to find that Stuart had not returned from his morning walk. Soon he came in; he passed his guest in a state of great agitation, and went straight to a closet, from which he took tobacco and a bundle of implements. With the aid of a grater and sieve he ground tobacco into snuff; hastily he took a large dose; his uncommon tremor seemed to forsake him, and, greeting his guest with renewed cordiality, he said, "What a wonderful effect a pinch of snuff has upon a man's spirits."

"You have Hull's likeness there," he observed, of the plate Edwin had completed from his portrait. "He always looks as if the sun was shining in his face, and he half shuts his eyes as he gazes at it."

But to Dunlap, who visited Boston that same year, Stuart admitted his disappointment that more war heroes were not asked of him. Those voted by the New York Common Council were entrusted to Jarvis.

XXVI

Mythomaniac

CONSCIOUS of his extraordinary skills and all he had been, the neglect he experienced in the sixth decade of his life added a very real pain to the disillusionment Stuart had felt for so long. Not far below the surface, always threatening to erupt in bad temper and violence was an immovable despair; and whereas in Philadelphia his chatter had been a transparent excuse for begging sympathy and at all times was of primary therapeutic value to himself, now it served a new purpose. John Quincy Adams noted the message that lay within the fancy wrappings of his loquaciousness. "He considers himself beyond all question the first portrait painter of the age, and tells numbers of anecdotes concerning himself to prove it, with the utmost simplicity and unconsciousness of ridicule." In a repertory that appeared to have become standardized, each story was told with considerable skill and conscious artistry. A phrase served as bland introduction to the subject and place—"When I resided in the Athens of America," was a common introduction to recollections of Philadelphia: "When I was in good practice and some repute in London," set the scene for tales of what now seemed to have been his most glorious era. Persons who heard his recitals agreed that on each occasion his wording was nearly identical, and, at the end, each tale was neatly rounded off by a line gracefully pointing the moral.

His memory was not famous for accuracy, and especially in the awkward passages in which his life had abounded he was apt to call fancy to its aid. Like all conscious artists, there also were those moments when he broke into free flight. One such concerned the summons he represented himself to have received in Ireland, to a castle where its occupant, a tailor whose peculations had made him newly rich, demanded portraits of his ancestors. "Why, what can be easier?" Stuart recounted his host explaining: "Set to work and paint such ancestors as I *ought* to have had"; which, he asserted, he thereupon did, producing a host of knights in armor, bushy-wigged judges, and high-born ladies with nosegays and nestling lambs. On occasion he saw lack of belief illumine his listener: "When Mr. Stuart related this anecdote to me," recounted Charles Fraser, the miniaturist, concerning the nostalgic tale of his organist's position in London, "he was sitting in his parlor, and as if to prove that he did not neglect the talent that had been so friendly to him in his youth, and in the days of extreme necessity, he took his seat at a small organ in the room, and played several old fashioned tunes with much feeling and execution." Equally, when he told how in West's studio Trumbull's drawing had revealed his defective vision, he attempted to force belief by a long dissertation on optics. Sully was inclined to dismiss these sound arguments as "one of Stuart's whims, who could lecture most eloquently on any subject, from the anatomy of a man to the economy of his shoe tie."

The reservations are instructive, and suggest that to those who knew him, and had lived with him, it was quite obvious Stuart did not adhere to the truth pedantically. The failing belonged to his character, traceable to earliest years, when, forcing his way into a world that knew only his talents, like Sheridan, he thought it necessary to put a better face on plain realities. He never knew the easy confidence that comes from security, financial and social, or the acceptance that derived from moving among equals, to whose social strata one was born. From first to last he was in a false position; and the inevitable discrepancy between appearance and reality had to be dealt with somehow. He managed with infinite resource, resolution, and courage, until the means he employed so brilliantly had ceased to serve him and took on their own life. His personality and character, and more unfortunately still, his mind, had become radically warped; his flights of fancy were uncontrollable, and worse, they were purposeless. The consequence was that inevitably he found himself in situations where truth, if it became known, would have been an acute embarrassment. He doubtless understood that himself, but he could not, of course, explain it to anyone else. Where once he had handled facts with an artistic dishonesty, now he looked on them with impudence, and his final resource, after a barrage of brazen lies, was anything from charm to anger.

Burbling and gobbling away, his spacious Georgian manner may sometimes have conveyed the impression of a walrus holding forth while half-submerged, yet also he conveyed by these ear-bashing exercises a most attractive warmth and sincerity, and a tremendous sense of personal involvement. At times content to pronounce elegant generalities with deceptive circumstance, he and the facts could equally become paradoxical antagonists, and his interventions in anyone else's conversation were so frequent and elaborate as to suggest the original speaker merely embroidered the steady flow of his interruptions. His recollections of Washington had grown to suggest an intimacy that had never existed; but even his inclinations to aggrandizement were punctuated by unexpected and paradoxical floods of truth, as when he was questioned on whether the numbers of his Washington portraits were painted from the first President. "If the General had sat for all these portraits he could have done nothing else; our Independence would have been a secondary matter, or out of the question!" When Dolly Madison rescued another portrait of Washington from flames spread through the White House by an invading British army, he then whimsically took the opposite course by elaborately pretending that this picture, the same he had fraudulently sold to Gardiner Baker after it was paid for in behalf of General Pinckney, was one of the Winstanley copies. How he could have obtained this knowledge he did not trouble to explain at all.

Indeed, the omissions from his tales and the subjects with which they did not concern themselves are equally instructive, for though he skillfully ridiculed persons he thought had done him harm, any vindictiveness he felt was reserved for Senator Bingham. The troubles he had encountered in London, his victorious combat with Reynolds, and the actual heights to which his career rose, never occurred in his anecdotage. Likewise, he did not occupy himself with the important questions of his youthful ambitions, nor the means by which he had advanced himself. He intimated that he "shared" patronage with Reynolds, Gainsborough, and Romney, but never mentioned that he was an equal, or, for a short period, London's lion rampant. The position of extraordinary eminence he had held in Ireland was unmentioned. Boastful as his anecdotes were in respect to his abilities and the fine things people had said of him, they were modest in respect to his career itself, for, in his absurd way, while a scoundrel, a liar, and a cheat, he preserved the standards of a gentleman. To those unaware of his former buccaneering intrepidity, indeed his gentlemanly bearing and air of breeding, the shabbier relict of his lordly austerity, were pronounced; Samuel Knapp thought, somewhat indulgently, "he never lost the manners of a gentleman on any occasion"; noting also that "his literary acquirements were of a high order for a professional man constantly employed, but his early education was good, and the foundations of a classical education were well laid . . ." Stuart's outbursts, in fact, frequently drew on his literary knowledge; the threat to paint a ring through the nose of Elizabeth Patterson Bonaparte was surely derived from Hogarth's earlier menace, when he informed a nobleman, "that unless he sent for . . . [his picture] within three days, he should dispose of it, with the addition of a tail, to Hare the wild-beast man." Even his more earthy forms of humor are counterparts of Sir Thomas Overbury, whom, at times, he quoted directly.

Discursive, reflective, amiable, his fancy mingling with and cheating reality, his careful recitals calculated to make the point that he was "the first portrait painter of the age," inanity at last had broken down the standard of Stuart's humor. And these final wanderings of wit were symptomatic of his own breakdown before the abnormal nervous state in which his last decades were lived. He pressed compulsively for his sallies, eagerly forcing himself to exude the old charm; but it was charm no longer. Dunlap, to whom he demonstrated his palette, asked if he used madder-lake; "I should be madder if I did," came his reply. Nothing could draw him more easily from the true line of his thought than the possibility of foolish play; "Good woman, I saw a *man go* in your cellar—the door is open," began another.

"What does he want there, the impudent fellow?" she replied, and, running to her cellar, found only the *mangoes* she had purchased from a green-grocer.

"Mr. Stuart, this is the greatest likeness I ever saw," remarked a casual visitor to his house, before the carefully preserved portrait of Washington.

"Draw aside that curtain, and you will see a greater," he indicated.

"There's no picture here!" exclaimed the unfortunate victim, finding only the aparatus for grinding snuff.

"But there's a *grater*," shrugged Stuart, content with his pun, and incontrovertible logic.

"When I first came to England," he recounted, "my clothing was half a century behind the fashion, and I was told, 'Now you are in England, you must dress yourself as the English do.' Next morning I presented myself with my stockings drawn over my shoes, and my waistcoat over my coat. Then the cry was, 'Boy, are you mad?' You told me to dress as the English do, and they always say,—put on your shoes and stockings—put on your coat and waistcoat; so I have followed the direction." He even recounted this episode as having occurred in West's studio. In truth, he had entered the silly season, and suffered his final transmutation into a foolish braggart; not merely a liar but a mythomaniac, who did not always know himself whether he was inventing or telling the truth.

When he told Fraser that the exhibition of his *Skater* at the Royal Academy caused Mr. Grant, the subject, to be so mobbed he was compelled to quit the gallery, he was embroidering on realities. An entirely different phenomenon was seen in the elaborate invention by which he patronized Copley, to whom Boston was still devoted. He never forgave that compatriot for an unflattering portrayal of his hands, in the portrait of Lord Mansfield; after much impatient posing, he felt his thumbnail was clawlike. Now his imagination took flight, and a friend recorded being told:

> Copley in his distress took counsel of Stuart, who after learning all the facts of the case, and knowing, as he said, something about Lord Mansfield, advised Copley, instead of leaving the hand as he had it sketched, to paint something scarcely human,—the worst claw and talons of a monster, in short, the worst looking hand he could draw: and having done that, to have a great deal to say to the other Peers as they came to him, about his deep regret that so many of their Lordships, and particularly My Lord Chief-Justice, appeared to so great disadvantage in the detail of their persons.
>
> Copley pursued this course, and managed to draw attention pretty generally to Lord Mansfield's shocking hand. This reached his Lordship's ears, who was not insensible to the beauty of his hand, nor unwilling to have justice done it. In a very short time Copley received a polite note from him fixing a time for a sitting, and as his Lordship happened then to have a little leisure, begging the artist, who had been so successful thus far, to take his own time.

THE INTIMATE VIEW, seen by his family, was always less edifying than his appearance before the public, to whom, in some respects, he maintained the inscrutability of his respectable poses. His devouring egotism and his devotion entirely to himself had, from the start, made him a bad risk for marriage; Charlotte Coates Stuart had demonstrated no talent for managing either his fervid self-approbation nor his emotional indulgences. They had wrecked that ill-matched, sad, mistaken nuptial, and now, acting on his career also, left him tantrum-inclined, gay and sulky, stranded on the New England coast. Any restraint he ever had been capable of practicing was a forgotten thing, while to his wife, daughters, and son Charles Gilbert, his reckless impetuosity of words and the vitality and endurance with which he roared them produced the horrifying impression of a man who lived in a permanent rage.

As older daughters took on an increasingly spinsterish look, their brother, too long held in check, broke loose. On entering his twenties, Charles Gilbert displayed the same irreverent abandon that had characterized his father. Refused instruction in portraiture for fear of the too-heavy influence he had been to other pupils, Gilbert Stuart's only son turned to landscape, learning at second hand from Sully and Henry Sargent the lessons with which his father was prodigal to strangers. Amid temptations and dissipations, the same early death that took at least six Stuart children claimed this son at twenty-six. Unable to provide even a modest burial, his father, stunned, laid him to rest March 13, 1813, in Strangers Tomb, under the old Trinity Church, in Summer Street.

The blow was a terrible one. Stuart recognized his error in raising the boy under an angry and disapproving eye, and felt he was to blame. He spent a considerable sum on the construction of a box after his own design, which he placed on his sitting-room table, where, in some way associated with his son, it became a perpetual reminder of his loss. A year later he was indignant to receive a bill for this curious talisman, and the more so when his wife suggested he might indeed have overlooked the payment.

"Tom," said he, "I *know* I paid that bill;—but what I have done with the receipt I cannot tell"; and in this instance his assertion was well-founded, for the receipt was discovered years after, inserted in a book he had been reading.

The spiritual desolation he experienced had the effect of exaggerating further his eccentricities. Irritability became an excessive belligerence; it took the form of seeking offense, and meeting it with his old formula of iron indignation and brazen lies:

My dear Sir   Boston Augt. 30, 1813
   Mr. Stewart the painter has this moment called on me to enquire what I recollect about applying to him some years ago at your request for a picture of Priestley. Mr. S. relates to me the following story: that at the request of Mr. J. Williams and yourself he undertook to paint the picture mentioned, that the yellow fever drove him into the country before the painting was finished and he took it; from thence he moved to Washington where after about two years when he was on the point of removing here, Mr. Caldwell made a demand on him . . . that Mr. Thornton became his bondsman, and afterwards settled the demand for him; that feeling offended by this conduct of Mr. Williams he has ever since refused to deliver the painting to him to be used as was intended by Mr. W. and yourself—but that some time after at the request of Mr. Barclay, he finished and delivered it to him to be sent to England . . .
   —Now his daughter has returned from Philadelphia and says you insulted her in company, by refusing to know her, as you are very angry with her father, who had behaved very ill, by disposing of the picture of Priestley to another person after it had been paid for by Mr. Williams. This he understands is a calumny you have been circulating for 7 years past, and he must insist on ample reparations . . .

The account thus sent John Vaughan, by Samuel Higginson, preserves the flavor of Stuart's reproaches and his lamentable indifference to truth even when it was generally known. Other discreditable incidents of the past also followed him; even the patient Thomas Jefferson, long in retirement, recollected that though he twice had sat to Stuart, and paid for his portrait, he had none.

                                          [August 9, 1814]
   You wished to retain the portrait which you were so kind as to make of me while in Washington, until you should have time to have a print copied from it. This, I believe has been done, at least I think I have seen one which appeared to have been taken from that portrait. Mr. Delaplane of Philadelphia is now engaged in a work relating to the general history of America, and, wishing it to be accompanied with prints, has asked permission to have one taken from the same original, adapted to the size of his volume. I have therefore authorized

him to ask for the portrait in your possession, to copy his print from it, and return it to me. This I have done on the supposition that I had not been mistaken in believing it had already answered in your hands the purpose you had meditated.

Because his picture long had been disposed of, it was predictable that Thomas Jefferson should receive no reply.

Even the pleasures of society no longer were granted him. Contemplating his London career with an obvious nostalgia, he remembered his entertainments, and characterized them as ". . . a delightful solace after such labor . . . the greatest of all human luxuries . . ." but such joys were unknown in his desolated sixties. His inability to dissemble his likes and dislikes, the fierceness of his glance, and the malice that surrounded his name made him a personality that verged on indecent exposure. Known as a compulsive liar through three countries, hosts always had been willing to accept him as such. A certain charm existed in his inventions, so often given in the form of dramatized imaginary conversation; the really unforgivable sin was his appalling and ruthless candors, delivered in a manner that dominated painting-room, salon, or the noisiest dinner-table. A part of his unsuspected naivete was that he never knew, nor cared to learn, how much dissimulation is required to make polite society palatable. Freedom of tongue drove from him many who might have been his friends, and alienated for a time even those who knew he had a warm heart, and that when the storm of indignation had passed, he would be himself again. It was this that finally made him impossible to any society but that of his greatest intimates. Though Boston had first received him with admiration and pleasure, in retrospect one realized he had been to all the great houses—*once*. It was one more paradox, in a career teeming with them, that Stuart, in his terrible old age, became a martyr to the truth.

Instead of consolidating his position by wit and charm, as once was the case, he shattered it almost every time he opened his mouth. Even the political sagacity that had distinguished him vanished. In December 1815 Boston's enthusiasm for secessionist measures, proposed at the Hartford Convention, ran so strong he found himself pleading for the opposed principles of his boyhood friend Benjamin Waterhouse; "Stuart vindicated me at the dinner and supper tables of the *Essex junto,* or *nullifiers,* of that day, amidst their insults and toasts." The first political stand he was ever known to have taken, its wisdom is attested by the verdict of history. But he was exposed professionally, and then obliged by an unwise expediency to join the majority and break with Waterhouse, who "withdrew from him and his hot-headed companions." The longest friendship of his life thus was ended.

As STUART finished a decade caged in Boston, he was less reliable than ever. And, in the summer of 1815, his portraits showed a sudden stuttering into prose. The broad beauty of Van Dyckian form had given way before an excess of petty observation that lowers his art into a secondary category; higher efforts became more rare, frequently falling to earth in commonplaces; the decline that was an inevitable corollary to each period of increased emotional tension finally had set in. Triviality of observation and faulty proportions were consistent; to fit so much into even smaller panels he made figures that resembled gnomes. Though on occasion he still could be roused from artistic torpor, he was, with frightening suddenness, an artist in full decline, and a man whom sitters found distasteful. With the generosity of their youth, the Misses Bartlett kept "in a perpetual laugh," though inclined to sneeze "with so much snuff about." Others found him an abomination:

> Stuart's slovenly apparel, his strong mark of intemperance, his filthy mode of taking snuff, and the stories he told of his intimacy with distinguished men, now and then repeated during the sittings, were almost too much for the patience of my father, and I had to force a laugh occasionally to keep up my father's spirits. When told he need not come again he was much gratified; and he left without scarcely looking at the picture . . .

recorded the son of Benjamin Tappan. And John Neal, an aspiring artist who called on him, found a discomforting figure:

> He insisted on my emptying a tumbler of old East India madeira, which he poured out from a half gallon ewer, like cyder in haying time; and this at an early hour of the day when cyder itself might have been too much for a youngster like me, brought up on the plainnest of wholesome food. At first, having heard much of his propensity for hoaxing, I could hardly believe him when he threw off about half a tumbler full and told me it was madeira which had been twice round the Cape. Nor did he believe me, I am sure, when I told him I never did anything of the sort, for he winked at me as

much as to say "Can't you trust me?" and then hoped for better acquaintance.

Amused by his visitor's discomfort, Stuart put him at ease by puns, then spoke of Washington, and finally, to play on Neal's simplicity, he administered deliberate shock by stating that at Philadelphia he had belonged to a club that came together once a year, each member bringing between a dozen and a score of bottles, "every drop of which it was a point of honor with them to drink before they separated."

His nephew and namesake, Gilbert Stuart Newton, his sister Anne's son, now practically lived with him, joining the long progression of pupil-assistants. So very much like a younger version of his uncle, he caused uneasiness in Stuart's household: "Do you think Newton has very fine talents?" Mrs. Stuart asked her husband.

"Undoubtedly he has, but he is such a consummate coxcomb, I have no patience with him. If I attempt to instruct him, invariably he contradicts me."

Little observant of his fierce uncle's mood, on one occasion Newton entered his studio abruptly, and flourishing his brush, cried, "Now, old gentleman! I'll teach you to paint!"

"You'll teach me to paint, will you?— And I'll teach you manners," was the instant response; and not at the time happening to suffer from his gout, Stuart kicked the youth out of the room.

Slovenliness of appearance, abruptness of address, meannesses and pettinesses are the matters with which Stuart's later years are filled. Slowly, even his autumn twilight had grown more dim, and, incapable of control over himself, he slipped off toward inexorable artistic extinction. The superb powers of Lawrence, now reaching their apex, had no equivalent in a Stuart who had abandoned every heroic pretension in his work. Even his bust portraits had grown smaller, to 21 by 26 inches, or 20 by 24 inches, and the full deployment of his resources meant hardly more than a prose parody of his once great art. His price of one hundred dollars had remained unchanged since he established it in Philadelphia, more than twenty years before. The full significance can only be gauged by comparison with Lawrence, knighted and at the behest of the Prince Regent, touring Europe with a prefabricated studio. Guaranteed terms of £500 for each full-length portrait of the Generals and crowned heads who had crushed Napoleon, plus £1,000 for out-of-pocket expenses, Lawrence's suite of glorious works would be housed in a chamber specially constructed at Windsor. Stuart, meantime, lived on into an old age of artistic degeneration and despondence, a module of confounded humanity, willfully following his own erratic, egocentric route to oblivion.

XXVII

Rogue in Retirement

THE DESTRUCTION of his talents added a final bitterness and futility to Stuart's existence. To understand the complexities of his behavior, it was necessary to see him through his own eyes, not as an aging and degenerating artist, but as a gentle and much wronged gentleman. His sense of honor, when he called on it, was itself an anachronism; but what he had learned in London was part of his substance, and as a Georgian gentleman he was unfailingly kind to inferiors and took more offense at a slight or at a lack of appreciation of his merits and position than at a real injury.

Unwilling to do anything but talk, irresponsible toward letters, unable to cope with his affairs, only the weekly visits of Isaac P. Davis, who remained devoted to him, saw that the most urgent requirements received attention. Even the question of keeping a roof over his untidy head became supremely complicated, as Stuart argued with landlords and probably failed to pay their accounts. He had been in three locations since 1810; and now, in 1817, his most recent home in Roxbury was purchased by a sitter, Mrs. Robert Hooper, who experienced difficulty in forcing him to vacate the premises. From William Gowan he rented a house called Washington Place in Medford, where local reports found him "indeed very eccentric, he loves a cheerful bottle and does no work in the afternoons, he is very dilatory in finishing his pictures; there is no economy, of course he is said to be poor."

President James Monroe, in July of 1817, was on an inspection tour of New England, and wished to join his predecessors in Stuart's gallery of immortals. Uncertain of its destination, the President's party stopped a country man seated on his cart to inquire for Mr. Stuart's house. "It is the President, I vow," said the man; and taking off his hat, he gave three loud cheers, before driving off, leaving the question unanswered. Eventually, Stuart's house was found, and Monroe passed his last three mornings in Boston with the painter. If the President expected his portrait would resemble earlier performances of Stuart's familiar to him in Washington, he was disappointed; and he may have been dismayed at the unkempt individual who rose up at four o'clock in the morning to be ready for his early sittings. Equally disillusioning may have been the discovery that after a dozen years in Boston Stuart occupied the position of a privileged lunatic, a fiery, respected, elder-statesman type, who lived, largely ignored, in his household of spinsterish daughters.

Impressed by the unfinished head of Washington, still in the studio, President Monroe purchased a replica; but his own small portrait, freshly eked out, though it drew attention once more to an artist threatened with total neglect, was a paltry thing beside that of his predecessor. On a panel whose dimensions were only 21 by 26 inches, it proved that coarsening of style had been paralleled by diminishing authority. A mere imitation of his own former self, even a President now failed to rouse Stuart to work as good as he once had done for the meanest member of Washington's cabinet.

HALF THE twelve children born to his marriage had not survived infancy, and after Charles Gilbert's death, only four daughters remained under his aggressively masculine dominance. Their emotional development followed retarded patterns, from which only Emma, born in Dublin, broke away at the age of twenty-six to essay marriage, April 8, 1816. Mather Brown's aunts reported: "We ought to mention that on the 4th Fast Day after morning service we had a wedding at Church, Miss Stewart, niece to Mrs. Newton, was married to a Mr. Stebbins," a New York merchant. The marriage, however, was of short duration, and later Emma returned to her father's stormy household.

The youngest child was Jane, born in Philadelphia, who entered her teens displaying the affectionate interest in her father typical of English antecedents. Among Stuart's daughters she was the most consistently interested in painting. When she was thirteen she obtained colors and an old panel one day, with which she attempted to copy the discarded masterpiece of Madame Bonaparte, which she discovered lying unstretched on the garret floor. Her enjoyment was hardly disturbed by a frightful roar that issued from the chimney, which had caught fire. She continued work even when her father nearly tore the door off the hinges in his haste to see what damage was likely to be done. An expression of astonishment crossed his face, but he passed on, pretending not to notice how little Jane was employed. On his return from the top of the house, however, he could not resist looking over her shoulder. "Why, boy," he said, for, in an all female household, this had become his name for her, "you must not mix your colors with turpentine; you must have some oil."

Jane's delight in her craggy, masculine father was frequently dampened by Mrs. Stuart. Urged to repeat tales of their youthful adventures in foreign lands, she felt "pain to remember anything associated with his reckless extravagance, or what she called *his folly*." Girlish efforts to imitate the paternal wanderings of wit were dealt with summarily; "I have been annoyed enough with your father's nonsense in this way; besides, it is very bad taste."

Fear him as they did, Stuart's family felt an awesome respect, if not affection, for him, and his own deeply paternal nature cannot be ignored. It found expression also in his relations with the young men, who, for thirty years, had come to him for training in his profession. His brush no longer wrought the marvelous imagery of earlier days, but the many works of his American prime, scattered through the country, assured his position as *the master*. Most recent of aspiring artists to arrive at Boston was Matthew Harris Jouett, who in the autumn of 1817 journeyed from Lexington, Kentucky. Stuart displayed the same fondness for this new apprentice, whom he called "Kentucky," that he had for so many predecessors: kindness he had shown a score of others flowed forth, and the poetry of his oracular utterances was carefully noted in Jouett's memorandum:

> Flesh is like no other substance under heaven. It has all the gayety of a silk-mercer's shop without its gaudiness of gloss, and all the soberness of old mahogany without its sadness. . . . Be ever jealous about truth in painting, and preserve as pure as possible the round, blunt stroke. . . . Drawing the features distinctly and carefully with chalk is loss of time; all studies should be made with the brush in

hand. It is nonsense to think of perfecting oneself in drawing before one begins to paint. When the hand is not able to execute the decision of the mind, a fastidiousness ensues, and on its back disappointment and disgust. This is one reason why the Italians never painted so well as other schools.

Himself a simple, direct craftsman, Stuart distrusted new chemical formulas, which he treated with contempt. Of one discovery, represented to have been employed by an Italian master, he said, "Take my advice and have nothing to do with anything of the kind, for certainly you cannot pretend to know what may be the ultimate effect on your work." Another "wonderful" concoction, left with him, he threw from the window; and for those less easily impressed, his imagination supplied fabulous details to illustrate the dangers of experiment:

> He had been commissioned to copy a very fine head by Sir Joshua Reynolds, and while at work on it, in a warm room, he thought he saw one of the eyes move, and take a downward course. A second glance showed this to be true, and it instantly occurred to him that Sir Joshua must have used wax with his colors, to give greater transparency. In an agony of mind, for the picture was one of great value, he hurried with it into the cold air, and gradually worked the eye back into its place.

With materials, palette, and brushes he took infinite care, and if implements were brought to him blemished or improperly arranged, his words were severe. No one was permitted to touch his easel nor enter his painting-room in his absence; if anyone moved a brush or a picture he was certain to notice, which made it a settled thing in the house to abstain altogether unless invited to enter.

Jouett's chief duty became providing copies after portraits of the Presidents: of Washington and Adams he created a small stock, and, retouched by Stuart, in some instances they were sold as sets, to augment faltering finances. Patronage remained scarce, and those sitters he did attract he frightened or offended. The illusions of Mrs. Humphrey Devereux quickly were shattered when in her presence Stuart replied to another sitter when she asked for some changes in drapery that he was "not a milliner." Four years later, when her own portrait was given her, Mrs. Devereux had her fabrics repainted by Chester Harding.

Now UNPATRONIZED and poverty-stricken, by past reputation alone Stuart continued to dominate the American scene, and already his intimate association with history was fixed. In June 1818, the Rhode Island General Assembly, meeting beneath one of his finest Washington full-lengths, passed a resolution "of esteem for the brilliant achievements of Commodore Oliver H. Perry, with a request that he sit for his portrait, to be taken by Gilbert Stuart." They too doubtless were surprised, and disappointed, by the meager 21- by 26-inch panel that he executed. In August of that year he began a prim likeness of Mrs. John Quincy Adams, and, in September, an unsuccessful, diffuse image of the future President:

> A continual storm of rain the whole day. I sat to Stuart before and after breakfast and found his conversation very interesting. His own figure is highly picturesque, with his dress always disordered, and taking snuff from a large round tin wafer box, holding perhaps half a pound, which he must use up in a day.

The case was less that Stuart had found a place in his country's history, than that while still alive, and living through the terrible decay of his abilities, he had become a part of history itself. Patient though he had been, Thomas Jefferson could no more let him be than he could allow that he had not been painted by the great delineator of heroes; and Stuart, living in the fantastic and melancholy afterlife of his departed greatness, retained no portrait of the former President. The life-study which preceded the Bowdoin picture long before had been sold to President James Madison; it was merely typical, and hardly worthy of note, that Stuart, with that awful consistency, had sold this portrait *twice*. Jefferson now wrote to his former Secretary of War, Henry Dearborn, who, retired to Boston, had married the widow of James Bowdoin:

> [October 27, 1818]
> Can you, without involving yourself in offense with Stuart, obtain thro' any channel a frank and explicit declaration on what ground he detains my portrait? In what term? And whether there is to be an end of it. I think he has now had it 10 or 12 years. I wrote to him once respecting it, but he never noticed my letter.

The artist's character suggested this mission was fraught with an unpleasantness better avoided; Dearborn induced his son, who perhaps knew Stuart more personally, to make the perilous call. A report went back to Jefferson, November 16, 1818:

> An interview took place, and after many trifling excuses for the long detention of the portrait, and its unfinished situation, he said that he could not finish it in cold weather, but would certainly complete it in the spring. We will endeavor to push him on, and if possible compel him to finish it as early in the spring as we can.

Quite exceptionally vague and waffling excuses, they were calculated to gain time that would become an eternity. Unable to provide the picture Jefferson demanded, Stuart had bent his efforts to perpetuate the fraud.

Boston experienced a flurry of interested curiosity when John Trumbull's enormous canvas of *The Signing of the Declaration of Independence*, executed for the Capitol in Washington, was brought north by its artist. Hung in Faneuil Hall, it drew crowds, and earned large receipts for Trumbull, with which he commissioned his likeness from Stuart. One wonders if this gesture was not intended to assist a proud comrade in need? Whatever his motive, Trumbull was handsomely rewarded by a profound statement, mingling ancient amity with perceptions of his arrogant, stiff nature. Executed in a staccato shorthand, the small panel showed, again, to what dimensions Stuart's abilities had shrunk; his art had become dots and jottings, that by inference, if not intention, seemed to prefigure later French developments. Old, ill, and embittered, with shaking hands, and much troubled by ailments that now included asthma, his personal impressionism was a new departure in art, at the same time paralleling certain of Rembrandt's later studies.

Recollections of Trumbull in London joined the repertory of Stuart's anecdotage, and the sense of having outlived his time was strengthened that January, 1819, when, at the advanced age of ninety-one, his mother died. The journey to Newport, for her burial, was filled with nostalgia: wandering the town, he found the shoemaker whose head, so long before, he had covered with blood squirted from a syringe. "No," said the shoe-maker, "I don't know as I ever seen you afore."

"My name is Stuart; don't you remember the boy Stuart?"

"Oh yes," said the man, with a noncommittal grunt; "well, if you're as good a man as you were a bad boy, you're a devilish clever fellow."

He remembered this visit's strange mixture of sentiments:

I passed along looking eagerly at the signs, hoping that I might read the names of old friends. People stared at me and I at them, but we could not identify one another. Beginning to feel rather blue over the wrecks of time, I thought I might while away a portion of my time in the Organ Loft of Old Trinity Church, and perchance by force of memory, and a vivid imagination, revive some of the sweet music that used to reach me in my humble pew . . .

I then visited the Stone Mill, and mentally reviewed my questioning respecting that strange and meaningless structure; cast a glance at the Redwood Library building, and admired its unique architecture, so classical, so refined; examined a few folios and reverently gazed at their pictorial embellishments.

From thence I roamed to the neighborhood of Brimley's ropewalks; visited the beach where I had so often bathed, and after exploring the inner and outer, and above and below, passages of that once, in my view, gigantic structure, the State House, I returned to my lodgings to muse over the scenes of my childhood . . . [then] finally exhausted the daylight in reading familiar names on the monuments in the churchyard.

The gulf between this sad, introspective man, searching for friends among the gravestones, and the provocative rogue who continued to withhold Thomas Jefferson's portrait, indicates the polarities of his ambivalence. From the external view, if he did not refuse to give Jefferson his picture, he exhibited a remarkable degree of reluctance. To himself the reasons for so much subterfuge were obvious, and irremediable: he had no picture to give.

And so the long duel of wills continued. When his promise to deliver the picture in the spring was not kept, Dearborn again addressed Jefferson, June 24, 1819:

Having not yet been able to prevail on Stuart to finish your portrait, I suspect that you have paid him in part, or in full, in advance; if so I should like to know it, as I might in that case address his pride with some chance of success. If you have not made any advance, and will authorize me to pay as soon as he shall complete it, I will address his poverty, which is now great, and by engaging to pay him and by frequent calls I should hope to succeed.

After reference to his account books, on July 5, 1819, Jefferson sent Dearborn a full statement of payments made to Stuart. Six months later, January 20, 1820, Dearborn reported his further tribulations:

> After frequent promises Mr. Stuart has again forfeited his engage-
> ment to finish your portrait. His last promise was made in October
> last, when he said he would have it done by the first of January . . .
> Feeling a little out of patience I observed to him that I would inform
> you that you must never expect to have it. I then indicated his having
> received pay for it. He said that you paid him an hundred dollars for
> one that you now have in your home, and that he received one hun-
> dred dollars for a Medallion, but had received nothing for the one
> he now has. That he painted this for himself. That he had no com-
> mission from anyone to paint it. I was too much out of temper to
> say anything more to him and retired.

The reflection Dearborn had made on Stuart's Georgian honor was
surely what occasioned the more brazen lies: in small ways, as in
large, his sense of honor operated persistently to his own disadvantage.
When he replied, February 5, 1820, Jefferson chose to see it as an
inadvertence:

> . . . He must have spoken without reflection, when he supposed
> it in my possession and hanging on my wall. The peculiarities of his
> temper and ideas render him a difficult subject to handle. In the en-
> closed letter I have endeavored to bring his recollection to rights as
> softly as I can. With respect to the first canvas portrait, I thought
> it a good one, and should have been contented with it, and still if he
> chooses to deliver that instead of the second, and if he will finish and
> deliver it, I shall be satisfied. I am sorry to give you this trouble,
> but if this letter does not effect a delivery the business may still be a
> while longer.

Dearborn no longer was willing to approach Stuart, sending his son
to deliver Jefferson's letter. To Stuart, there was still no possible
remedy; he continued to negotiate elliptically and inconclusively,
and, a wily and resourceful opponent, he invented circumstances
calculated to confuse his adversaries. On March 3, 1820, Dearborn
wrote again to Jefferson:

> He now owns that he had been mistaken, and that he has received
> one hundred dollars for the portrait, which you have not received,
> and only wants to know whether you would prefer a common por-
> trait or one of half the length of the body, the former at $100, the
> latter $300. He said he would write to you on the subject, but he may
> neglect it as he has the finishing of the picture. If you will inform me
> which of the two you would prefer I will inform him.

Then, new elements entered the situation, to render its successful conclusion more possible. The sets of Presidents, executed by Jouett, once more had created demand for Presidential likenesses, following which, about 1820, John Doggett, a Boston frame-maker and art dealer, boldly ordered from Stuart a larger set of five half-lengths. To fill this more lucrative order Stuart considered obtaining from one of his own earlier works a likeness of Jefferson: from this he could pass a new study to the former President. But the nearest available image of Jefferson, from his own hand, was the half-length painted for James Bowdoin, which had been transported to Maine!

To Bowdoin College, at Brunswick, Maine, Stuart brought wood panels, on which to carry away likenesses of Jefferson and Madison. Ever equivocal, to Professor Packard, in whose keeping the portraits had been placed, he declared "that he regarded them as good as originals"; a statement remarkable for committing him to nothing.

CANVAS ONCE more was available in America, and on Stuart's return from Maine, its use suddenly refreshed him. He enjoyed feeling again the yielding sensation beneath his brush; vigor re-entered his work. The head of Washington, for the first of Doggett's half-lengths, signaled an amazing return to the qualities of his prime. His heads became firm and true, and after borrowing a hand from Reynolds' *Charles James Fox*, he threw aside completely the Davidian manner that had become associated with his decline. A sense of relief is evident, as he adopted once more the familiar Georgian art of his youth, touched now by Regency romanticism. Half-lengths of Adams and Jefferson followed, the latter executed with torsoless body—a failure consistent since Sir William Barker, with whom it had begun thirty years earlier.

In his last reply to General Dearborn, dated March 26, 1820, Jefferson had expressed a definite preference for his first portrait, painted in Philadelphia:

> I have no doubt Mr. Stuart's justice will think me entitled to the original, and not merely a copy. There was something pleasanter in the aspect of that portrait which I liked better than the second drawn at Washington.

This unexpected complication the artist ignored. On August 14th, noting that Captain Peyton, of Richmond, was headed for Boston,

Jefferson instructed him, too, to speak to Stuart, "as a stimulus to deliver to you, in obtaining which I am sure Mr. Dearborn will lend his kind assistance." By May, 1821, Stuart had advanced the Doggett series sufficiently to contemplate giving up the study-head of Jefferson, brought back from Maine; Dearborn forwarded this welcome news to Virginia; after twenty-one years, Jefferson would have a portrait.

> I have procured your picture from Mr. Stuart at last, and shipped it on board the brig Richmond, S. Hill, Master, for Richmond to the care of Capt. B. Peyton.

Receipt at Monticello was acknowledged by Jefferson, August 17th, "in due time and good order and claims; for this difficult acquisition, the thanks of the family." The paint was still fresh, and Jefferson's daughter, Mrs. Randolph, immediately suspected the imposition. Stuart met the charge with deafening indignation, vehemently expressing his mortification that she supposed him guilty of such a thing. He gave Mrs. Randolph definite assurances he had sent the original, and this final untruth, to which his behavior invariably reduced him, was supported by a specially invented humbug: "he often left the accessories to be filled in just before it was sent home."

And so, after twenty-one years and a long list of personal services, among them the rescuing of his Philadelphia household, and the engraved gold watch he had pawned in Boston, Gilbert Stuart again had deceived Jefferson. How much more honest had he admitted his earlier faults, and repaired them honorably; what reason was sufficient to account for such unspeakable perverseness? Like so many acts in his long career, it brought him no profit once again to be guilty of bad faith. Vanity, levity, subterfuge, artifice, want of veracity, indifference to the truth—the long indictment was complete. And nobody, in fact, had suffered from it more than he himself, who, for sixteen years since his flight from Washington, had passed a futile existence in isolation and neglect. He had suffered unspeakably in disappointments and slights. Now he was old and in difficulties, suffering physically, with only the tragic ruins of his great career and his once-transcendent talents to draw on. Bitterness and frustrations accounted for these last of his vagaries, and, even in their latest and most disquieting form, they were only the same phenomena that had marked his long career.

THE PORTRAIT of George Washington, for which the first President had sat at Mrs. Bingham's request, now hung, without a frame, behind the door of Stuart's painting-room. Still brilliant, unfinished, and widely considered to be the only faithful record of the father of the nation, its shabby circumstance was symbolic of its creator's reduced fortunes. Any rival artist who came to Boston could strip him of sitters, as Chester Harding did in 1822, and both Stuart's house and his painfully afflicted, gout-ridden self were eloquent of material circumstances declining still further.

Ill-humor played about him, despite intermittent efforts to be more obliging towards the few sitters who dared apply. The sudden death of James Perkins, whose sessions had been passed in conversation, left an unfinished head: "Very well, Mr. Stuart; you have inflicted an irreparable loss by your dilatoriness, and I shall never enter your studio again," barked Perkin's brother. By force of memory the face was completed, then he employed a morning visit from Dunlap to paint in two hands from nature: the result was so successful a replica was asked, and he received a subscription of $285 raised by forty-six gentlemen, who presented the picture to the Athenaeum, of which Perkins had been a founder. Jonathan Mason, son of the Senator at whose invitation Stuart had come to "visit" Boston, one day called, while the artist sat fretfully playing his chamber-organ. After introductory remarks the guest implied he had some favor to ask: one that his friends laughed at him for.

"What is it? Let's have it," snapped Stuart, as he stopped playing.

"To ask you to paint for me a copy of your Washington."

Stuart took a pinch of snuff. He was not averse to his old cat and mouse game; "Will you be here the end of next week?" he asked.

"Certainly, Mr. Stuart, if I can be of any service to you."

Uncertain in what state the negotiation stood, Mason returned punctually, to find the painter affable. Suddenly Stuart rose from his chair, and taking a wood panel that was facing the wall, he placed it on an easel. "Now let them laugh at you!" he exclaimed.

He even delivered the portrait of Elizabeth Patterson Bonaparte, when her father came to Boston: "I am very glad that Stuart has given up the picture, and obliged to you for taking the trouble of getting it from him. It is the only likeness that has ever been taken of me. My other pictures are quite as like anyone else as me," wrote Madame Bonaparte, and, when her picture reached Philadelphia, Sully repaired damages suffered by the long discarded canvas.

The melancholy so marked in these neglected years attached itself to endless lesser causes, in addition to those that were fundamental. He spoke often of his son, Charles Gilbert, whose loss seemed never far from his mind; a tormented nature seeks excuses for its moods, and others existed in the passing of Benjamin West, who in March, 1820, went to learn how accurate had been his representations of eternity. Before Stuart traveled again to Newport, in 1822, for the interment of his sister, Anne Newton, he learned through Trumbull that recollections of him lingered in London.

G. Stuart, Esq. New-York, 25th March, 1821
My dear Sir:—

A few days ago I received a letter from our old acquaintance, Sir Thomas Lawrence (who is painting for the Academy here, a full length portrait of Mr. West), in which is a passage which I am sure will give you great pleasure:

"I am glad to hear that Mr. Stuart is still in good health, and practicing his profession. He is one of my very earliest recollections in London; if you ever see him, pray tell him that Mr. Kemble still retains a most extravagant partiality for him."

I hope you and your family enjoy good health, after this murderous winter, and that your daughter is making progress in the Arts worthy of her beginning.

I am faithfully yours,
Jn. Trumbull

Flattering as were Lawrence's words, his ill-concealed surprise that Stuart was still alive echoed sensations not unknown in America. Not yet sixty-five, he had outlived his contemporaries and the world that had been his. In the winter of his years, older than his age, asthmatic and frequently gout-stricken, he seemed a survival of an earlier, less tattered age. Perhaps it was these realizations, wounded pride, and the sudden impetus he felt when able once more to work on canvas, that made the Doggett series of Presidents so impressive. His impressionistic jot and squiggle was replaced by a firm touch; and for the picture of James Monroe it is notable that the hands, the same that had appeared in his first New York canvases (one of which derived from Raphael, by way of Reynolds), were carefully adjusted and restudied from nature. Thrice-familiar elements that had filled his canvases over many years developed new force and sureness: was it the arrival of engravings after Lawrence's newest efforts that drew Stuart away from the French classicism of his wood-panel works to his own previous high-Rigaud manner? Did he at last think the struggle had been in vain, and the soaring romanticism of Lawrence proved the essential rightness of what he had done himself, in the final great Washington full-length, painted two decades before at Germantown? Whatever the case, one senses feelings of relief.

OFTEN IN these years of neglect Stuart expressed a desire to leave Boston for the greener pastures that he once had known in New York. Despite the numbers of capable artists grown up and settled there, among them Trumbull and Jarvis, there is no doubt that Stuart's re-emergence on the national scene would have signaled much new patronage for a legendary figure; gout, asthma, and indolence were sufficient causes for him not to do, at sixty-seven, what he had failed to do for nearly twenty years past.

Occasionally he finished old pictures that had been in his studio three and four years, and in December 1822, he was requested by the Trustees of the Massachusetts General Hospital to paint its benefactor, William Phillips, which, by the following October, he had accomplished in a large half-length. His celerity was surprising, and indicative of idleness and need; it was the more remarkable at a period when, in an effort to bring himself back into patronage and doubtless fortified by the success of the Doggett pictures, he moved again into the center of Boston. From John Wilson, a tailor, he rented a three-story brick house at 59 Essex Street, and the numbers of small canvases that again came off his easel attest the relative wisdom of this change. By August he was well installed, and active about town; on August 21, 1823, Josiah Salisbury reported, "I have called three times upon Stuart, without being able to see him. He has lately removed to Essex Street which I suppose has interrupted his labors," but the portrait of Stephen Salisbury, for which he received payment in July, was duly delivered to Worcester in September. Though well-characterized, it shows another sudden loss of force, and certainty. His trembling hand and diminished vision are evident in all the works of this time; also, that to make good in his subject's absence what he failed to accomplish at sittings, he now consistently painted onto each head, male or female, his own large ears, their distinctive trailing lobes lying flat against the upturned jaw. An old expedient, traceable even to the London portrait of *Sir William Burton Conyngham,* it was hardly proper to tamper with the authenticity of a head's characteristics in this way. Only the most urgent necessity, and the need to disguise his faltering vision, made it a consistent practice. One last shred of integrity, the "truth" of his heads, thus fell by the way.

On weekly visits, Isaac P. Davis dealt with incessant problems. His affection for the difficult artist was sincere, and not unmixed with sympathy; once, when Stuart departed Davis' house, leaving behind his oversized snuff-box, Davis humorously hired a porter to return it in a handcart. In March, 1823, therefore, Davis was present when Timothy Williams, whose brother, the merchant-banker Samuel Williams of London, had come into possession of the Lansdowne full-length of Washington after the Marquis' death, called on Stuart for verification of the picture's authenticity. The Williams brothers sought to establish that they owned an original portrait of Washington, *painted from life;* a condition to which, in strictest fact, no full-length by Stuart could conform. Five years later Stuart was indebted to Timothy Williams for the considerable sum of $487.04, which, if already owed to the merchant, may have been a factor on this occasion, for he acquiesced in what was asked of him.

Among his papers Stuart discovered Washington's letter of April 11, 1796, fixing the first sitting for the head which still hung in his studio. Quaking hands made writing too difficult: Davis was accustomed to act as secretary, preparing letters, and receipts, for his trembling signature. From Stuart's dictation, he now added an extraordinary line of untruths to Washington's note:

> In looking over my papers to find one that had the signature of Geo. Washington, I found this, asking me when he should sit for his portrait, which is now owned by Samuel Williams, of London. I have thought it proper it should be his especially as he owns the only original painting I ever made of Washington, except one I own myself: I painted a third but rubbed it out.
> I now present this to his brother Tim. Williams, for said Samuel.
> Boston, 9th Day March 1823   G. Stuart

Washington himself thus became a signatory to falsehoods: the final triumph of Stuart's many years' devotion to trading in villainy, this paradox is delightful as it is disturbing. To accomplish such a strange, distasteful perversion, Stuart denied Georgian art its basic principles, of which, in his better days, he had been so much a master. Complacently he allowed the Williams brothers to represent that the Lansdowne portrait had precedence over the Bingham and Constable versions, and was painted from the living person—casting aside the concept of classic allusion, and all the grandiose scholarly principles he had himself brought to America.

But also, by his inference, he had created a new portrait for which Washington himself had given sittings. He thus faced the necessity of asserting the authenticity of his own carefully retained life-head; and that first brilliant effort, which had so startled Philadelphia by its superbly restrained violence of mood, he bastardized by the statement it was "rubbed out"—a hopelessly unnecessary falsehood, thrown in as an afterthought, because of the earlier too-free wording. An extraordinary pernicious brew, added to a letter written by the American national hero reputed never to have told a lie, it confused Stuart's own fame for nearly a century and a half. One hardly knows whether laughter or tears are more appropriate.

XXVIII

Expiation

THE CIRCUMSTANCES of Stuart's last sad years cast their gloom over his entire career. Everything had resolved into this final failure, and failure, in retrospect, seemed writ large across his life. He never had found the material rewards he had seen others enjoy: he never had dominated, except fleetingly, the knowledgeable artistic world of London, where alone his supreme gifts might have been fully appreciated: nor had gold ever filled his pockets to the extent his exertions deserved. Now, aware that the race was nearly run, he reflected that he would be able to leave his wife and four daughters not even the meannest provision, and he began to view differently his carefully preserved study of Washington. When one of his last pupils asked if he intended ever to finish the coat and background, he replied, "No: and as this is the only legacy I can leave my family, I will let it remain untouched"—to distinguish its superb fresh observation from the five-score replicas he had ground out and authorized.

Seldom had he evinced any vanity about his works, but now he spoke frequently of the *Macbeth* for which Kemble had posed in London, regretting that he had never learned its fate. And with his heart turned once more, ever regretfully, to London, he recollected how the Duke of Kent might have been his sitter at Halifax, and looked upon declining that offer as the most signal error of his life; though, in effect, acceptance would have precluded his painting Washington. There are delicacies of interpretation inherent in this to which he may not have been sensitive, or perhaps already he recognized himself that his career had become too much a question of history, and that he had ceased to be regarded as the brilliant artistic phenomenon he was. Had he not painted Washington, were that eternal linkage unforged, had he returned to London in good time, unquestionably his supreme artistry with the portrait would have rung through with more force. Chester Harding realized this when he wrote from London, in January, 1825: "This is the place where I think you should have remained, and the place where I think if you were to come now, you would command any price for your labors, and I don't hesitate to say that you would stand ahead of all, unless it be Sir Thomas Lawrence." Yet, however fondly this view was entertained, it was vain, for the fault lay not in the fact that his mature years had been given to his native land, but that he had been deficient in judgment. Throughout his career he failed to respond properly to the succession of overwhelming successes he gained. Even in America, had he organized a functioning studio at Philadelphia, Washington, or Boston, he would not have ended his existence as he was, wedged into a cul-de-sac. His principal errors were not that he declined offers such as Kent's, nor even that he offended patrons and practiced such lamentable deceits on them, but that more opportunities than ever came to his contemporaries were allowed to slip through his fingers. His supreme gifts failed to win just rewards because, at each stage of his life, he exhibited a fundamental incompetence to deal with his own promising affairs.

To the end Stuart remained a watchful and ever-interested observer of the motions of his own mind. He saw himself, as he saw everything else, with the special view of genius, if, indeed, with an added measure of self-indulgence. His failure and poverty were a torment to his final years; but, from a perspective hidden from him, another view of his life found it a series of accomplishments too splendid to be the work of one man. Throughout the English-speaking world he was the unique painter-laureate of revolutionaries and those who opposed oppression, whether successfully, as in America, or unsuccessfully, in Ireland. Single-handed he recorded the Shelburne Whigs who destroyed the personal rule of King George III, the rebellious Irish whom Pitt suppressed, and the generation of Americans who brought forth a new nation. With twinkling eye and twisted lip, they are an international heritage, treasures to an entire civilization, valuable to all those peoples who speak the English language. Alone, too, he had brought across the ocean his superb technique, Europe's studio traditions, and the distilled artistic thought of centuries. In thirty years of dominance he saw his art take root, firmly grounding his native land in a great tradition at its moment of flowering. No other colonial center had the continued advantage of an artist of his caliber; the lead the United States thereafter took in portraiture, with its own tradition that outlived all others and flourishes yet, was due entirely to him. Finally, and it is no small thing, he painted many individual masterpieces and heads rarely equaled and never surpassed, over a working span of fifty years.

The neglect of his later years was not salutary; in Boston he grew stale, peered over engravings after the works of London rivals, adapted himself to their ideas, became a follower of those he once led, and industriously deteriorated. While John Adams observed in a letter to Dr. Waterhouse, one fancies not without a suppressed smile, "Mrs. Morton says genius is sorrow's child," and though the state to which he had fallen was of his own making, the growth of younger rivals caused Stuart to observe, pettishly, ". . . fifty years hence you will not be able to kick a dog-kennel but out will start a portrait-painter." Since Van Dyck, those artists who occupy themselves with portraits have suffered from nervous afflictions attributable to the tensions of their profession. And whereas artists as a category live long, portrait artists tend to be extinguished in their prime. The melancholy that was a part of Gainsborough's gay personality gives a bittersweet flavor to his work; early in the decade of the nineties Romney collapsed in a storm of nerves, never to recover. Reynolds, cold of disposition and robust of frame, lost his vision suddenly, surviving only a year; Lawrence soon was snuffed out, without warning, at sixty. It is difficult to see how a person of Stuart's inherent instability, could, under any circumstances, have withstood the strains of his calling. The seeds of his final decay had been within him from the start; they were propagated by the harsh test of his profession, but his appalling collapse into deceit and dishonor was a personal development, on private traits. Never an honest man, now he shuffled and prevaricated so lamentably that even the magnificent achievements of his past sank into the mire of this final degeneration. At Boston, having muddled and tricked himself out of the fruits of his genius and exertions, he learned where God had found his model for Hell.

MOMENTS OF visual clarity and greater manual control still punctuated years of dimming sight and pathetically declining capacities. If his place in history already was an acute embarrassment to his living self, also, on occasion, it sprang up to rescue him from idleness and poverty. Among those who retained a surprising faith in him, despite earlier astringent observations, was John Quincy Adams, who, September 3, 1824, noted in his diary:

> I called . . . upon Stuart, the painter, and engaged him to go to Quincy and there paint a portrait of my father. More than twenty years have elapsed since he painted the former portrait, and time has wrought so much change on his countenance that I wish to procure a likeness of him as he is now. Stuart started some objections of trivial difficulties,—the want of an easel, of a room properly adapted to the light, but finally promised that he would go and take with him his best brush, to paint a picture of affection and of curiosity for future times.

The light he found at Quincy was *not* good, and its very inappropriateness provided new stimulus. The long-retired second President was seen half-shrouded in shadow, a departure almost unique among Stuart's works, immeasurably contributing to the subtlety of this portrayal. His supreme understanding of form had free play, and midst the sag of ancient flesh he glimpsed the living spirit shining through Adams' feeble body. Nearing his eighty-ninth birthday, the former President told Boston's Mayor, Josiah Quincy, he was well pleased to sit: "for he lets me do just what I please, and keeps me constantly amused by his conversation"; a moment when Stuart's "abundance of superfluous breath" proved its worth. In the evening of his powers, he achieved a work of the greatest profundity, and his quaking hand, which put pigment to canvas in sudden thrusts, created an impressionistic vibration of color that persuaded he was painting better than ever.

Only a small proportion of his recent works rose to these heights, but, like the Doggett series of Presidents and *William Phillips*, canvases spaced along the route of his obvious deterioration showed his final development advantageously. Boston stirred slightly at the revelation of Stuart's continued gifts, and, in November 1824, urged by his daughter, Josiah Quincy came to sit. Stuart had first painted him ten years earlier, and it was a gentler, chastened, artist who again greeted Boston's Mayor, with obvious pleasure at receiving a public official. Canvas was ready on the easel; he sketched a bold outline, and worked while conversing rapidly. The Rigaud manner was what he intended, and presently a tone of bright blue appeared: his explanation was carefully phrased to suggest his exalted place among artists: "Your father is an active man, and likes to be in the open air; he shall have blue sky behind his head. Few artists would attempt to give effect to a portrait with such a light background. It is a bold effort; but I will try it."

Though he appeared inclined to dispute the fact of his sad fate, fortune had a broad back, and had turned it inexorably on Gilbert Stuart. His late brilliance offended that angry Goddess, who too long had been troubled by the preposterous man; early in 1825 he suffered a stroke, which left his hands trembling more violently than before, the left arm slightly paralyzed, and a fixed, lionlike expression on the fallen right side of his face. Josiah Quincy's unfinished image remained in the studio, and, anxious to demonstrate he could still paint, despite much weakness, he asked for a drawing of the new Boston market that Quincy, as Mayor, was erecting opposite Fanueil Hall. Just as he had painted the ruined Kilcooley Abbey behind Sir William Barker, now he painfully drew the market's façade, too large, into Quincy's picture. Visitors saw him stand before it, his wrist on a rest, from which the hand vibrated—then, when it had become tolerably steady, a sudden dash of the brush touched color to canvas. Washington Allston reassuringly told Quincy's daughter "the head was worthy of the old masters," a remark she proudly repeated to Stuart.

"And am I not an old master, Miss Quincy?" was his response, given with a sharp glance. Was it his pride that brought forth this rebuke, or had he intended only a pun that made him an aged master of his craft? Whatever his thought, he saw dismay in Miss Quincy's face, and added, "You deserve half the credit of the portrait, as you persuaded your father to sit to me a second time. You must always say that *we* painted that portrait."

At intervals, newly completed canvases still left his studio; in April he received $200 for Ward Nicholas Boylston's portrait. And as works were completed, he was obliged, like a beginner, to seek their replacement on his easel by soliciting orders. History came to his rescue and sent him, early in February, when too ill to deal with it, a request for a full-length of Washington. Anxious, weak, and infirm, he was forced to embrace all opportunities:

Dear Sir,
                                                      Boston Mar. 6, 1825
A serious and continual indisposition has prevented an acknowledgement of yours of Feb. 8th respecting a portrait of Washington, and I am now reminded by your letter to my friend Mr. Davis that an answer to the honored call of your Committee cannot be delayed any longer. While I am sensible to this honor, I am sensible also of the uncertainty of the health that is so necessary to the completion of the work. This uncertainty makes it proper that all my engagements respecting it be conditional.

Should I regain my strength; I propose to commence a full-length portrait by the 1st of May, and be allowed 2 years at least for the completion of it. That I receive two thousand dollars for the picture and be protected in the exclusive benefit of copies of it by engraving through fourteen years. I make this last condition with feelings injured by repeated attempts by others to copy my works, (to which I have devoted much time and expense,) not only without remuneration but without my consent. To you I need not dilate upon the feelings and rights of authors nor upon the protection to which they are entitled and which in this country are so openly violated, and so seldom defended without sacrificing the value of the right contended for.

Should these considerations meet the approbation of your Committee, I will endeavor to fulfill their expectations.

I subscribe myself,

                                                      their Obt Servt
                                                      G. Stuart

Though only the signature is from Stuart's quaking hand, the letter rings with his unmistakable phrasing. That in this late moment of his life he could attempt a full-length portrait, a genre untouched for eighteen years, was surely illusory, and, with what strength he could muster, he returned to the posthumous images ordered by Bostonians sympathetic with his plight. The Trustees of the Massachusetts General Hospital requested him to view the dead body of another benefactor, John McLean, and though he found it distasteful, he reluctantly consented. "I can paint that man's portrait," he commented. "I remember seeing him one day on State Street, with his head out of a carriage window, in earnest conversation with a gentleman, and was struck with the expression of his face."

"THAT'S A BOBBISH PICTURE," Stuart opined when young John Neagle, accompanied by Longacre, the engraver, arrived from Philadelphia, with letters of introduction and a sample of his work. He received his callers with much courtesy, but the terrible expression of his mask-like face made his comment impossible to interpret. Mrs. Stuart came to Neagle's aid: "Quiet your fears. If that is what he said, he paid you a high compliment. With him *bobbish* means remarkably fine."

Troubled increasingly by his vision, Stuart asked Neagle to read out a letter, which proved to be from an artist named Parker, who wished permission to copy the Bingham version of his Washington full-length, now deposited with the Pennsylvania Academy. The very application was treated as an affront; "If I am not much mistaken, this man has not the essentially requisite feelings for a good artist," he observed, and dictated his negative reply to Neagle: "My answer will be found in a number of the *Spectator*," he intoned; ". . . and my feelings understood by referring to that paper. The only difference is that Addison speaks of pirating the works of an author; substitute for *author* the word *painter*." So rapidly introduced into Stuart's affairs, both Neagle and Longacre were also received by his family: "Spent the evening most agreeably indeed in the rich and constructive conversation of Mr. Stuart," Longacre recorded in his diary, Sunday, July 24, 1825; and the following day, "from 12 to 2 with Mr. Stuart's daughters." Tuesday he noted again, "Took a carriage at eight o'clock, called for the daughters of Mr. Stuart . . ." and after dinner that night, and the night following, he "spent the evening with Mr. Stuart. . . . His age does not appear to have impaired his faculties so far as judgement and conversation are concerned. His powers are still displayed in his most recent pictures; they are full of likeness and animation"; but, for all the amiability they displayed, Neagle could not fail to notice, "his family appeared to fear him."

No mention is made of any work in progress, though Neagle's concern over how Stuart directed his trembling hand implies he saw him in action. With rare indulgence, Stuart allowed Neagle to paint him, an honor of which the younger man was most conscious. Under the excuse of advising on principles, Stuart suggested that the contracted side of his face be turned away, "for the sake of perspective representation." An essential melancholy quickly manifested itself in Neagle's image; in confirmation of older habits, it caught his head inclined at the same angle seen by Archer-Shee in Dublin. When Stuart stepped out of the room, Neagle placed beside his picture the unfinished one of Josiah Quincy.

"What is that?" Stuart asked on his return.

"One of your portraits."

"Oh, my boy, you should not do that!"

"I beg your pardon, Mr. Stuart. I should have obtained your permission before I made this use of it; but I have placed it so carefully that it cannot suffer the least injury."

"It is not on that account . . ." said Stuart. "I have every confidence in your care: but why do you place it there? . . . Does my face look like Mr. Quincy's?"

"No, sir, not at all in the expression, nor can I say that the coloring is even like; but there is a certain air of truth in the coloring of your work . . . and I was in hopes of catching something from the work of the master without imitating it."

". . . Tell me what suggested this method."

"Some parts of the lectures of Sir Joshua Reynolds . . ."

"I knew it," said Stuart. "Reynolds was a good painter, but he has done incalculable mischief to the rising generation by many of his remarks. . . . While you have nature before you as a model, paint what you see, and look with your own eyes. However you may estimate my works, depend on it they are very imperfect; and the works of the best artists have some striking faults . . ."

As the sittings advanced, every act seemed to bring forth an anecdote; even when Neagle asked for a pinch of snuff: "I will give it to you," Stuart replied, "but I advise you not to take it. Snuff-taking is a pernicious, vile, dirty habit, and, like all habits, to be carefully avoided."

"Your practice contradicts your precept, Mr. Stuart."

"Sir, *I* can't help it. Shall I tell you a story?" An account of his accident on the Black Rock coach followed, and, when he recounted how, on being seized, the "corpse" roared to life with the words, "Let me alone; I'm not hurt—I was born so," Stuart added, ". . . *I* was born so"; and, taking an enormous pinch of snuff, neatly finished his story, "*I was born in a snuff mill.*"

His box of snuff had become *two*, each nearly as large as the top of a small hat, and he offered Neagle a pinch from each. Asked the difference, he droned, "One box is common, and the other superior.

The first is for common every-day acquaintance, the second for particular friends; therefore, take you a pinch of the best."

Nor could he resist the temptation of one last whopper at the expense of Washington. Neagle recorded:

> Mrs. Washington called often to see the General's portrait, and was desirous to possess the painting. One day she called with her husband, and begged to know when she might have it. The General himself never pressed it, but on this occasion, as he and his lady were about to retire, he returned to Mr. Stuart and said he saw plainly what advantage the picture was to the painter; he therefore begged the artist to retain the painting at his pleasure.

A useless flight of fancy, he was explaining away things *unnecessary* to explain, for the study of Washington had become his, by right, when Senator Bingham decided on a larger canvas. Yet fact and fiction were intermingled in his mind to such a degree he was incapable of discerning the truth, and his family, at their peril if they had not, supported him in every rash assertion. His own aged London ruffles of Brussels lace, long tattered, had been divided and parceled out for souvenirs among the admirers of Washington. "My father asked Mrs. Washington if she could let him have a piece of lace, such as the General wore, to paint from," explained Jane; "she said 'certainly,' and then enquired if it would make any difference if it were *old*." The calculation of this last point is delicate, for the London ruffle obviously was older than Washington's portrait. "Keep it; it may be of use for other pictures," Mrs. Washington is then said to have told the painter. And Mrs. Stuart nobly supported questionable histories recounted by husband and daughter, asserting that the first time she saw Washington, in Philadelphia, "he was dressed in black velvet, with white lace ruffles . . ."

UNDER A pressure of mounting debt, Stuart was not without honor in Boston, where, if his word was known to be untrustworthy, and his gurgling talk at times was a bore, the haunting power of his earlier works retained for him the respect due a declining master. Contumely was not his lot, and it is a credit to Boston that her institutions sought to give him patronage, and such honors as could safely be conferred. His name ornamented the committee formed to erect a monument at Bunker Hill, and, serving as chairman, he was intimate with architects and Massachusetts' political leaders, among them Daniel Webster, whose portrait he began. The commission, however, came from Isaac P. Davis, and Webster himself adopted the ambivalent attitude of the practical politician. One day while visiting Davis, he stood some time before the picture, and finally, bowing low, said, "I am willing *that* should go down to posterity"; but at home he differed, for his wife wrote of "Stewart's portrait, about which I agree with Daniel, who said the other evening that he should rather see the other side of the canvas."

At Lafayette's visit to Boston, in June 1825, a rare moment of elation came to Stuart as the cornerstone of the Bunker Hill monument was laid in a pageant of civic display. As the surviving authority on Washington appearance, he earlier had assisted the French sculptor, Binon, who essayed a portrait, "aided by the condescending instructions of this great master, whose *mind's eye* still beholds the countenance which his immortal pencil had saved from the grave to transmit to posterity." Mobilization of his artistic prestige remained significant; his judgment still bore weight throughout the country, and was fiat in Boston. He submitted to the near suffocation of plaster poured over his face, for a life-mask, when Henri Browere visited Boston; the formidable ogre who emerged, his intensity of expression fixed for all time, is the best likeness of Stuart in his terrible old age. And however unflattered, he knew the value of what was done:

> Boston, 29th Nov., 1825
> Mr. Browere has made a bust of me from the life, with which I am perfectly satisfied; and which I hope will remove any illiberal representations which may prevent the nation from possessing records of more important men.
> G. Stuart

Yet, however potent his word in behalf of others, for himself he was forced to solicit work by whatever means he could, and in October he traveled to Quincy, to see a portrait of Copley that might assist a posthumous image of Josiah Quincy, Jr., who had perished at sea in 1775. The picture was one previously refused.

"Here is a family, Mr. Stuart, who are looking to you for a head," was the gracious greeting of Mayor Quincy, and Stuart appeared pleased.

"It is seventeen years since I was here last," he replied, "and I am very glad to find myself here again."

The intimation of mortality passed unnoted, and on Quincy's wall he noted a print from Benjamin West's *Battle of the Boyne,* which cued him to anecdoting: he recalled posing for two of its figures, and remembered an Irishman who thought West had erred by omitting the monument he had seen on the battlefield! John Quincy Adams, who, since their last meeting, had succeeded James Monroe as President of the United States, joined the company for lunch, and spoke at length of Lafayette's visit. But also, with remarkable faith in his feeble dinner companion, the President requested a full-length portrait of himself. Out of pride, and, perhaps, an unwillingness to admit his state, and surely, too, from pleasure that a *sixth* American President made call on him, Stuart agreed.

A brave effort to turn back the clock, the full-length portrait of John Quincy Adams was begun: beyond his powers physically, and nervously, inevitably it remained a head, left isolated, high up on a large bare canvas. Winter saw him growing more weak; "I fear this poor fellow will not live to paint another . . ." wrote Thomas Handasyd Perkins, March 12, 1826. "He is quite feeble and has not used his pencil for some months." Ill though he was, penury was his taskmaster, and in May he delivered to the Massachusetts General Hospital a replica of John McLean's posthumous image. His efforts lacked clarity and authority: advancing a head of Thomas Motley, he asked petulantly if the subject had any Scotch blood. On receiving a negative reply, he exclaimed, "Well, I've a damned Scotchman *here,*" and laid aside his essay for a second attempt. How much more than the head of any picture was from his own brush is open to question, for his daughter Jane had assumed a large role in the studio, and the only purpose of father and daughter now was to ease the family's poverty, which was proverbial: "Mr. Stewart being the tenant, I must conclude but a small part of the value has been paid," occurs in a letter pertaining to his Essex Street house.

Aware of the assistance Jane gave him, and the praises that had greeted her *Magdalene,* exhibited in 1823, he contemplated sending her to London, to the care of Beechey, with whom he opened a correspondence: ". . . how very happy I was to receive a letter from my old friend in Boston, after an absence of one hundred and fifty years . . ." was the warm response, and ruminating his daughter's prospects, "he then very earnestly advised and urged that I should obtains heads painted by Romney," remembered Jane, "as being exceedingly beautiful, and more true to nature than any others he had ever seen, not even excepting those of Sir Joshua, much as he admired the latter." But Jane never left America.

A MORE COMPLETE paralysis of his left arm increased Stuart's distress, and though his mind was clear and active, the damage to his morale was severe when he found his arm becoming useless. "If I could live and have my health," he repeated, "I could paint better pictures than I have ever done." Fretfully reflecting his reasons, so slight, unworthy, and ridiculous, for endless lapses from high quality, he doubtless saw how true this might have been. Rarely had he employed his abilities to the full, a thought disturbing now as he grew dim and meager. Occasionally something amusing passed his lips, but the natural flow of spirits that had marked him from earliest times, was gone. Still he tried to paint heads, and those he succeeded in rubbing in, like *Jared Sparks* in its diffuse edgelessness, show how poor his vision had become. In the mood of regret and reverie that overcame him, he even fancied one of his last sitters, Mrs. John Forrester, bore a resemblance to Mrs. Benjamin West, to whom he once tendered boyish affection. The few faces he finished were given to Jane, to add dry, uninspired shoulders and accessories; poverty and failing abilities thus added further indignity to a graceless end.

To visitors, Stuart still elaborated on his relations with Washington and at any mention of Senator Bingham or the engraving after the Lansdowne portrait, agitatedly paced the room. The fixed expression of his face was so severe it terrified some: "Oh, your father has such a searching look that I am frightened to death," one lady admitted to his daughter Anne. Occasionally he ventured out in a hired carriage, and in 1827 visited the first exhibition at Boston's Athenaeum. His sickly appearance brought out the man in charge of the gallery, who, with a courtesy undesired by Stuart, assisted him up the steps. At the landing place he turned with such a withering look it seemed to annihilate the Samaritan, as Boston's artists with difficulty restrained their laughter. Memorable remarks were reserved for a portrait of Napoleon: "How delicately the lace is drawn; did one ever see a richer satin? The ermine is wonderful in its finish;

and, *by jove*, the thing has a head!"

Stuart lingered through another winter in a shocking state of emaciation. When asked about his health by Washington Allston, for the only time in his life he called attention to his malformed leg. "Ah," said he, "you can judge"; and he pulled up his pantaloons. "You see how much I am *out of drawing*." New symptoms developed in the spring, accompanied by pain in his chest and stomach, where Dr. Warren thought his gout had settled. He bore his physical torment with much fortitude, then, slowly, exhausted from the tortures of a painful cancer, at the age of seventy-two he crumbled, and on the ninth day of July, 1828, he departed to the ultimate expiation of his sins.

Sources Employed by Gilbert Stuart

The *Apollo Belvedere*

Pope Leo X and Two Cardinals, Raphael

Hands were taken from the following works by Raphael: *The Disputa* (An Angel); *The Alba Madonna*; *The Sistine Madonna*

Pope Paul III, Titian

Pesaro Family Altarpiece, Titian

Decius Mus Sending Away the Lictors, Rubens

Triple Portrait of Charles I, Van Dyck

Prince d'Arenberg, Van Dyck

The Earl of Bristol and the Duke of Bedford, Van Dyck

Bishop Bossuet, by Rigaud (engraved by Pierre Imbert Drevet)

Charles d'Hozier, by Rigaud (engraved by Edelinck)

François Gigot de Lapeyronnie, Rigaud

Mrs. Rous, Sir Peter Lely

Queen Marie D'Este (or Countess of Westmoreland), Sir Peter Lely

Queen Marie-Antoinette (seated full-length) Vigée-Lebrun

Queen Marie-Antoinette with a Rose, Vigée-Lebrun

Self-portrait before her easel, Vigée-Lebrun

Madame Mole-Raymond, Vigée-Lebrun

Madame Louise Lefevre, dite la Dugazon, Vigée-Lebrun

La Comtesse de Provence, Vigée-Lebrun

Duchess de Polignac, Vigée-Lebrun

"*La Tricoteuse*," J. L. David

La Marquise D'Orvilliers, J. L. David

Portrait of a Man, Francis Cotes

Queen Charlotte and Her Children, Benjamin West

Mrs. Siddons, Gainsborough

Self-portrait, James Barry

Mrs. Milles, Romney

Mrs. "Perdita" Robinson, Romney

Admiral Keppel, Reynolds

Josiah Wedgwood, Reynolds

Prince of Wales (1785), Reynolds

Duchess of Ancaster, Reynolds

Percival Pot, Reynolds

Charles James Fox (1784), Reynolds

"*Heads of Angels*" (Miss F. I. Gordon), Reynolds

The Marlborough Family, Reynolds

The Angerstein Family, Reynolds

Richard Brinsley Sheridan, Reynolds

Lord Rawdon, Reynolds

Thomas Tomkins, Reynolds

Countess of Dartmouth, Reynolds

The Irish House of Commons, engraving by Mazell

Notes

PROLOGUE

THIS INTERPRETATION of Georgian art and its special character derives from the author's observation, experience, and technical knowledge in the practice of portraiture.

The English do not have the same pride in their own artists exhibited by Italians, French, and Dutch; only an assiduous study in museums, private homes, and at the Witt Library in London, will familiarize one with the vast treasures that exist. For earlier efforts in this direction see "A Hidden Treasure in Britain," Charles Merrill Mount, *The Art Quarterly*, Autumn 1959, and "A Hidden Treasure in Britain," Part II, Charles Merrill Mount, *The Art Quarterly*, Spring 1961.

The principal sources concerning Reynolds are *Reynolds*, by Ellis K. Waterhouse, London, 1941, and *Sir Joshua Reynolds*, by Derek Hudson, London, 1958; Reynolds' letter explaining his sittings, written to Daniel Daulby, September 1777, from the latter. More enlightening concerning "attitudes" and the question of plagiarism from sources is *The Lives of the Most Eminent British Painters, Sculptors, and Architects*, by Allan Cunningham, London, 1854, but the work of tracing from what sources Reynolds and the other artists of the period derived their pictures has been the author's own throughout. Gainsborough has been treated in a limited edition of reproductions, with catalogue, *Gainsborough*, by Ellis K. Waterhouse, London, 1958; and *Lely*, by R. B. Beckett, London, 1951, is helpful with that admirable artist. Romney has fared less well; except for books now half a century old and generally unobtainable, there is only the catalogue of the recent Iveagh Bequest exhibition at Kenwood, *George Romney*, London County Council, 1961.

PART ONE
Chapter I

THE MOST considerable source concerning Stuart's early life is the biography begun by his daughter, Jane Stuart, and completed in 1879 by George C. Mason as *The Life and Works of Gilbert Stuart*. With the assistance of an extensive manuscript prepared by Dr. Benjamin Waterhouse and information supplied by Sully, Trott, Trumbull, Neagle, Edwin, Longacre, and Fraser, the biography of Stuart contained in *The His-*

334 *Notes*

tory of the Rise and Progress of the Arts of Design in the United States, by William Dunlap, New York, 1834, is more revealing concerning the first years. Mabel Munson Swan has published what is known of the missing Waterhouse manuscript itself in "Scraps—The Missing Waterhouse Biography of Gilbert Stuart," *Art in America,* 1953, Vol. 41, no. 2, pages 88–91. Waterhouse's reflections on her father aroused Jane Stuart to refutation, and her heated treatment of him is all the more remarkable for having waited forty years! Before turning the work over to Mason, however, she was herself responsible for three articles in *Scribner's Monthly:* "The Stuart Portraits of Washington," "The Youth of Gilbert Stuart," and "Anecdotes of Gilbert Stuart" (XII, 1876, pp. 367–74; XIII, 1876–7, pp. 640–6; XIV, 1877, pp. 376–82). None of these are anything but historical raw materials, and require careful consideration. Another effort to set forth Stuart's early years is that by John Hill Morgan, prefaced to Lawrence Park's *Gilbert Stuart,* New York, 1926, a work chiefly memorable for its bulk and useful illustrations.

John Smibert's portrait of the Rev. Dr. McSparren is at the Metropolitan Museum, New York; that Stuart celebrated his birthday at Easter is inherent in his letter to Benjamin West. Material on Fontenoy and the Highland Rising of '45 is taken from *England In The Eighteenth Century* (1714–1815) by J. H. Plumb, Harmondsworth, Middlesex, 1950; its aftermath is well treated in "The Northern Campaign of the '45," by R. J. Adam, *History Today,* June 1958, and "Going to America," by J. W. Blake, *History Today,* June 1958. Some background on the settlements in Nova Scotia is found in "New England Architecture in Nova Scotia," by Alan Gowans, *The Art Quarterly,* Spring 1962. Through much of the years 1961 and 1962 the author conducted a search of Irish country houses, and was impressed by the remarkable likeness he found between the works of the "Colonial" period in Ireland and America; thanks to the present-day antiques trade, many American heirlooms have in fact come from Ireland.

To William T. Whitley (*Gilbert Stuart,* Cambridge, Massachusetts, 1932) goes credit for a remarkable tenacity in searching contemporary sources and newspapers. Whitley first discovered the date of Alexander's death; my own efforts to find Stuart's name in the registers of several Scottish universities were not fruitful. Two examples of Alexander's earlier works (dated 1760 and signed) are in the National Gallery of Scotland, Edinburgh. Precisely what Alexander did in America with his "optical glasses" is open to surmise, but his route indicates that he was taking tracings of the Gibbs-inspired churches for some purpose; see *The Life and Work of James Gibbs,* by Bryan Little, London, 1955. Mather Brown's letter (dated March 2, 1817) is in the Byles and Brown letters, Massachusetts Historical Society, published by Mabel M. Swan in "Gilbert Stuart in Boston," *Antiques,* February 1936. The presence of Stuart's name in Joseph Anthony's account book, July 1775, shows his southerly route (*Dictionary of American Biography,* New York, 1936). I have been unable to locate this account book.

Chapter II

JOHN PALMER's address appears in one of Stuart's own anecdotes, recounted many years later in Boston and recorded by Dunlap. The stylish green overcoat was remembered by Wharton, present when Stuart called on West; Wharton told Sully, who recorded it for Dunlap. In another anecdote Stuart himself mentioned how outdated was his apparel. It is significant that while Stuart suffered in London, Zoffany and Tilly Kettle found their way to India, and Hickey, Pack, Angelica Kauffman, and Robert Home to Dublin. Mrs. Stuart's petition appears in Whitley in full text and Morgan (Park) excerpted, both recounting it from *Narragansett Historical Register*, Vol. VII, and *Rhode Island Colonial Records*, Vol. VII.

Probably Waterhouse was reliable, though his revelations aroused the ire of Stuart's family, who made highly unpleasant insinuations. Still, it seems strange that in view of his direct assertion that Stuart twice was seized and confined in "sponging houses," the records of the Middlesex Quarter Sessions and the Middlesex Old Bailey Sessions for the years 1775–78 do not mention his name (letter from Miss E. D. Mercer, County Archivist, November 26, 1962). Records of less formal establishments, called "lock-ups," have not been preserved; letter from the Secretary, Public Records Office, London, October 31, 1962. Dr. Fothergill's practice is reported with his death in *The Gentleman's Magazine*, London, 1781.

The exact sequence of Stuart's earliest contacts with West has been much disputed by his family and those who followed. Waterhouse is authority for his own visit to West, and probably is accurate. That Stuart wrote West "my hopes from home blasted" infers he had expectations, presumably from his rich uncle Joseph Anthony. That he visited West on the strength of Waterhouse's earlier interview, and before he had written his beseeching letter, is clear from the talk he had with Wharton. It is significant that this part of the narrative comes not from Stuart, nor Waterhouse, but Wharton—a disinterested party.

Stuart himself recounted the episode of the organist's position in Dublin, and James Dowling's recollection of this tale is embodied in his memoir, *Irish Varieties*, J. D. Herbert (pseud.), London, 1836. This book was known to Stuart's daughter, who placed it at the disposal of Mason. Expurgated and authorized versions of Dowling's anecdotes thus are those known and used by previous authors, who were not aware Stuart had said West refused to believe he had won the organist's position until shown proof. This episode therefore falls into the period *after* Stuart's meeting with West, proving West did not immediately provide for him, nor did the meeting alter Stuart's fortunes. Dowling quotes Stuart as saying he kept the post only three months. Mason is source for the use of Grant as Stuart's reference on this occasion, a fact not contained in Dowling's original memoir, and possibly only an assumption by Jane Stuart. The additional information concerning William Duncombe is from *Dictionary of American Biography*.

Stuart's remarkable and revealing letter, on the back of which West sketched designs in pencil, is preserved in the New York Historical Society, who kindly provided photostats; its face is reproduced in Park, Vol. I, page 29. The internal evidence of this letter, previously ignored by others following the disputed Jane Stuart or Waterhouse versions, is that Stuart already was acquainted with West when he wrote it. Thus "The Benevolence of your disposition encourageth me," implies he knew this quality in West, and, "Let me beg that I may not forfeit your good will," also implies acquaintance. A further clue to the date lies in the fact it is marked "Monday evening," and states "I've just arrived at the age of 21," highly significant when one recalls he was baptized on Easter Sunday and probably was writing, therefore, on the Easter Monday holiday, which set his sufferings in greater relief. Jane Stuart says her father became West's pupil shortly before the summer of 1777, which in this context seems a further evidence of the letter having been written at Easter.

Chapter III

As Dunlap is the principal source for the American painters of this period—much that passes under the names of other authors is merely his material re-presented—so Allan Cunningham rendered the same inestimable service for English painters. His short biographies of West and Copley, Vol. II and Vol. V of *The Lives of the Most Eminent British Painters, Sculptors, and Architects,* are the most considerable sources employed here. Of interest also is *Benjamin West and the Taste of his Times,* by Grose Evans, Carbondale, 1959.

William Coates and his father, Thomas Coates, appear in records at the Royal College of Surgeons of England, London. The examination book of the older Surgeon's Company shows that in 1776 William Coates passed the company's examination for Surgeon's Mate in the Royal Navy; The Royal College of Surgeons, on its founding in 1800, listed Thomas Coates as a member resident in Salisbury (letter, January 23, 1963, from R. S. J. Gilbert, Secretary). The family continued in Salisbury, each generation producing doctors and solicitors, until the end of the nineteenth century (letter, G. Scholfield, City Librarian, Salisbury, Wilts., Eng., March 4, 1963).

Jane Stuart was born at Philadelphia and her information on earlier periods of her father's career naturally was hearsay. Thus she writes that her father stayed at Syon House with the Duke of Northumberland before his apprenticeship to West, putting this highly significant episode out of proper chronology by ten years. Her information always must be separated from her interpretations of it. Another example is her statement that her father went to stay with West the summer of 1777. Probably this misleading idea stems from the arrangement at Windsor during that and subsequent *summers,* for a considerable body of evidence negates any idea that Stuart actually lived in West's house in London. West's establishment at Windsor, and those present, is treated in "Two Letters from Ralph Earl, with notes on his English Period," by William and Susan Sawitzky, the *Worcester Art Museum Annual,* Vol. VIII, 1960. West's view of the Queen was noted in her diary by Fanny Burney, who was an attendant: *The Diary and Letters of Madame D'Arblay,* London, 1890.

Hyacinthe Rigaud's portrait of Bishop Bossuet is in the Louvre, where I was fortunate in being able to examine it carefully. A copy of the famous Drevet engraving belongs to the British Museum, who photographed it for me; its very significant position in the history of French engraving is treated in *La Gravure Originale au XVIIIe Siècle,* by Jean Adhemar, Paris, 1963, but Rigaud remains one of the forgotten giants of art. Despite the enormous influence he exerted on the artists of his own country, and the English Georgian painters, only one small work on him is known to me: *H. Rigaud,* Pierre Lafitte & Cie., Paris (undated); its excellent short text is unsigned. West's portrait of the Queen appears to have Stuart's brushing in portions of the drapery; the vast impression this picture made on the young man implies he did indeed have a hand in its actual execution.

The Domestic and Artistic Life of John Singleton Copley, R. A., by Marthe Babcock Amory, Boston, 1882, is the most comprehensive source, and indispensable, because the documents on which it drew have been destroyed. Benjamin West's self-portrait is now in the National Gallery of Art, Washington (Mellon Collection). Stuart's self-portrait was given to Waterhouse, in whose house, at Cambridge, Mass., Stuart found it again in later years. Mr. Sidney C. Hutchison, the genial Librarian of the Royal Academy, kindly searched the Minutes for the dates of Copley's elections, at variance with those frequently published.

Copley's mannerisms and very individual brushing, appear in works by several other painters of this time, attesting to his activities among the London studios where he sought work. This free time was eventually absorbed by his own large historical works. Naturally no mention of such undignified employ reached the papers published by Mrs. Amory, and despite my own efforts (see "A Hidden Treasure in Britain," Part II), much remains to be clarified about this first phase of Copley's English career. The hands in Nathaniel Dance's portrait of Captain Cook, at the National Martime

Museum, Greenwich, are surely by Copley, and *two* versions of Reynolds' 1779 portrait of Keppel (The National Portrait Gallery, London, and formerly with Agnews) show that Copley was in fact employed by Reynolds to proliferate this popular picture, rather than merely carrying out studies.

Peter Denying Christ, painted by Copley and Stuart in West's studio is in the Royal Collection; Peter's head is employed by Copley for his own *Samuel and Eli* at the Wadsworth Athenaeum, Hartford, Conn., dated 1780 (letter of August 27, 1962, Mrs. Janet S. Ballard, Secretary to the Curators, Wadsworth Athenaeum). Titian's *Pesaro Altarpiece* in the Church of the Frari, Venice; Guercino's *Jacob Blessing the Sons of Joseph* collection of Denis Mahon, Esq.

John Trumbull's entry into West's studio recounted in *The Autobiography of Colonel John Trumbull,* edited by Theodore Sizer, New Haven, 1953. Reports on Trumbull exist in British Archives printed by the Historical Manuscript Commission, and his own story has been filled out by his recollections as given to Dunlap. The portrait of King George that Stuart painted for West was surely not an original work of his own.

Chapter IV

THE MATERIALS on the Committee of American Loyalists and Joseph Galloway's activities, are from Sizer and further information on Galloway from the *Encyclopaedia Britannica,* edition 1948. Ralph Earl's embarrassing presence is recounted in Sawitzky, whose source is "Ralph Earl, Loyalist," by John M. Phillips, *Art in America,* October 1949. Trumbull recounts King George's conversation with West (Sizer); presumably he heard of it when Stuart visited him in prison. Trumbull told Dunlap of his call on the apparently ill Stuart, as Waterhouse did Stuart's failure to write to his family.

The Gainsborough portrait in the National Gallery, London, said to be Gainsborough Dupont, is surely of Gilbert Stuart. Every feature plots out perfectly against the known portraits of Stuart, and especially the highly individual squared planes beside the nose tip. This same young man appears in various of West's pictures, and would therefore not be Gainsborough Dupont in any case. Gainsborough's letters addressed to his friend Jackson are quoted from Waterhouse.

The curtain behind Gainsborough's lost portrait of the Earl of Abercorn, 1778, known in mezzotint by John Dean, is surely from Rigaud's *Bossuet,* as, in inverted form, is the drapery held in the hand of *Mrs. Elliott* (Metropolitan Museum). More striking still is the use of draperies in Gainsborough's portrait of Admiral Rodney (Rosebery Collection) where the Admiral's left hand is Bossuet's. Almost invariably the extraneous draperies and the flowing additions to women's skirts were taken by Gainsborough from some portion of Rigaud's *Bossuet,* a habit which Stuart and Sir Thomas Lawrence adopted. Two of Lawrence's most sumptuous early works, the 1790 portrait of Queen Charlotte in the National Gallery, London (see the two extraneous pieces of overskirt which have been added to each side of the Queen's frock) and the arrangement of clouds behind and to the left of *Eliza Farren* (1790), in the Metropolitan Museum, all flow from *Bossuet.*

The portrait of Henry Lambert is significant for being the earliest example known in which Stuart's ruffle and cuffs of Brussels bobbin lace appears; it is also somewhat more frontal in position than most of Stuart's heads, which soon became resolutely three-quarter face. The date of Dr. Fothergill's demise comes from *The Gentleman's Magazine.*

Alderman Boydell plays a supporting role in many biographic works without ever having been assigned a lead. His Shakespeare Gallery is treated at some length in *Shakespeare and the Artist*, W. Moelwyn Merchant, London, 1959, but this touches on only part of his activities. Stuart's "tolerable likeness" jibe was recalled in 1795 in a London paper; quoted by Whitley, page 33, who unfortunately does not identify it further. Whitley's remarkable discoveries are marred by inadequate identification of sources and his inability to organize a coherent text.

Chapter V

"CHAMBERS was the son of a merchant of Scottish descent who had settled in Gothenburg; he felt himself as much Swedish as British"; *Sir Joshua Reynolds*, by Derek Hudson. "An exceedingly fine picture and a strong likeness of a Swedish gentleman to be seen about town; if we are not mistaken the original would not like to carry the copy of himself to Stockholm" (Whitley, page 31, quoted from a contemporary journal). This would appear to be a reference to Chambers' striking success in London as an architect in Royal favor. He was a rival for influence rather than a friend to Reynolds; the latter complained Chambers was the real force behind the Royal Academy whose new quarters in Somerset House he designed. *The Homes of the Royal Academy*, by Sidney C. Hutchison, London, 1956, is most informative. Whitley, whose discoveries cannot be too much praised nor his incoherence too much deplored, is likewise the source for quotes on the success of the *Skater* at the Royal Academy. Mrs. Hoppner's letter is from Dunlap.

Stuart called himself *Charles* to sitters such as Sir John Dick; *Gabriel* is almost consistent on the engravings of his works at this period; and *George* is the name in the Westminster rate books. "Judging from the light background of the lace . . . one might tentatively suggest that it is a piece of Brussels bobbin lace . . ." letter from G. F. Wingfield Digby, Keeper, Department of Textiles, Victoria & Albert Museum, July 26, 1962. Reynolds' "shameful" prices are noted by Burney, the remark made by *Mr. B----y*, "I don't want to run the man down; I like him well enough in his proper place; he is as decent as any man of that sort as I ever knew; but for all that, sir, his prices are shameful. Why, he would not do *your* head under seventy guineas!"

I am obliged to my friend Major Eric Peel for taking me to see the Cartwright home, Aynho Park (November 1958); the portrait of William Ralph was attributed to Gainsborough until I reclaimed it for Stuart (see "A Hidden Treasure in Britain"). See also *Aynho Park: An Illustrated Survey*, English Life Publications, Ltd., Derby (undated). Sir Harry Parker's portrait was likewise called a Romney. Stuart's use of turpentine as a medium with his whites remained consistent throughout life.

Sheridan, by Lewis Gibbs, London, 1947, contributed much to this and other chapters, and I am under particular obligation to Lord Spencer, who permitted me to have the Van Dyck portrait of *Prince d'Arenberg* photographed. Many guides to British politics have been employed, including numerous articles in the 1948 *Encyclopaedia Britannica* about Shelburne, Fox, Pitt, Hood, etc., and Plumb. Lord George Germaine's letter, August 1, 1782, is from *Historical Manuscripts Commission*, Vol. VI, 1904. Copley's sittings with Lord North and his wife are in Amory, though the portrait is not known to exist today. His *Elkanah Watson*, a work of extraordinary beauty and power, is in the Metropolitan Museum.

Chapter VI

STUART's longer hair and supercilious air are well fixed in the portrait of him at the Tate Gallery, previously identified as Marie-Auguste Vestris (1760–1842), a dancer. The identification rested on the likeness to some engravings. But "Ellis Waterhouse, incidentally, simply refers to it as a portrait of an unknown man, probably by Dupont" (letter from Dennis Farr, Assistant Keeper of the Tate Gallery, June 14, 1962). A further relationship between Stuart and Dupont would seem implied by W. Ward's engraving of a portrait of Lord Carnarvon, the legend on which reads, "Gainsborough and Stuart." With the permission of the present Lord Carnarvon I had the picture photographed, and it proved to be a Stuart head with additions in the hand of Dupont. The "picture surely was enlarged and Duponted after 1793, when Lord Porchester became Earl of Carnarvon and wanted to be shown in his new robes—so that no direct Dupont/Stuart connexion is likely" (letter of July 9, 1962, from E. K. Waterhouse, with which I am happy to agree).

A selection of works by Vigée-Lebrun that Stuart and his English contemporaries employed can be found in *Madame Vigée-Lebrun*, by André Blum, Paris (undated). Mlle. Marie Gerthoffer kindly obtained this for me in Paris while I worked in Ireland. The portrait of Marie Antoinette holding a rose, used by Stuart in three countries, remains at Versailles and is a popular post card.

Cunningham and Whitley supply information concerning the Incorporated Society of Artists; burrowing into newspapers of that period, Whitley unearthed most of the materials relative to Stuart's relations with this society without, unfortunately, collating them into the obvious pattern. The portrait of the Duke of Manchester is now known only in the engraving by John Jones, a photo of which was prepared for me by the British Museum. The highly important portrait of John Pitt, 2nd Earl of Chatham, painted in 1783 and the real prototype of all Stuart's seated male three-quarter lengths I discovered only in July 1963, on my return from New York where this book was prepared for print. Thus it has not been able to take its significant place in the text, both artistically, and as Stuart's introduction to the Pitt family.

Mason mentions the Moses painted by Stuart from West's design, and a Christ paired with it, both executed for the Fitzroy Chapel, London. This building no longer stands, and I am obliged to Professor Helmut von Erffa of Rutgers, an authority on Benjamin West, for bringing to my attention the panels of the same description at St. Margaret's, Westminster (his letter, May 1, 1962.). With assistance from Dr. Peter Murray of the Witt Library, Prof. von Erffa and I successfully pressed the Canon for photos of these pictures, and feel confident they are the ones described by Mason. Prof. von Erffa also brought to my attention West's drawing of Stuart, in the British Museum, inscribed "Mr. Stewart, painting Mr. West's portrait, 1783."

Mather Brown's known portraits of this period, in particular his John Adams (Boston Athenaeum) and Thomas Jefferson (collection of Charles Francis Adams, Esq.) except for their heavier facture are avowed imitations of Stuart. John Hoppner's portrait of Miss Frances Beresford (Gulbenkian Collection) said to have been painted about 1785, is a good example of whites handled in imitation of Stuart. Hoppner remained, of course, a more resourceful and glowing colorist. Lord Mansfield's portrait, one of Copley's masterpieces, is in the National Portrait Gallery, London, to which I am indebted for preparing a detailed photo of one hand and cuff.

Raeburn's portrait of the Rev. Robert Walker skating belongs to the National Gallery of Scotland, Edinburgh, and his development from brevity suggestive of Stuart to his own bravado brilliance can be seen in reproductions published with *Sir Henry*

Raeburn, by R. S. Clouston, London (undated). William Bingham's career is covered by the *Dictionary of American Biography* and the *Encyclopaedia Britannica.* Material on William Pitt is taken from *Pitt,* by Lord Rosebery, London, 1898. Reynolds' yearly exhibition lists at the Royal Academy are in Waterhouse (*op. cit.*) and the dates of his sittings to Stuart given by Whitley (*op. cit.*) from Reynolds' sitting books at the Royal Academy. For another picture of Reynolds evidently worked on by Stuart at a fourth and last sitting, see "A Hidden Treasure in Britain."

Whitley first established the location of Stuart's house; information from the relevant rate books of 1785 and 1786 was provided me by the Archives Department of the Westminster Public Library. The house has been demolished, but fortunately a photo showing it as it was in 1898 has been preserved in the Westminster History Collection. The history of the house was provided by the London County Council's *Survey of London* staff, from a volume to be published on this area. The drawing room is illustrated as plate 69, "Drawing Room at Richard Chandler's" in Isaac Ware's *Complete Body of Architecture,* 1756. In Boston Stuart still possessed ocular instruments given him at this time by Humphreys.

Chapter VII

JOHN OPIE is another of the painters whose life has been preserved by Cunningham, Vol. II; more recently the Arts Council has circulated an exhibition of his works with a modest catalogue prepared by Mary Peter (London, 1962). Lord Mulgrave's boast was noted by Fanny Burney (*op. cit.*). Temple Franklin's letter from Park is the only information concerning this portrait, which is not known to have reached America in the sitter's lifetime. Probably it is the picture now at the Butler Art Institute, Youngstown, Ohio. Prof. von Erffa of Rutgers kindly brought to my attention the West picture of *Moses As The First Law-Giver,* now in the House of Commons, London.

Stuart's talk of his London home took place in Dublin, to James Dowling, who recorded it in his *Irish Varieties,* from whence it was retailed by Mason and all subsequent efforts. For Mrs. Siddons see Yvonne ffrench's *Mrs. Siddons Tragic Actress,* London, 1936 and 1954. Dowling is authority for the statement that Stuart's speech was an actual imitation of Kemble, a fact about which Dowling, himself a professional thespian in later life, would be accurate. The examples of Kemble's drawl are from *John Philip Kemble,* by Herschel Baker, Cambridge, Mass., 1942. The particular speech of the Deb's Delight was pointed out to me by Miss Sylvia Ellison-Macartney.

"The group [of the Bingham Family] was never finished owing, it is said, to Stuart taking offense at some directions Mrs. Bingham wished him to follow in the arrangement of the picture." This statement is Park, Vol. I, page 155. John Jay's unfinished portrait was discovered by Trumbull in an attic after Stuart's flight, and completed by him; National Gallery of Art, Washington, D.C. Reynolds' annotations to Dufresnoy's treatise appeared in 1783; a copy is in the National Library, Kildare Street, Dublin, and excerpts are given by Cunningham. In Boston Stuart said he found instruction in Reynolds' works, though he appears not to have suggested that he was employing engravings after them in his own production. The full-length of Captain Gell has been cut down to a bust, and was attributed to Reynolds until re-discovered.

Gainsborough's decreasing numbers of male sitters is seen clearly in the catalogue prepared by Waterhouse. Reynolds' portrait of Captain Gell is at the National Maritime Museum, Greenwich; greater generalization of features and forms, and the bad drawing of the eyes, prove it to have come after the Stuart it follows. Gainsborough's picture of Mrs. Siddons is in the National Gallery, London; Romney's Mrs. Perdita Robinson is in the Wallace Collection.

To the Witt Library I owe an especial gratitude for their answers to my thousands of queries, and the final courtesy of photographing their extensive Stuart files on my behalf; to Dr. Peter Murray, Mr. Kemp, Miss Edmundson, Mrs. Phyllis Borland, and particularly Miss Norma Bevin, who showed an unique talent for digging out obscure materials, profound thanks.

Chapter VIII

THE MEETING with Lord Shelburne was recounted by Stuart in America and reached print in Dunlap, with the peer's name left a blank, an omission due to the faulty memory of Dunlap's informant. The description of Shelburne—"his shabby black dress and respectful politeness"—is too much the work of a portraitist to fail in recognition. Thomas Jefferson's visit to London from *The Life Portraits of Jefferson and Their Replicas*, Fiske Kimball, Philadelphia, 1944.

The date of Stuart's marriage is given by Jane Stuart, whose words must be accepted, for every effort to verify it, locate the marriage line, or even discover at what parish the Rev. Dr. Springate officiated, has failed. He was not in the Berkshire triennial lists for 1783, 1786, or 1789, though such a clergyman did exist. He was educated at Bradfield, Berks., receiving a Bachelor of Arts degree in 1751 (research by A. M. Colliard, genealogist, his letters of October 22 and December 19, 1962), but no further light can be shed on Jane Stuart's assertion. Presumably the place of the wedding was an obscure one because of Charlotte Coates' advanced condition.

Stuart mentioned his income to W. T. Parke, *Musical Memoirs*, 1830, recounted in Whitley; the comparable earnings of Romney and Reynolds are taken from Cunningham; in Dublin Stuart received thirty guineas for a bust portrait,—Dowling records him sending home a Bishop's portrait by his servant, with instructions to get the fifteen-guinea balance. Stuart averaged about twenty-five portraits a year through his life; though surely he varied somewhat from year to year, his exertions and routine would appear always to have accommodated the same approximate numbers. Alderman Boydell's call on Reynolds in June 1786 mentioned page 6, *Sir Edwin Landseer*, by Frederic George Stephens, London, 1883. Trumbull's acquaintance with Lawrence is recounted on page 85 of *The Autobiography of Col. John Trumbull*. In Boston Stuart recollected his "damned little things" to Mrs. Basil Hall, who set it down under date of Sunday, October 14, 1827; see *The Aristocratic Journey*, New York, 1930 and pages 208-9, Whitley. Lawrence's use of Rigaud is mentioned in notes to Chapter IV. Francis Cotes' excellent portrait of Lord St. Vincent, signed and dated 1769, is in the National Portrait Gallery, London. *Stokes' Cyclopedia of Music and Musicians*, L. J. de Bekker, London, 1911, is enlightening concerning Mrs. Billington, a very fine portrait of whom by Reynolds graces the Lennox Collection of the New York Public Library.

Chapter IX

The Dictionary of National Biography is enlightening concerning the Duke of Northumberland, and I am obliged to the present Duke, who kindly looked through his ancestor's private accounts (letter, November 15, 1962). Stuart's first effort at Mrs. Siddons for long was called a Hoppner, and was published as such in *Les Chefs-*

d'Oeuvre de Hoppner, Paris, 1926, plate 57. I have been unable to locate this picture, but judging from that reproduction (credited to Shepherd Bros., London) and the larger photo provided by the Witt Library, it appears to be Stuart's own work intact. It is amusing therefore to note that by contrast the second portrait of Mrs. Siddons, in the National Portrait Gallery, London, obviously has been much reworked by John Hoppner! Conditions at Drury Lane from *Mrs. Siddons Tragic Actress* and *Sheridan.*

Lawrence's quote, "I knew Stuart well," from "Autobiographical Recollections," C. R. Leslie, London 1860, as given on page 67, Whitley (*op. cit.*), "I believe the real cause of his leaving England was his having become tired of the inside of our prisons," —which gaps in his chronology at this point would make possible. A search of all entry and discharge books kept at London prisons of this period, carried out in 1958 at the Public Records Office, London, revealed nothing that could have been considered a reference to Stuart in any of the possible variations and spellings of his name. This is mentioned in my "A Hidden Treasure in Britain," but the absence of records from the less formal "lock-ups" must be noted.

R. H. Bridgeman-Evans, M.C., a partner of Fribourg and Freyer, kindly searched the old ledgers for me. That for 1787 has not survived, but Stuart's name (in all possible variations) failed to appear either before or after this date, which is conclusive (letter, November 20, 1962).

Jane Stuart mentions Fuseli's praises for her mother's singing; Parke's recollections are from "Musical Memories"; his brother John Parke appears in *Stokes' Cyclopedia of Music and Musicians.* Dunlap mentions the birth of the *second* child in London, thus establishing that Charlotte bore two within sixteen months after her marrige (May 1786 to September 1787, when the London period ended). The first child, a boy, seems not to have survived childhood; Agnes lived until 1850. All quotes from English newspapers were discovered by Whitley. The Northumberland Family picture, too has often been called a Hoppner.

"*Saturday 27th April 1805* His Lordship [St. Vincent] mentioned how great a Patron he had been to American Stuart while he painted Portraits in England, and said Stuart had received through their recommendations at least £2,000—and that Stuart had behaved most ungratefully to him." This statement is from the *Farington Diaries,* typescript in the British Museum.

Chapter X

THE EXTRAORDINARY pageant surrounding Rutland's death is well covered by the Irish newspapers of that period in the National Library, Kildare Street, Dublin, where I was also fortunate in discovering a copy of the complete text of Dowling's "Memoir of Stuart, Portrait-Painter," pages 226–248 of *Irish Varieties.* This is the most substantial source on Stuart in his Irish years. Many of the anecdotes, and much of the dialogue in the following chapters has been drawn from it, and except for Jane Stuart, who preferred to suppress it, and Mason, who followed her wishes, I believe I am the first to have seen and made use of this remarkable text in its original form. Two caveats must be noted; Dowling (1762–1837), writing at the end of his life, shows an Irishman's love of a good tale, and he wrote after having seen Dunlap.

Robert Home (1752–1834) and other artists working in Ireland are well treated in the *Dictionary of Irish Artists,* Walter G. Strickland, Dublin and London, 1913, a pioneer work with the usual faults of one. Strickland frequently fails to identify the sources of his materials and quotations, nor is he always reliable as to fact. His Dictionary contains a useful effort at a catalogue of Stuart's Irish works, marred by misinformation and errors of judgment.

Christopher Faithful Pack (1750–1840) had indeed worked with Reynolds, and that same year (1787) had been recommended by Reynolds to the Duke of Rutland (Strickland). Both Pack and Stuart therefore were new to Dublin, and at the dinner both were intent upon impressing their Dublin hosts—because both had recommendations to Rutland, for the moment they were serious rivals.

It is particularly unfortunate that no effort was made to trace Stuart in Ireland at an earlier date. When I went to Ireland in February 1961, specifically to do so, I discovered the "trouble" of 1921–22 had destroyed masses of documents stored at The Four Courts in Dublin, including not only those from the former government of Ireland but even Parish records that had been collected together. Thus the expected records of his children's baptisms and perhaps their interments can never be seen. Only the Kings' Inn records, consisting principally of deeds (and leases and bankruptcies, which are registered as deeds), survived and yielded up their secrets. Miss Rosemary ffolliott, dean of Irish genealogists, very kindly assisted my searches throughout.

The letter passed to Stuart from Mason, who had access to Stuart's papers before their loss by fire in Jane Stuart's studio. It is highly significant that Stuart had kept in his possession papers from his Irish years on. Together with his later careful use of appointment books, one senses a less haphazard personality than otherwise has appeared. Stuart had a definite literary taste, and a style of his own that is very strong in his letters and even at second hand in his repeated anecdotes. Mabel Munson Swan, in her "Scraps—The Missing Waterhouse Biography of Gilbert Stuart" (*op. cit.*), feels that Stuart as a youth kept a diary, called his "Book of Judges." She deduces this from an ambiguous passage in Waterhouse's diary: "My old companion of my boyhood Gilbert (Charles) Stuart . . . used to predict as he told me after he found that his predictions failed and derided his judgement, he put me down in his Book of Judges that Ben Waterhouse would never rise over thirty years of age . . ." One feels such a passage may be mere pompous phrasing, and surely it cannot be trusted with certainty.

The meetings and membership of the Irish Parliament as used here are from *Proceedings and Debates of the House of Commons of Ireland,* Dublin, 1787–1793. My friend Jocelyn Proby was of inestimable assistance. Other sources employed include *The End of the Irish Parliament,* Joseph R. Fisher, London, 1911; *The Leaders of Public Opinion in Ireland,* W. E. H. Lecky, London, 1871; *Correspondence of the Rt. Hon. John Beresford,* London, 1954; *British History in the Nineteenth Century,* G. M. Trevelyan, London, 1922; "Georgian Dublin," by John M. Hunt, *The Irish Tatley & Sketch,* October 1962; *England in the Eighteenth Century,* and *Pitt.*

The Pill Lane address from Jane Stuart; efforts to verify Stuart's presence there through leases registered at Kings' Inn, or Parish Registers, failed. Stuart's appearance at this time from the Archer-Shee portrait (Tate Gallery, where unfortunately it is still called Stuart) is strengthened by the fact that he habitually painted the coats in his portraits from himself, so that one is aware of his own changing proportions at all periods of his career. At times in Ireland he forgetfully left coat and vest buttons as they appeared in the mirror—on the wrong side, as he did again in America with the portrait of Horace Binney. Archer-Shee's recollections quoted from "The Life of Sir Martin Archer-Shee, P.R.A.," London, 1860, Whitley, pages 81–2. His date of departure comes from Strickland, Vol. II, page 331, and Archer-Shee's letter from *A Century of British Painters,* Richard & Samuel Redgrave, London, 1947 (first edition, 1866). Jane Stuart mentions her father's love of teasing his wife.

For his time Stuart was a man unusually tolerant in questions of religion; Quakers,

Catholics, Presbyterians, and Jews all played their role in his life, and it is probable that in Ireland he fitted into the prevailing scheme passively and without partisanship, as he did elsewhere. My own years in Ireland, during which I visited many of the older Georgian Houses searching for Stuart's works, have familiarized me with the pattern of this vanished civilization; one has the same sense of wonder as Xenophon before the abandoned walls of Babylon. See also *The Irish Career of Gilbert Stuart*, by Charles Merrill Mount, Bulletin of the Irish Georgian Society, January–March, 1963.

Chapter XI

STRICKLAND first noted that Stuart had a Dublin monopoly, a fact that my own searches through the country have verified overwhelmingly. On the purely mathematical basis of his average production throughout his lifetime, which comes to 25 portraits per year, it is possible that another forty to fifty of his Irish works remain to be found. A small grant given me by the Archives of American Art in 1962 was not sufficient to search more than three of Ireland's 26 countries. It was most productive, however, and since February 1961 I have found upwards of forty portraits listed in this catalogue; the majority are registered in photos at the Archives of American Art in Detroit. Special thanks must be extended to Michael O'Reilly, my worthy photographer, who in my wake has traveled as much of Ireland as I did myself.

Sources for Irish and British political events are cited in the previous chapter. Trumbull (*op. cit.*) recounts Rawdon's cutting statement. Fitzgibbon's dinner comes originally from Dowling (*op. cit.*) and is retailed by Mason and all subsequent authors, who failed to realize Fitzgibbon's significance. It is probable that Stuart was asked to do at least one replica of the Fitzgibbon portrait; to inspect the version hung high up in the Examination Hall of Trinity College closely is now impossible, but despite much bad varnish one feels it is Stuart's own. Presented by the subject in 1801, probably it is the version that Chester Harding saw in 1824: ". . . and a very fine picture it is, in a good state of preservation," he wrote to Stuart from London, January 6, 1825 (Mason, page 73). Dean Beatson's letter is also from Mason, page 75; his portrait is another that I have recently rediscovered.

Jane Stuart asserts that her father had promised to do further portraits when he returned to London. As generally it is her correlations that are at fault, this isolated fact may well be reliable. Hodges' engravings after Stuart are listed in Strickland and Whitley. Most of them are represented in the Joly Collection of engravings, National Library, Dublin, and it is not uncommon to find them hanging still in Irish country houses. Lord Carysfort is well treated in *The Complete Peerage*, London, and the *Dictionary of National Biography*. I am particularly obliged to his great great grandson, my friend Jocelyn Proby, for assistance in unraveling this portion of Stuart's career, as well as to his brother Sir Richard Proby, Bart., present possessor of Elton Hall, with its Carysfort collections. Sir Richard's son, Claud Proby, very kindly loaned me the Carysfort leases surrounding the area where Stuart resided, thus allowing me to fill out my knowledge. The lease to Richard Sinclair was registered in the Deed Books at Kings' Inn, Dublin (no. 419.276), but various features of the seal used by Sinclair, and his signature, made Claud Proby question whether he existed at all. Surrounding leases do show that in 1792 Sinclair himself was not on the property, when it was called "Moore's"; the lease to Sinclair, however, was renewed in 1853, accompanied by a slight diagram showing the irregular outline of a modest house which does not appear on the earliest Ordnance Map of the district (1837, sheet 23). The house appears to be the one Stuart was given under the original Sinclair lease of 1790, and which was razed sometime during the growth of gardens which surround the red brick pile now occupied by the Oblate Fathers. In a corner of this garden the obelisk still stands. Dowling fortunately records details of Stuart's farming, and the actual position of his house was discovered by tracing the route he employed to reach it from Black Rock. Then, as now, only one road leads from the coastal village of Black Rock up the hill to Stillorgan; "as I walked up the narrow road that leads to that quarter from the Black Rock," is a description that brings one to the land leased by Sinclair. Jane Stuart's truthfulness is again vindicated, despite Whitley's heated re-buttals, for she stated that her family lived at *Stillorgan Park*, which is indeed correct.

No clue to the actual location of Stuart's Dublin painting-room has been found, ex-cept for Dowling's context, "Get your hat, and come with me to West's house; *it's not far* . . ." Robert Francis West lived at 31, Exchequer St. (Strickland), not far from the Irish Parliament, which implies that Stuart also was in the area surrounding it.

Dowling has evidently misinterpreted something Stuart said regarding the Van Dyck portrait of Charles I at Hampton Court, now at Windsor Castle. There is no such "stream of light" in Van Dyck's picture; however, the archway which is the chief architectural feature of this imposing work is derived from one by Veronese, in *The Adoration of the Magi*, National Gallery, London, and here indeed is a "stream of light" that cuts across the canvas to shine on Mother and Child. Stuart's reference therefore must have been to this work that was Van Dyck's source. I am obliged to Miss Geraldine Willis, Assistant Librarian of the Representative Body of the Church of Ireland, for help in identifying various of Stuart's Bishops. Robert Fowler was Archbishop of Dublin 1779–1801.

Chapter XII

THE VIEWS of Kilcooley in the Barker portraits have been responsible for an assump-tion (Park) that Stuart painted them *in situ*, in the manner of the nineteenth century. This would be contrary to the practices of an eighteenth-century artist, who always preferred to work in the studio and from engravings or drawings. Even had Stuart visited Kilcooley, it is more than likely he would have painted the views from draw-ings rather than before the scene. However, various drawings of Kilcooley were avail-able to him in Dublin at the time, including one published as an engraving slightly later (June 23, 1792, by S. Hooper). That Stuart actually has misplaced several of the roof shapes was pointed out to me by Major George Ponsonby, present owner of Kilcooley and the pictures. I am obliged to James White, Director of the Municipal Gallery of Modern Art, Dublin, who enabled me to see the Ponsonby Collection.

The incident of the coach was recounted by Stuart to John Neagle, Boston, 1825. As printed by Dunlap it began "You were neither of you ever in *England*—so I must describe an English stagecoach of my time"; but since Mason, page 43, records it was in Ireland that "Stuart . . . was suffering from the effects of a fall. He had been thrown from a vehicle, and had broken his arm . . ."—one sees the reference was to the Black Rock coach, a daily part of his life, and used by Dowling when he visited Stillorgan. Confusion exists about the identity of the doctor who treated Stuart suc-cessfully; the names Haughton and Hartigan both have been given, and both John Haughton and William Hartigan are listed by *Watson's Almanack*, 1790, as practicing in Dublin. I have favored John Haughton, 78 Stephen Street, because he is listed as "practicioner in midwifery" which probably means he had the Edinburgh training mentioned and therefore knew how to deal with infection.

The picture in the National Gallery, Washington, said to be this Dublin doctor who treated Stuart (identified as William Hartigan) is surely a New York period work, and not of him. It is not a pair with the picture said to be "Mrs. Hartigan," in which repaints were discovered by an x-ray taken at my request under the direction of William Campbell, the Gallery's most helpful Assistant Chief Curator. Mr. Campbell also provided details of Stuart's treatment (his letter, April 24, 1963) found in a letter from Lucie Lull Oliver, August 11, 1914, to Charles Henry Hart: ". . . Stuart seriously injured his right hand and various surgeons declared it must be amputated to save his life. One alone, Dr. Hartigan, differed in opinion and thought he could save it. He took the artist into his own home and by constantly pouring fresh water on the wound conquered the inflamation and saved the hand."

Van Dyck's portrait of *Sir John Suckling*, in the Frick Collection, immediately comes to mind as an equivalent of Stuart's new thin manner, though any of Van Dyck's later English heads will demonstrate the same flat use of pigment and reserved texture, plus the mannerism of giving accent to the eyes alone. Dowling, of course, is authority for the activities of the bailiffs and Stuart's bravado. Some confusion has existed over the Bishop of Ossory; Mason recalls Stuart's rebuff, and the snuffbox is now in the Boston Museum of Fine Arts. With the aid of the Representative Society of the Church of Ireland I was able to establish that at this date Ossory was the Hon. William Beresford, and his portrait, found in torn and darkened condition, I was able to identify through a miniature copy at Balinacor, the home of Captain and Mrs. Kemmis. Cased with this miniature is another of what appears to be a Stuart portrait of his daughter, with a blue background. The possibility that Dowling, writing forty years later, may have meant "Ossory" when he wrote the "Archbishop of Dublin," must therefore be entertained.

Chapter XIII

WILLIAM BLAKE expressed the minority view on Reynolds' death:

> When Sir Joshua Reynolds died
> All nature was degraded;
> The King dropped a tear into the Queen's ear
> And all his pictures faded.

Lawrence has fared better than most painters of that age, in large part due to the understanding and energy of Kenneth Garlick, whose major work, *Sir Thomas Lawrence*, London, 1954, has been followed by model catalogues (Worcester Art Museum 1960 and the Royal Academy Diploma Gallery, 1961), while he prepares a definitive edition for the Walpole Society. Also of interest are the *Farington Diaries; Regency Portrait Painter*, by Douglas Goldring, London, 1951; *Romney and Lawrence*, by Lord Ronald Gower, London, 1892; and Cunningham.

Walter Robertson had been undergoing financial troubles for some time; conveyances registered at Kings' Inn, Dublin, include 447-10-287211 (May 1, 1791) property on the south side of Great Britain Street, Dublin; 447-45-287213 and 449-11-287214, the same property. The Grange of Baldoyle is transferred April 20, 1791 (445-442-287295) and July 1, 1791 (445-455-287346 and 459-157-293221), in which he is described as a gentleman, and has evidently recently moved from Dublin to Dalkey. His actual bankruptcy is registered September 8, 1792 (459-170-293313), and in four further deeds he is listed as brickmaker, dealer, and chapman (peddler), a bankrupt.

I have accepted as authentic Dowling's account of his visit to Stillorgan, though with misgivings about his quotations of Stuart's future plans to "make a fortune by

Washington alone. I calculate upon making a plurality of his portraits, whole lengths
. . ." It could well be that Stuart went to America specifically to paint Washington,
or even to paint him at full length; every artist knew the advantages of such an undertaking and Stuart surely carried out this intention at the very first opportunity. But,
events in America imply the initiative for the full-lengths was not his own, and one
must remember that Dunlap, published in 1834, was available to Dowling, whose
memoir appeared in 1836. Dowling was thus aware of what Stuart actually had done
in America. His decision to include in his memoir a separate section on Stuart, and a
lengthy one, certainly came about when he realized to what eminence his old employer had risen in America. Whether his own recollections remained uncolored by
these new impressions is a neat problem for the historian.

The New York Historical Society carefully transcribed the Marine Register of the
Daily Advertiser for me; Miss Rosemary ffolliott discovered that Captain Collins was
from Cork; the *Cork Hibernian Chronicle*, May 3, 1781, says: "married last Monday
in Cove, Mr. John Roche, Jr. to Miss Collins, daughter of Captain Collins of said
place . . . handsome fortune." "On Tuesday last at Cove died Mrs. Collins, relict of
the late Captain Collins," *Cork Mercantile Chronicle*, January 23, 1809. Shipboard life
is mentioned by Dunlap.

The full-length portrait of Henry Grattan, in the Dining Hall at Trinity College,
was among the first Stuarts I discovered on my arrival in Ireland. The Provost very
kindly permitted me to have it photographed, and recently, while the pictures in the
Dining Hall were being cleaned, I examined it and found how much it has suffered
through overcleaning and repainting. The attribution to Nicholas Kenny is from *A
Descriptive Catalogue of the Pictures, Busts, and Statues in Trinity College, Dublin
and in the Provost's House*, by W. G. Strickland, Dublin, 1916.

PART II
Chapter XIV

I am most obliged to James J. Heslin, Director of the New York Historical Society,
and his staff, who searched directories and newspaper files in my behalf. The first reports of Louis XVI's death arrived at Charleston March 14 by the ship *James*, Captain
Murray; this information comes from the New York *Daily Advertiser*, March 29,
1793. New York's historic position is very well outlined in the *Encyclopaedia Britannica*, edition 1948, and other information bearing on the period is found in *The
Birth of the United States*, R. B. Nye and J. E. Morpurgo, Harmondsworth, Middlesex, 1955 and 1961; and in *George Washington*, by John Alexander Carroll and Mary
Wells Ashworth (completing the biography by Douglas Southall Freeman), New
York, 1957 (Vol. VII); these authors regrettably do not reply to questions. In out-
lining the role of Hamilton, Jay, and Madison, the reader will note that I was much
impressed by Charles Beard's *An Economic Interpretation of the Constitution*.

The number of children who accompanied Stuart and his wife on their journeys is
problematic, as the actual figure increased and declined drastically. At this point with
them surely were Agnes, born in London; Charles Gilbert, born about 1787 either in
England or Ireland; and Emma, born in Ireland in 1790. As none of the known children
was born in Ireland after Emma, presumably there was some baby from the years
1791-93, or possibly two. Stuart's address is recorded in the New York City Directory
for 1794; *Stewart, Gilbert, limner, 63 Stone St.*

Thomas Barrow is mentioned in *John Vanderlyn*, by Marius Schoonmaker, Kingston, New York, 1950, and his previous role during the revolution outlined in many

state papers published by Historic Manuscript Commission (National Library, Dublin). Farington's diary reference is undated, page 187 of the British Museum typescript (*op. cit.*). John Shaw lived at 85 Water Street, according to the New York City Directory, 1793. Stuart's letter to Joseph Anthony, dated November 2, 1794, presupposes an earlier visit to Philadelphia: ". . . the object of my journey is only to secure a picture of the President, & *finish* yours." (Italics mine.) The Massachusetts Historical Society kindly provided a photostat of this highly significant document, which varies in eleven particulars from what Whitley gives as "exactly as written."

Mrs. Yates' cap had been used in Dublin on an unusual portrait of Mrs. Dobbyn, recently discovered in the cellar of the National Gallery of Ireland, where it is attributed to the miniaturist John Comerford. His lopping off of Mrs. Yates' elbow is the start of a mannerism that became very strong; from this point on, the elbows in his portraits are invariably lopped off by the addition of some bit of drapery or furniture.

Col. Smith, Citizen Genêt, and Jefferson and Hamilton's reactions are taken from *George Washington* (*op. cit.*). Breakfast with John Jay is mentioned in Mrs. Jay's letter of August 2, 1794 (Mason). Jane Stuart is the original source of the suggestion Jay arranged for Washington's sittings, and all authorities have followed. Jay's own letters (at the Library of Congress, Columbia University Library, and the New York Historical Society) unfortunately are silent regarding Stuart. Mrs. Gabriel Manigault's diary was first brought to my attention by Miss E. Nancy Day, of the Albright-Knox Art Gallery, Buffalo, who gallantly copied those portions available to her, and a set of letters which I quote from extensively. Joseph P. Monigle presented an edited version of the diaries to the faculty of the University of Delaware as his master's thesis, June 1959. I am exceedingly grateful for his kindness in sending me a copy of this thesis.

Chapter XV

Mrs. Manigault's mention of Sir Thomas Overbury (1581–1613) in her diaries points to a new side of Stuart not recorded elsewhere, though in Boston Neagle recorded him quoting from the *Spectator* (Dunlap). Just what Stuart had been reading remains a mystery however, for the Overbury apocrypha at one period grew vast, falsely attributing to him quantities of slightly earthy maxims and droll tales. The passage Stuart quoted appears nowhere in Overbury's most famous work, *Characters,* as it is now known, and the question arises whether it was an invention he found, or for which he was himself responsible! It will be noted that many of his own rejoinders were cast in the same mode; "You bring . . . a potato and expect (I) . . . will paint you a peach!"

All Manigault letters are quoted from a three-volume typescript (at the Charleston Museum, South Carolina) compiled by Louis Manigault; a copy of pages 15–27 of Volume III was made by the Albright-Knox Art Gallery, Buffalo, in whose collection two of the Manigault portraits are found, and from which Miss E. Nancy Day kindly copied these for me.

The portrait of Clarkson is derived from Francis Cotes' *Portrait of a Man,* Tate Gallery, and it hung for many years in the American Wing of the Metropolitan Museum where it is one of the most vivid recollections of my early years. The second portrait of Mrs. Manigault, recorded in her diary, is unknown.

The elder Gilbert Stuart's death is recorded in the Providence Gazette of November 9, 1793; the news may have taken time to travel from Halifax. The fate of his lands became a matter of record February 5, 1811, when Andrew William Cochrane, of Halifax, petitioned for his abandoned holdings against counter claims by heirs of the McMasters brothers. For this and details of Prince Edward, Duke of Kent's visit to Halifax, I am much obliged to C. Bruce Fergusson, Provincial Archivist, Halifax, Nova Scotia, who also provided information on the Newton family.

Washington's military display from *George Washington*. Stuart's illness is recorded in his own letter to Joseph Anthony, Mrs. Jay's letter of August 2, 1794, by Mason. When writing about the portrait of Jaudenes, which I likened to that of Sir William Barker, I had not yet discovered the portrait of John Pitt, 2nd Earl of Chatham, which of course is the closer prototype. One feels Mrs. Jaudenes' hands and arms must have been painted with the assistance of Mrs. Stuart, whose heavy arm is apparent; even so the hands themselves are direct from Marie Antoinette. Park states the signatures on these two pictures are not Stuart's own, an impression with which, on viewing them fresh in June 1963, I was inclined to disagree.

Robertson's presence in Philadelphia is shown by *Charles Willson Peale*, Charles Coleman Sellers, Philadelphia, 1947, Vol. II; Professor Sellers' familiarity with this period and its sources was of great assistance. Aaron Burr's letter is from Park.

Chapter XVI

THIS CHAPTER, with all its technical details, is framed in the strong belief that the portrait of Washington from the Mellon Collection, in the National Gallery of Art, Washington, is in fact the first life-portrait painted at Philadelphia. Stuart's motives in claiming later to have effaced it are discussed in chapter twenty-seven. Jane Stuart is the original source of the list of "gentlemen" which subsequently was used by Mason. Dunlap is authority for the tale of Stuart's visit to Peale while painting Washington; Vanderlyn's part and Aaron Burr's letter are from *John Vanderlyn*.

Chapter XVII

MATERIAL ON Washington and the complexities of his second administration is from *George Washington*. Jane Stuart gave the motivation of Stuart's quarrel with Robertson; Chief-Justice Shippen's letter is from Park. William Bingham is well treated in the *Encyclopaedia Britannica* and his wife's role is outlined in *Martha Washington*, by Anne Hollingsworth Wharton, London, 1897, from which Abigail Adams and Bingham's cold reply to Louis Philippe are quoted.

Thomas Maythem of the Museum of Fine Arts, Boston, very kindly measured the "Athenaeum" portrait of Washington for me. After verifying that it is on a canvas of three-quarter length proportion I had no choice but to admit that a picture of this size was what Senator Bingham originally requested. All Stuart's other study heads intended for the full-length were on his usual small canvases. Washington's own letter of April 11, 1796, a photostat of which was given me by Lady Rosebery, possessor of the original, clearly implies the picture had been ordered by the Binghams: "I am under promise to Mrs. Bingham, to set for you tomorrow . . ." cannot be interpreted otherwise in the light of Washington's precise literary style.

Jane Stuart told much of the social nature of these sittings and Mason gives the tale of her brother Charles' interview with Washington. Stuart himself recounted his patter to Mrs. Hall, October 14, 1827 (*The Aristocratic Journey*, New York, 1931), recounted in Whitley, pages 208–9.

Chapter XVIII

ALL PRINCIPAL sources recount the move to Germantown, and in *Gilbert Stuart's Portraits of George Washington*, by Mantle Fielding, Philadelphia, 1923, the location has been more definitely established. This book, however, can only be employed with the utmost caution, as the author piles hypothesis on supposition and does not distinguish the genuine among masses of pictures attributed to Stuart.

The faults of the Bingham full-length, now at the Pennsylvania Academy, Philadelphia, prove it to be the original; comparison of the head with the "Athenaeum" portrait will show it to be taken from that work, as was Stuart's custom with his larger works. Washington's rigid attitude towards Stuart showed him to be less than generous about sittings. To claim the Bingham portrait's head as a life portrait is an historical absurdity and contrary to precedents of Stuart's usage and the evidence of the picture itself. Mason lists persons who contributed to Washington's figure; the wax cast of the hand is mentioned in Mason and in *Charles Willson Peale*. According to Jane Stuart the silver mountings of de Noailles' sword were finally made into spoons by her mother. Though I have followed her assertion that this nobleman (whose presence in Philadelphia is recounted in *George Washington*) wished Stuart to keep his sword, it would have been equally in character for Stuart to have neglected to return it. Mason mentions Stuart's breakdown while at work on the Washington full-length.

The Constable version of the full-length is now in the Brooklyn Museum, where at the age of fourteen I first became involved with Stuart by copying his portrait of Mrs. Auchmuty. Daniel McCormack is found in Mason. The inventory taken of Lord Lansdowne's estate, in 1804, showed he possessed a bust portrait of Washington in addition to the full-length sent by Bingham (Whitley). I am much obliged to the American Philosophical Society, Philadelphia, for a photostat of Lord Lansdowne's letter to Vaughan. A postscript, added by Vaughan himself, explains the further details. The papers of Rufus King are in the New York Historical Society.

Chapter XIX

WASHINGTON's New Year's reception is taken from *George Washington*, as is his call on Stuart. The wildest assertions have been made from this, the only recorded call that Washington made on Stuart. Stuart's acquaintance with Washington was limited; it comprised only the six sittings granted by the President, his initial conversation at High Street at one of Washington's regular Tuesday evening receptions, the unfortunate meeting when Washington sat to all the Peales, and this last call—the only time Washington ever saw his own full-length portrait. Nothing else is recorded, and the many assertions of great intimacy, or other sittings, are pure fancy.

Pinckney's movements and Adams' inauguration are from *George Washington;* Rufus King's papers are in the New York Historical Society. Mason provides the excerpt from Lord Lansdowne's letter to Major Jackson, who was Washington's secretary, and married to Mrs. Bingham's sister. Dance's proposal (undated) is on page 988 of the typescript of Farrington's diary, British Museum. The London newspaper quote is from Whitley, and the New York Historical Society kindly supplied me a photostat of William Bingham's letter of July 10, 1797. Adams' "A solemn scene . . ." is from *Martha Washington*.

The Constable-Vaughan receipt is reprinted in Mason; Robert Hare's experience is in Dunlap. Timothy Pickering's letter comes from the Massachusetts Historical

Danby. My efforts to contact the actual present owner of the watch and letter (Mr. James M. Swartz of Baltimore is mentioned by Kimball) failed.

Mabel Swan's *Gilbert Stuart in Boston* discusses the question of his various addresses, which is also touched on in all the principal sources. "To be delivered when finished" was written in the receipt given for payment on the portrait of Mrs. Otis; the Massachusetts Historical Society provided a photostat. The ambivalent vexations are from Mason and Dunlap; I have supplied the name of Governor *Sullivan* in the belief that nothing of the sort could be said about a member of the *Sargent* family, the only other possibility. Mrs. Peabody's letters are given by Park. Sully, Eicholtz, and Washington Allston are found in Dunlap and Whitley, the latter of whom recounts the episode of the gentleman who changed his opinion of a picture on discovering it was not by Stuart. The "theory of shadow" was propounded to Miss Eliza Susan Quincy, whose interesting memoir is printed on pages 243–47 of Mason.

David's *Marquise d'Orvilliers*, in the Louvre, passed the war years at the Metropolitan Museum in New York, where I became acquainted with it; Reynolds' *Lady Frances Finch*, later Countess of Dartmouth, is the property of Mrs. H. Terrell van Ingen, New York. David Edwin's Boston visit in company with Jarvis is from Dunlap, and further details are found in *John Wesley Jarvis*, by Harold Dickson, New York, 1949.

Chapter XXVI

EXCERPTS FROM John Quincy Adams' diary are from Park and from Whitley. Charles Fraser's memoirs were given by Dunlap, who also mentions Sully's impression. The same source is the origin of Stuart's claim that the White House portrait was not by him. Samuel Knapp is quoted in Whitley. The final wanderings of wit are also recounted by Dunlap, many of them as notes. The episode of Copley and Lord Mansfield is preserved at the Massachusetts Historical Society in an unsigned copy of a letter to Lord Campbell, dated February 11, 1851, and sent me in a photostat.

All the principal sources contribute parts to the sad tale of Charles Gilbert Stuart; his actual death as recorded in the Boston register was found by Mabel M. Swan, and is printed in her *Gilbert Stuart in Boston*. Samuel Higginson's letter to John Vaughan belongs to the American Philosophical Society. Thomas Jefferson's letter is from Kimball, and the Bartlett and Tappan recollections from Park; John Neal's recollections (said to be from the *Atlantic Monthly*) are quoted on page 155, Whitley. Lawrence's astonishing position in Europe is mentioned in *Sir Thomas Lawrence*.

Chapter XXVII

STUART'S DIFFICULTIES with landlords, neighbors reports on him, and his daughter's marriage, are from *Gilbert Stuart in Boston*. Whitley found the newspaper reports of President Monroe's visit. Jouett's memorandum of Stuart's remarks has been printed in many places; the first appears to be that in Mason, pages 67–70, which I have used. Adams' diary excerpts are from Park; Thomas Jefferson's many letters, and the replies, from Kimball.

Stuart's mother died January 18, 1819 (*Gilbert Stuart in Boston*) and Stuart's sentimental journey to Newport is quoted by Whitley from *Early Recollections of Newport* by George G. Channing. Material on John Doggett and Professor Packard is from Kimball. Reynolds' portrait of Fox, exhibited at the Royal Academy of 1784, is now in the collection of the Earl of Ilchester, Holland House. Jefferson's letter to Captain Peyton (Monticello, August 14, 1820) is in the Massachusetts Historical Society, which provided a photostat. Dunlap saw the now frameless portrait of Washington when he visited Stuart himself. Anne Newton's death reported to me in enclosures with the letter of February 20, 1963, by C. Bruce Fergusson, Provincial Archivist of Nova Scotia. Trumbull's letter is from Mason. Park provides details of the Phillips portrait's order, and Stuart's final move back into Boston is detailed by Mabel M. Swan, who also gives the Salisbury letters.

Stuart's actual indebtedness to Williams is outlined in the list of claims against his estate, the total of which was $1778.34, filed in the probate Court. This was found and published by John Hill Morgan in "The Date of Stuart's Death, The Place of His Burial, and the Inventory of His Estate," *Antiques,* March 1934.

Chapter XXVIII

NEAGLE'S RECOLLECTIONS were given Dunlap; those of Longacre, with whom he traveled to Boston, were published in *The Pennsylvania Magazine of History and Biography,* 1905, and are recounted by Whitley. John Adams' letter to Waterhouse, dated May 21, 1821, appears in "John Adams as He Lived," *The Atlantic Monthly,* Vol. 139, page 783. Despite this curious observation, Adams would not appear to be referring to the relationship between Stuart and Mrs. Morton. John Quincy Adams' diary is quoted in Mason, page 125. Josiah Quincy's sittings are described in his daughter's memoir, quoted in Mason, pages 243-7. Stuart's letter of March 6, 1825, was communicated to me as a photostat from the collection of the Massachusetts Historical Society.

Bunker Hill and Daniel Webster are recounted by Whitley; quotations from the latter are from Park; the Browere letter is from Whitley; Stuart's visit to Quincy is from a memoir by Eliza Susan Quincy (Mason). T. H. Perkins' letter is in the Massachusetts Historical Society collection, which kindly sent me a photostat. Accounts of the McLean and Motley portraits are from Park, who also mentions Mrs. John Forrester's likeness. Beechey's genial letter is in Mason; Jane Stuart is authority for her own history.

The Works of Gilbert Stuart

THIS CATALOGUE of the entire known works of Gilbert Stuart is divided into three parts: English and Irish works, the American works of Stuart's youth and prime, and, as a separate category, his portraits of Washington.

Asterisks (*) mark those pictures I have been unable to see or to examine in photographic form. While in each case the available information has seemed to warrant inclusion of the picture, I am unable to verify the authenticity of these works from personal knowledge. (D) denotes those new works added to these lists through my own searches and discoveries; they are pictures previously unknown or attributed to other artists from whom they have been reclaimed.

A special effort has been made to exclude from these lists any picture that in the opinion of the author is not authentic. Unless otherwise specified the medium is oil on canvas, and the size 25 x 30 inches.

An effort has been made to bring the ownership of each picture up to date. Museums in America and the British Isles have been circularized concerning their holdings and private collections in their area, and whenever they could be traced, printed notices have been sent to those parties, or their heirs, listed in previous catalogues. Difficulty in tracing families and sales has resulted in some lacunae; the failure of persons to reply in others. When the ownership has not been brought down to the present, a date indicates when the picture last was located.

ENGLISH & IRISH WORKS

Abdy, Sir William.
    National Maritime Museum, Greenwich.
Acton, Thomas, of West Aston. (D)
    Charles Acton.
Annesley, Hon. Richard.
    Not located, though evidence indicates he was painted in Dublin.
Armit, John.*
    In 1916 belonged to John D. M'Ilhenny, Philadelphia.

Barker, Sir William, 4th Bart.
    (1) approx. 50 x 40; Major George Ponsonby.
    (2) approx. 12 x 14; small-scale replica of head, in different costume; Major George Ponsonby. (D)
Barker, Lady.
    Approx. 50 x 40; Major George Ponsonby.
Barré, Col. Isaac.
    (1) 36¼ x 28¼; Brooklyn Museum.

(2) Replica, The National Portrait Gallery, London.

(3) Copy by another hand, Marquis of Lansdowne, Bowood.

Barrington, Admiral the Hon. Samuel.
(1) Saltram House.
(2) Yale University Art Gallery.

Barrington, Sir Jonah.
John Herron Museum of Art, Indianapolis.

Barrington, the 2nd Lord.
G. T. Couger, M.D.

Barwell, Richard. (D)
The Wernher Collection, Luton Hoo.

Beatson, Dean. (D)
20 x 24; private collection, Dublin.

Beatson, Mrs.
Probably painted in Dublin; letter from Dean Beatson to Stuart, pp. 75–6 Mason, speaks of "our pictures."

Bective, The Earl of. (D)
Lady Headfort.

Bennett, William (Bishop of Cork & Ross).
Emmanuel College, Cambridge.

Beresford, Lady Catherine.*
Not located. Said to have been sold by Dublin dealer, B. Watkins, November 1850.

Beresford, Rt. Hon. John.
(1) The Marquis of Waterford, Curragh-more. Two replicas: one formerly Lewis & Simmons, New York; the other, Hugh Maude.
(2) In oval form: sold at Christies—copy at the National Gallery of Ireland.

Billington, Mrs.
Mentioned by *Morning Post* (1786) as seen in Stuart's house. Not located.

Bingham, Anne Louisa.
17¼ x 18; Alexander Grant, Rome.

Bingham, Anne Willing (Mrs. William).
(1) 19 x 15; Philadelphia Museum, loaned by Mr. & Mrs. Robert L. McNeail. Study head for the London group.
(2) 36 x 26 inches; with her baby; a piece cut from the unfinished London group. Robert Melezieux-Dehon, Paris.

Bingham, William.
17 x 17; head cut from the unfinished London group. Robert Melezieux-Dehon, Paris.

Bisse, Thomas.
Leggatt's (1932).

Bisse, Mrs. Thomas.
Leggatt's (1932).

Blades, Mrs., and her daughter.
Mr. Albert R. Jones.

Bowles, General.*
Not located. Sold in Dublin from collection of Lord Fitzgerald & Vesci, August 1843.

Boydell, John.
(1) 35¾ x 33. Henry W. Sage.
(2) Peter Nicolson.

Boydell, Josiah, Jr.
(1) Rhode Island School of Design.
(2) exh. Royal Academy, winter 1956–7. Reprod. in *The Art Quarterly*, autumn 1959. (D)

Brown, ------.
Stuart said to have painted two heads on one canvas of two young men from Liverpool; Mason, p. 152.

Browne, John.
Not located. An engraver said to have been painted for Boydell.

Browne, Arthur.
Not located. An engraving issued July 1805, in Joly Collection, National Library, Dublin, appears to be from a Stuart portrait of this boyhood friend from Newport.

Brownlow, Rt. Hon. William.
36½ x 31½; Lord Lurgan.

Caldwell, Andrew, of New Grange. (D)
National Gallery of Ireland.

Carleton, Hugh.
The Earl of Normanton.

Carnarvon, Henry 1st Earl of.
Approx. 40 x 50; The head by Stuart, enlarged by G. Dupont. The Earl of Carnarvon.

Cartwright, William Ralph. (D)
Aynho Park.

Carysfort, John Joshua Proby, 1st Earl of. (D)
Jocelyn Proby.

Carysfort, Countess of.
National Gallery of Ireland (as "Portrait of a Lady").

Chatham, John Pitt, 2nd Earl of.
40 x 50 inches. (D) Private Collection, Dublin.

Cleaver, Euseby (Bishop of Cork).
Not located; engraved in mezzotint by J. Grozer, 1790.

Clinton, Sir Henry.*
Albert Rosenthal, Philadelphia.

Clive, Lady Charlotte.
Not located. Mason mentions this work (p. 159), presumably from family sources.

Clonmell, John, 1st Earl of.
Frank T. Sabin, London.

Clonmell, Countess of.
Frank T. Sabin, London.

Cobbe, Mr. (Charles? M.P. for Swords).
Not located. Mason gives the name Cobb, asserting it was painted in Ireland. Probably the reference is to the Newbridge House family.

Cobbe, Mrs.
Not located.

Cockburn, Captain George.
Formerly Knoedler's.

Coffin, Richard.
 Saltram House.
Colvill, William. (D)
 Captain J. C. Colvill.
Colvill, Mrs. William. (D)
 Captain J. C. Colvill.
Conyngham, Sir William Burton.
 (1) New York Art Market, 1922; the life
  portrait, painted in London. 36 x 28.
 (2) The National Gallery of Ireland; 36
  x 26 inches.
Copley, John Singleton.
 The National Portrait Gallery, London.
Cruikshank, William Cumberland.
 Not located. Strickland says this picture
  was engraved by W. Say, 1801.
Curtis, Dr. William.
 Said by Waterhouse to have been painted
  in London, probably the autumn of
  1776.
Dabzac, Henry.
 (1) Sold at Parke-Bernet, N.Y., March 28,
  1946.
 (2) Provost's Lodge, Trinity College,
  Dublin. (D) As neither of these ap-
  pear to be the life-portrait it is pos-
  sible the first version is unknown.
Dartrey, Thomas Dawson, Lord (Viscount
 Cremorne).
 (1) Howard Young Gallery.
 (2) 36 x 28. Montclair Museum. (D)
Dartrey, Lady (Viscountess Cremorne).
 Howard Young Gallery.
Dalton, Captain John. (D)
 Reprod. in *Art Quarterly*, autumn 1959.
Dawson, Lucius.*
 Strickland credits to B. T. Balfour,
  Townley Hall, Drogheda.
De Vesci, Thomas, First Viscount.*
 Viscount de Vesci.
Devon, Earl of.
 Joseph Grafton Minot.
Dick, Miss, and her cousin, Miss Forster.
 36 x 37.
Dick, Sir John, of Braid.
 (1) National Gallery of Art, Washington
  (Mellon Coll.). 36 x 28.
 (2) Messrs Mitchell, sold at Christie's; 35
  x 27.
Dick, Mrs. Samuel, and daughter Charlotte
 Anna.
 John Nicholson; 36 x 29½.
Dobbyn, Mrs. (D)
 Approx. 20 x 24; National Gallery of
  Ireland.
Dufferin and Ava, Marchioness of.
 Museum of Fine Arts, Boston.
Earlom, Richard.
 Not located. Engraved in mezzotint by
  T. Lupton, 1819.
Facius, Georg Sigmund.
 35 x 27; Ehrick Galleries, 1933.
Facius, Johann Gottlieb.

36 x 28; Mrs. Rutherford Stuyvesant.
Farnham, John James, 2nd Earl of.
 Charles B. Fox.
Farran, Charles.
 G. C. Farran.
Farran, Mrs. Charles.
 G. C. Farran.
Farren, Elizabeth (Countess of Derby).
 George Evans Tenen.
Fisher, Jonathan.
 Not located. In his memoir Dowling
  mentions this among the first three
  portraits Stuart painted in Dublin.
Fitzgibbon, John, Lord (Earl of Clare).
 (1) Kleeman Thorman Galleries.
 (2) 96½ x 60⅝; Cleveland Museum of Art.
  (replica) Trinity College, Dublin.
  (replica) 42¾ x 26¾ prepared for en-
  graver. Mr. & Mrs. William Wallace.
Flecke, Count.
 Not located. Listed by Mason as "Count
  Fluke."
Foster, Rt. Hon. John.
 (1) 83½ x 59⅝; William Rockhill Nelson
  Gallery.
 (2) Stuart surely painted another picture
  of Foster in three-quarter face to left;
  a poor copy is at Lisnavagh, Co. Car-
  low, and various engravings at National Library, Dublin, reflect Stuart's
  standard seated composition.
Fothergill, Dr. John.
 36 x 28; Pennsylvania Academy.
Fowler, Robert, Archbishop of Dublin.
 Not located. Mentioned in Dowling's
  memoir.
Fowler, Miss.
 Not located. Mentioned in Dowling's
  memoir.
Franklin, Temple.
 His letter of November 9, 1784, tells his
  grandfather he is sitting to Stuart.
  Picture otherwise unknown, but
  probably is the "Portrait of a Gentle-
  man" (also called Webb, Sr., or Lord
  Webb) at The Butler Art Institute.
Gardner, Henry Farington.
 Not located. Mentioned in Farington
  diary, Dec. 20, 1802.
Gell, Captain John. (D)
 Sir Dennis Stucley, Bart.
 Miss Eleanor Gordon. 40 x 60; Hirschl &
  Adler.
Grant, Sir Alexander.
 Not located. Mentioned by Waterhouse
  and Mason.
Grant, William of Congalton. (The Skater)
 96⅝ x 58¼; National Gallery of Art, Wash-
  ington (Mellon Coll.).
Grantham, Thomas, Lord.
 Saltram House.
Grattan, Henry.
 (1) Engraved by Hodges; not located.

(2) sold Hearn Coll., American Art Galleries, 1918 as a Zoffany. The study for the full-length. (D)

(3) approx. 90 x 60; Trinity College, Dublin; repainted extensively by Nicholas Kenny. (D)

Grenville, General Sir Richard.
Not located.

Grenville, William Wyndham (Baron). (D)
Published in *Art Quarterly*, autumn 1959. Previously called Rt. Hon. George Greville, by Romney.

Grierson, Charlotte.
Charles Kinahan.

Grierson, George.
Charles Kinahan.

Hall, John (the engraver).
35½ x 27; National Portrait Gallery, London.

Hamilton, George.
48½ x 37; Mrs. Ormsby-Hamilton.

Hamilton, Mrs. George.
Mrs. Ormsby-Hamilton.

Hamilton, Hugh, Dean of Armagh.
(1) John Levy Gallery, 1938.
(2) in clericals; not located; engraved by W. Evans, 1807.

Hamilton, Mrs. Hugh.
John Levy Gallery, 1938.

Hart, Sir John.
Saltram House.

Hamilton, James of Sheephill and Holmpatrick. (D)
Lord Holmpatrick.

Hannay, Sir Samuel.
Not located. *The London World*, April 18, 1787, lists portraits of "Sir Samuel and other Hannays."

Harvey, Captain John.
Not located; engraved by J. Murphy, 1795.

Heath, James.
Wadsworth Athenaeum, Hartford.

Heathcote, George.
36 x 28; Henry W. Wehrhane.

Henderson, John.
Not located. Dunlap says Stuart sketched Henderson as Iago, which was engraved by Bartolozzi.

Hood, John Willet, Admiral.
Louis Bamberger.

Hotham, Chancellor Sir Beaumont.
Lord Hotham.

Hotham, General George.
Lord Hotham.

Hotham, Dr. John.
Lord Hotham.

Hotham, Admiral William.
Lord Hotham.

Hughes, Vice-Admiral Sir Edward.
48 x 39; John Herron Museum, Indianapolis.

Humphrey, Ozias.

Wadsworth Athenaeum, Hartford.

"Humphries," Mr.
M. R. Schweitzer Gallery.

Jay, John.
50½ x 39¾; John Clarkson Jay, on loan to National Gallery, Washington.

Kemble, John Philip.
(1) National Portrait Gallery, London.
(2) as Richard III; mentioned by *Morning Chronicle*, 1786.
(3) as Orestes; mentioned in Boaden's *Life of Kemble* (1825); in possession of the Rev. C. Este.
(4) As Macbeth; not located.

Kemble, Mrs. John Philip.
Mason (page 209) asserts Stuart painted her "several times and in various characters."

Lambert, Henry.
Minneapolis Institute of Arts.

Lansdowne, Marquis of (as Earl of Shelburne).
Not located. Mentioned in the *World* of April 18, 1787.

La Touche, William Digges.
Knoedler's.

La Touche, Mrs. Digges.
Knoedler's.

Lees, Sir John.
(1) Irish Post Office. (D)
(2) Studio replica; Mrs. Herbert V. Jones.

Lees, Mary.
Possibly a studio replica; Mrs. Herbert V. Jones.

Legge, Rt. Hon. Heneage.
John Levy Gallery, 1920.

Leinster, The Duke of.
(1) The Duke of Leinster.
(2) 32 x 26; Montclair Museum.

Leland, The Rev. Doctor. (D)
20 x 24; The National Gallery of Ireland (attributed to Thomas Hickey). A studio replica.

Leslie, Charles Powell.
36 x 30; Mrs. William King.

Lettsom, Dr. John C.
Waterhouse mentions an unfinished half-length.

Locker, Captain William.
(1) Ginsburg & Levy.
(2) National Maritime Museum, Greenwich (replica), also a copy by another hand.

Loftus, Col. Sir Edward.
Addison Gallery of American Art, Phillips Academy (studio replica).

Loftus, Edward.
John Herron Art Museum, Indianapolis. The sitter is more probably Henry Loftus, M.P. for Bannow, 1790.

Logan, John.
Knoedler's.

Longford, Edward, Baron.
(1) The Duke of Wellington. (D)

(2) Mrs. E. H. Patterson.

Macartney, George, Earl of.
The Earl of Normanton.

Mackenzie, Sir Alexander.*
University Club, New York.

McClintock, John. (D)
Lord Rathdonnell.

Malcolm, Dugald. (D)
Colonel George Malcolm.

Malton, Thomas.
Not located; engraved by J. Jones, 1790, and W. Barney, 1806.

Manchester, The Duke of.
Not located; engraved by J. Jones, 1790, and J. Collyer, 1794.

Manigault, Joseph.*
Miss Joanna Manigault.

Matcham, George.
Mrs. Booth Tarkington.

Miller, William.*
Sold Parke-Bernet, March 28, 1946.

Montagu, Hon. John.
(1) The Earl of Sandwich. (D)
(2) National Gallery of Ireland. (D)

Montagu, Hon. Augusta.
Mrs. Booth Tarkington.

Moira, The Earl of (as Lord Rawdon).
Major S. P. H. Simonds.

Molesworth, Sir T.
Ehrick Newhouse Galleries.

More, Hannah.
Westmore Collection.

Mulgrave, Constantine John Phipps, Lord.
Mrs. B. F. Jones, Jr.

Newdigate, Francis.*
Temple House, Arbury.

Normanton, The Earl of (Archbishop of Dublin, as Lord Somerton).
The Earl of Normanton.

Normanton, Jane Countess of.*
The Earl of Normanton.

Northland, Hon. Anna Vesey, Viscountess. (D)
Lewis Motley.

Northumberland, The Duke of.
(1) Not located; engraved by Charles Turner.
(2) The Duke of Northumberland, Syon House.

Ormonde, Countess of.
Mason (page 233) mentions "Lady Ormand."

Ossory, Lord Bishop of (Hon. William Beresford). (D)
Julian Peck.

Park, John.
Museum of Fine Arts, Boston. Possibly repainted by John Trumbull, who added the dog.

Parke, William Thomas.
Arnot Art Gallery, Elmira, New York.

Parker, Sir Harry, 6th Bart. (D)
Sir Hyde Parker.

Parker, Sir Edward.

William Rockhill Nelson Gallery.

Paton, Richard.
36 x 28; James H. Hammond.

Pearson, Captain Richard.
Vose Gallery, Boston.

Percy Family.
Approx. 90 x 50; the children of the Duke of Northumberland; The Duke of Northumberland, Syon House.

Pery, Edmund Sexton, Viscount.
(1) 38 x 26; sold at Sotheby's June 9, 1932.
(2) National Gallery of Ireland; studio replica, perhaps by Dowling.

Phipps, General.
Not located. Dunlap asserts Stuart painted General Phipps for his brother, Lord Mulgrave.

Pole, Admiral Sir Charles.
Saltram House.

Ponsonby, Chambré Brabazon, Sr.
Not located. A copy at Kilcooley Abbey.

Ponsonby, Chambré Brabazon. (D)
Major George Ponsonby.

Ponsonby, Lady Harriet. (D)
Major George Ponsonby.

Portrait of a Gentleman (Perhaps Sir William Chambers).
Not located; Royal Academy, 1782, number 417.

Portrait of a Gentleman.*
C. Dillon.

Portrait of a Gentleman (called Mr. Webb, Jr.).
Sold at Parke-Bernet, March 18, 1961.

Portrait of a Gentleman.*
Stevenson Scott.

Portrait of a Man.
Frank T. Sabin.

Portrait of a Man (perhaps Sir Desmond Barrington).
The Newark Museum.

Portrait of a Man.*
Robert G. Kales.

Portrait of a Man.
Not located; copy in possession of Julian Peck.

Portrait of a Naval Officer (called St.-Vincent).
T. J. Coolidge.

Portrait of a Girl with Bonnet.*
Max Saffron.

Portrait of Two Sisters (as Comic and Tragic Muses).
Mentioned by Waterhouse; not located.

Portrait of a Little Girl.
Not located; Royal Academy, 1779, no. 318.

Portrait.
Not located; Royal Academy, 1779, no. 318 "a head."

Preston, Reverend William (Bishop).
Preston Davie.

Pringle, Admiral Thomas.
Not located; engraved by Orme, Jr., 1797.
Rainier, Admiral Peter.
Museum of Fine Arts, Boston.
Rainsford, Brig.-General Charles.
Leggatt, 1946.
Reynolds, Sir Joshua.
(1) 36 x 30; National Gallery of Art, Washington (Mellon Coll.).
(2) formerly Major Eric Peel; see *Art Quarterly*, autumn 1959. (D)
Richardson, John.
Museum of Fine Arts, Boston.
Ringgold, Mrs. Mary.
Hirschl & Adler.
Rodney, Admiral Baron.
Mentioned in London newspaper, 1787, as collection of Sir John Taylor, Jamaica.
Rowley, Rt. Hon. Hercules Langford.
40 x 50; destroyed by fire, 1921.
Robinson, The Hon. Frederick.
Saltram House.
Russell, Admiral Thomas Mac Namara.
Engraved by H. R. Cook, 1806.
St. Vincent, John Jervis, Rear-Admiral, Earl of.
(1) full-length, engraved by John Raphael Smith, 1797.
(2) National Maritime Museum, Greenwich; study head for the full-length, left unfinished.
Serres, Dominic.
Approx. 30 x 36; P. Jackson Higgs (1928). Reprod. *N.Y. Times Magazine*, Aug. 21, 1928, by W. Sawitzky as Adam Walker, but surely the picture exh. R.A. 1782, no. 164, "in the act of fresh pointing his pencil" (*London Courant*).
Sharp, William (the Engraver).
Not located; listed by Park from Fielding.
Shaw, Bernard.
Knoedler's (London, 1930).
Shaw, Robert, of Terenure.
(1) Knoedler's (London, 1930-).
(2) George Bernard Shaw; studio replica.
(3) National Gallery of Ireland; studio replica (Dowling).
(4) L. H. Shaw; studio replica (Dowling).
Shaw, Mrs. Robert.
Knoedler's (London, 1930).
Sheridan, Richard Brinsley. (D)
Approx. 40 x 90; Lady Beaverbrook.
Sheridan, Thomas, A. M.
Not located; engraved by Scott, 1789.
Copy 10 x 8½; Garrick Club, London.
Siddons, Mrs. Sarah.
(1) Not located; Shepherd Bros. (D)
(2) National Portrait Gallery; finished by Hoppner.
Smith, Matthew.*

Not located.
Smith, Mrs., of Gaybrook. (D)
Major George Ponsonby.
Smith, T.
Not located; mentioned in "Musical Memoirs" of W. T. Parke.
Staples, Sir Robert, 5th Bart.
Major George Ponsonby.
Staples, Sir Robert, 6th Bart. (D)
Major George Ponsonby.
Stronge, Helen, Lady.*
Sold in London 1929-30 to H. Blaker.
Stuart, Gilbert (self-portrait).
(1) Redwood Library.
(2) Tate Gallery.
Sydney, Thomas, Baron (First Viscount Sydney).
36 x 28; Walter Jennings.
Symes, Richard, Brig.-General. (D)
Edward Bayley.
Taylour, The Hon. -----. (D)
Major George Ponsonby.
Thayendanegea (Joseph Brandt).
(1) Mrs. John Hayes Simonds.
(2) The Duke of Northumberland, Syon House.
Tottenham, Charles, of Ballycurry. (D)
Charles Tottenham.
Tottenham, The Hon. Mrs. Loftus.
Addison Gallery of American Art, Phillips Academy.
Townshend, John.
Not located; engraved by John Young.
Tracy, Nathaniel.*
Newburyport Public Library.
Trumbull, John.
Pilgrim Society, Plymouth, Mass.; completed by Trumbull.
Vane, Henrietta Elizabeth Frederica.
65⅞ x 35⅝; Smith College Museum of Art.
Ward, James.
Minneapolis Institute of Arts.
Warre Malet, Sir Charles.
Howard Young Galleries.
Warren, Dr. Richard.
Theodore W. Bennett.
Waterford, Marquis of.
(1) Marquis of Waterford, Curraghmore.
(2) Herbert E. Gale.
(3) F. R. Mayer.
(4) Micheletti, N.Y.
(5) Peacock, New Zealand.*
(6) Hugh Maude (in St. Patrick's robes). (D)
Waterford, Marchioness of.
(1) The Marquis of Waterford, Curraghmore.
(2) F. R. Mayer.
Waterhouse, Dr. Benjamin.
(1) Redwood Library; 22 x 18.
(2) Waterhouse mentions Stuart *began* a three-quarter length with a skull.
(3) Metropolitan Museum (called "Man

in a Green Coat").

Weldon, The Hon. Mrs. Steuart.
Not located; mentioned in *Evening Herald*, Dublin, 1789.

West, Benjamin.
(1) 35½ x 27½; The National Portrait Gallery, London.
(2) 35 x 27½; The Tate Gallery. *Copy, perhaps by Mather Brown, at Annamary Brown Memorial Gallery.*

Westmeath, The 8th Earl of (as a child).
Approx. 40 x 50; Knoedler's.

Westmeath, George Frederick, Earl of
Reprod. by W. Sawitzky, *The N.Y. Times Magazine,* Aug. 12, 1928.

Westmeath, Countess of.
Not located; listed by Mason, page 276.

Whichcote, Lady.*
Mrs. Benjamin Thaw, (1914).

White, Luke.
The National Gallery of Art, Washington (Mellon Coll.).

White, Mrs. Luke, and child.
Scott & Fowle; possibly unfinished. Several copies and partial replicas are known.

Whitefoord, Caleb.
Montclair Museum.

Wilson, Mrs.
Not located. Listed by *London World,* 1787.

Woolet, William (the engraver).
35 x 27 inches; National Gallery, London.

Young, John.
Knoedler's (1925).

Young, William.
Lord Talbot de Malahide.

Historical Works

Moses.
St. Margaret's, Westminster.

Christ.
St. Margaret's, Westminster.

Air, Water, Earth, and Fire.
Five panels originally designed for Somerset House, by B. West, executed by Stuart; The Royal Academy.

Peter Denying Christ.
St. James' Palace, London; painted in cooperation with J. S. Copley, from design by B. West.

AMERICAN WORKS

Adams, John.
(1) The first portrait from life (1798) National Gallery of Art, Washington.
(2) (Replica) panel, 25½ x 21⅛; T. J. Coolidge.
(3) 50 x 40; painted for dealer John Doggett, destroyed in fire of Congressional Library, 1851.
(4) The second life portrait (1824), Charles Francis Adams.
(5) (Replica of 1824 portrait) National Collection of Fine Arts (Smithsonian Institution).*

Adams, Mrs. John.
(1) Begun 1798, delivered 1812; National Gallery of Art, Washington.
(2) Unfinished study, presumably from same 1798 sittings; John Adams.

Adams, John Quincy.
(1) 26¾ x 22; panel (1818); Mrs. Arthur Adams.
(2) 95⅝ x 60¼; begun 1825, head only by Stuart, completed by Sully. Harvard University Portrait Collection.

Adams, Mrs. John Quincy.
Panel; August 1818; Mrs. Arthur Adams.

Allen, Andrew.
Sully records him sitting to Stuart in 1807.

Allen, Jeremiah.
Panel. Massachusetts Historical Society.

Allston, Anne.
Miss Elizabeth W. Ball (1927).

Allston, Washington.
24 x 21½; Metropolitan Museum (Unfinished).

Ames, Fisher.*
(1) Smithsonian Institution.
(2) 27⅝ x 22½; Harvard Memorial Hall.

Amory, John, Jr.
Panel, 25½ x 21½; Museum of Fine Arts, Boston.

Amory, Mrs. John, Jr.
Panel, 25½ x 21½; Museum of Fine Arts, Boston.

Amory, Jonathan.
Panel, 26⅝ x 20¼; Vose Gallery.

Amory, Mrs. Thomas.
Panel; exh. Musuem of Fine Arts, Boston (1928).

Amory, Thomas.
Mrs. O. H. Ernst.

Amory, Thomas Coffin.
Panel; exh. Museum of Fine Arts, Boston (1928).

Anthony, John.
Ehrick Galleries, (1931).

Anthony, Captain Joseph.

(1) 35½ x 28; National Gallery of Art, Washington (Mellon Collection).
(2) 28 x 22; Pennsylvania Academy.
(3) Lawrence J. Morris.

Anthony, Mrs. Joseph.
Mentioned by Mason, page 129; not located.

Anthony, Judge Joseph, Jr.
Metropolitan Museum.

Anthony, Mrs. Joseph, Jr.
Metropolitan Museum.

Anthony, Joseph, III.
Frederick Brooks (1926).

Appleton, Nathan.
Panel, 27½ x 22⅜; Longfellow House Trust, Cambridge.

Appleton, Mrs. Nathan.
Panel, 27⅞ x 22⅝; Longfellow House Trust, Cambridge.

Arden, Mrs. James.
Bordeaux Museum.

Ashburton, Lord (as Alexander Baring).
Not located. Mentioned by Mason, page 130.

Ashburton, Lady.
Not located. Mentioned by Mason, page 130.

Ashe, Col. John Baptista.
36 x 27⅞; National Gallery of Art, Washington (Mellon Collection).

Ashley, John (formerly called Sir Cropley Ashley-Cooper).
(1) Dallas Museum of Fine Arts.
(2) (Replica) Toledo Museum.

Ashley, Mrs. John.
Dallas Museum of Fine Arts.

Aspinwall, William.
Panel 28 x 22⅝; exh. Museum of Fine Arts, Boston (1928).

Astor, John Jacob.
(1) The Brook Club, New York.
(2) Lord Astor.

Atherton, Charles Humphrey.
Amherst Town Library (1926).

Auchmuty, Mrs. Robert Nicholls.
34 x 28; Brooklyn Museum.

Babcock, Adam.
Panel, 32¼ x 26¼; Museum of Fine Arts, Boston.

Babcock, Mrs. Adams.
Panel, 32¼ x 26¼; Elizabeth F. Head (1926).

Bainbridge, Commodore William.
Panel, 29 x 23; J. H. Whitney.

Baker, Admiral Sir Henry Lorraine.
Panel, 26 x 21; Pennsylvania Academy.

Bannister, John.
36 x 20; Redwood Library, Newport.

Bannister, Mrs. John, and Her Son.
36 x 20; Redwood Library, Newport.

Barclay, Hon. John.
Mrs. Alfred C. Prime.

Bard, Mrs. James.
20½ x 16½; Montclair Museum.

Barry, Miss Ann.
National Gallery of Art, Washington.

Barry, James David.*
W. T. Walters (1880).

Barry, Commodore John.
Mrs. Leiper, on loan to the White House, Washington.

Barry, Miss Mary.
National Gallery of Art, Washington.

Bartlett, Miss Ann (Mrs. Dwight).*
Panel, 28½ x 22⅝; Museum of the City of New York.

Bartlett, John, M.D.
Panel, 28¾ x 23¼ inches. Knoedler's, (1929).

Bartlett, Mrs. John.
Panel, 28¾ x 23½; Theoda F. Bush.

Bartlett, Maria.
Panel, 20⅞ x 16¼; Museum of Fine Arts, Boston.

Bartlett, Thomas, M.D.
Panel, 28½ x 23½; Museum of Fine Arts, Boston.

Bartlett, Mrs. Thomas.
Panel, 27⅝ x 23⅛; Museum of Fine Arts, Boston.

Battelle, Mrs. Ebenezer.
Panel, 31⅝ x 25½; Museum of Fine Arts, Boston.

Bayard, Mrs. Nicholas.
Mason says a portrait "probably" was done.

Bayard, William.
36 x 28; Mrs. Howard Townsend.

Bayard, Mrs. William, Jr.
Panel, 36 x 27; Howard Townsend (1933).

Bayley, Dr. Richard.
Not located.

Beach, Miss Clementina.
Panel, 26 x 21; Carnegie Library, Fort Worth, Texas.

Bean, Stephen.
F. W. Buck, (1926).

Benson, Judge Egbert.
(1) Mrs. Arthur Iselin.
(2) Panel, 28½ x 24½; New York Historical Society.

Bethune, Dr. George.
Panel, 27 x 21⅝; Dr. F. S. Weisse (1926).

Bethune, Mrs. George.
Panel, 27⅛ x 21¾; Mrs. Roger I. Lee.

Bingham, Mrs. William.
Pennsylvania Academy

Binney, Hon. Horace.
National Gallery of Art, Washington.

Binney, Miss Mary.
Panel, 28⅜ x 22¾; Mrs. Elizabeth Sargent Miller (1926).

Blodget, Mrs. Samuel.
Pennsylvania Academy.

Blodget, Mrs. Samuel and Her Daughter.
Not located.

Bonaparte, Jerome, Jr.
  Mason asserts such a picture was done.
Bonaparte, Jerome, Prince (King of Westphalia).
  (Unfinished) Mrs. W. A. Harriman.
Bonparte, Madame Jerome (Elizabeth Patterson).
  Count Adam Moltke-Huitfeldt.
Bond, Nathan.
  Panel, 25 x 21; Museum of Fine Arts, Boston.
Bond, Mrs. Nathan.
  Panel, 25 x 21; Musuem of Fine Arts, Boston.
Booth, Kirk.
  Panel, 28¼ x 22⅞; Francis R. Welsh (1926).
Bordley, Elizabeth Beale.
  Pennsylvania Academy.
Borland, Mrs. Leonard Vassall.
  Panel, 27 x 21½; William A. Jeffries (1926).
Bowditch, Dr. Nathaniel.
  (Unfinished) Mrs. R. L. Bowditch.
Bowdoin, James.
  Bowdoin College.
Bowdoin, Mrs. James.
  Bowdoin College.
Bowdoin, James Temple.*
  Princess di Pandolfino (1875).
Bowdoin, Mrs. James Temple.
  Bowdoin College.
Boylston, Ward Nicholas.
  (1) Panel, 21 x 17; Museum of Fine Arts, Boston.
  (2) 32 x 28; Museum of Fine Arts, Boston.
  (3) 36 x 27¾; Harvard Medical School.
Brackenridge, Hugh Henry.
  Panel, 28 x 24; Jos. McKibben (1890–).
Bradlee, Josiah.
  Panel, 28⅜ x 22⅝; Frederick J. Bradlee.
Bradlee, Mrs. Josiah.
  Panel, 29 x 23; Frederick J. Bradlee.
Breck, Mrs. Samuel.
  26 x 21; Mrs. Paul Tuckerman (1926).
Brewster, Mrs. Oliver.*
  William Brewster (1926).
Bromfield, Mrs. John.*
  Formerly at Bromfield House, Harvard.
Brooks, Gov. John.
  Panel, 31⅛ x 25⅜; on loan at the White House.
Brooks, Peter Chardon.*
  (1) Mrs. Mary O. Adams (1926).
  (2) Destroyed by fire.
Brown, Moses.
  (1) Panel, 31 x 25; Historical Society of Beverly, Mass.
  (2) Panel, 32¾ x 25¾; sold in New York, April 1920.
Buckminster, Rev. Joseph Stevens, D.D.
  (1) Panel, 33 x 26 inches; Boston Athenaeum.
  (2) (Replica) panel, 33 x 26 inches; Cincinnati Art Museum.
Bullus, Dr. John.
  Robert L. Fowler, Jr. (1926).
Bullus, Mrs. John.
  Robert L. Fowler, Jr. (1926).
Burdett, Sir Francis.*
  Boston art market (1918).
Burr, Aaron.
  (1) New Jersey Historical Society, Newark.
  (2) (Replica) Museum of History of Art, Princeton.
Burr, Theodosia.
  Yale University Art Gallery.
Burroughs, Rev. Charles, D.D.
  George Burroughs (1926).
Bussey, Benjamin.
  Panel, 32 x 26½; Harvard University Hall
Bussey, Mrs. Benjamin.
  Panel, 32¼ x 26¼; Miss Katherine P. Motley (1926).
Bussey, Benjamin, Jr.
  Panel, 32⅝ x 26; Mrs. Willoughby H. Stuart, Jr.
Callender, John.*
  Miss Mary R. Callender (1919).
Callender, Thomas.*
  Miss Mary R. Callender (1919).
Calvert, George.
  Dr. T. Morris Murray (1926).
Calvert, Mrs. George and Her Daughter Caroline.
  Dr. T. Morris Murray, (1926).
Campbell, John.
  36 x 28; New York Public Library.
Carroll, Archbishop John.
  Georgetown University.
Cary, Mrs. Samuel.
  Panel, 26¾ x 21⅞; Mrs. Lewis Iselin, Jr.
Channing, Walter.
  Panel, 28 x 22; on loan at Museum of Fine Arts, Boston (1926).
Channing, Mrs. Walter.
  Panel, 26 x 22; exh. at Museum of Fine Arts, Boston (1928).
Channing, Rev. William Ellery.
  Mrs. John Amory Jeffries (1926).
Chase, Judge Samuel.*
  Mason says it was in possession of Dudley T. Chase, (1879).
Chauncey, Commodore Isaac.
  Panel, 24 x 20; Annapolis Naval Academy.
Chestnut, Col. John.
  (1) Herbert L. Pratt, (1926).
  (2) (Replica) John F. Braun (1926).
Chestnut, Col. James, Sr.
  Mrs. Meredith Hare (1926).
Chestnut, Mrs. James.
  Mrs. Meredith Hare (1926).
Cheverus, Bishop John.

36⅜ x 28½; Museum of Fine Arts, Boston.
Chew, Mr.
Not located. C. W. Peale reported Stuart painted this man smoking, then was forced to paint out the cigar and smoke.
Chipman, Ward.
Panel, 25½ x 21¼; Christopher Gray.
Chipman, Mrs. Ward.
Not located. Listed by Mason.
Chipman, Ward, Jr.
Panel, 25¾ x 21⅛; John C. Gray.
Clarkson, General Matthew.
36 x 28; Metropolitan Museum.
Clement, Thomas, Sr.
Panel, 26¼ x 21⅜; Boston Athenaeum.
Clymer, Mrs. Henry.
(1) Alexander Grant, Rome (1926).
(2) (Replica) Mrs. Thomas F. Bayard (1926).
Cobb, General David.
Panel, 28¼ x 22¾; Miss Julia Cabot Wilde (1926).
Codman, Charles Russell.
(1) Panel, 31 x 24¾; Mrs. Charles R. Codman.
(2) 35½ x 28½; Mrs. C. C. Ely (1926).
Coffin, Admiral Sir Isaac.
Panel, 33 x 26½; Mr. William Amory.
Coffin, Dr. Nathaniel.
Panel, 28 x 22; Miss Harriot S. Curtis.
Coffin, Mrs. Nathaniel.
Panel, 27¼ x 21¾; Miss Harriot S. Curtis.
Colburn, Mrs. James Smith.
Panel, 28 x 22; Museum of Fine Arts, Boston.
Collins, Jonathan.
Not located. Engraved by John Chester Buttre.
Constable, William Kerin.
(1) Metropolitan Museum.
(2) National Gallery of Art, Washington (Mellon Coll.).*
Cony, Daniel.
Panel, 28 x 24; Old Williams House, Augusta, Maine.
Cooke, George Frederick.
Panel, 27 x 22; Garrick Club, London.
Coolidge, Joseph.
(1) National Gallery, Washington (Mellon Coll.).
(2) Panel, 27½ x 22½; J. R. Coolidge.
Cooper, Thomas Apthorp.
Panel, 28½ x 22¾; Player's Club, New York.
Cooper, Judge William.
36 x 28; Henry S. F. Cooper, M.D.
Cordis, Thomas.*
Cordis Estate, Longmeadow, Mass.
Cordis, Mrs. Thomas.*
Cordis Estate, Longmeadow, Mass.
Cottringer, Mrs.
Listed by Mason, page 165. Not located.
Craig, Mrs. William.
Not located. Listed by Mason, page 165.
Crocker, Allen.
Mrs. F. Reed Dickerson.
Cruger, Matilda Caroline.
36¼ x 28¼; National Gallery of Art, Washington, (Mellon Coll.).
Cunningham, Mrs. Joseph Lewis.
Mr. & Mrs. Francis I. Amory.
Curtis, ------.
Not located. Mentioned by Mason, page 166.
Cushing, Mrs. Thomas.
Panel, 26 x 21⅛; George M. Cushing, Jr.
Cutts, Richard.
Mrs. Walter Farwell (1926).
Cutts, Mrs. Richard.
George B. Cutts (1926).
Dabney, Mrs. Charles William.
Panel, 26⅛ x 21; Misses Sarah and Ellen Dabney (1926).
Dallas, Alexander James.
Pennsylvania Academy.
Dallas, Mrs. Alexander James.
Mrs. Dennis McCarthy (1926).
Danforth, Dr. Samuel.
35½ x 29⅜; Museum of Fine Arts, Boston.
Daschkoff, Count André.
Not located. Listed by Mason, page 168.
Davis, Aaron.
Panel, 28⅛ x 22⅞; Museum of Fine Arts, Boston.
Davis, Mrs. Aaron.
Panel, 28 x 22¾; Dr. Edward Brinley Kellog (1926).
Davis, General Amassa.
Panel, 32 x 26; Detroit Art Institute.
Davis, Mrs. Cabel.
Panel, 26 x 21; Henry L. Shattuck.
Davis, Charles.
Panel, 32 x 26; Mrs. Lawrence Park (1926).
Davis, Mrs. Charles.
Panel, 32 x 26; Mrs. Lawrence Park (1926).
Davis, Mrs. Eleanor.
Not located. Listed by Mason, page 168.
Davis, Mr. Isaac P.
His name appears in the page of Stuart's journal printed by Mason; presumably he was a sitter in 1808.
Davis, Mrs. Isaac P. & Her Sister Mrs. Bernard Henry.
Panel 26½ x 26½; Gordon Chickering Prince.
Davis, William.
W. J. A. Bliss (1926).
Davis, Mrs. William.
W. J. A. Bliss (1926).
Dawes, Colonel Thomas.
Panel, 32 x 26; Fred. D. Stetson (1926).
Dawes, Judge Thomas.
Panel, 32 x 26; Fred. D. Stetson (1926).

Dearborn, Major-General Henry.
  (1) Panel, 28 x 22; Chicago Art Institute.
  (2) Panel, 28 x 22; (replica) L. D. M.
    Sweat Memorial Gallery, Portland.
  (3) Panel, 28 x 22 (in civil dress); Henry
    Ford Museum & Greenfield Village,
    Dearborn.
Dearborn, Major-General Henry Alexander
  Scammell.
  Panel, 28 x 22½; Bowdoin College.
Dearborn, Mrs. Henry Alexander Scammell.
  Panel, 28 x 22½; Bowdoin College.
Decatur, Commodore Stephen.
  (1) National Collection of Fine Arts
    (Smithsonian Institution).
  (2) Robert Bryan (1926).
Decatur, Mrs. Stephen.
  Mrs. William F. Machold.
Delano, Abisha.
  26 x 22 inches; Fairhaven Homestead
    (1890).
Delano, Mrs. Abisha.
  26 x 22 inches; Wilson G. Hunt Heath
    (1926).
Dennie, Thomas.
  Museum of Fine Arts, Boston.
Dennie, Mrs. Thomas.
  Museum of Fine Arts, Boston.
Derby, Captain John.
  Panel, 28 x 22⅝; Dr. Frederick Shattuck
    Bigelow.
Derby, Mrs. Richard C.
  New York Historical Society.
Devereux, Humphrey.
  Panel. Nathaniel Devereaux Silsbee
    (about 1900).
Devereux, Mrs. Humphrey.
  Panel. Russell W. Nowels. Drapery re-
    painted by Chester Harding.
Dexter, Andrew.
  Mrs. Stanley R. McCormick.
Dexter, Mrs. Andrew.
  Panel. National Gallery of Art, Washing-
    ton (Mellon Coll.).
Dexter, Samuel.
  Gordon Dexter (1926).
Doggett, Samuel.
  Panel, 28⅜ x 23¼; Santa Barbara Museum
    of Art.
Doggett, Mrs. Samuel.
  Panel, 25⅝ x 23¼; Santa Barbara Museum
    of Art.
Dorr, Mrs. Sullivan.
  Mason lists such a work, and in 1867 it
    was in possession of Sullivan Dorr.
    The possibility must be entertained
    that Mason was in error.
Dorsey, Mrs. Hammond.
  Reproduced in *The Pickering Genealogy*,
    1897.
Duane, Col. William.
  Destroyed by fire (1886).
Dunn, Counsellor John.

  (1) National Gallery of Art, Washington
    (Mellon Coll.).
  (2) Museum of Fine Arts, Boston.
  (3) Panel, 23 x 19; Mrs. J. Montgomery
    Sears (1905).
Dunn, Samuel.
  Panel, 27⅞ x 22⅞; Rhode Island School of
    Design.
Dunn, Mrs. Samuel.
  Panel, 27¾ x 22¾; Rhode Island School of
    Design.
Durant, Maria Cornelia.
  Exh. Museum of Fine Arts, Boston
    (1928).
Dutton, Francis Lowell.
  Panel, 26⅞ x 22; Henry R. & Elizabeth L.
    Dalton (1926).
Dutton, Mrs. Warren.
  Panel, 27 x 23; Miss Sarah L. Barnard
    (1926).
D'Yrugo, Marquis.
  (1) Philadelphia Museum of Art.
  (2) Duke of Sotomayor, Madrid, (1926).*
  (3) According to Charles Henry Hart,
    in possession of a sister to the Duke of
    Sotomayor, Madrid.*
D'Yrugo, Marchioness.
  (1) Philadelphia Museum of Art.
  (2) Duke of Sotomayor, Madrid, (1926).*
  (3) According to Charles Henry Hart, in
    possession of a sister to the Duke of
    Sotomayor, Madrid.*
Eliot, Miss Mary Harrison.
  (1) Panel, 28 x 23; Eliot Farley (1926).
  (2) Said to differ in details; Albert Ro-
    senthal (1926).
Eliot, Samuel.
  (1) Panel, 32 x 28; Richard C. Paine.
  (2) (Replica) 36 x 28; Massachusetts Gen-
    eral Hospital.
Eliot, Mrs. Samuel.
  Panel, 32 x 28; Richard C. Paine.
Eliot, William Havard.
  24 x 20 inches; Mrs. John Holmes Morri-
    son (1926).
Ellery, John Stevens.
  Panel, 26¼ x 21⅝; John Turner Sargent.
Elliot, James Henderson.
  Panel, 28¾ x 23¼; Mrs. H. Thomas Bal-
    lantine, Jr.
Erskine, Hon. David Montague (Baron).
  Philadelphia Museum.
Erskine, Hon. Mrs. (Lady Fanny).
  (1) Philadelphia Museum.
  (2) Herbert Lee Pratt; said to be a
    partial replica.*
Eustaphieve, Alexis.
  Panel, approx. 21 x 26; Miss Mary E.
    Milligan.
Eustaphieve, Mrs. Alexis.
  Panel, approx. 21 x 26; Miss Mary E.
    Milligan.
Eustis, William.

Metropolitan Museum.
Everett, Mrs. Alexander Hill.*
    Listed by Park and Fielding; not located.
Everett, Edward.
    (1) Panel, 27 x 21½ inches; Fogg Museum.
    (2) Head only; Massachusetts Historical
        Society.
    (3) 24 x 20; head only; Wadsworth Ath-
        enaeum (called Portrait of a Gentle-
        man).
Fales, Samuel.
    Panel, 28½ x 23½; Haliburton Fales.
Fenwick, General John R.
    J. Coleman Drayton (1926).
Flint, Mrs. Simon.*
    Panel, 26½ x 21½; Pontus H. Conradson
        (1922).
Ford, Mrs. James.*
    Mrs. Heloise Chamberlain (1897).
Forrest, Edwin.*
    Edwin Forrest Public School, Philadel-
        phia.
Forrester, Mrs. John.
    Panel, 26¾ x 21½; only head said to be by
        Stuart; Essex Institute, Salem, Mass.
Francis, Thomas Willing.*
    John F. Braun (1926).
Francis, Mrs. Thomas Willing.*
    Mrs. Frank H. Brown (1914).
Franks, Colonel Isaac.
    Pennsylvania Academy.
Freeman, Rev. James.
    Engraved by Kilburn, 1881.
Gallatin, Albert.
    Metropolitan Museum.
Gansevoort, Leonard.*
    Rowland N. Moore (1918).
Gansevoort, General Peter.
    Rowland N. Moore (1918).
Gardiner, Reverend John S. J.
    (1) Panel, 27¾ x 22½; Boston Athenaeum
        (facing left).
    (2) 35½ x 27½ (facing right); Robert H.
        Gardiner.
Gardner, Samuel Pickering.
    Sidney Coolidge (1926).
Gardner, Mrs. Samuel Pickering.
    Panel, 28 x 22½; exh. Museum of Fine
        Arts, Boston, 1928.
Gates, General Horatio.
    44 x 36; Metropolitan Museum.
Gatliff, Samuel.
    Pennsylvania Academy.
Gatliff, Mrs. Samuel and Her Daughter Eliza-
    beth.
    Pennsylvania Academy.
Gerry, Elbridge.
    The Misses Gerry (1879).
Gerry, James Thompson, U.S.N.
    The Misses Gerry (1879).
Gerry, Thomas Russell, U.S.N.
    The Misses Gerry (1879).
Gibbs, George, Sr.

(1) Paul Tuckerman (1926).
(2) Mrs. Stephen H. Pell (1926).
Gibbs, Mrs. George, Sr.
    Paul Tuckerman (1926).
Gibbs, Col. George.
    Panel, 26 x 20; Bayard Tuckerman, Jr.
Giles, Col. Aquila.
    Wadsworth Athenaeum, Hartford.
Gilmor, Robert.
    (1) John Gilmor.
    (2) Philipse Manor Hall, Yonkers.
Gilmor, Robert, Jr.
    Panel, 25 x 21; Museum of Fine Arts,
        Boston.
Goldsborough, Mrs. Charles.
    Listed by Mason, page 185.
Gore, John.*
    Not located. A copy at Museum of Fine
        Arts, Boston.
Gore, Mrs. John.
    Museum of Fine Arts, Boston.
Gouverneur, Isaac.*
    Gouverneur Paulding (1879).
Grafton, Major Joseph.
    Panel, 26 x 21; J. Grafton Minot (1926).
Grafton, Mrs. Joseph.
    Panel, 26 x 21; J. Grafton Minot (1926).
Grant, Patrick.
    (1) Panel, 26 x 21 inches; Mrs. David
        Scull.
    (2) (Replica) Panel, 26 x 21 inches;
        Robert Grant.
Gratz, Mrs. Michael.
    Henry Joseph (1926).
Gray, John Chipman.
    35 x 27; John C. Gray.
Gray, William.
    (1) Panel, 31 x 25 inches; Roland Gray,
        Jr.
    (2) 32 x 26 inches; Mrs. George Ehrhorn.
Gray, Mrs. William.
    32 x 26; Roland Gray, Jr.
Gray, William Rufus.
    32 x 26; Francis Gray Leonard.
Greenleaf, James.
    (1) Pennsylvania Academy (with curtain).
    (2) Lewis S. Greenleaf, Jr.
Greenleaf, Mrs. James.
    (1) Metropolitan Museum.
    (2) Pennsylvania Academy.
    (3) Philadelphia Museum of Art.
    (4) Destroyed in San Francisco earth-
        quake (1906).
Greenough, David Stoddard.
    (1) Panel, 25 x 21; Horatio G. Curtis
        (1926).
    (2) Panel, 33 x 26; Mrs. D. S. Gree-
        nough.*
Greenough, David Stoddard, Jr.
    Panel, 26½ x 22½; sold at Christies', Octo-
        ber 27, 1961.
Greenough, Mrs. David Stoddard, Jr.
    Panel, 26½ x 22½; sold at Christies', Octo-

ber 27, 1961.
Griffin, Samuel.
  Pennsylvania Academy.
Griffith, Robert Egglesfield.
  R. E. Griffith (1926).
Griffith, Mrs. Robert Egglesfield.
  R. E. Griffith, (1926).
Griswold, Alexander Viets, Bishop.*
  Head only said to be Stuart; Frederic B.
  Robinson.
Guillemard, John. (D)
  National Portrait Gallery, Edinburgh.
Hale, William.
  Panel, 27 x 21; Fogg Museum.
Hallam, Mrs.*
  Mrs. Charles Steadman Hanks (1926).
Hollowell, Robert.
  Panel; Robert H. Gardiner.
Halsey, James Moore.
  Panel, 26 x 21; M. Knoedler (1924–5).
Hammond, George.
  50 x 39; the Hon. Misses Hammond
  (1926).
Hare, Robert, Sr., and His Daughter Martha.
  47 x 37; Charles Hare.
Harman, Mrs. Thomas Leader.*
  The Hon. Frances Louise Eaton (1926).
Harrison, Richard.*
  J. H. E. Coffin (1880).
Hatch, Mercy Shiverick.
  Panel, 27 x 22; The Newark Museum.
Hartigan, Dr. William (so-called).
  National Gallery of Art, Washington
  (Mellon Coll.).
Hartigan, Mrs. William (so-called).
  National Gallery of Art, Washington
  (Mellon Coll.).
Haven, John.
  New York Public Library.
Haven, Mrs. John.
  New York Public Library.
Haven, Nathaniel Appleton.*
  William Jones Ladd (1923).
Hays, Judah.
  Panel, 28 x 23; Mrs. William C. Preston
  (1926).
Hayward, Mrs. Lemuel.
  Sidney W. Hayward.
Head of a Child.
  18 x 15 (unfinished); Charles Pelham
  Curtis (1926).
Head, Joseph.
  Panel, 32 x 26; National Collection of
  Fine Arts (Smithsonian Institution).
Heard, John.
  Joseph Grafton Minot (1925).
Henry, Mrs. Bernard.*
  (1) Panel, 5½ x 5½; Barklie McKee Henry.
  (2) Morton P. Henry (1887).
Hicks, Zachariah.
  Museum of Fine Arts, Boston.
Higginson, Stephen.*
  George Higginson (1926).

Hinckley, Anne Outram.
  Exh. Museum of Fine Arts, Boston, 1928.
Hinkley, David.
  Panel, 28 x 22; Mrs. David Hinckley
  Bangs.
Hoffman, Josiah Ogden.*
  In 1880 said to have been owned by his
  widow.
Holker, John.
  Panel, 25 x 21; Mrs. Hugh Mortimer
  Nelson (1915).
Holker, Mrs. John.
  Panel, 25 x 20; Mrs. Hugh Mortimer
  Nelson (1915).
Holley, Rev. Horace.
  Panel, 30 x 25; possibly destroyed in Bos-
  ton fire of 1872.
Holman, Joseph George.*
  Listed by Strickland.
Hooper, Robert.
  Mentioned by Mason (who possibly was
  in error).
Hooper, Mrs. Robert.
  Credited by Mason to possession of Rev.
  Charles Robbins (1879).
Hopkinson, Joseph.
  Panel, 29 x 24; Pennsylvania Historical
  Society.
Hopkinson, Mrs. Joseph.
  Panel, 29 x 24; Pennsylvania Historical
  Society.
Howard, Dr. John Clark.*
  Panel, 27 x 22; Miss Susan H. Pickering
  (1926).
Howard, Mrs. John Clark.
  Springfield Museum.
Hughes, Christopher.
  Panel, 28 x 22; sold at Anderson Gal-
  leries, New York, 1925.
Hull, Commodore Isaac.
  Philadelphia Museum (A copy at the
  Metropolitan Museum).
Hull, General William.
  Mrs. Lucy Smith (1915).
Humphreys, General David.
  Panel, 39 x 29½; Yale University Art
  Gallery.
Hunt, Mrs. William.
  Panel, 26½ x 21; Museum of Fine Arts,
  Boston.
Hurlburt, Rev. Joseph.*
  Not located. In possession of his daugh-
  ter, 1880.
Inches, Miss Elizabeth.
  Panel, 31 x 25; Mrs. Oric Bates.
Izard, Miss Ann.
  Albany Institute of History and Art.
Izard, Mrs. George.*
  Arkansas Arts Center, Little Rock.
Jackson, Frances James.
  Panel, 32 x 26; Orrin W. June.
Jackson, Mrs. Francis James.
  Mason notes this was seen by Judge

Hopkinson. Not located.

Jackson, General Henry.
Panel, 33 x 26; Mrs. Francis W. Sargent (1926).

Jackson, Mrs. William.
(1) Pennsylvania Academy.
(2) In dark dress; Princess Poniatowska. (D)

Jarvis, Rev. Samuel Farmar.
Head only by Stuart; Wadsworth Athenaeum, Hartford.

Jaudenes y Nebot, Don Joseph de.
50 x 40; Metropolitan Museum.

Jaudenes y Nebot, Matilda Stoughton.
50 x 40; Metropolitan Museum.

Jay, John.
50½ x 41¾; National Gallery of Art, Washington. At least three copies, or replicas, are recorded; but confusion exists over whether they are of this picture or the earlier effort completed by Trumbull.

Jefferson, Thomas.
(1) The first life-portrait, sold to S. Smith, 1803; known only by engraving by W. Nettling.
(2) The second life-portrait, 1805. Williamsburg Collection, Williamsburg, Virginia.
(3) 46½ x 38¾; enlarged replica of second life portrait; Bowdoin College.
(4) Panel, 26½ x 21¾; replica painted from the Bowdoin College version and sent Jefferson, 1821. Estate of Percy S. Straus.
(5) Panel, 25⅝ x 21½; T. J. Coolidge.
(6) Studio replica, perhaps by Jouett; the White House.
(7) The third life-portrait, as a classic medallion, 1805; an aqueous medium on paper; Fogg Museum.

Johnson, Dr. William Samuel.
35 x 27; Milch Gallery (1925).

Jones, Judge Stephen.
Panel, approx. 20 x 25; F. A. Richards (1909).

Jones, Mrs.
Listed by Mason, page 208.

Jouett, Matthew Harris.
Stuart is believed to have painted this pupil.

Kane, Oliver de Lancey.
Panel, 28 x 22½; The Misses Kane (1926).

Kane, Mrs. Oliver de Lancey.
Panel, 28 x 22½; The Misses Kane (1926).

Keppele, Michael.
Mrs. Bayard Kane (1926).

Keppele, Mrs. Michael.
Mrs. John K. Mitchell (1926).

King, Rufus.
(1) Panel; Frederick Gore King (1926).
(2) Panel; New York Public Library.
(3) 36 x 29; Frederick Lennig, Jr.

King, William.
W. K. Richardson (1926).

King, Mrs. William.
W. K. Richardson (1926).

Kirkland, Rev. John Thornton.
Panel, 32 x 25; private collection, Boston.

Kirkpatrick, Sir William.
Mrs. Jonathan Kearsley Webster (1926).

Knapp, Captain Charles.
Panel, 27 x 21¼; Yale University Art Gallery.

Knox, Major General Henry.
Panel, 47 x 38½; Museum of Fine Arts, Boston.

De Lancey, James.
Not located.

Lardner, John.
Panel, 29 x 24; Mrs. Edwin L. Reakirt (1926).

Lathrop, Rev. John.
Mrs. Algernon Brinsley Sheridan.

Law, Thomas B.
Herbert L. Pratt (1926).

Law, Mrs. Thomas B.
William H. Ball.

Lawrence, Augustine Hicks.
33 x 26; New York Historical Society.

Lawrence, Captain James.
(1) (Uncompleted) Washington Headquarters, Morristown, New Jersey.
(2) Panel, 28 x 22; United States Naval Academy, Annapolis.

Lea, Mrs. Thomas.
Lea McIlvaine Luquer.

Lear, Benjamin Lincoln.
Exhibited at Metropolitan Museum (1896).

Le Conte, Mrs. William.
Panel; Miss Mary H. Penington (1888).

Lee, Charles (?).
Metropolitan Museum.

Lee, Mrs. Charles.
18 x 16 (unfinished); Mrs. Charles F. Harrison (1922).

Lee, Mrs. George Gardiner.
Mrs. Charles J. Paine (1879).

Lee, Major General Henry.
Carter Lee Refo.

Lennox, Miss Elizabeth Sproat.
Panel, 28 x 23; New York Public Library. (A second version, at Virginia Museum of Fine Arts, I have not seen.)

Lennox, Miss Isabella Henderson.
Panel, 28 x 23; New York Public Library.

Lewis, Mrs. Lawrence.
Mrs. Edwin Augustus Stevens Lewis (1926).

Lewis, William.
Engraved by C. Goodman and R. Piggot, 1820.

Liston, Robert.
National Gallery of Art, Washington (Chester Dale Coll.).

Liston, Mrs. Robert.
National Gallery of Art, Washington
(Chester Dale Coll.).
Livingston, Rev. John Henry.
New York Historical Society.
Livingston, Mrs. Robert.
(1) 36 x 28; Brigadier General John Ross
Delafield (1926).
(2) 36 x 28; Stephen Henry Olin (d.
1925).
(3) 36 x 27½; C. V. Livingston (1926).
(4) 36 x 28 (with addition of black lace
scarf); Museum of the City of New
York.
Livingston, Robert R.
(1) 36 x 28; John Henry Livingston
(1926).
(2) 36 x 28; New York Historical Society.
Lloyd, Dr. James.*
Panel, 33 x 26; National Gallery of Art,
Washington. (Mellon Coll.).
Lloyd, Mrs. James.*
Aspinwall Gallery, New York (1879).
Logan, Dr. George.
Historical Society of Pennsylvania.
Lopez.
Mason states that Stuart painted mem-
bers of this family at Newport prior
to 1775.
Lopez, Mrs. Aaron, and Her Son Joshua.
26 x 21½; Detroit Institute of Arts.
Loring, Caleb.
Panel, 26 x 21; Augustus P. Loring.
Loring, Mrs. Caleb.
Panel, 26 x 21; Augustus P. Loring.
Low, David.
Charles Frederick Roper (1926).
Lowell, John.
Ralph Lowell.
Lowndes, Thomas.
Carolina Art Association (Gibbs Art Gal-
lery).
Lowndes, Mrs. Thomas.
Carolina Art Association (Gibbs Art Gal-
lery).
MacDonald, James.
Howard Young Galleries.
Macdonough, Commodore Thomas.
35¾ x 27½; National Gallery of Art, Wash-
ington. (Mellon Collection).
Madison, James.
(1) Williamsburg Collection, Williams-
burg, Va.
(2) 46 x 38; Bowdoin College.
(3) 40 x 32; (from Doggett set) Herbert
Lee Pratt, (1926).
(4) Panel, 25⅝ x 21; T. J. Coolidge, Jr.
Madison, Mrs. James (Dolly).
Pennsylvania Academy.
Malbone, Francis and His Brother Saunders.
35 x 43; Mrs. Lucy R. Blodgett, (1926).
Manigault, Gabriel.
Destroyed during the Civil War.

Manigault, Gabriel.
(1) Albright-Knox Art Gallery (In
spotted coat).
(2) Captain Lewis Morris (Blue coat).
Manigault, Mrs. Gabriel.
(1) Albright Knox Art Gallery.
(2) Sittings recorded in Mrs. Manigault's
diary. Not located.
Mason, Miss Anna Powell.
(1) 33 x 27; Mrs. Courtlandt Parker.
(2) Panel, 32 x 26; Francis C. Gray.
Mason, Jeremiah.
Panel, 32 x 25¾; Mrs. Gordon Knox Bell
(1926).
Mason, Mrs. Jeremiah.
Panel, 32 x 25¾; Mrs. Gordon Knox Bell
(1926).
Mason, Rev. John Mitchell.
Panel, 28 x 22; Liberty Hall, Louisville,
Kentucky.
Mason, Mrs. John Thomson.
Cleveland Museum.
Mason, Jonathan.
Panel, 32 x 25; Henry Sears.
Mason, Mrs. Jonathan.
Panel, 28 x 23; Miss Honora Winthrop
Mason (1928).
May, Colonel John.*
Listed by Park.
May, Mrs. John.
Panel, 28 x 23; not located.
May, Colonel Joseph.
Valentine May (1910).
McCall, Richard.
Panel; George McCall (1926).
McCormick, Daniel.
Photo at Witt Library, London.
McKean, Gov. Thomas.
Panel, 29 x 25; John Hill Morgan (1926).
McLean, John.
(1) The McLean Hospital, Belmont,
Mass.
(2) (Replica) The McLean Hospital, Bel-
mont, Mass.
McLean, Mrs, John.
The McLean Hospital, Belmont, Mass.
Meade, Richard Worsam.
Destroyed during the Civil War.
Meade, Mrs. Richard Worsam.
Destroyed during the Civil War.
Meeker, William.
28 x 23; Mr. & Mrs. Robert I. Gale, Jr.
Meircken, Peter.
29 x 24; Pennsylvania Academy.
Meircken, Mrs. Peter.
29 x 24; Pennsylvania Academy.
Merritt, Charles.*
Panel, 24 x 19; Albert Rosenthal (1926).
Merry, Anthony.
Not located.
Merry, Mrs. Anthony.
Don José de Lazaro, Madrid (1926).
Mifflin, General Thomas.

Alexander James Dallas Dixon (1926).
Miles, Colonel Samuel.
Panel, 29 x 23½; Corcoran Gallery.
Monroe, James.
(1) Panel, 26 x 21; (the life-portrait) Pennsylvania Academy.
(2) Panel, 25⅝ x 21½; (replica) T. J. Coolidge, Jr.
(3) 40 x 32; (from the Doggett set) Metropolitan Museum.
Montgomery, William.
Pennsylvania Academy.
Montgomery, Mrs. William.
Pennsylvania Academy.
Morris, Miss Hetty and Miss Maria.
37 x 51; Philadelphia Museum of Art.
Morris, Robert.
Mrs. Richard B. Tinsley (1926).
Morris, Mrs. Robert.
(Unfinished—head only); New York Public Library.
Morton, Mrs. Perez.
(1) Panel, 29½ x 24; probably the life-portrait; Henry Francis Dupont Winterthur Museum.
(2) 29 x 22⅝; Museum of Fine Arts, Boston.
(3) 28 x 24; unfinished; Worcester Museum.
Moses, Solomon.
28 x 24; Mrs. Ethel Olive Elwell.
Moses, Mrs. Solomon.
28 x 24; Mrs. Ethel Olive Elwell.
Motley, Thomas.
(1) (Unfinished) Miss Prentiss Shepherd.
(2) 27 x 22; Thomas Motley.
Murray, John R.
Metropolitan Museum.
Murray, Mrs. John R.
37 x 32; Mrs. W. Wilton Phipps (1926).
Murray, Miss Julia Maria.
37 x 32¾; Mrs. Warfield T. Longcope (1926).
Myers, Moses.
Panel, 33 x 26¼; The Norfolk Museum.
Myers, Mrs. Moses.
Panel, 33 x 26; The Norfolk Museum.
Myers, Samuel.
Panel, 27 x 22; Mrs. John Hill Morgan (1926).
Newton, Edward.
Edward Newton Perkins (1880).
Nicholas, Wilson Cary.
(1) Mrs. Leonard Hewitt (1926).
(2) R. Carter Nicholas.
Nichols, Mrs. Charles Colton.
(Completed by Jane Stuart). Harry W. Watrous (1926).
Nicklin, Philip.
Mrs. Russell Thayer (1926).
Nicklin, Mrs. Philip.
Mrs. Arthur Emlen Newbold.
Nichols, Henry.

Carnegie Institute, Pittsburgh.
Nixon, Colonel John.
Pennsylvania Academy.
Ogden.
Such a picture is listed by Mason, page 233.
Ogilvy, James.*
Panel, 28 x 22. Sold at Parke-Bernet, December 1953.
Oliver, Ebenezer.
Panel, 28 x 23; Mrs. Francis Cole.
Oliver, Mrs. Ebenezer.
Panel, 28 x 22; Mrs. Francis Cole.
Orne, William.
Panel, 26 x 20½; Museum of Fine Arts, Boston.
Otis, George Alexander.
Panel, 27 x 22; Mrs. Ruth Graves Ernst.
Otis, Mrs. George Alexander.
Panel, 28 x 22½; Mrs. Ruth Graves Ernst.
Otis, Harrison Gray.
Panel, 32 x 26; Museum of Fine Arts, Boston.
Otis, Mrs. Harrison Gray.
Panel, 32 x 26; Mrs. Albert A. H. Meredith and Mrs. William Platt.
Otis, Samuel Alleyne.
Panel, 27½ x 22½; Robert H. Thayer.
Paine, Robert Treat, Jr.
Engraved by Elkanah Tisdale, 1812.
Palmer, Mrs. William Lamb.*
Said to be in Ireland (1926).
Parker, Daniel Pinckney.*
The Estate of Edmund Quincy (1879).
Parker, Mrs. Daniel Pinckney.
Panel, 23¾ x 21¼; Doll & Richards (1924).
Parker, John, Sr.
J. Harleston Parker.
Parkman, Samuel.
(1) Panel, 28 x 23; exh. Museum of Fine Arts, Boston, 1928.
(2) (Replica) * Miss Mary G. Parkman (1915).
Parkman, Mrs. Samuel.
(1) Panel, 28 x 23 (facing right); exh. Museum of Fine Arts, Boston, 1928.
(2) (Replica) * Mrs. Quincy A. Shaw.
(3) Panel, 29 x 24 (facing left); probably with the participation of Jane Stuart; The Misses Cordner, (1926).
Parsons, Chief Justice Theophilus.
(1) Panel, 25 x 21 (unfinished); National Collection of Fine Arts (Smithsonian Institution).
(2) Panel, 25 x 21; Mrs. Neilson Abeel.
Patten, Miss Sally.
Panel, 26 x 21; Museum of Fine Arts, Boston.
Patterson, William.
Mrs. Elisha Dyer (1926).
Peabody, Mrs. Stephen.
Panel, 27 x 21; Mrs. Henry A. Cook.
Peirse, Sarah Ann.

Ehrick Galleries (1929).
Pennington, Miss Anne.
    32 x 28; Society for the Preservation of
    Landmarks of Philadelphia; Powell
    House Museum.
Pennington, Edward.
    Panel, 29 x 23½; Historical Society of
    Pennsylvania.
Perkins, James.
    (1) 35 x 27½; Mrs. Edward Perkins.
    (2) (Replica) 43½ x 33½ inches; Boston
    Athenaeum.
Perkins, Thomas.
    Panel, 28 x 23; Mrs. Daniel Catlin.
Perkins, Mrs. Thomas.
    Panel, 19 x 10 (cut down); Mrs. Daniel
    Catlin.
Perkins, Thomas Handasyd.
    (1) Panel, 28 x 23; Mary Geraldine
    Cabot.
    (2) 36 x 28; Mrs. Henry W. Minot.*
Perkins, Mrs. Thomas Handasyd.
    Panel, 29 x 23¾; Mrs. Henry W. Minot.
Perry, Commodore Oliver Hazard.
    Panel, 26¾ x 21¾; Museum of Fine Arts,
    Boston.
Peters, Mrs. Richard, Jr.
    Pennsylvania Academy.
Pettit, Colonel Charles.
    Mrs. Charles Henry.
Philips, Mrs. Henry.
    Charles Henry Hart was told it was in
    possession of James T. Montgomery.
Philipse, Captain Frederick.
    51½ x 40½ (?); The Misses Philipse (1907).
Phillips, John.
    Destroyed by fire, 1914.
Phillips, William.
    (1) 44 x 34; Treadwell Library, Mass.
    General Hospital.
    (2) Panel, 7 x 5½; Rhode Island School
    of Design * (preliminary study).
Phillips, Mrs.
    Listed by Mason, page 240.
Pickering, Colonel Timothy.
    (1) Panel, 28 x 22½; Arthur T. Lyman.
    (2) Miriam S. D. Manning (1930–).
Pickering, Mrs. Timothy.
    Panel, 31 x 24; Carnegie Institute.
Pinckney, Charles.*
    32 x 25; Alexander Smith Cochran
    (1926).
Pinckney, General Charles Cotesworth.
    47 x 38; head only by Stuart; Julian
    Mitchell.
Plumstead, George.
    Pennsylvania Academy.
Plumstead, Mrs. George.
    Pennsylvania Academy.
Pollock, George.
    36¼ x 28¼; National Gallery of Art, Wash-
    ington (Mellon Coll.).
Pollock, Mrs. George.

36 x 28¼; National Gallery of Art, Wash-
    ington (Mellon Coll.).
Porter, William.
    Panel, 26½ x 21; exh. Museum of Fine
    Arts, Boston, 1928.
Porter, Mrs. William.
    Mrs. William H. McLellan (1880).
Portrait of a Gentleman.
    Pastel, 15 x 13 (signed); Essex Institute,
    Salem, Mass.
Portrait of a Gentleman.
    James A. Mornaghan.
Portrait of a Gentleman.*
    Panel, 28 x 23 inches. Albert Rosenthal.
Portrait of a Man.
    Ehrick Galleries (1926).
Portrait of a Man.
    J. Gillingham Fell (1880).
Portrait of a Gentleman.
    Panel, 27 x 21; Vose Gallery.
Portrait of a Gentleman.
    Metropolitan Museum.
Portrait of a Lady.
    Panel, 28 x 23; unfinished head; Mrs.
    Ward Thoron (1926).
Portrait of a Lady.
    Destroyed by fire in Executive Mansion,
    Albany, 1961.
Portrait of a Lady.*
    National Collection of Fine Arts (Smith-
    sonian Institution).
Powell, Mrs. Ann Catherine.
    Mrs. Alice Mason (1879).
Prescott, Judge William.*
    (1) 37 x 28; John Endicott Lawrence.
    (2) (Separate bust-length portrait) Mrs.
    Franklin Dexter (1926).
Priestley, Joseph.
    Mrs. Susan Lowndes-Marques.
Purviance, Mrs. William Young.
    Not located.
Quincy, Josiah, Jr.
    35½ x 27½; Edmund Quincy.
Quincy, The Hon. Josiah.
    (1) Facing left; panel, 30 x 24; Fogg Mu-
    seum.
    (2) Facing right; 36 x 28; Museum of
    Fine Arts, Boston.
Quincy, Mrs. Josiah.
    Panel, 30 x 24, Mrs. Henry Philips
    Quincy (1926).
Rabbi (A).
    Said to have been painted at Newport,
    before 1775.
Randolph, John.
    National Gallery of Art, Washington.
Rawle, Mrs. William.
    Panel, 29 x 23; Henry Rawle.
Ricketts, Mr.
    Head only, with sketched horses heads
    behind; National Gallery of Art,
    Washington.
Redwood, William.

35 x 29; Redwood Library.
Reed, William.*
Mrs. Henry Edward Waite (1900).
Reed, Mrs. William.
Panel; Mrs. Henry Edward Waite (1900).
Reid, J.
Exhibited at Stuart Memorial Exhibition, Boston Athenaeum, 1828.
Reigart, Mrs. Adam.
Panel (unfinished head). Not located.
Reignold, George.
Panel, 29 x 24; Pennsylvania Academy.
Revere, Joseph Warren.
Panel, 27 x 22; Margaret A. & Anna P. Revere.
Revere, Paul.
Panel, 27 x 20; Museum of Fine Arts, Boston.
Revere, Mrs. Paul.
Panel, 27 x 20; Museum of Fine Arts, Boston.
Reynolds, Dr. Edward.
Exhibited at Boston Athenaeum Stuart Memorial Exhibition, 1828.
Rice, Captain Henry.
Panel, 26 x 21; Metropolitan Museum.
Rice, Colonel Nathan.
Panel, 24 x 20⅝; Nathan W. Rice (1926).
Richards, John.
Panel, 29 x 23; Francis Ashburner Richards (1926).
Richards, Mrs. John.
29 x 24; Francis Ashburner Richards (1926).
Ridgely, Commodore Charles Goodwin.
Panel, 24½ x 20; Mrs. Charlotte Cahill Thorp.
Rivera, Jacob Rodriguez.
Redwood Library.
Rivington, James.
Not located. A copy by Ezra Ames at the New York Historical Society.
Robinson, Mrs. William.
Panel, 28¼ x 22¾; National Gallery of Art, Washington (Mellon Coll.).
Rodman, Mrs.
Listed by Mason, page 250.
Rogers, Daniel Denison.
Panel, 33 x 26; Dr. John Rogers (1926).
Rogers, Mrs. Daniel Denison.
Panel, 32 x 26; Samuel Cabot Sedgewick.
Rogers, Rev. John.
Engraving published by Annim & Smith.
Roosevelt, Isaac.
38 x 29; Franklin D. Roosevelt Library.
Rotch, Mrs. William J.
Mrs. Thomas Dunn (1926).
Russell, Nathaniel Pope.
Museum of Fine Arts, Boston (on loan to Springfield Museum).
Rutledge, Miss Mary.
Destroyed during the Civil War.
Salisbury, Samuel.

(1) Panel, 29 x 23; Miss Laura Heermance (1926).
(2) 27½ x 22½; Theodore Salisbury Woolsey (1866).
(3) Panel, 31¾ x 25¾; Worcester Museum.
Salisbury, Stephen.
(1) 28 x 23; Worcester Museum.
(2) 27½ x 22½; Prof. Theodore F. Woolsey (1926).
Salisbury, Mrs. Stephen.
Panel, 31¾ x 25¾; Worcester Museum.
Sargent, Gov. Winthrop.
33 x 27; Anderson Dana (1926).
Sargent, Mrs. Winthrop.
33 x 27; Anderson Dana (1926).
Savage, Mrs. Samuel.
Panel, 28¼ x 22¾; Mrs. Francis Tiffany Bowles (1926).
Schuyler, Philip Jeremiah.
New York Historical Society.
Schuyler, Mrs. Philip Jeremiah.
New York Historical Society.
Searle, Mrs. George.*
Panel, 25½ x 21½; Mary and Elizabeth Marquand (1926).
Sears, David.
(1) Panel, 27¾ x 22¼; Dr. Henry F. Sears (1926).
(2) Panel, 28½ x 23½; (replica) Dr. Henry F. Sears (1926).
Sears, David.
Metropolitan Museum of Art.
Sears, Mrs. David (Miriam Mason).
Panel, 22 x 16; Dr. Henry F. Sears (1926).
Sedgewick, Theodore.
Museum of Fine Arts, Boston.
Selfridge, Thomas Oliver.
Panel, 27 x 22; Museum of Fine Arts, Boston.
Seton, William.
Reproduced, *Art in America*, 1933, pages 83–4.
Shattuck, Dr. George Cheyne.
Dr. George Cheyne Shattuck.
Shaw, John.
(1) 36 x 28; Mrs. Lawrence H. Pugh.
(2) 32 x 26; (copy or replica?) National Gallery of Ireland.
Shaw, Robert Gould.
Panel, 32½ x 26½; Mrs. Henry Lyman.
Shaw, Mrs. Robert Gould.
Panel, 32½ x 26½; Mrs. Henry Lyman.
Shaw, William Smith.
35⅝ x 27½; Boston Athenaeum.
Shepherd, Rezin Davis.
(1) Shepherd Brooks.
(2) 24¾ x 20¾; Leverett Saltonstall.
Shippen, Chief Justice Edward.
Corcoran Gallery of Art, Washington.
Shippen, Thomas Lee.
National Collection of Fine Arts (Smithsonian Institution).
Shippen, Dr. William, Jr.

National Collection of Fine Arts (Smithsonian Institution).

Shubrick, Admiral William Branford.

Panel, 24 x 20; Mrs. Thomas F. Bayard (1926).

Shurtleff, Dr. Samuel A.

Dr. Augustine Shurtleff (1879).

Sigourney, Mrs. Andrew.

Herbert Lee Pratt (1926).

Slade, Mrs. Jacob Tilton.*

Panel, 27¾ x 22; Margaret B. Slade (1926).

Smith, Abiel.

The Rev. Robert Lewis Weis (on loan to Rhode Island School of Design).

Smith, Mrs. Abiel.

The Rev. Robert Lewis Weis (on loan to Rhode Island School of Design).

Smith, Barney.

Panel, 38¾ x 29½; Roger Ernst.

Smith, Mrs. Barney.

Panel, 36½ x 26½; Roger Ernst.

Smith, Henry Barney.

(1) Panel, 27¼ x 25⅝; Mrs. George Robert Russell Rivers.

(2) 24 x 19¾; sold 1922 by Lucinda Smith Otis.

Smith, Miss Lydia.

Panel, 32¼ x 28¾; Mrs. George Robert Russell Rivers.

Smith, General Samuel.

Dr. B. Noland Carter.

Smith, Mrs. Samuel.

Dr. B. Noland Carter.

Smith, Mrs. Samuel.

Panel, 32½ x 26½; Museum of Fine Arts, Boston (on loan to Springfield Museum).

Smith, Dr. William.

37 x 60; Dr. Ward Brinton (1926).

Smith, William Loughton.

Carolina Art Association (Bibbs Art Gallery).

Smith, Colonel William Stephens.

(1) Herbert Lee Pratt (1926). (In civil dress.)

(2) Yale University Art Gallery (in uniform). Both are life portraits.

Smith, Mrs. Robert.

Not located. Mentioned in letter from Mrs. Cutts to Dolly Madison (May 7, 1804).

Sparks, Jared.

(Uncompleted—head only) New Britain Museum of American Art.

Spring, Mrs. Marshall Binney.

Panel, 26¼ x 21¼; Mrs. Henry St.-John Smith (1926).

Stackpole, William.

Panel, 28⅜ x 23¼; J. Lewis Stackpole.

Stevens, Mrs. John, II.

36 x 28; New York Historical Society.

Stewart, Mrs. Charles.

Mrs. William Tudor (1926).

Stillman, Mrs. Samuel.

Panel, 25½ x 21; Boston Society for the Care of Girls.

Storrow, Thomas Wentworth.

Panel, 27½ x 22½; Thomas W. Storrow.

Story, Joseph.

Panel, 32½ x 26; Harvard Memorial Hall.

Story, Mrs. Joseph.

Panel, 32¾ x 25¾; George H. Webster (1926).

Stow, Edward.

Panel, 29 x 23⅝; National Gallery of Art, Washington (Mellon Collection).

Stow, Mrs. Edward.

Panel, 29½ x 23½; Thomas B. Clarke (1926).

Strong, Governor Caleb.

Panel, 26⅝ x 21¼; Frederick Strong Moseley (1926).

Stuart, Gilbert, Sr.

Not located. Said by Mason to have been painted when the artist was sixteen.

Stuart, Gilbert (self-portrait).

10⅝ x 8; Metropolitan Museum.

Stuart, Gilbert (self-portrait).

Not located. An ink drawing on the back of an envelope, reproduced in Mason.

Stuart, Dr. James.

Panel, 32¾ x 26; Cleveland Museum of Art.

Stuart, Mrs. James.

Panel, 32¾ x 26; Cleveland Museum of Art.

Sturgis, Russell (three separate portraits).

(1) Mrs. William Smith Carter, (1926).

(2) Mrs. E. Sturgis Hinds.

(3) Worcester Museum.

Sturgis, Mrs. Russell.

Mrs. William Smith Carter.

Stuyvesant, Peter.

New York Historical Society.

Sullivan, Governor James.

(1) Panel, 32¼ x 26; Massachusetts Historical Society.

(2) Panel 33 x 26¾ (replica); Museum of Fine Arts, Boston.

Sullivan, Mrs. Richard.

Exhibited Boston Museum of Fine Arts, 1880.

Sullivan, Mrs. William.

35 x 28; Yale University Art Gallery.

Sutcliffe, Mr.

Weston Art Galleries (New York) 1924.

Swan, Colonel James.

Museum of Fine Arts, Boston.

Swan, Mrs. James.

Panel, 31⅞ x 25⅝; Museum of Fine Arts, Boston.

Swan, James Keadie.

Panel, 32¼ x 26½; Prof. Henry Thatcher Fowler (1926).

Swett, Col. Samuel.

33 x 27; Newburyport Public Library.

Swett, Mrs. Samuel.
33 x 27; John F. Braun (1920).
Talbot, Silas.
William R. Talbot (1912).
Tappan, Benjamin.
Panel, 28 x 33; Anna and Margaret Hulett (1926).
Tappan, Mrs. Benjamin.
Panel, 28 x 23; Bowdoin College (on loan).
Tayloe, Colonel John.
Edward D. Tayloe (1926).
Tayloe, Mrs. John.
Edward D. Tayloe (1926).
Taylor, Rev. Doctor.
Destroyed by fire, 1832.
Temple, Sir Grenville, 9th Bart.
Mentioned by Mason, page 266.
Temple, Sir John.
Panel, 28 x 23 (the head copied from Trumbull); Mrs. Henry W. Sage (1926).
Temple, Lady John.
(1) Panel, 29 x 25; George Temple Bowdoin (1926).
(2) 49½ x 35½; Mrs. Joseph Grafton Minot (1926).
(3) Panel, 28⅞ x 23½; Mrs. Henry W. Sage (1926).
Thayer, Rev. Nathaniel.
Adele G. Thayer (1926).
Thorndike, Colonel Israel.
(1) Panel, 32½ x 25¾; Dr. Augustus Thorndike (1926).
(2) Panel, 31¼ x 25⅛; Massachusetts Historical Society.
Thorndike, Mrs. Israel.
36 x 27; Walter Aikman.
Thorndike, Mrs. Israel, Jr.
Panel, 33 x 26½; Harvard University Portrait Collection.
Thornton, Sir Edward.
According to Dictionary of National Biography (1909), in possession of the family.
Thornton, Dr. William.
National Gallery of Art, Washington (Mellon Coll.).
Thornton, Mrs. William.
National Gallery of Art, Washington (Mellon Coll.).
Tilden, Bryant Parrott.
Panel, 29 x 24; Berkshire Museum.
Tillotson, Dr. Thomas.
John Tillotson Wainwright (after 1880).
Torrey, Miss Frances.
Panel, 20 x 20; exhibited Museum of Fine Arts, Boston (1928).
Touro, Abraham.
(1) Massachusetts General Hospital.
(2) Samuel W. Weiss (1926).
Townsend, Alexander.
Panel, 33¼ x 26½; Minneapolis Institute.
Trask, Israel Elliott.
Panel, 27½ x 22¼; Mrs. Robert M. Tappan.
Trask, Mrs. Israel Elliott.*
25 x 19⅝; Mrs. Frederick H. Tappan (1926).
Travis, John.
Miss Fanny Travis Cochrane.
Travis, Mrs. John.
Pennsylvania Academy.
Trumbull, John.
Panel, 25½ x 21½; Yale University Art Gallery.
Tuckerman, Edward.
Panel, 27 x 22¾; Victor Spark.
Tuckerman, Mrs. Edward (Hannah M. Parkman).
Panel, 26 x 22; Victor Spark.
Tuckerman, Mrs. Edward (Sophia May).
(1) Completed by Chester Harding; Prof. William Est (1926).*
(2) Dr. Frederick Tuckerman (1926).
Tuckerman, Rev. Joseph.
Panel, 27¾ x 22¾; Walter R. Tuckerman (1926).
Tudor, William, Jr.
Robert Hallowell Gardiner.
Tyng, Dudley Atkins.
Francis Higginson Atkins (1891).
Upham, Mrs. Thomas Cogswell.
Bowdoin College.
Van Ness, John Peter.
John Van Ness Philip (1926).
Van Rensselaer, Stephen.
(1) A. Rueff, (1926).
(2) Mrs. Arthur Iselin, (1926).*
(3) National Gallery, Washington.
Vaughan, John.
John F. Vaughan (1926).
Volney, Count Constantin François.
Pennsylvania Academy.
Waddington, Joshua.*
Ogden Codman, (1915).
Wager, Philip.
Panel, 28¼ x 23¼; Charles Edward Brown (1926).
Wager, Mrs. Philip.
Panel, 28¼ x 23¼; Charles Edward Brown (1926).
Walcott, Mr.*
Albert Rosenthal (1926).
Walker, Alexander William.
A. W. Erickson (1926).
Walker, Mrs. Alexander William.
A. W. Erickson (1926).
Walley, Mrs. Samuel Hall.
The National Academy of Design.
Ward, William.
Panel, 32¼ x 26; Thomas Wren Ward (1926).
Warren, Dr. John Collins.
32 x 26; Dr. Richard Warren.

Warren, Mrs. John Collins.
Panel, 18 x 14¾ (cut down); Museum of Fine Arts, Springfield, Mass.
Washington, Marthe.
48 x 37; Museum of Fine Arts, Boston.
Waterston, Robert.
Museum of Fine Arts, Boston.
Waterston, Mrs. Robert.
Museum of Fine Arts, Boston.
Watson, Captain Horace Howard.
Panel, 27¼ x 21¼; Henry Watson Kent (1926).
Webster, Daniel.
(1) Panel, 30 x 24 (unfinished); Francis Parkman.
(2) 36 x 28; with participation of Jane Stuart; exhibited at Metropolitan Museum, 1924.
Weems, Miss (?).
Formerly Milch Galleries.
Welch, Francis.
Panel, 26 x 21½; Francis Welch (on loan to Museum of Fine Arts, Springfield, Mass.).
Welch, Mrs. Francis.
Panel, 26 x 21½; Francis Welch (on loan to Museum of Fine Arts, Springfield, Mass.).
Wells, Rev. William.
Panel, 29 x 23; Loren C. White.
Wetmore, Judge William.
Panel, 27 x 21½; Mrs. Elaine Story (1926).
Wheeler, Moses.
Panel, 26¼ x 21⅜; Herbert Rogers Wheeler (1904).
Wheeler, Mrs. Moses.
Panel, 26¼ x 21⅜; Herbert Rogers Wheeler (1904).
White, Bishop William.
36 x 31¾; Pennsylvania Academy.
Whitney, Elisha.
Panel, 27¾ x 23; The Misses Whitney (1926).
Wickham, Mrs. John.
33 x 26⅝; Judge Thomas Ashby Wickham (1926).
Wildman, William.
Rhode Island Institute.
Wilkes, Charles.
Metropolitan Museum.
Williams, Cumberland Dungan.
Panel, 28¼ x 22; William G. Warden (1926).
Williams, Mrs. Cumberland Dungan.
Panel, 28¼ x 23; William G. Warden (1926).
Williams, Mrs. George.
(1) 36 x 28; Museum of Fine Arts, Boston.
(2) 36 x 28 (replica, the hands altered); The Misses Sears (1926).
(3) 36 x 28; (unfinished) Mrs. Cyril Bathurst Judge (1926).
Williams, George.
Panel, 26¼ x 21½; Miss Julia Bell Williams (1926).
Williams, Mrs. George.
Panel, 26½ x 21½; Museum of Fine Arts, Boston.
Williams, Henry Howell.*
Lithographed by J. H. Bufford, 1858.
Williams, John.
Miss Anne Williams (1880).
Williams, Colonel Joseph.
Panel, 26¾ x 21¼; Mrs. Wallace Lanahan (1926).
Williams, Mrs. John.
Panel, 26⅞ x 21⅜; Museum of Fine Arts, Boston.
Williams, Samuel King.
27 x 22; Fogg Museum.
Williams, Mrs. Samuel King.
27 x 22⅜; Fogg Museum.
Williams, Miss Susan Mae.
Panel, 25½ x 21½; Sarah Bell Williams (1926).
Williamson, William.
Rhode Island School of Design.
Willing, Thomas.
(1) Princess Poniatowska.
(2) Temporarily deposited at Independence Hall (1879).
Wilson, Commodore Joseph.
Panel, 26⅝ x 22; Mrs. Edward G. Gardner (1926).
Winthrop, Elizabeth Temple.
Massachusetts Historical Society.
Winthrop, Grenville Temple.
Unfinished on Stuart's death. Not located.
Winthrop, Joseph.
Mentioned by Mason, page 281.
Winthrop, Sarah Bowdoin (Mrs. George Sullivan).
Mentioned in Mason, pages 265–7. Possibly the picture exhibited at Boston Museum, 1880, as Mrs. "Richard" Sullivan.
Winthrop, Mrs. Thomas Lindall.
28½ x 23½; Miss Clara B. Winthrop (1926).
Winthrop, William.
36 x 28; Grenville Lindall Winthrop (1926).
Wolcott, Hon. Oliver, Jr.
27½ x 23¼; Yale University Art Gallery.
Yates, Lawrence Reid.
(1) National Gallery of Art, Washington (Mellon Coll.).
(2) Huntington Collection, San Marino.
Yates, Richard.
National Gallery of Art, Washington (Mellon Coll.).
Yates, Mrs. Richard.
(1) National Gallery of Art, Washington

(Mellon Coll.).
(2) Museum of Fine Arts, Boston.*
Young, Judge John.
    Mrs. William H. la Boyteaux.

Young, Mrs. John.
    Mrs. William H. la Boyteaux.
Young, Robert.
    Phillipse Manor Hall, Yonkers (1926).

PORTRAITS OF GEORGE WASHINGTON

The "Vaughan" Type

National Gallery of Art, Washington. Probably the original portrait painted from life at Philadelphia (Washington's house in High Street), 1795.

REPLICAS

Mrs. George F. Tyler (1921).
Henry Francis Dupont Winterthur Museum.
The National Gallery of Art, Washington.
The Metropolitan Museum.
Mrs. I. Sheldon Tilney (1926).
The Frick Collection.
Edward S. Harkness.
Walter O. Briggs.
G. Dawson Coleman (1926).
Herbert Lee Pratt (1926).
Mrs. George L. Rives (1926).
Willard D. Straight (1898).
John F. Braun (1926).
Art House, Inc. (1926).
Phillips Manor House, Yonkers (1926).
Metropolitan Museum.
Mr. and Mrs. Eli Lilly.

The "Athenaeum" Type

Museum of Fine Arts, Boston. The second portrait of Washington, Stuart painted from life, Philadelphia, April 1796. Purchased from the artist's family, 1831; 48 x 37.

REPLICAS

Yale University Art Gallery.
Toledo Museum.
The American Philosophical Society.
Pennsylvania Historical Society.
George Elkins (1922).
W. W. Carnill (1918).
Cincinnati Art Museum.
John D. Rockefeller, Jr.
The Brook Club, New York.
The University Club, New York.
C. du Bois Wagstaff (1926).
Metropolitan Museum.
Corcoran Gallery.
Washington Cathedral.
Huntington Collection, San Marino, Calif.
Philadelphia Museum of Art.
Lambert Cadwalader (1926).

Herbert Lee Pratt (1916).
Dr. Henry K. Dillard (1922).
Miss Mary R. Coles (1926).
New York Historical Society.
Henry P. Davison.
Hon. Oscar S. Straus (1926).
Lord Monk Bretton.
Maryland Historical Society.
The Walters Art Gallery.
Miss G. K. McCall and Mrs. Keating.
(Mrs.) Charles W. Henry (1926).
United States Military Academy, West Point.
Peter Nicolson.
Rhode Island School of Design.
Fogg Museum.
William K. Bixby (1926).
Landon C. Bell.
National Portrait Gallery, London.
The Philadelphia Club.
John H. Earley (1926).
Mrs. Wilfred P. Mustard (before 1926).
National Gallery of Art, Washington.
Mrs. J. I. Cooper (1926).
Mrs. H. Irvine Keyser (1923).
F. S. Tainter (1926).
Pennsylvania Academy.
The Capitol Building, Washington; office of
    Senate Majority Leader.
United States Senate, Washington; main
    corridor.
Macbeth Galleries (1922).
New York Art Market (1905).
Sterling & Francine Clark Institute.
Estate of Col. Alexander Biddle (1926).
Horatio Rubens (1924).
W. D. Craig Wright (1926).
Private Collection, Boston (1926).
Fredericksburg Lodge No. 4, Masons.
Mount Vernon.
Mrs. Woods King.
Mrs. C. L. F. Robinson.
New York Chamber of Commerce.
Mrs. Ferree Brinton (1926).
George F. Baker.
Bowdoin College.
Mrs. Vance McCormick (1926).
Joseph Pulitzer.

The following "Athenaeum" type replicas, painted on wood, must be considered a special category because of the frequent participation of Matthew Harris Jouett.

Huntington Collection, San Marino, Calif.; panel, 22 x 27.

Thomas Jefferson Coolidge, Jr.; panel, 22 x 26.

Museum of Fine Arts, Boston; panel, 25¼ x 21.

Museum of Fine Arts, Boston; panel, 25¾ x 21¼.

Dudley Leavitt Pickman (1926).

The Berkshire Museum; panel 24 x 30.

Albert Rosenthal (1926); panel; 23½ x 28.

Albert H. Wiggin (1917).

G. M. Heckscher (1926).

Charles T. Fisher.

The Full-Lengths

Pennsylvania Academy of Fine Arts. Painted for Senator Bingham; the first effort at full-length; 96 x 60.

Brooklyn Museum; 96¼ x 60¼. Painted at the same time as the Bingham original.

The Earl of Rosebery; 96 x 60. The second improved effort, painted for shipment to Lord Lansdowne.

The White House, Washington. Replica of the Lansdowne portrait prepared for General Pinckney.

New York Public Library. The third fresh effort at a full-length, and Stuart's finest such picture of Washington.

The State House, Providence; approx. 95 x 60 (third type).

The State House, Newport; approx. 95 x 60 (third type).

The State House, Hartford; approx. 95 x 60 (third type).

Museum of Fine Arts, Boston. "Washington at Dorchester Heights," panel, 108 x 72.

Heirs of Ignatius Sargent; "Washington at Dorchester Heights," 24 x 36.

Half-Lengths

New York Public Library; 40 x 50.

Mrs. Alfred G. Wilson; 34 x 44 (from the Doggett set).

James Speyer (1940–), 46 x 37.

Index

DATE DUE

NO 0 5 '86			
GAYLORD			PRINTED IN U.S.A